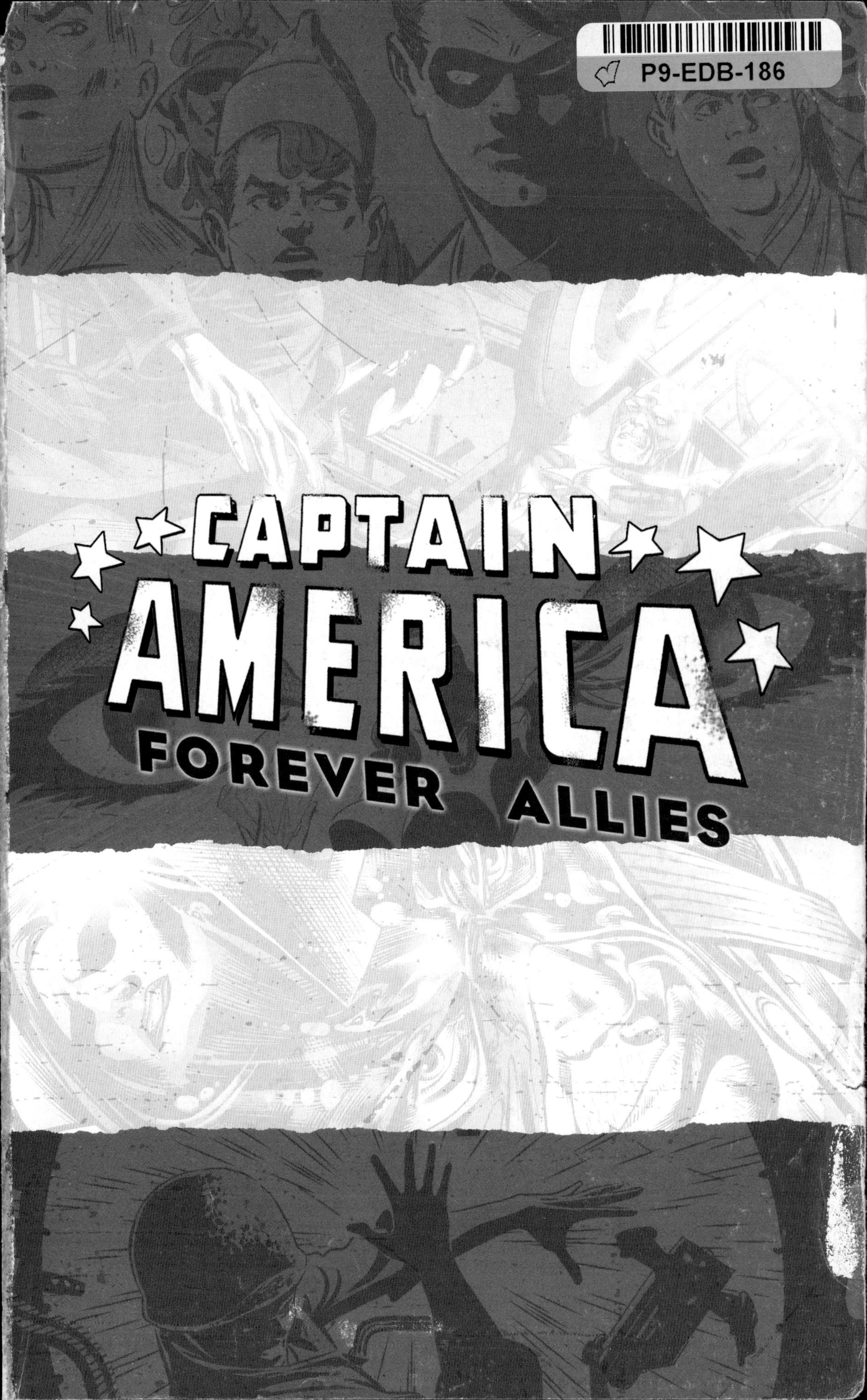
CAPTAIN
AMERICA
FOREVER ALLIES

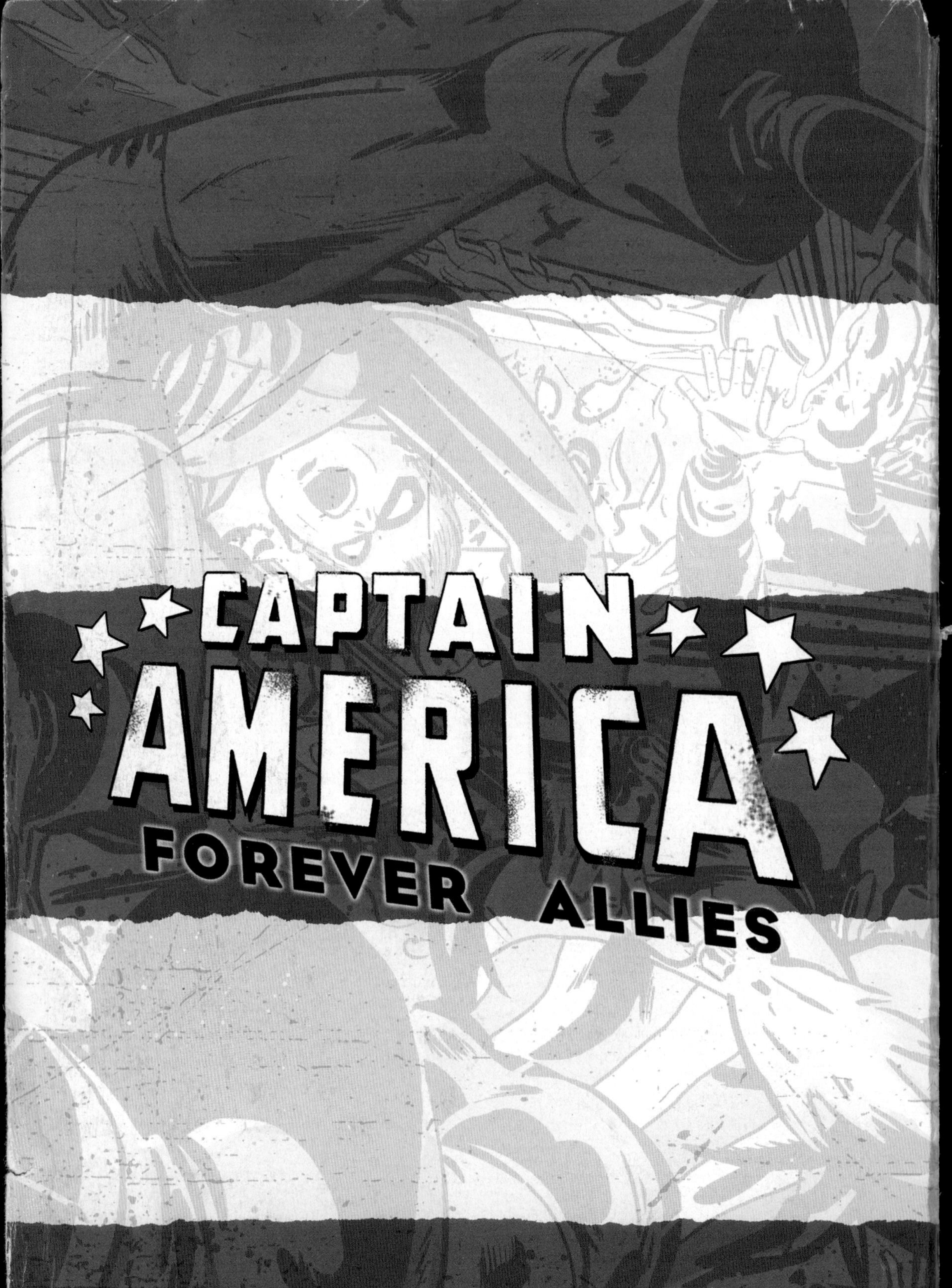

CAPTAIN
AMERICA
FOREVER ALLIES

CAPTAIN AMERICA: FOREVER ALLIES. Contains material originally published in magazine form as CAPTAIN AMERICA: FOREVER ALLIES #1-4, YOUNG ALLIES COMICS 70TH ANNIVERSARY SPECIAL #1 and YOUNG ALLIES #1. First printing 2011. ISBN# 978-0-7851-4702-2. Published by MARVEL WORLDWIDE, INC., a subsidiary of MARVEL ENTERTAINMENT, LLC. OFFICE OF PUBLICATION: 135 West 50th Street, New York, NY 10020. Copyright © 1941, 2009, 2010 and 2011 Marvel Characters, Inc. All rights reserved. $19.99 per copy in the U.S. and $21.99 in Canada (GST #R127032852); Canadian Agreement #40668537. All characters featured in this issue and the distinctive names and likenesses thereof, and all related indicia are trademarks of Marvel Characters, Inc. No similarity between any of the names, characters, persons, and/or institutions in this magazine with those of any living or dead person or institution is intended, and any such similarity which may exist is purely coincidental. **Printed in the U.S.A.** ALAN FINE, EVP - Office of the President, Marvel Worldwide, Inc. and EVP & CMO Marvel Characters B.V.; DAN BUCKLEY, Publisher & President - Print, Animation & Digital Divisions; JOE QUESADA, Chief Creative Officer; JIM SOKOLOWSKI, Chief Operating Officer; DAVID BOGART, SVP of Business Affairs & Talent Management; TOM BREVOORT, SVP of Publishing; C.B. CEBULSKI, SVP of Creator & Content Development; DAVID GABRIEL, SVP of Publishing Sales & Circulation; MICHAEL PASCIULLO, SVP of Brand Planning & Communications; JIM O'KEEFE, VP of Operations & Logistics; DAN CARR, Executive Director of Publishing Technology; SUSAN CRESPI, Editorial Operations Manager; ALEX MORALES, Publishing Operations Manager; STAN LEE, Chairman Emeritus. For information regarding advertising in Marvel Comics or on Marvel.com, please contact John Dokes, SVP Integrated Sales and Marketing, at jdokes@marvel.com. For Marvel subscription inquiries, please call 800-217-9158. **Manufactured between 9/28/2011 and 10/17/2011 by R.R. DONNELLEY, INC., SALEM, VA, USA.**

10 9 8 7 6 5 4 3 2 1

YOUNG ALLIES COMICS 70TH ANNIVERSARY SPECIAL #1

WRITER: **ROGER STERN**
ARTIST: **PAOLO RIVERA**
LETTERS: **JARED K. FLETCHER**
COVER ART: **PAOLO RIVERA**
EDITOR: **THOMAS BRENNAN**
CONSULTING EDITOR: **STEPHEN WACKER**
EXECUTIVE EDITOR: **TOM BREVOORT**

CAPTAIN AMERICA: FOREVER ALLIES

WRITER: **ROGER STERN**
ART, 1940S: **NICK DRAGOTTA** WITH **BRAD SIMPSON**
PENCILS, PRESENT: **MARCO SANTUCCI**
INKS, PRESENT: **MARCO SANTUCCI & PATRICK PIAZZALUNGA**
COLORS, PRESENT: **CHRIS SOTOMAYOR** WITH **ANDREW CROSSLEY**
LETTERS: **JARED K. FLETCHER**
COVER ART: **LEE WEEKS** WITH **MATT HOLLINGSWORTH & DEAN WHITE**
EDITOR: **THOMAS BRENNAN**

YOUNG ALLIES #1 (SUMMER 1941)

SCRIPT: **OTTO BINDER**
CHAPTER 1 PENCILS: **CHARLES NICHOLAS WOJTKOWSKI**
CHAPTER 2 TITLE PAGE ART: **JOE SIMON & JACK KIRBY**
CHAPTER 2 PENCILS: **CHARLES NICHOLAS WOJTKOWSKI**
CHAPTER 3 TITLE PAGE ART: **JOE SIMON & JACK KIRBY**
CHAPTER 3 PENCILS: **CHARLES NICHOLAS WOJTKOWSKI**
CHAPTER 4 TITLE PAGE ART: **ERNIE HART**
CHAPTER 4 PENCILS: **CHARLES NICHOLAS WOJTKOWSKI**

CHAPTER 5 TITLE PAGE ART: **JOE SIMON & JACK KIRBY**
CHAPTER 5 PENCILS: **UNKNOWN**
CHAPTER 6 TITLE PAGE ART: **JOE SIMON & JACK KIRBY**
CHAPTER 6 PENCILS: **CHARLES NICHOLAS WOJTKOWSKI & UNKNOWN**
"CROOKS ARE COWARDS" SCRIPT: **UNKNOWN**
"UNSOLVED MYSTERIES" SCRIPT: **STAN LEE**
"UNSOLVED MYSTERIES" ART: **UNKNOWN**

CAPTAIN AMERICA CREATED BY **JOE SIMON & JACK KIRBY**

COLLECTION EDITOR: **JENNIFER GRÜNWALD**
EDITORIAL ASSISTANTS: **JAMES EMMETT & JOE HOCHSTEIN**
ASSISTANT EDITORS: **ALEX STARBUCK & NELSON RIBEIRO**
EDITOR, SPECIAL PROJECTS: **MARK D. BEAZLEY**
SENIOR EDITOR, SPECIAL PROJECTS: **JEFF YOUNGQUIST**
SENIOR VICE PRESIDENT OF SALES: **DAVID GABRIEL**
SVP OF BRAND PLANNING & COMMUNICATIONS: **MICHAEL PASCIULLO**
BOOK DESIGN: **JEFF POWELL**
EDITOR IN CHIEF: **AXEL ALONSO**
CHIEF CREATIVE OFFICER: **JOE QUESADA**
PUBLISHER: **DAN BUCKLEY**
EXECUTIVE PRODUCER: **ALAN FINE**

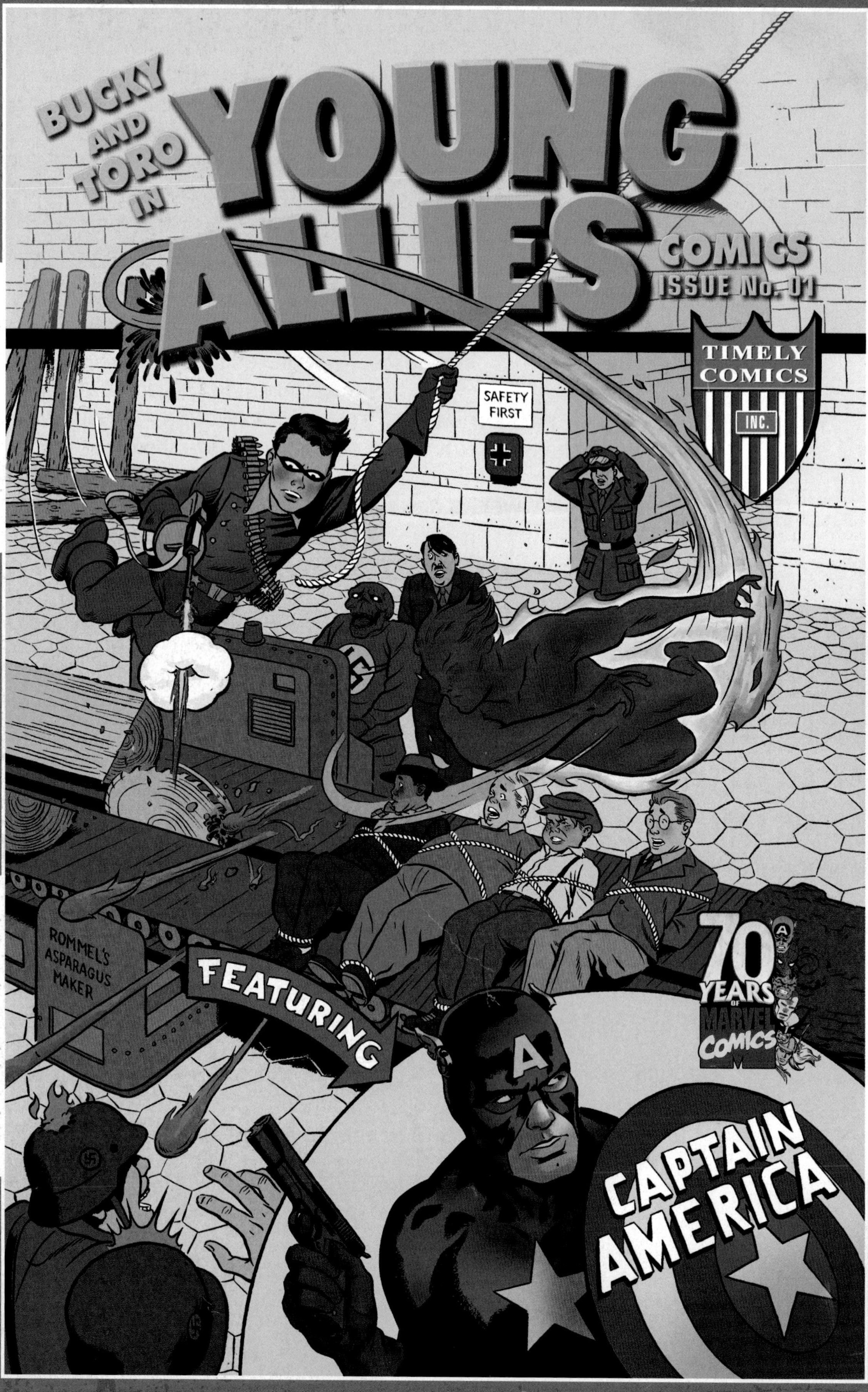
BUCKY AND TORO IN
YOUNG ALLIES
COMICS
ISSUE No. 01
TIMELY COMICS
INC.
SAFETY FIRST
ROMMEL'S ASPARAGUS MAKER
FEATURING
70 YEARS OF MARVEL COMICS
CAPTAIN AMERICA

YOUNG ALLIES COMICS 70TH ANNIVERSARY SPECIAL #1

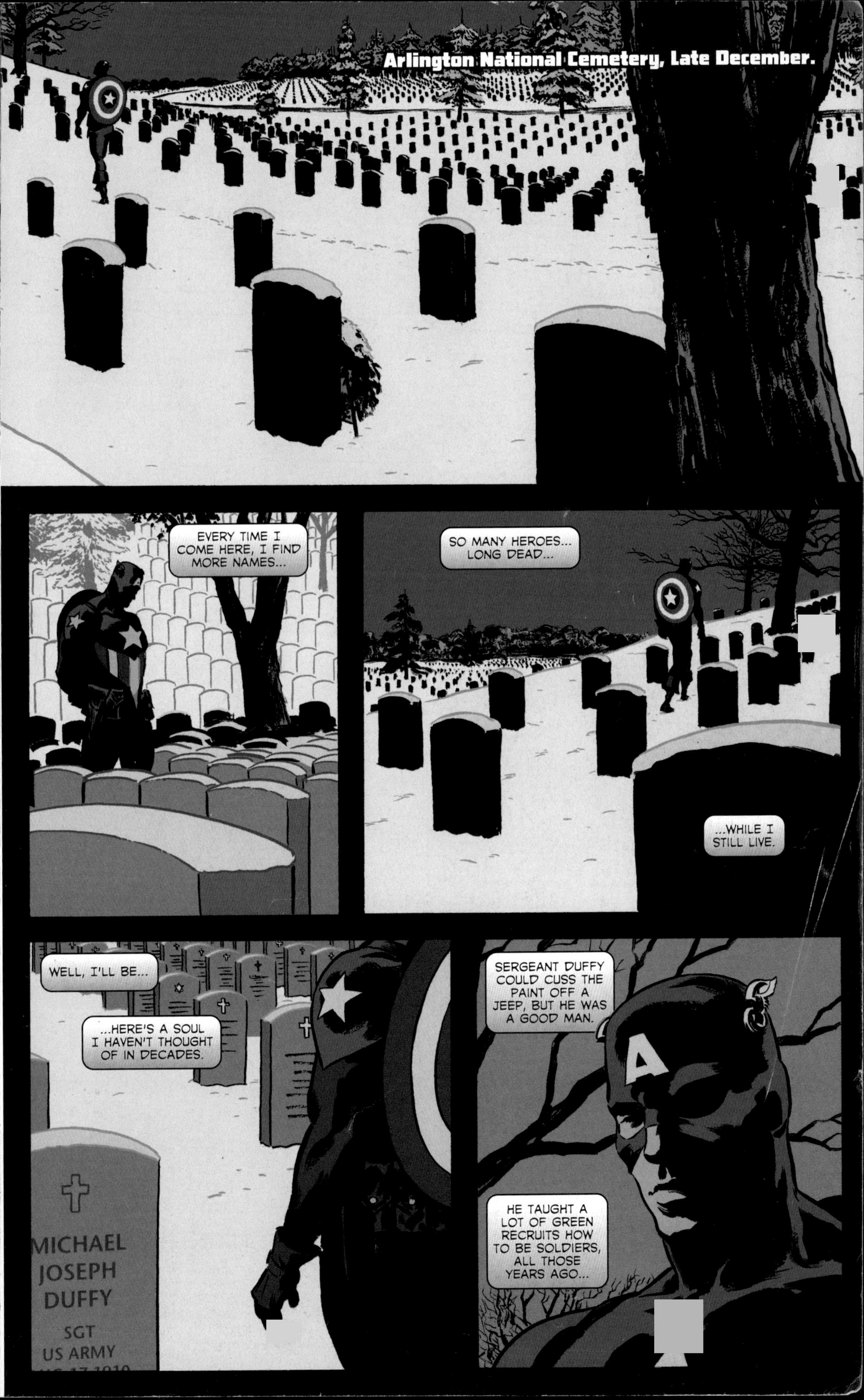
Arlington National Cemetery, Late December.
EVERY TIME I COME HERE, I FIND MORE NAMES...
SO MANY HEROES... LONG DEAD...
...WHILE I STILL LIVE.
WELL, I'LL BE...
...HERE'S A SOUL I HAVEN'T THOUGHT OF IN DECADES.
MICHAEL JOSEPH DUFFY
SGT US ARMY
SERGEANT DUFFY COULD CUSS THE PAINT OFF A JEEP, BUT HE WAS A GOOD MAN.
HE TAUGHT A LOT OF GREEN RECRUITS HOW TO BE SOLDIERS, ALL THOSE YEARS AGO...

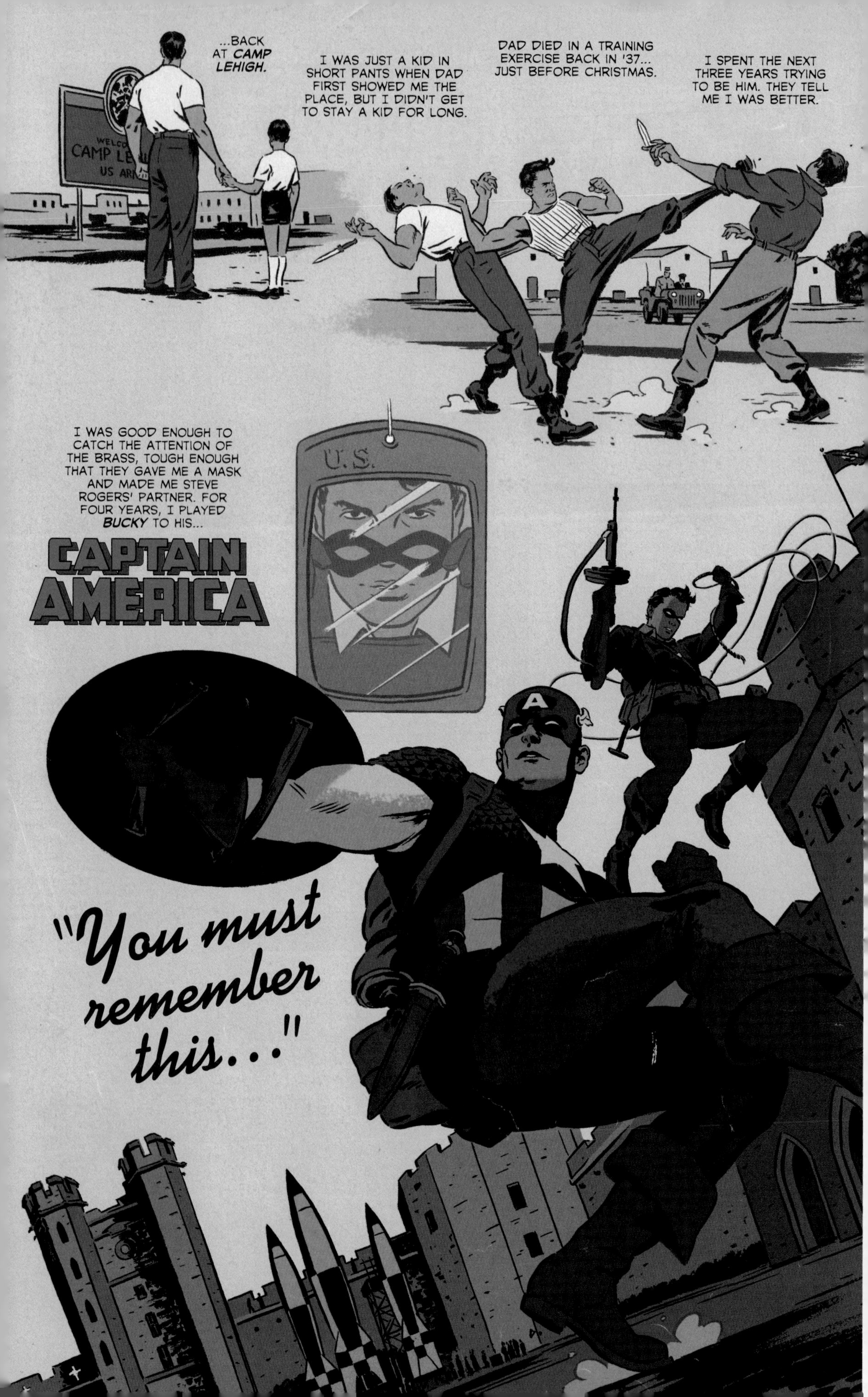

...BACK AT CAMP LEHIGH.
CAMP LE
US ARM
I WAS JUST A KID IN SHORT PANTS WHEN DAD FIRST SHOWED ME THE PLACE, BUT I DIDN'T GET TO STAY A KID FOR LONG.
DAD DIED IN A TRAINING EXERCISE BACK IN '37... JUST BEFORE CHRISTMAS.
I SPENT THE NEXT THREE YEARS TRYING TO BE HIM. THEY TELL ME I WAS BETTER.
I WAS GOOD ENOUGH TO CATCH THE ATTENTION OF THE BRASS, TOUGH ENOUGH THAT THEY GAVE ME A MASK AND MADE ME STEVE ROGERS' PARTNER. FOR FOUR YEARS, I PLAYED BUCKY TO HIS...
CAPTAIN AMERICA
U.S.
"You must remember this..."

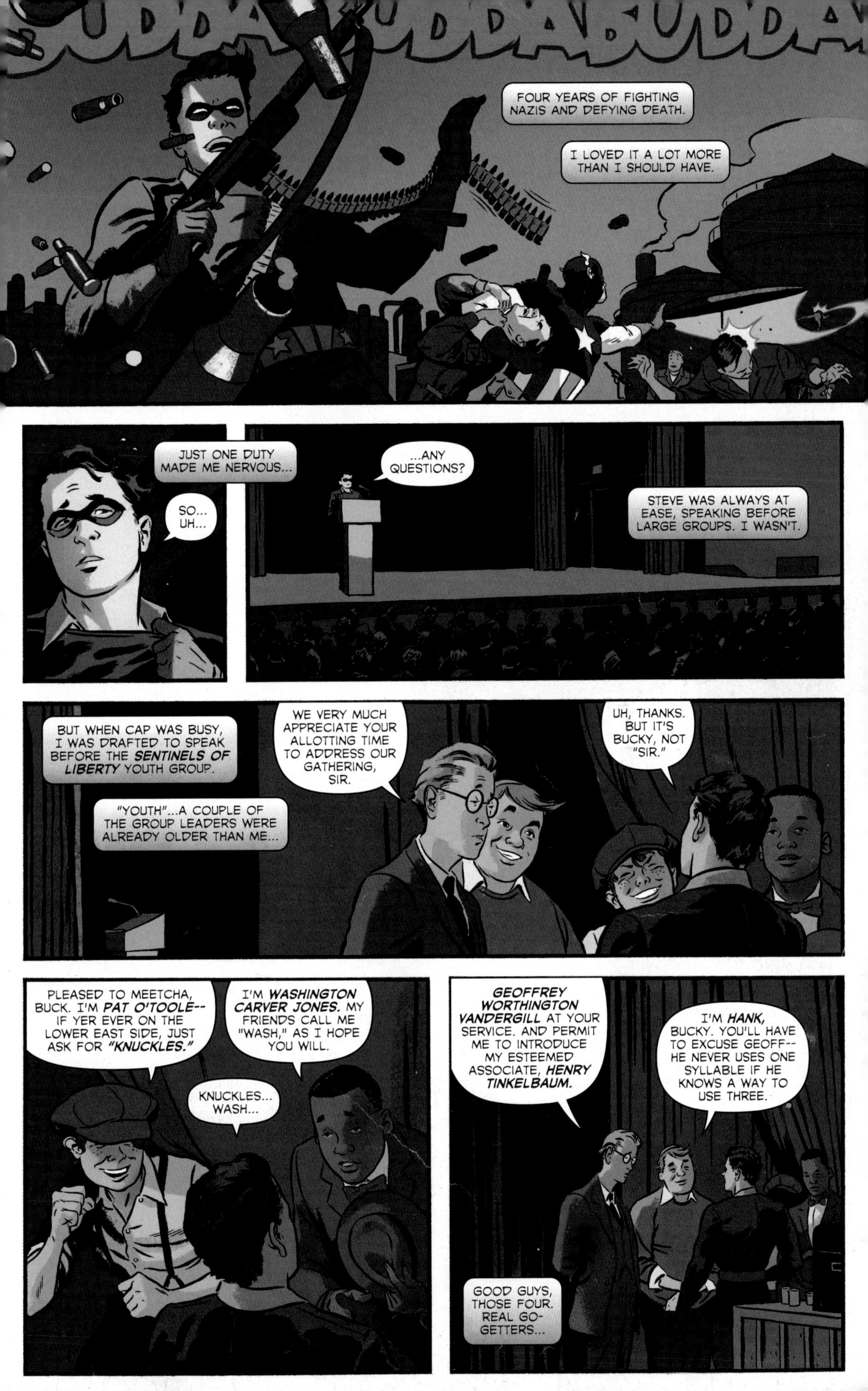

BUDDABUDDABUDDA
FOUR YEARS OF FIGHTING NAZIS AND DEFYING DEATH.
I LOVED IT A LOT MORE THAN I SHOULD HAVE.
JUST ONE DUTY MADE ME NERVOUS...
SO... UH...
...ANY QUESTIONS?
STEVE WAS ALWAYS AT EASE, SPEAKING BEFORE LARGE GROUPS. I WASN'T.
BUT WHEN CAP WAS BUSY, I WAS DRAFTED TO SPEAK BEFORE THE SENTINELS OF LIBERTY YOUTH GROUP.
"YOUTH"...A COUPLE OF THE GROUP LEADERS WERE ALREADY OLDER THAN ME...
WE VERY MUCH APPRECIATE YOUR ALLOTTING TIME TO ADDRESS OUR GATHERING, SIR.
UH, THANKS. BUT IT'S BUCKY, NOT "SIR."
PLEASED TO MEETCHA, BUCK. I'M PAT O'TOOLE-- IF YER EVER ON THE LOWER EAST SIDE, JUST ASK FOR "KNUCKLES."
I'M WASHINGTON CARVER JONES. MY FRIENDS CALL ME "WASH," AS I HOPE YOU WILL.
KNUCKLES... WASH...
GEOFFREY WORTHINGTON VANDERGILL AT YOUR SERVICE. AND PERMIT ME TO INTRODUCE MY ESTEEMED ASSOCIATE, HENRY TINKELBAUM.
I'M HANK, BUCKY. YOU'LL HAVE TO EXCUSE GEOFF-- HE NEVER USES ONE SYLLABLE IF HE KNOWS A WAY TO USE THREE.
GOOD GUYS, THOSE FOUR. REAL GO-GETTERS...

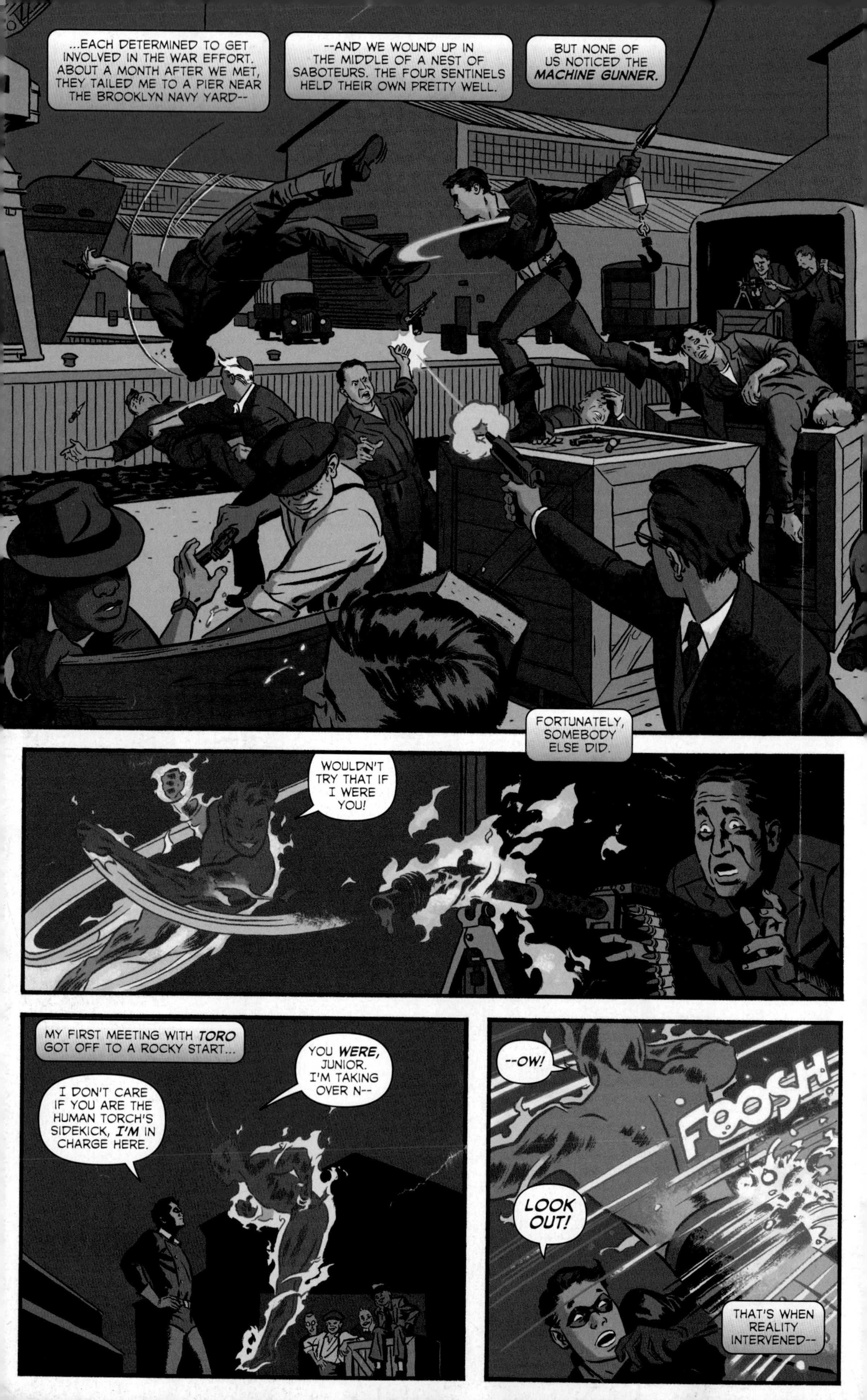
...EACH DETERMINED TO GET INVOLVED IN THE WAR EFFORT. ABOUT A MONTH AFTER WE MET, THEY TAILED ME TO A PIER NEAR THE BROOKLYN NAVY YARD--
--AND WE WOUND UP IN THE MIDDLE OF A NEST OF SABOTEURS. THE FOUR SENTINELS HELD THEIR OWN PRETTY WELL.
BUT NONE OF US NOTICED THE *MACHINE GUNNER.*
FORTUNATELY, SOMEBODY ELSE DID.
WOULDN'T TRY THAT IF I WERE YOU!
MY FIRST MEETING WITH *TORO* GOT OFF TO A ROCKY START...
I DON'T CARE IF YOU ARE THE HUMAN TORCH'S SIDEKICK, *I'M* IN CHARGE HERE.
YOU *WERE,* JUNIOR. I'M TAKING OVER N--
--OW!
FOOSH
LOOK OUT!
THAT'S WHEN REALITY INTERVENED--

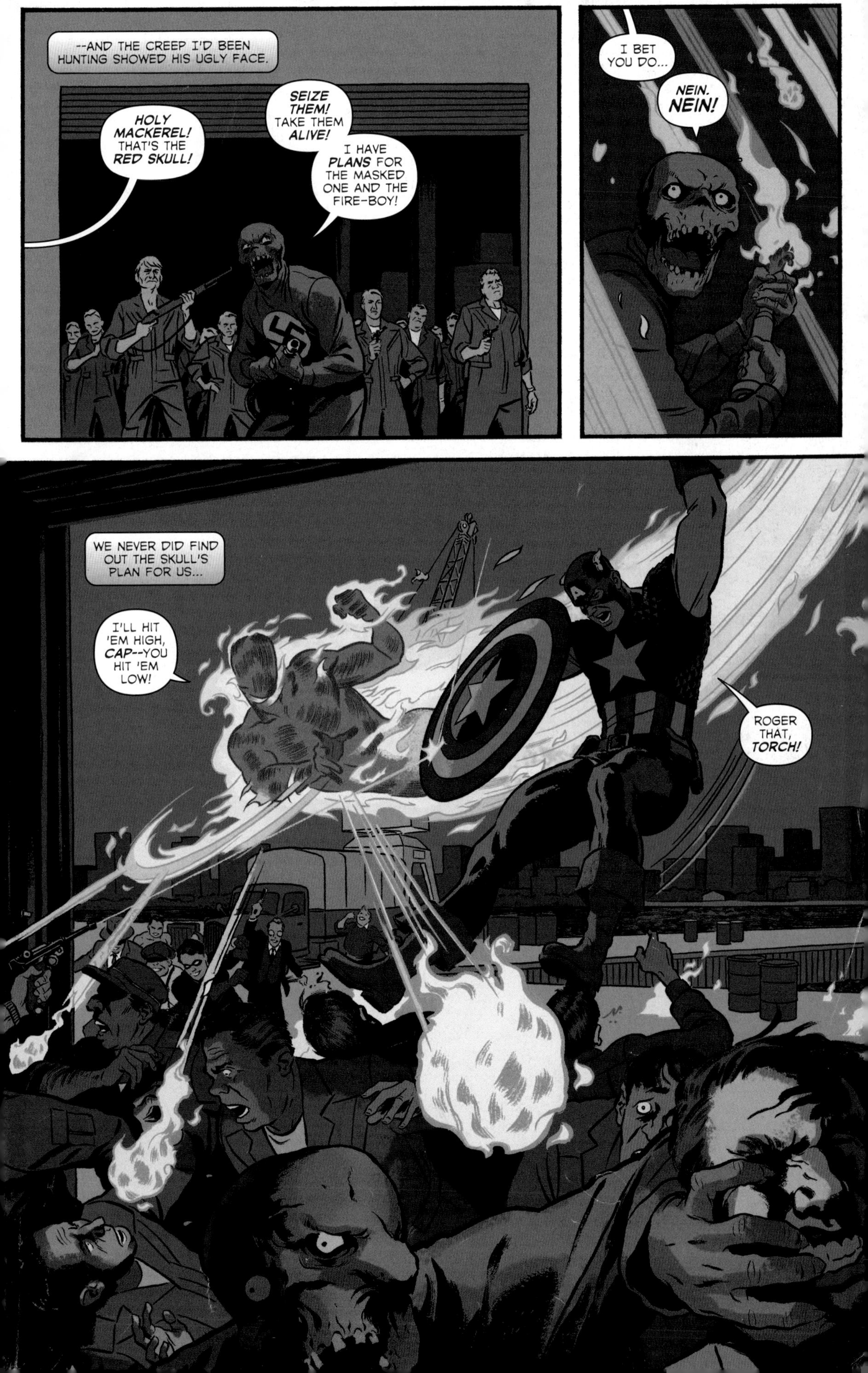
--AND THE CREEP I'D BEEN HUNTING SHOWED HIS UGLY FACE.
HOLY MACKEREL! THAT'S THE RED SKULL!
SEIZE THEM! TAKE THEM ALIVE!
I HAVE PLANS FOR THE MASKED ONE AND THE FIRE-BOY!
I BET YOU DO...
NEIN. NEIN!
WE NEVER DID FIND OUT THE SKULL'S PLAN FOR US...
I'LL HIT 'EM HIGH, CAP--YOU HIT 'EM LOW!
ROGER THAT, TORCH!

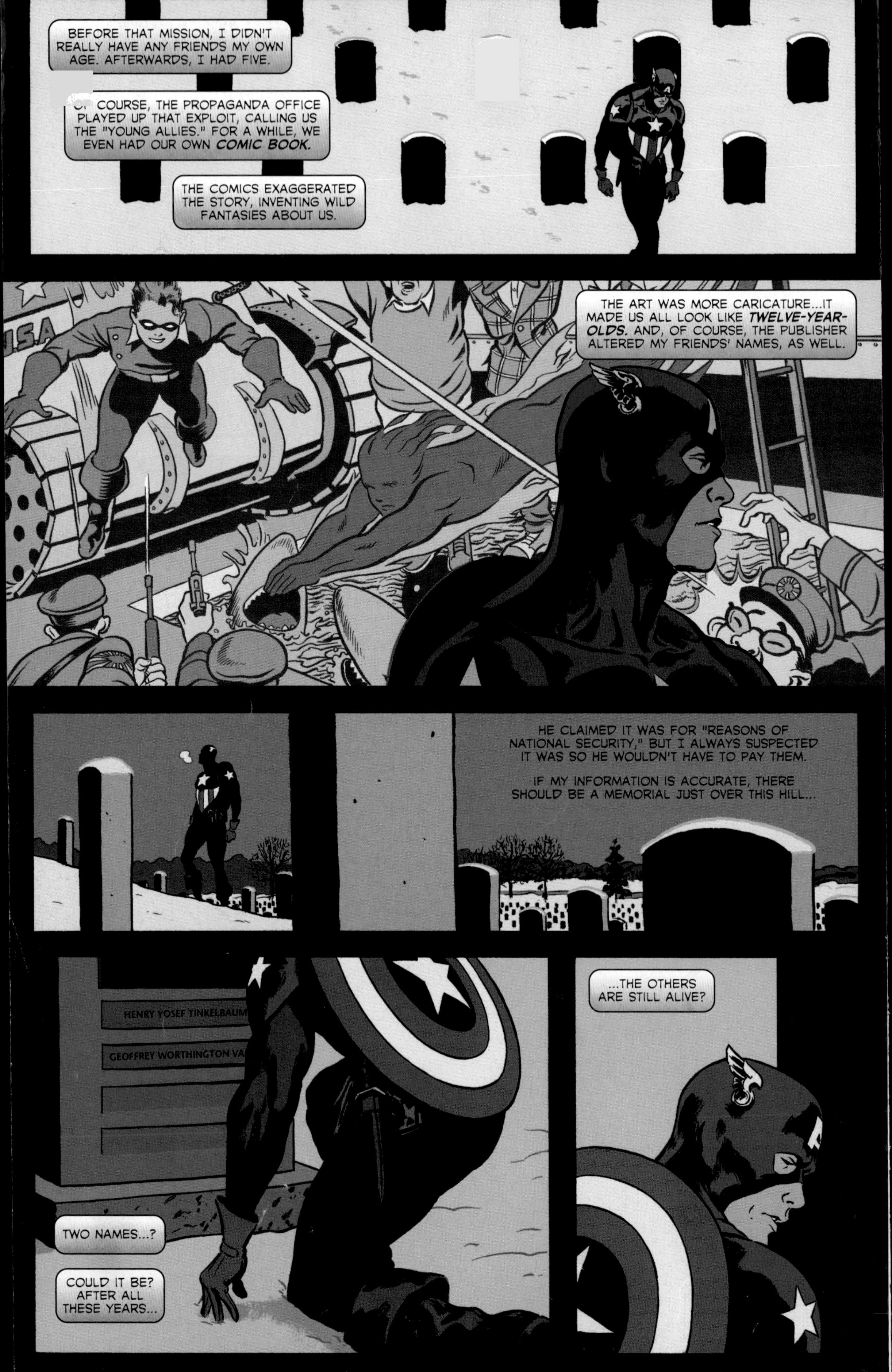
BEFORE THAT MISSION, I DIDN'T REALLY HAVE ANY FRIENDS MY OWN AGE. AFTERWARDS, I HAD FIVE.
OF COURSE, THE PROPAGANDA OFFICE PLAYED UP THAT EXPLOIT, CALLING US THE "YOUNG ALLIES." FOR A WHILE, WE EVEN HAD OUR OWN COMIC BOOK.
THE COMICS EXAGGERATED THE STORY, INVENTING WILD FANTASIES ABOUT US.
THE ART WAS MORE CARICATURE...IT MADE US ALL LOOK LIKE TWELVE-YEAR-OLDS. AND, OF COURSE, THE PUBLISHER ALTERED MY FRIENDS' NAMES, AS WELL.
U.S.A
HE CLAIMED IT WAS FOR "REASONS OF NATIONAL SECURITY," BUT I ALWAYS SUSPECTED IT WAS SO HE WOULDN'T HAVE TO PAY THEM.
IF MY INFORMATION IS ACCURATE, THERE SHOULD BE A MEMORIAL JUST OVER THIS HILL...
HENRY YOSEF TINKELBAUM
GEOFFREY WORTHINGTON VA
TWO NAMES...?
COULD IT BE? AFTER ALL THESE YEARS...
...THE OTHERS ARE STILL ALIVE?

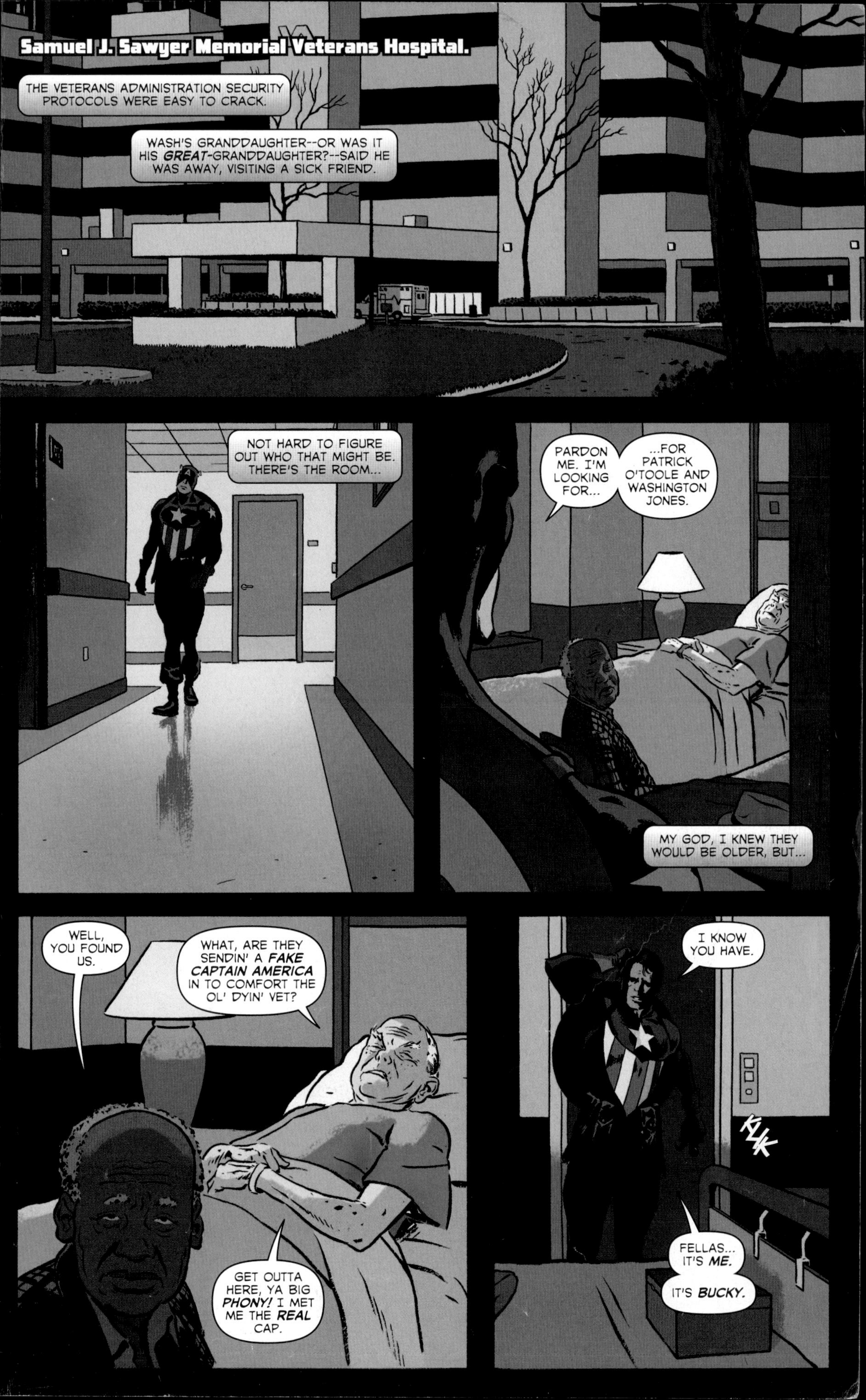
Samuel J. Sawyer Memorial Veterans Hospital.
THE VETERANS ADMINISTRATION SECURITY PROTOCOLS WERE EASY TO CRACK.
WASH'S GRANDDAUGHTER--OR WAS IT HIS *GREAT*-GRANDDAUGHTER?--SAID HE WAS AWAY, VISITING A SICK FRIEND.
NOT HARD TO FIGURE OUT WHO THAT MIGHT BE. THERE'S THE ROOM...
PARDON ME. I'M LOOKING FOR...
...FOR PATRICK O'TOOLE AND WASHINGTON JONES.
MY GOD, I KNEW THEY WOULD BE OLDER, BUT...
WELL, YOU FOUND US.
WHAT, ARE THEY SENDIN' A *FAKE CAPTAIN AMERICA* IN TO COMFORT THE OL' DYIN' VET?
GET OUTTA HERE, YA BIG *PHONY!* I MET ME THE *REAL* CAP.
I KNOW YOU HAVE.
KLIK
FELLAS... IT'S *ME.*
IT'S *BUCKY.*

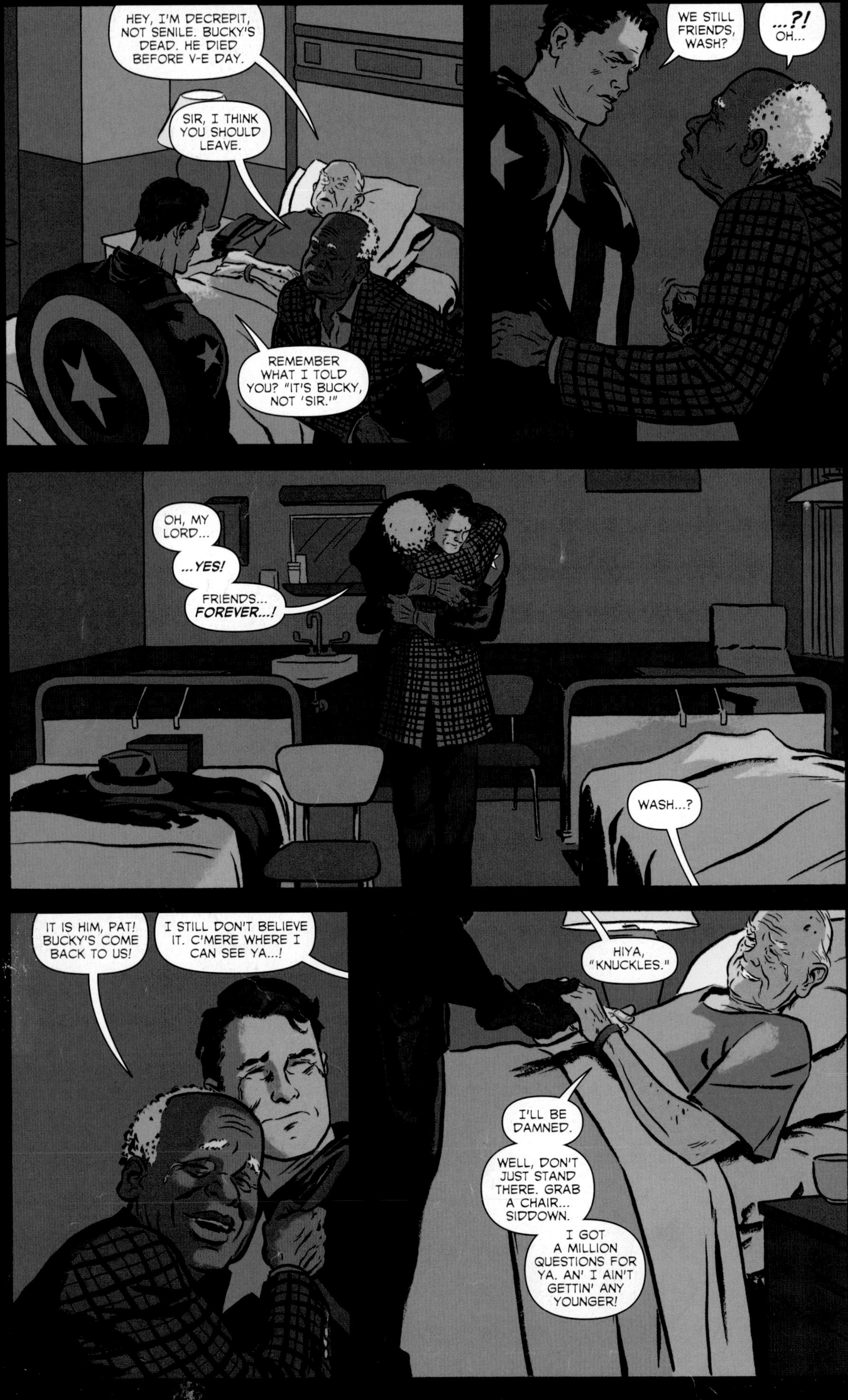
HEY, I'M DECREPIT, NOT SENILE. BUCKY'S DEAD. HE DIED BEFORE V-E DAY.
SIR, I THINK YOU SHOULD LEAVE.
REMEMBER WHAT I TOLD YOU? "IT'S BUCKY, NOT 'SIR.'"
WE STILL FRIENDS, WASH?
...?!
OH...
OH, MY LORD...
...YES!
FRIENDS... FOREVER...!
WASH...?
IT IS HIM, PAT! BUCKY'S COME BACK TO US!
I STILL DON'T BELIEVE IT. C'MERE WHERE I CAN SEE YA...!
HIYA, "KNUCKLES."
I'LL BE DAMNED.
WELL, DON'T JUST STAND THERE. GRAB A CHAIR... SIDDOWN.
I GOT A MILLION QUESTIONS FOR YA. AN' I AIN'T GETTIN' ANY YOUNGER!

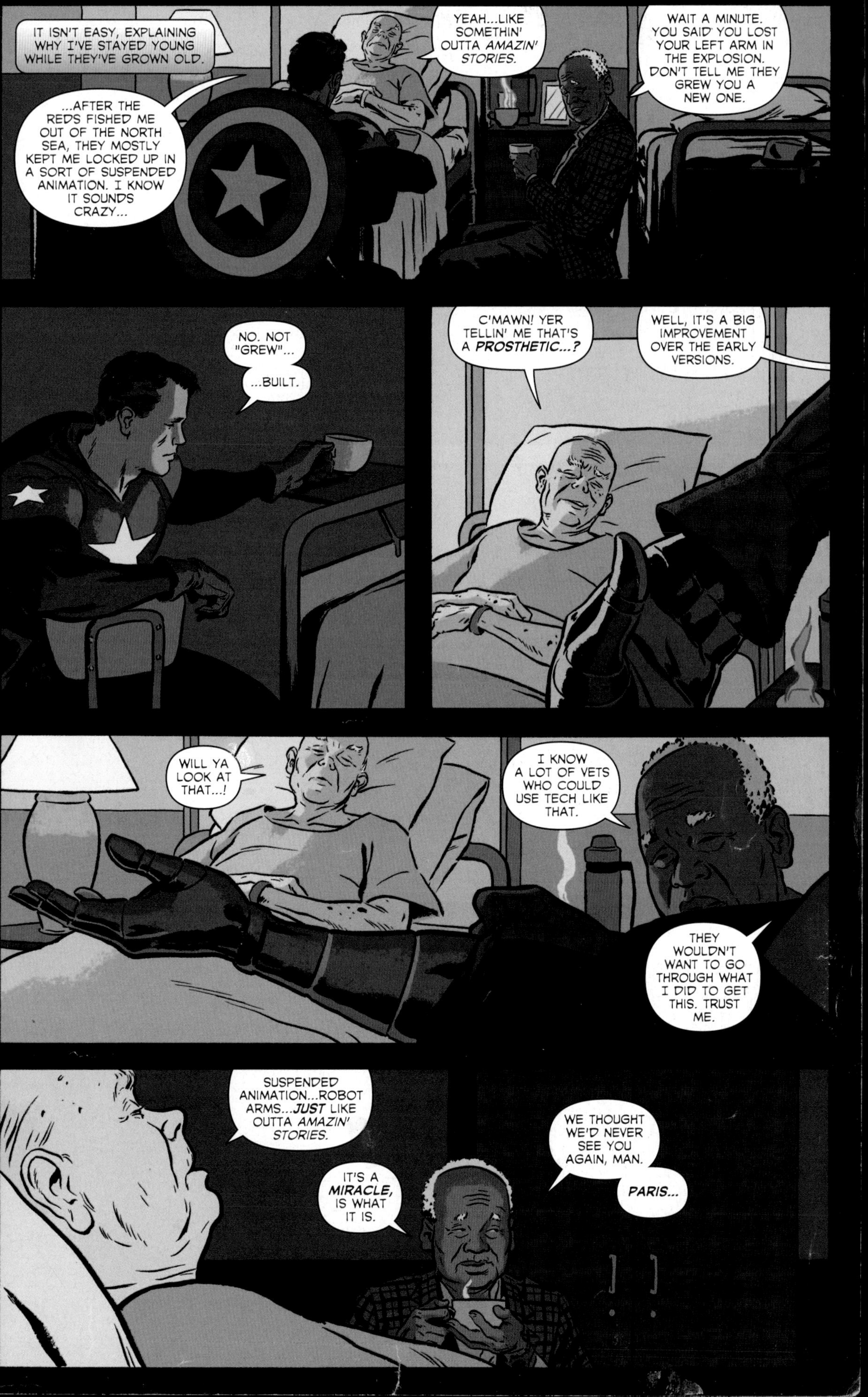
IT ISN'T EASY, EXPLAINING WHY I'VE STAYED YOUNG WHILE THEY'VE GROWN OLD.
...AFTER THE REDS FISHED ME OUT OF THE NORTH SEA, THEY MOSTLY KEPT ME LOCKED UP IN A SORT OF SUSPENDED ANIMATION. I KNOW IT SOUNDS CRAZY...
YEAH...LIKE SOMETHIN' OUTTA *AMAZIN' STORIES.*
WAIT A MINUTE. YOU SAID YOU LOST YOUR LEFT ARM IN THE EXPLOSION. DON'T TELL ME THEY GREW YOU A NEW ONE.
NO. NOT "GREW"...
...BUILT.
C'MAWN! YER TELLIN' ME THAT'S A ***PROSTHETIC...?***
WELL, IT'S A BIG IMPROVEMENT OVER THE EARLY VERSIONS.
WILL YA LOOK AT THAT...!
I KNOW A LOT OF VETS WHO COULD USE TECH LIKE THAT.
THEY WOULDN'T WANT TO GO THROUGH WHAT I DID TO GET THIS. TRUST ME.
SUSPENDED ANIMATION...ROBOT ARMS...***JUST*** LIKE OUTTA *AMAZIN' STORIES.*
IT'S A ***MIRACLE,*** IS WHAT IT IS.
WE THOUGHT WE'D NEVER SEE YOU AGAIN, MAN.
PARIS...

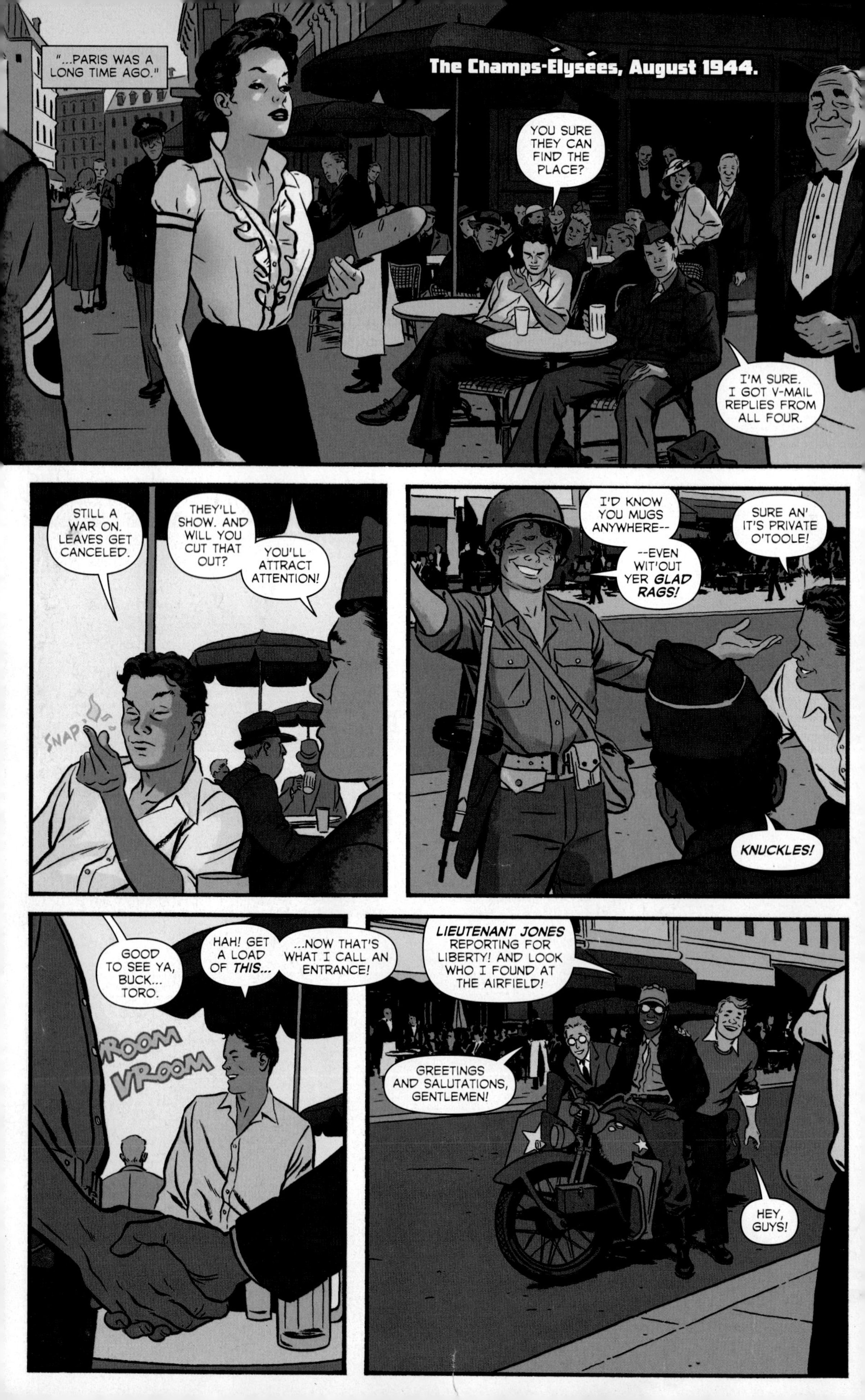
"...PARIS WAS A LONG TIME AGO."
The Champs-Elysées, August 1944.
YOU SURE THEY CAN FIND THE PLACE?
I'M SURE. I GOT V-MAIL REPLIES FROM ALL FOUR.
STILL A WAR ON. LEAVES GET CANCELED.
THEY'LL SHOW. AND WILL YOU CUT THAT OUT?
YOU'LL ATTRACT ATTENTION!
SNAP
I'D KNOW YOU MUGS ANYWHERE--
--EVEN WIT'OUT YER GLAD RAGS!
SURE AN' IT'S PRIVATE O'TOOLE!
KNUCKLES!
GOOD TO SEE YA, BUCK... TORO.
HAH! GET A LOAD OF THIS...
...NOW THAT'S WHAT I CALL AN ENTRANCE!
VROOM VROOM
LIEUTENANT JONES REPORTING FOR LIBERTY! AND LOOK WHO I FOUND AT THE AIRFIELD!
GREETINGS AND SALUTATIONS, GENTLEMEN!
HEY, GUYS!

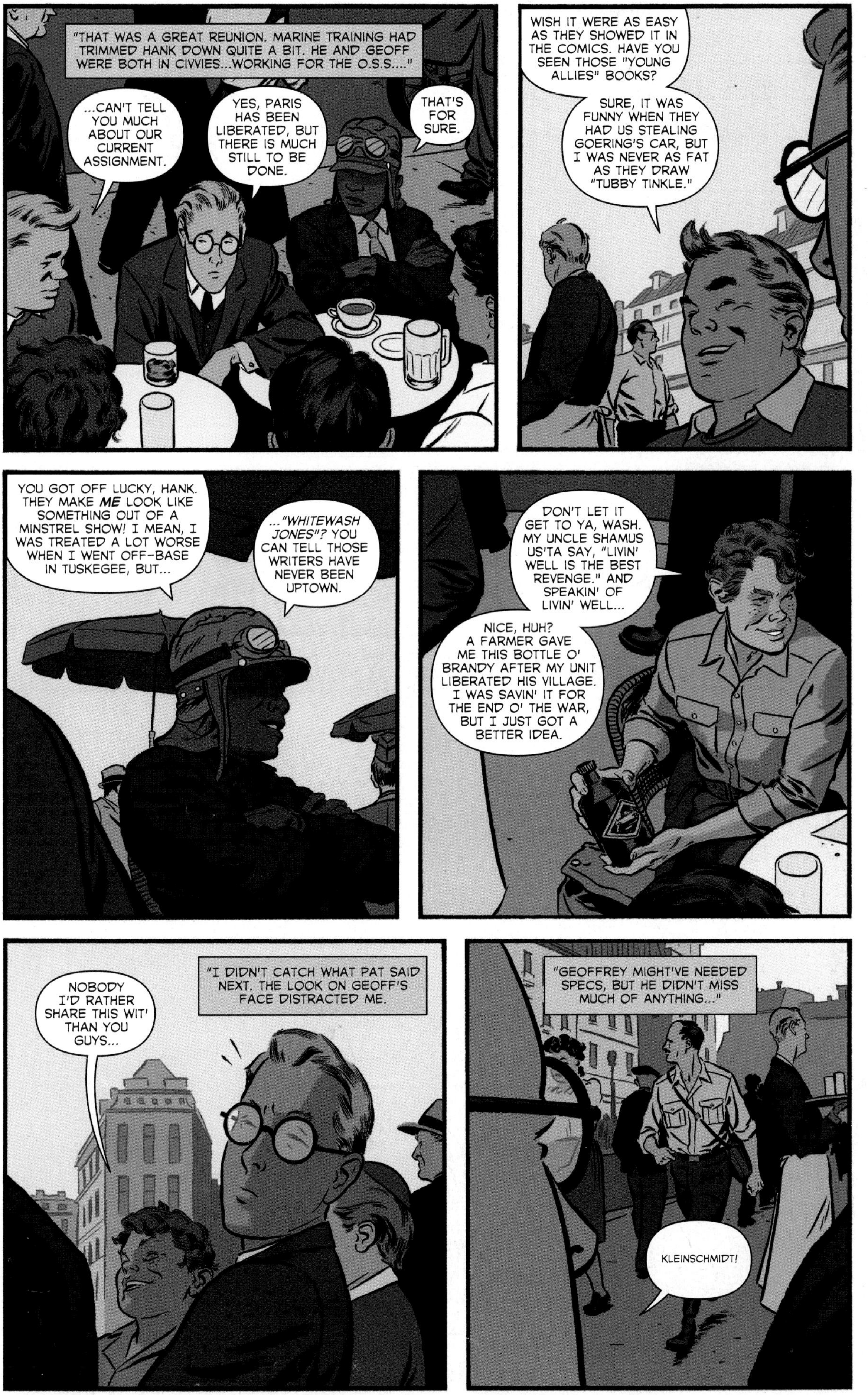

"THAT WAS A GREAT REUNION. MARINE TRAINING HAD TRIMMED HANK DOWN QUITE A BIT. HE AND GEOFF WERE BOTH IN CIVVIES...WORKING FOR THE O.S.S...."
...CAN'T TELL YOU MUCH ABOUT OUR CURRENT ASSIGNMENT.
YES, PARIS HAS BEEN LIBERATED, BUT THERE IS MUCH STILL TO BE DONE.
THAT'S FOR SURE.
WISH IT WERE AS EASY AS THEY SHOWED IT IN THE COMICS. HAVE YOU SEEN THOSE "YOUNG ALLIES" BOOKS?
SURE, IT WAS FUNNY WHEN THEY HAD US STEALING GOERING'S CAR, BUT I WAS NEVER AS FAT AS THEY DRAW "TUBBY TINKLE."
YOU GOT OFF LUCKY, HANK. THEY MAKE ME LOOK LIKE SOMETHING OUT OF A MINSTREL SHOW! I MEAN, I WAS TREATED A LOT WORSE WHEN I WENT OFF-BASE IN TUSKEGEE, BUT...
..."WHITEWASH JONES"? YOU CAN TELL THOSE WRITERS HAVE NEVER BEEN UPTOWN.
DON'T LET IT GET TO YA, WASH. MY UNCLE SHAMUS US'TA SAY, "LIVIN' WELL IS THE BEST REVENGE." AND SPEAKIN' OF LIVIN' WELL...
NICE, HUH? A FARMER GAVE ME THIS BOTTLE O' BRANDY AFTER MY UNIT LIBERATED HIS VILLAGE. I WAS SAVIN' IT FOR THE END O' THE WAR, BUT I JUST GOT A BETTER IDEA.
NOBODY I'D RATHER SHARE THIS WIT' THAN YOU GUYS...
"I DIDN'T CATCH WHAT PAT SAID NEXT. THE LOOK ON GEOFF'S FACE DISTRACTED ME.
"GEOFFREY MIGHT'VE NEEDED SPECS, BUT HE DIDN'T MISS MUCH OF ANYTHING..."
KLEINSCHMIDT!

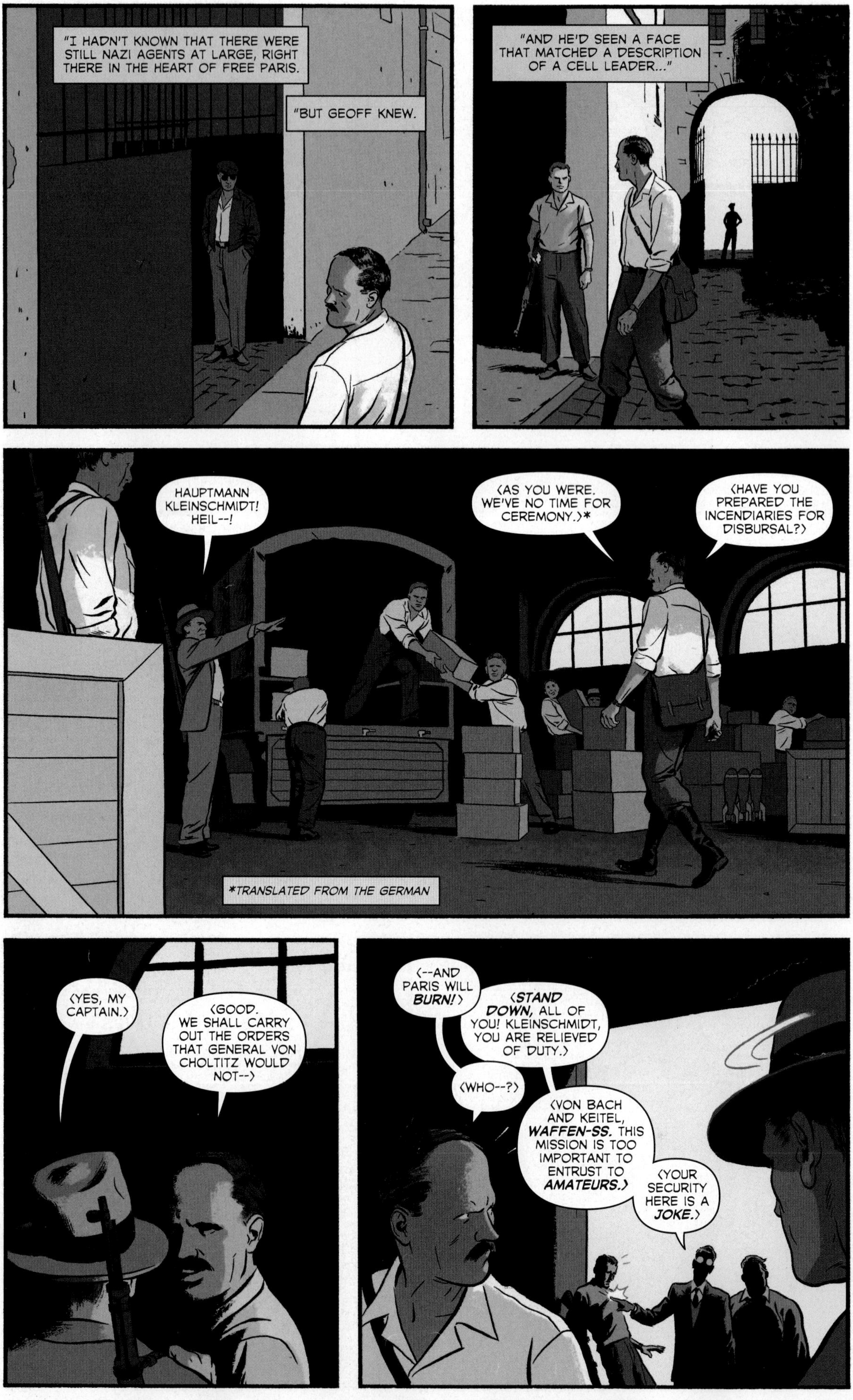
"I HADN'T KNOWN THAT THERE WERE STILL NAZI AGENTS AT LARGE, RIGHT THERE IN THE HEART OF FREE PARIS.
"BUT GEOFF KNEW.
"AND HE'D SEEN A FACE THAT MATCHED A DESCRIPTION OF A CELL LEADER..."
HAUPTMANN KLEINSCHMIDT! HEIL--!
<AS YOU WERE. WE'VE NO TIME FOR CEREMONY.>*
<HAVE YOU PREPARED THE INCENDIARIES FOR DISBURSAL?>
*TRANSLATED FROM THE GERMAN
<YES, MY CAPTAIN.>
<GOOD. WE SHALL CARRY OUT THE ORDERS THAT GENERAL VON CHOLTITZ WOULD NOT-->
<--AND PARIS WILL BURN!>
<STAND DOWN, ALL OF YOU! KLEINSCHMIDT, YOU ARE RELIEVED OF DUTY.>
<WHO--?>
<VON BACH AND KEITEL, WAFFEN-SS. THIS MISSION IS TOO IMPORTANT TO ENTRUST TO AMATEURS.>
<YOUR SECURITY HERE IS A JOKE.>

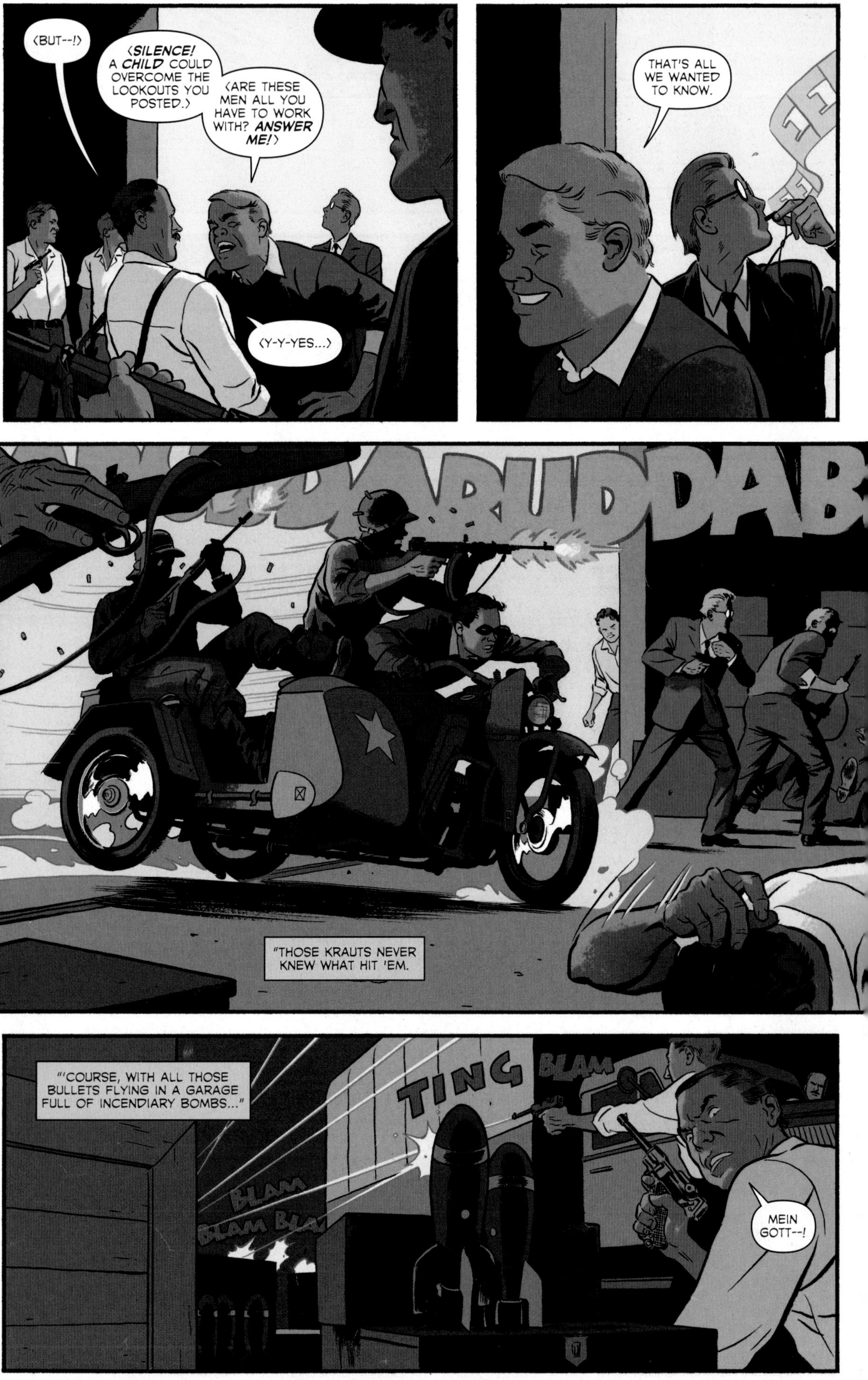
‹BUT--!›
‹SILENCE! A CHILD COULD OVERCOME THE LOOKOUTS YOU POSTED.›
‹ARE THESE MEN ALL YOU HAVE TO WORK WITH? ANSWER ME!›
‹Y-Y-YES...›
THAT'S ALL WE WANTED TO KNOW.
DARUDDAB
"THOSE KRAUTS NEVER KNEW WHAT HIT 'EM.
"'COURSE, WITH ALL THOSE BULLETS FLYING IN A GARAGE FULL OF INCENDIARY BOMBS..."
TING
BLAM
BLAM
BLAM BLAM
MEIN GOTT--!

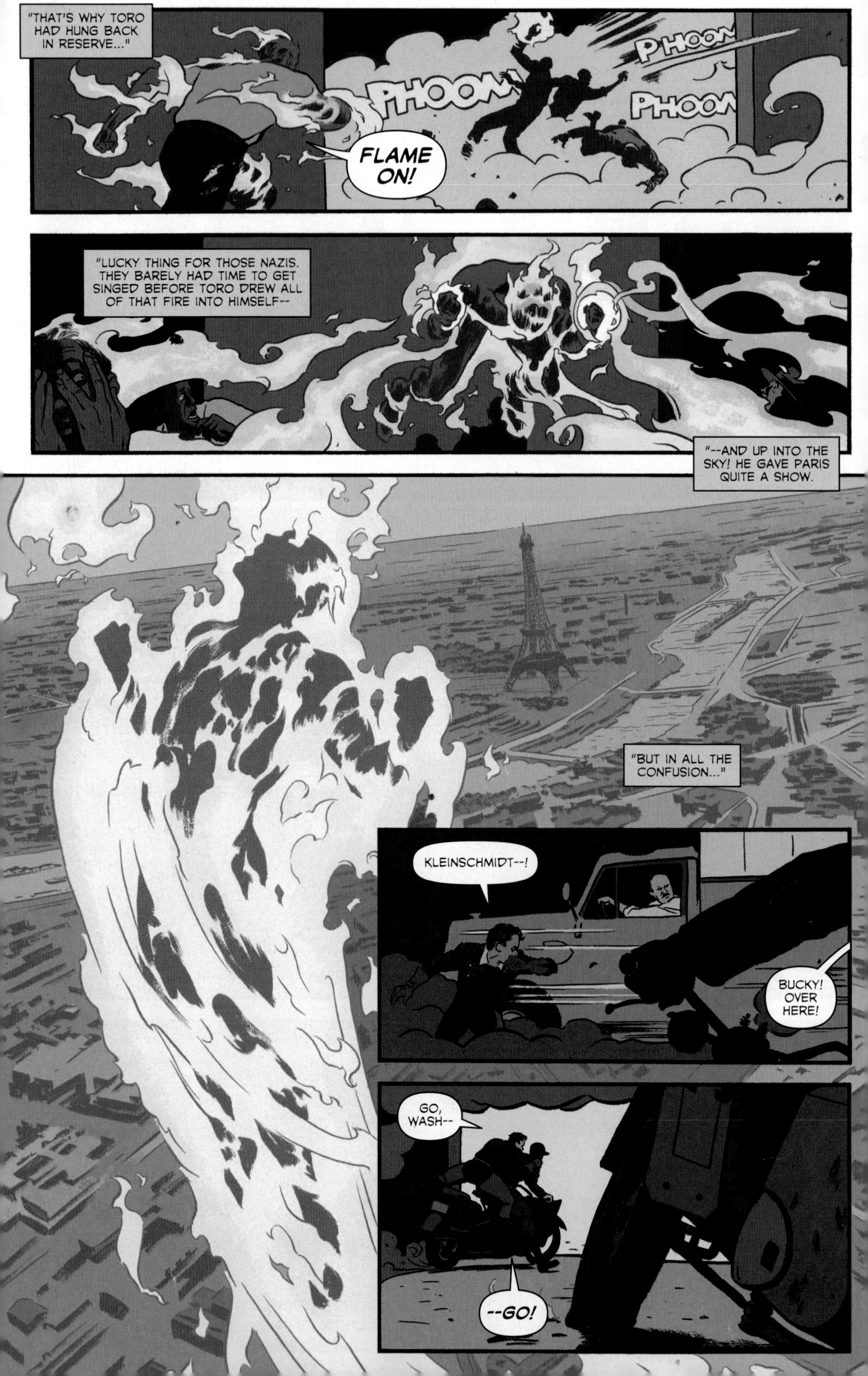
"THAT'S WHY TORO HAD HUNG BACK IN RESERVE..."
PHOOM
PHOOM
PHOOM
FLAME ON!
"LUCKY THING FOR THOSE NAZIS. THEY BARELY HAD TIME TO GET SINGED BEFORE TORO DREW ALL OF THAT FIRE INTO HIMSELF--
"--AND UP INTO THE SKY! HE GAVE PARIS QUITE A SHOW.
"BUT IN ALL THE CONFUSION..."
KLEINSCHMIDT--!
BUCKY! OVER HERE!
GO, WASH--
--GO!

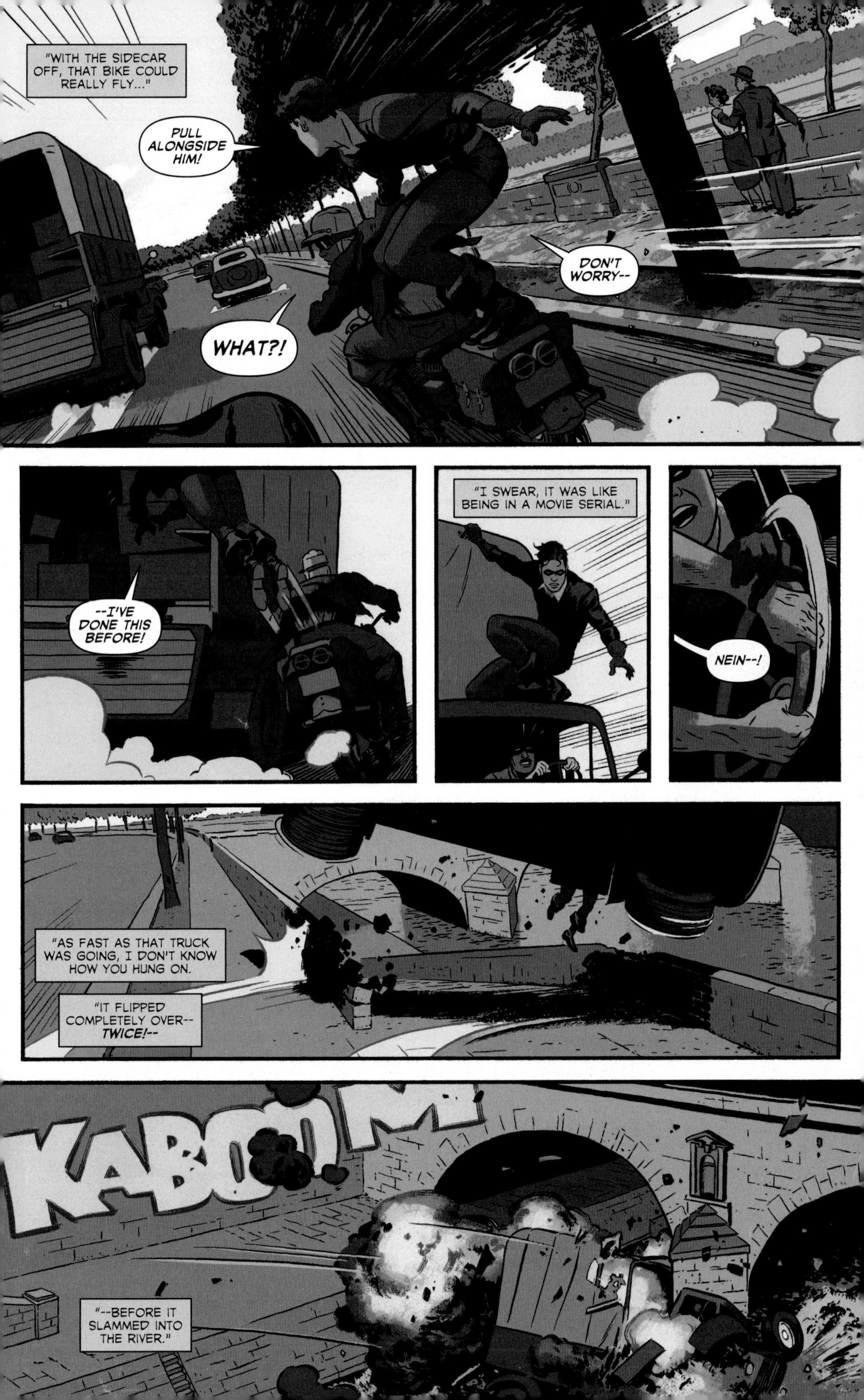
"WITH THE SIDECAR OFF, THAT BIKE COULD REALLY FLY..."
PULL ALONGSIDE HIM!
WHAT?!
DON'T WORRY--
--I'VE DONE THIS BEFORE!
"I SWEAR, IT WAS LIKE BEING IN A MOVIE SERIAL."
NEIN--!
"AS FAST AS THAT TRUCK WAS GOING, I DON'T KNOW HOW YOU HUNG ON.
"IT FLIPPED COMPLETELY OVER-- TWICE!--
KABOOM
"--BEFORE IT SLAMMED INTO THE RIVER."

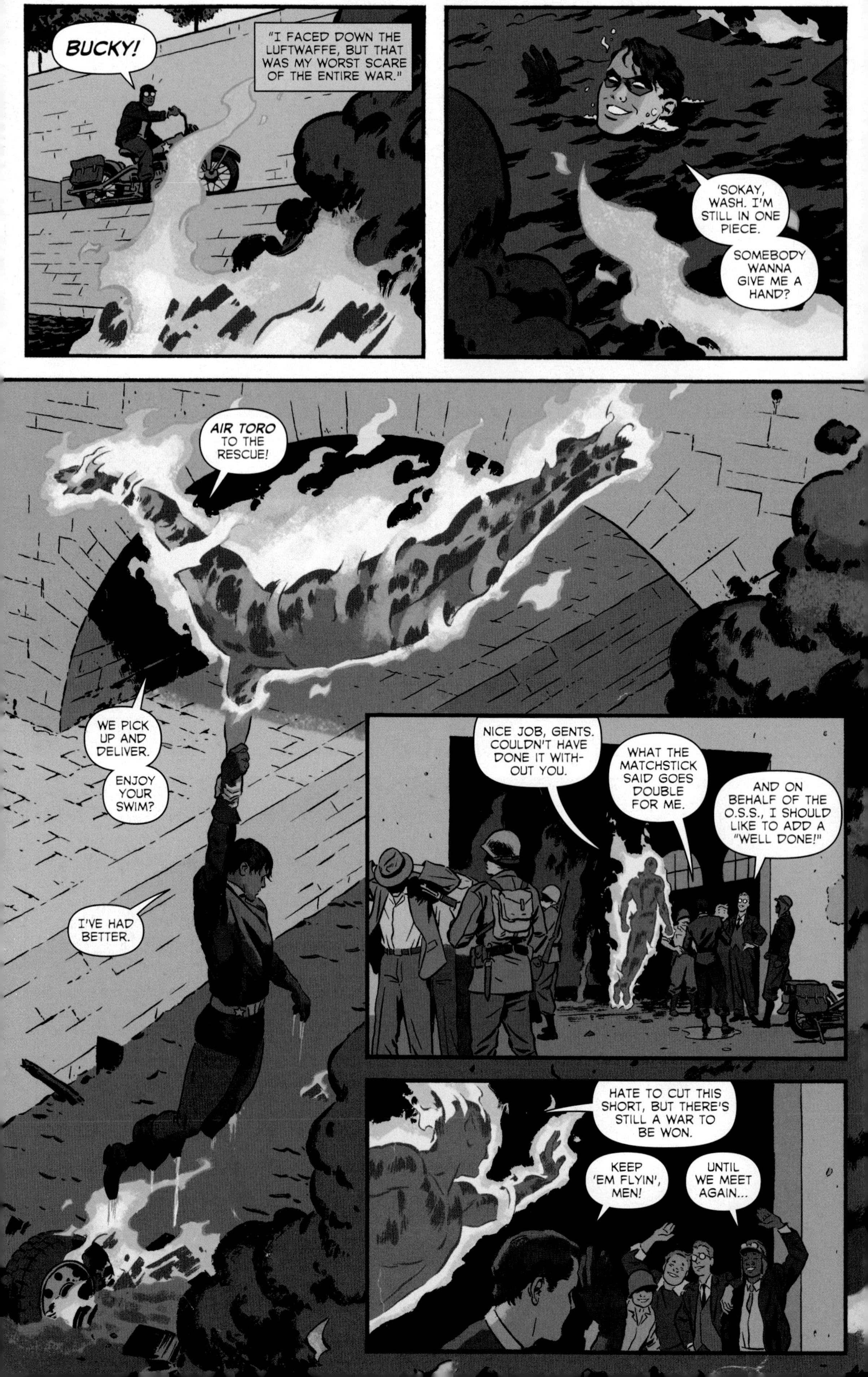

BUCKY!
"I FACED DOWN THE LUFTWAFFE, BUT THAT WAS MY WORST SCARE OF THE ENTIRE WAR."
'SOKAY, WASH. I'M STILL IN ONE PIECE.
SOMEBODY WANNA GIVE ME A HAND?
AIR TORO TO THE RESCUE!
WE PICK UP AND DELIVER.
ENJOY YOUR SWIM?
I'VE HAD BETTER.
NICE JOB, GENTS. COULDN'T HAVE DONE IT WITH-OUT YOU.
WHAT THE MATCHSTICK SAID GOES DOUBLE FOR ME.
AND ON BEHALF OF THE O.S.S., I SHOULD LIKE TO ADD A "WELL DONE!"
HATE TO CUT THIS SHORT, BUT THERE'S STILL A WAR TO BE WON.
KEEP 'EM FLYIN', MEN!
UNTIL WE MEET AGAIN...

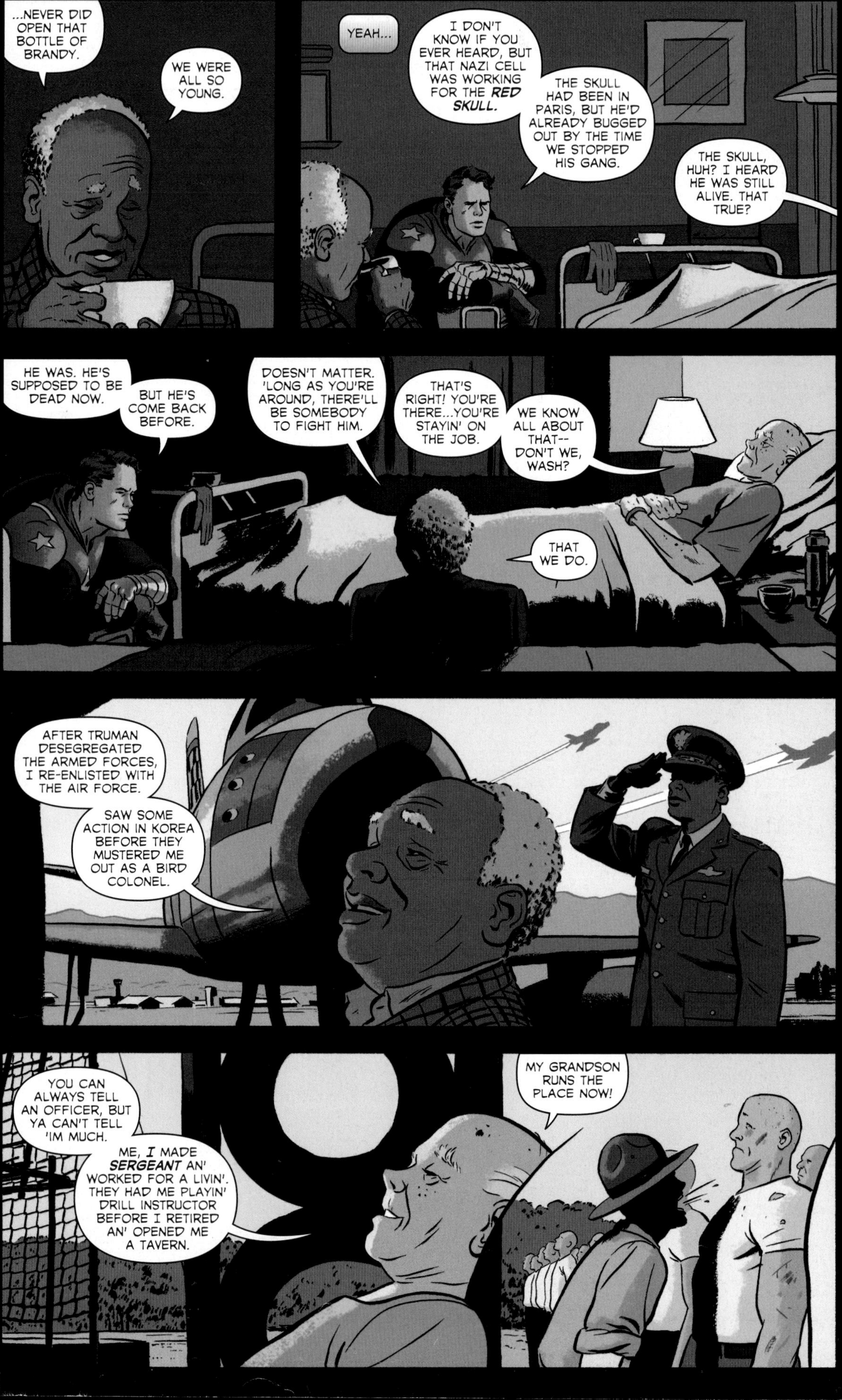
...NEVER DID OPEN THAT BOTTLE OF BRANDY.
WE WERE ALL SO YOUNG.
YEAH...
I DON'T KNOW IF YOU EVER HEARD, BUT THAT NAZI CELL WAS WORKING FOR THE RED SKULL.
THE SKULL HAD BEEN IN PARIS, BUT HE'D ALREADY BUGGED OUT BY THE TIME WE STOPPED HIS GANG.
THE SKULL, HUH? I HEARD HE WAS STILL ALIVE. THAT TRUE?
HE WAS. HE'S SUPPOSED TO BE DEAD NOW.
BUT HE'S COME BACK BEFORE.
DOESN'T MATTER. 'LONG AS YOU'RE AROUND, THERE'LL BE SOMEBODY TO FIGHT HIM.
THAT'S RIGHT! YOU'RE THERE...YOU'RE STAYIN' ON THE JOB.
WE KNOW ALL ABOUT THAT-- DON'T WE, WASH?
THAT WE DO.
AFTER TRUMAN DESEGREGATED THE ARMED FORCES, I RE-ENLISTED WITH THE AIR FORCE.
SAW SOME ACTION IN KOREA BEFORE THEY MUSTERED ME OUT AS A BIRD COLONEL.
YOU CAN ALWAYS TELL AN OFFICER, BUT YA CAN'T TELL 'IM MUCH.
ME, I MADE SERGEANT AN' WORKED FOR A LIVIN'. THEY HAD ME PLAYIN' DRILL INSTRUCTOR BEFORE I RETIRED AN' OPENED ME A TAVERN.
MY GRANDSON RUNS THE PLACE NOW!

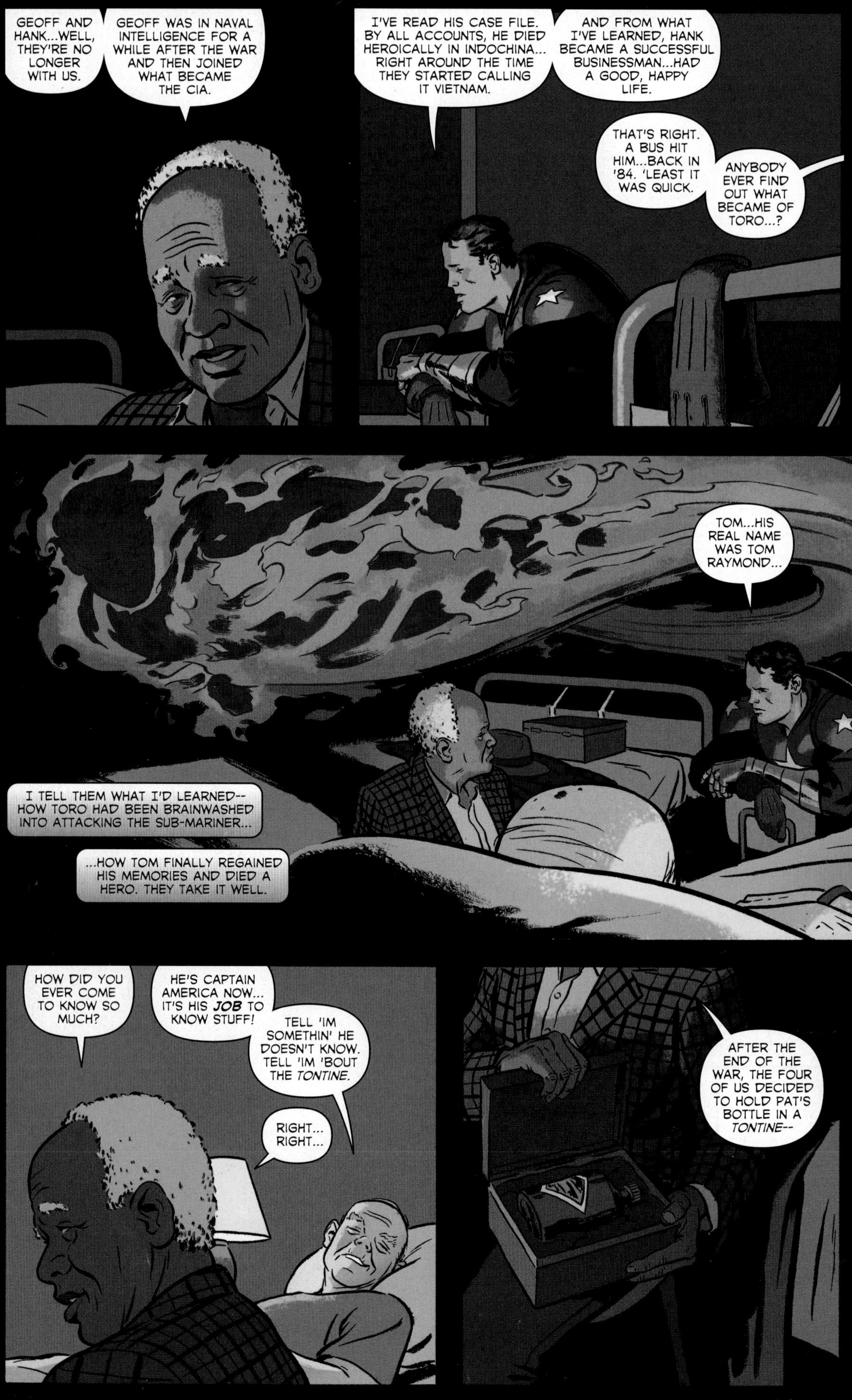
GEOFF AND HANK...WELL, THEY'RE NO LONGER WITH US.
GEOFF WAS IN NAVAL INTELLIGENCE FOR A WHILE AFTER THE WAR AND THEN JOINED WHAT BECAME THE CIA.
I'VE READ HIS CASE FILE. BY ALL ACCOUNTS, HE DIED HEROICALLY IN INDOCHINA... RIGHT AROUND THE TIME THEY STARTED CALLING IT VIETNAM.
AND FROM WHAT I'VE LEARNED, HANK BECAME A SUCCESSFUL BUSINESSMAN...HAD A GOOD, HAPPY LIFE.
THAT'S RIGHT. A BUS HIT HIM...BACK IN '84. 'LEAST IT WAS QUICK.
ANYBODY EVER FIND OUT WHAT BECAME OF TORO...?
TOM...HIS REAL NAME WAS TOM RAYMOND...
I TELL THEM WHAT I'D LEARNED-- HOW TORO HAD BEEN BRAINWASHED INTO ATTACKING THE SUB-MARINER...
...HOW TOM FINALLY REGAINED HIS MEMORIES AND DIED A HERO. THEY TAKE IT WELL.
HOW DID YOU EVER COME TO KNOW SO MUCH?
HE'S CAPTAIN AMERICA NOW... IT'S HIS **JOB** TO KNOW STUFF!
TELL 'IM SOMETHIN' HE DOESN'T KNOW. TELL 'IM 'BOUT THE *TONTINE.*
RIGHT... RIGHT...
AFTER THE END OF THE WAR, THE FOUR OF US DECIDED TO HOLD PAT'S BOTTLE IN A *TONTINE--*

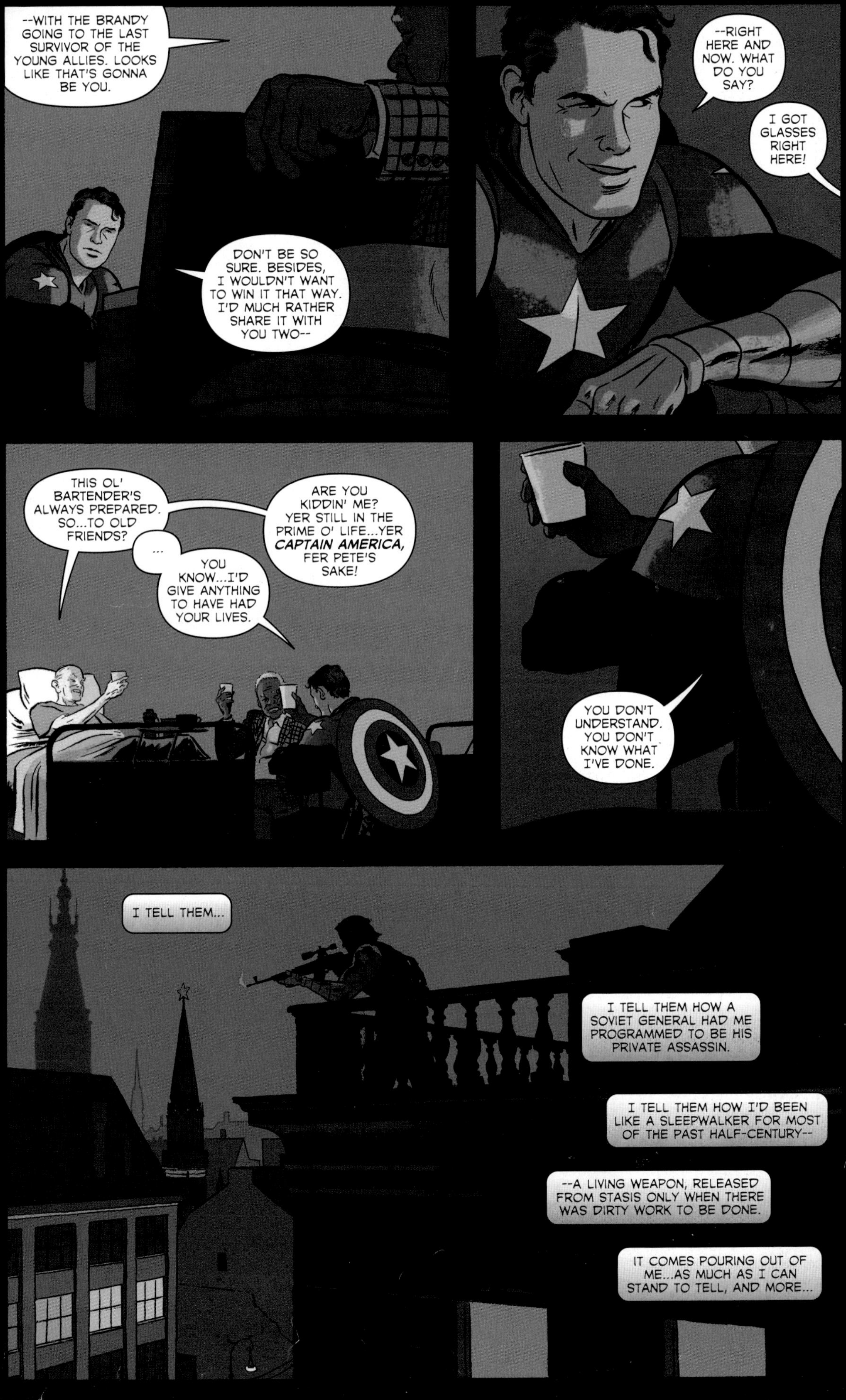
--WITH THE BRANDY GOING TO THE LAST SURVIVOR OF THE YOUNG ALLIES. LOOKS LIKE THAT'S GONNA BE YOU.
DON'T BE SO SURE. BESIDES, I WOULDN'T WANT TO WIN IT THAT WAY. I'D MUCH RATHER SHARE IT WITH YOU TWO--
--RIGHT HERE AND NOW. WHAT DO YOU SAY?
I GOT GLASSES RIGHT HERE!
THIS OL' BARTENDER'S ALWAYS PREPARED. SO...TO OLD FRIENDS?
...
ARE YOU KIDDIN' ME? YER STILL IN THE PRIME O' LIFE...YER CAPTAIN AMERICA, FER PETE'S SAKE!
YOU KNOW...I'D GIVE ANYTHING TO HAVE HAD YOUR LIVES.
YOU DON'T UNDERSTAND. YOU DON'T KNOW WHAT I'VE DONE.
I TELL THEM...
I TELL THEM HOW A SOVIET GENERAL HAD ME PROGRAMMED TO BE HIS PRIVATE ASSASSIN.
I TELL THEM HOW I'D BEEN LIKE A SLEEPWALKER FOR MOST OF THE PAST HALF-CENTURY--
--A LIVING WEAPON, RELEASED FROM STASIS ONLY WHEN THERE WAS DIRTY WORK TO BE DONE.
IT COMES POURING OUT OF ME...AS MUCH AS I CAN STAND TO TELL, AND MORE...

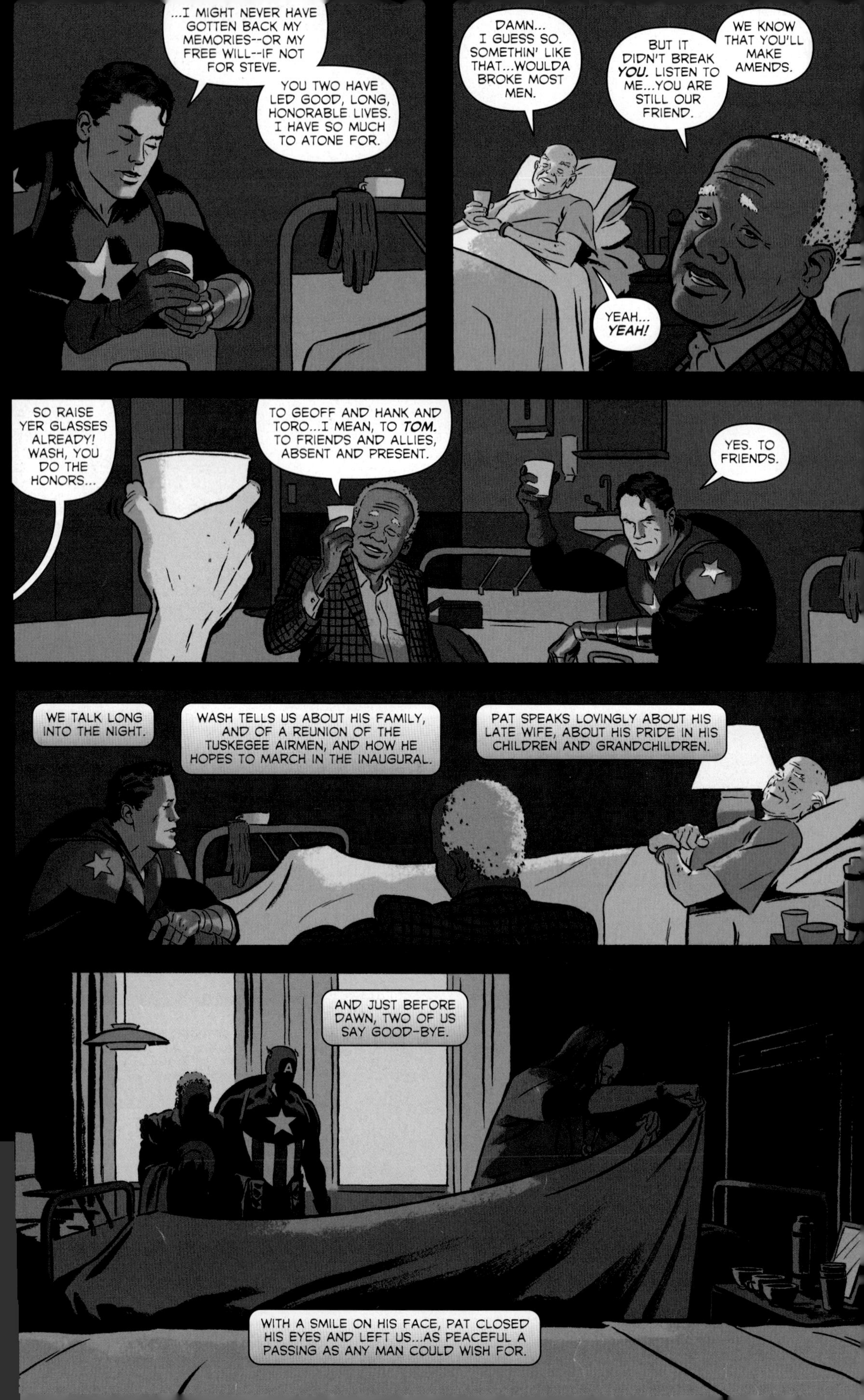
...I MIGHT NEVER HAVE GOTTEN BACK MY MEMORIES--OR MY FREE WILL--IF NOT FOR STEVE.
YOU TWO HAVE LED GOOD, LONG, HONORABLE LIVES. I HAVE SO MUCH TO ATONE FOR.
DAMN... I GUESS SO. SOMETHIN' LIKE THAT...WOULDA BROKE MOST MEN.
BUT IT DIDN'T BREAK YOU. LISTEN TO ME...YOU ARE STILL OUR FRIEND.
WE KNOW THAT YOU'LL MAKE AMENDS.
YEAH... YEAH!
SO RAISE YER GLASSES ALREADY! WASH, YOU DO THE HONORS...
TO GEOFF AND HANK AND TORO...I MEAN, TO TOM. TO FRIENDS AND ALLIES, ABSENT AND PRESENT.
YES. TO FRIENDS.
WE TALK LONG INTO THE NIGHT.
WASH TELLS US ABOUT HIS FAMILY, AND OF A REUNION OF THE TUSKEGEE AIRMEN, AND HOW HE HOPES TO MARCH IN THE INAUGURAL.
PAT SPEAKS LOVINGLY ABOUT HIS LATE WIFE, ABOUT HIS PRIDE IN HIS CHILDREN AND GRANDCHILDREN.
AND JUST BEFORE DAWN, TWO OF US SAY GOOD-BYE.
WITH A SMILE ON HIS FACE, PAT CLOSED HIS EYES AND LEFT US...AS PEACEFUL A PASSING AS ANY MAN COULD WISH FOR.

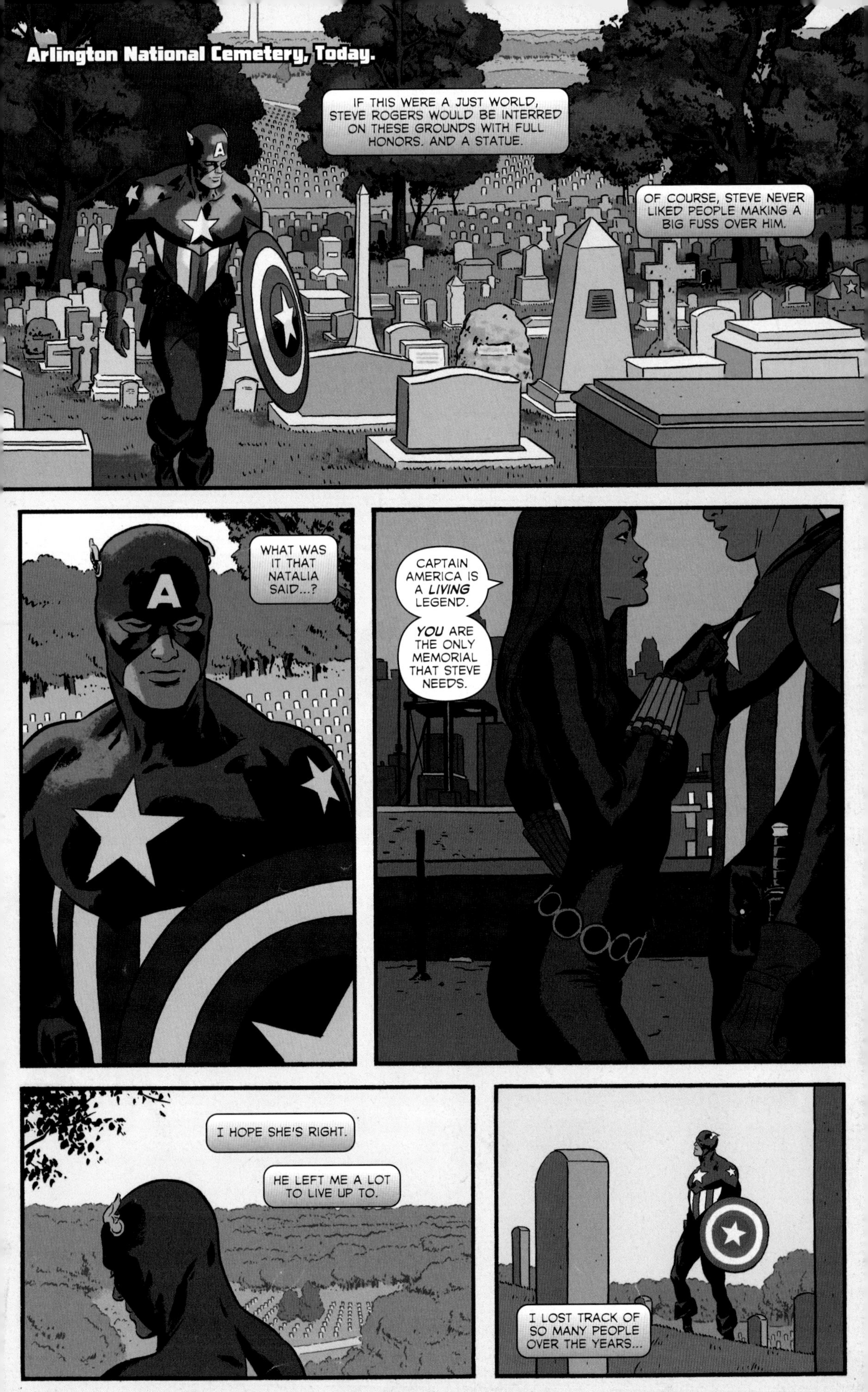
Arlington National Cemetery, Today.
IF THIS WERE A JUST WORLD, STEVE ROGERS WOULD BE INTERRED ON THESE GROUNDS WITH FULL HONORS. AND A STATUE.
OF COURSE, STEVE NEVER LIKED PEOPLE MAKING A BIG FUSS OVER HIM.
WHAT WAS IT THAT NATALIA SAID...?
CAPTAIN AMERICA IS A *LIVING* LEGEND.
YOU ARE THE ONLY MEMORIAL THAT STEVE NEEDS.
I HOPE SHE'S RIGHT.
HE LEFT ME A LOT TO LIVE UP TO.
I LOST TRACK OF SO MANY PEOPLE OVER THE YEARS...

FOREVER ALLIED IN THE SERVICE OF THEIR NATION

...IT'S GOOD THAT I FOUND PAT AND WASH BEFORE THE END.

STRANGE TO SEE MY FACE THERE AMONG THE OTHERS. STILL, IT'S FITTING. IN A WAY, THAT BUCKY IS DEAD, TOO.

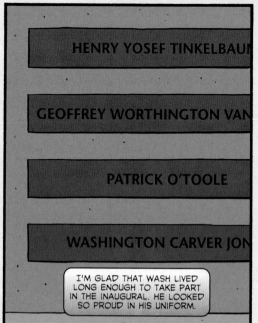

HENRY YOSEF TINKELBAUM

GEOFFREY WORTHINGTON VAN

PATRICK O'TOOLE

WASHINGTON CARVER JON

I'M GLAD THAT WASH LIVED LONG ENOUGH TO TAKE PART IN THE INAUGURAL. HE LOOKED SO PROUD IN HIS UNIFORM.

AND I'M GLAD WE DIDN'T FINISH THE BRANDY THAT NIGHT.

REST WELL, MY YOUNG ALLIES.

IT WAS A PRIVILEGE TO SERVE WITH YOU.

FOREVER ALLIED IN THE SERVICE OF THEIR NATION

Your lost friends are not dead, but gone before, advanced a stage or two upon that road which you must travel in the steps they trod.,

-Aristophanes

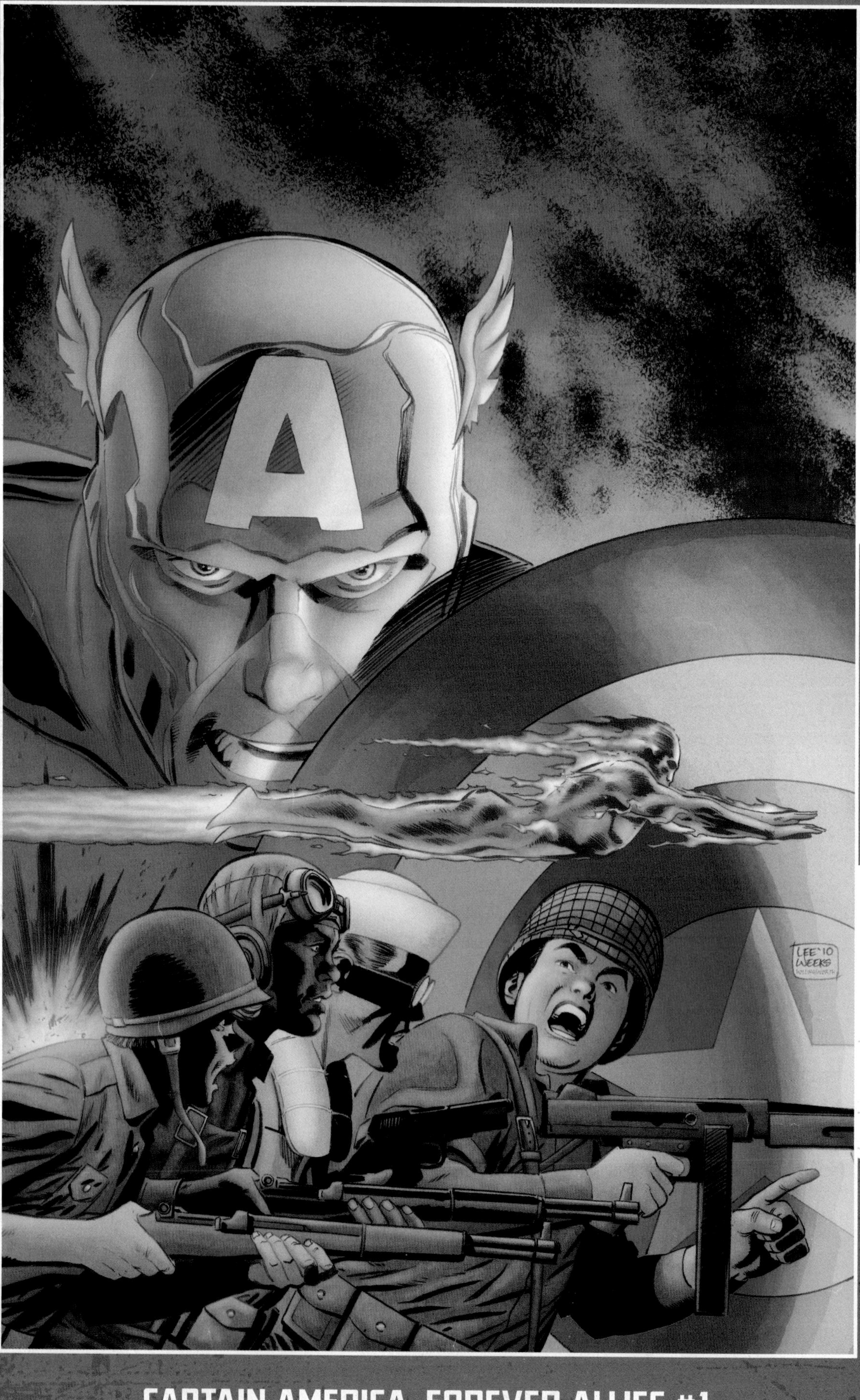
LEE '10
WEEKS

CAPTAIN AMERICA: FOREVER ALLIES #1

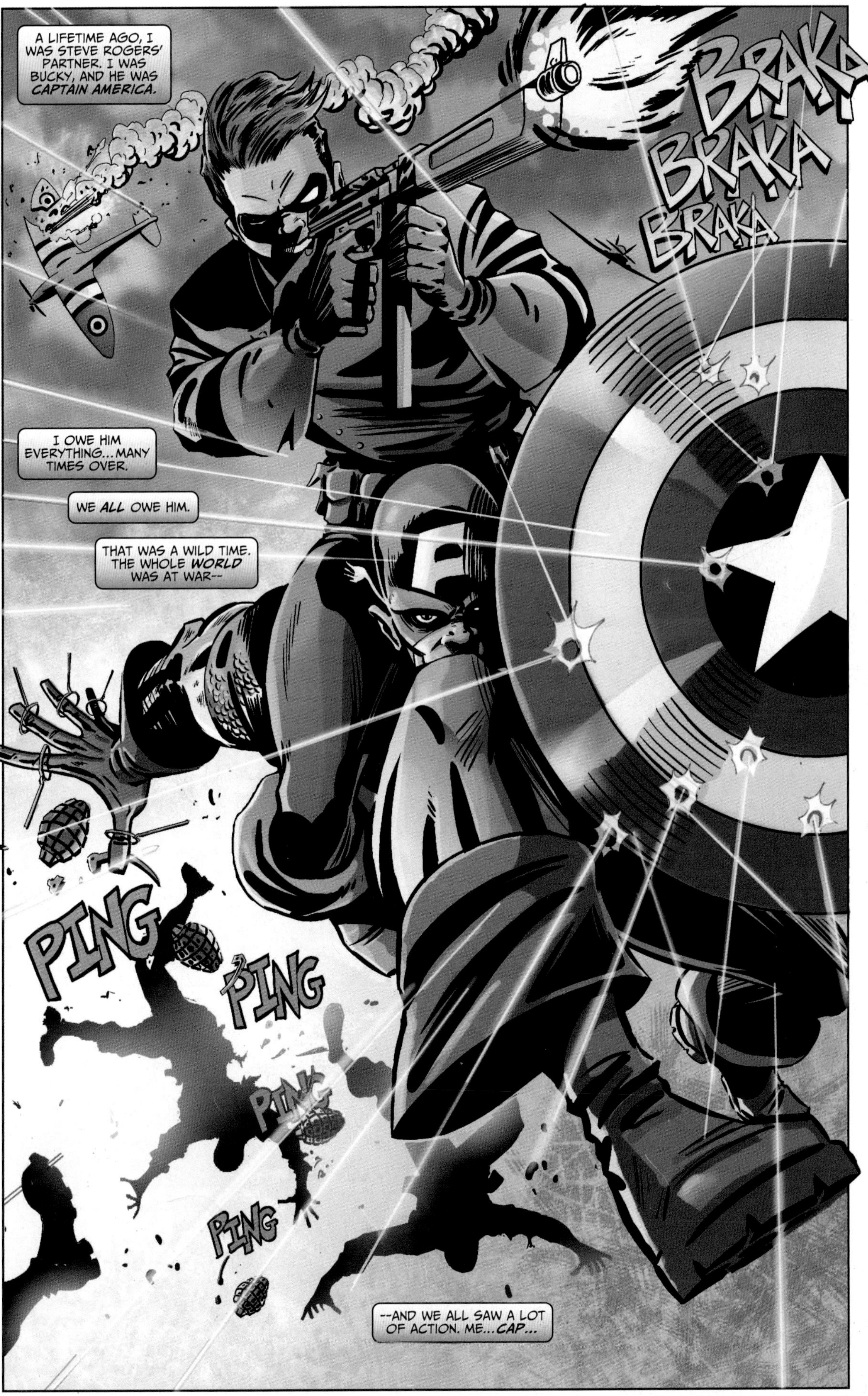
A LIFETIME AGO, I WAS STEVE ROGERS' PARTNER. I WAS BUCKY, AND HE WAS CAPTAIN AMERICA.
BRAKA
BRAKA
BRAKA
I OWE HIM EVERYTHING... MANY TIMES OVER.
WE ALL OWE HIM.
THAT WAS A WILD TIME. THE WHOLE WORLD WAS AT WAR--
PING
PING
PING
PING
--AND WE ALL SAW A LOT OF ACTION. ME... CAP...

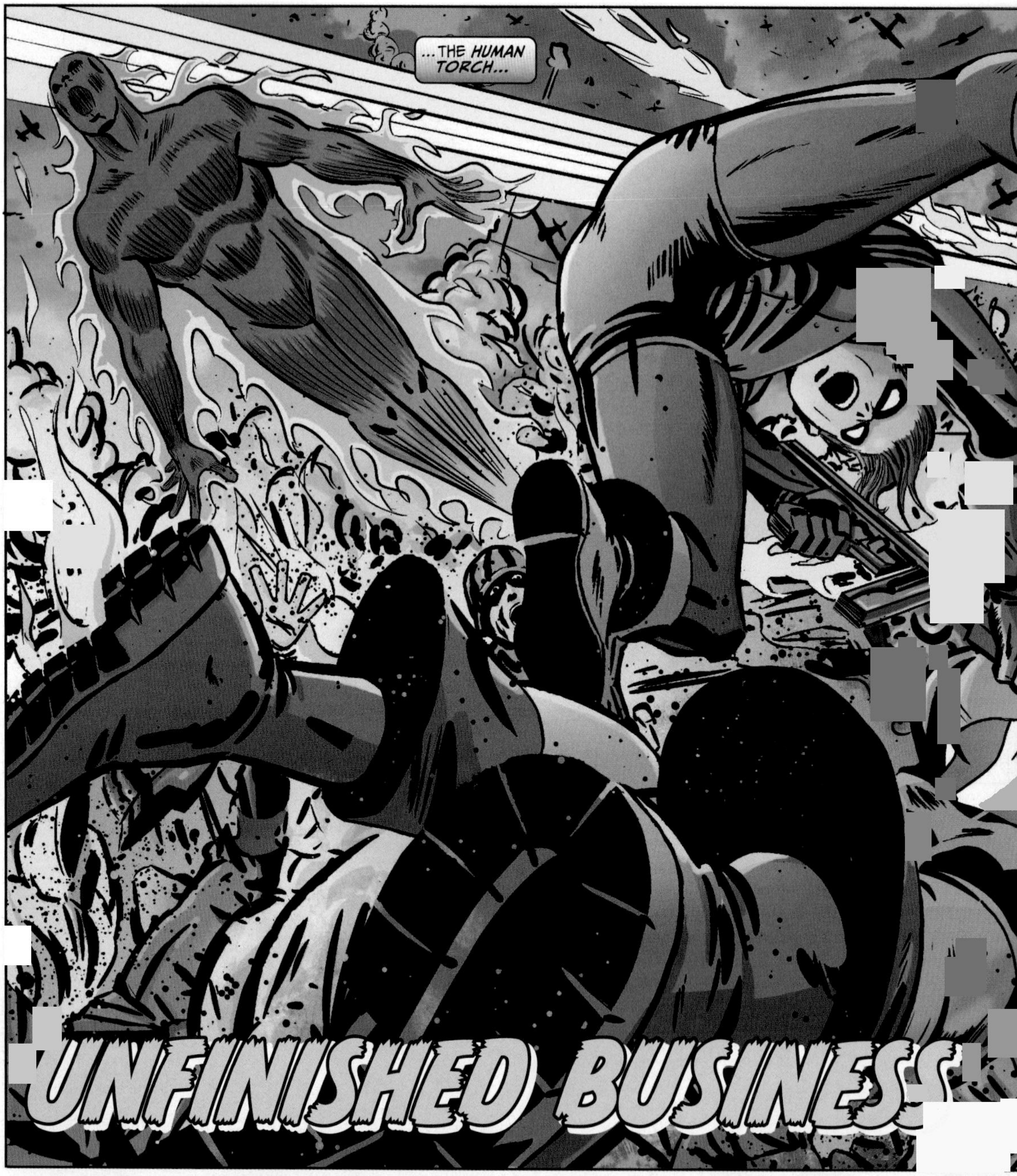
...THE HUMAN TORCH...
UNFINISHED BUSINESS

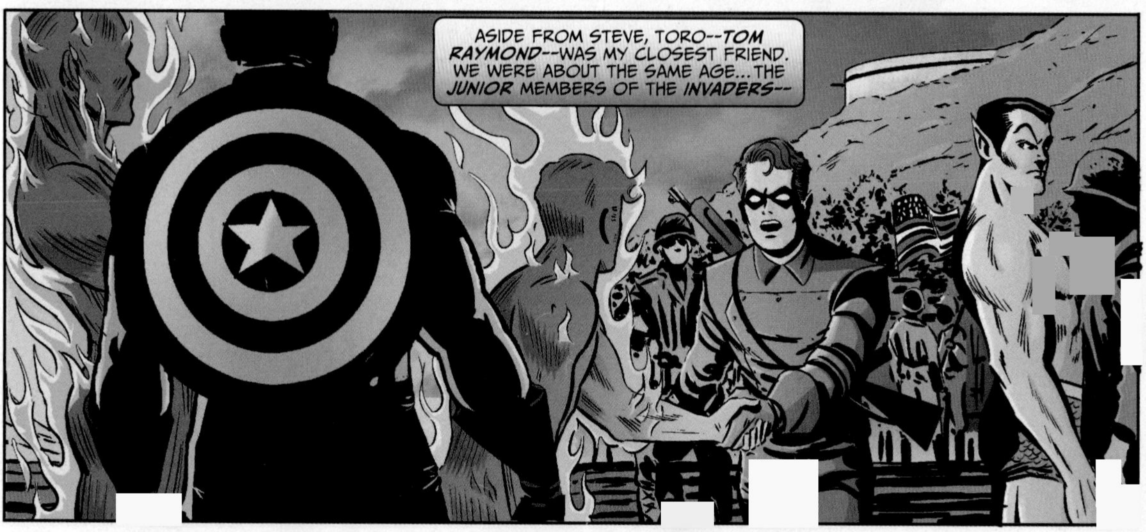
ASIDE FROM STEVE, TORO--TOM RAYMOND--WAS MY CLOSEST FRIEND. WE WERE ABOUT THE SAME AGE...THE JUNIOR MEMBERS OF THE INVADERS--

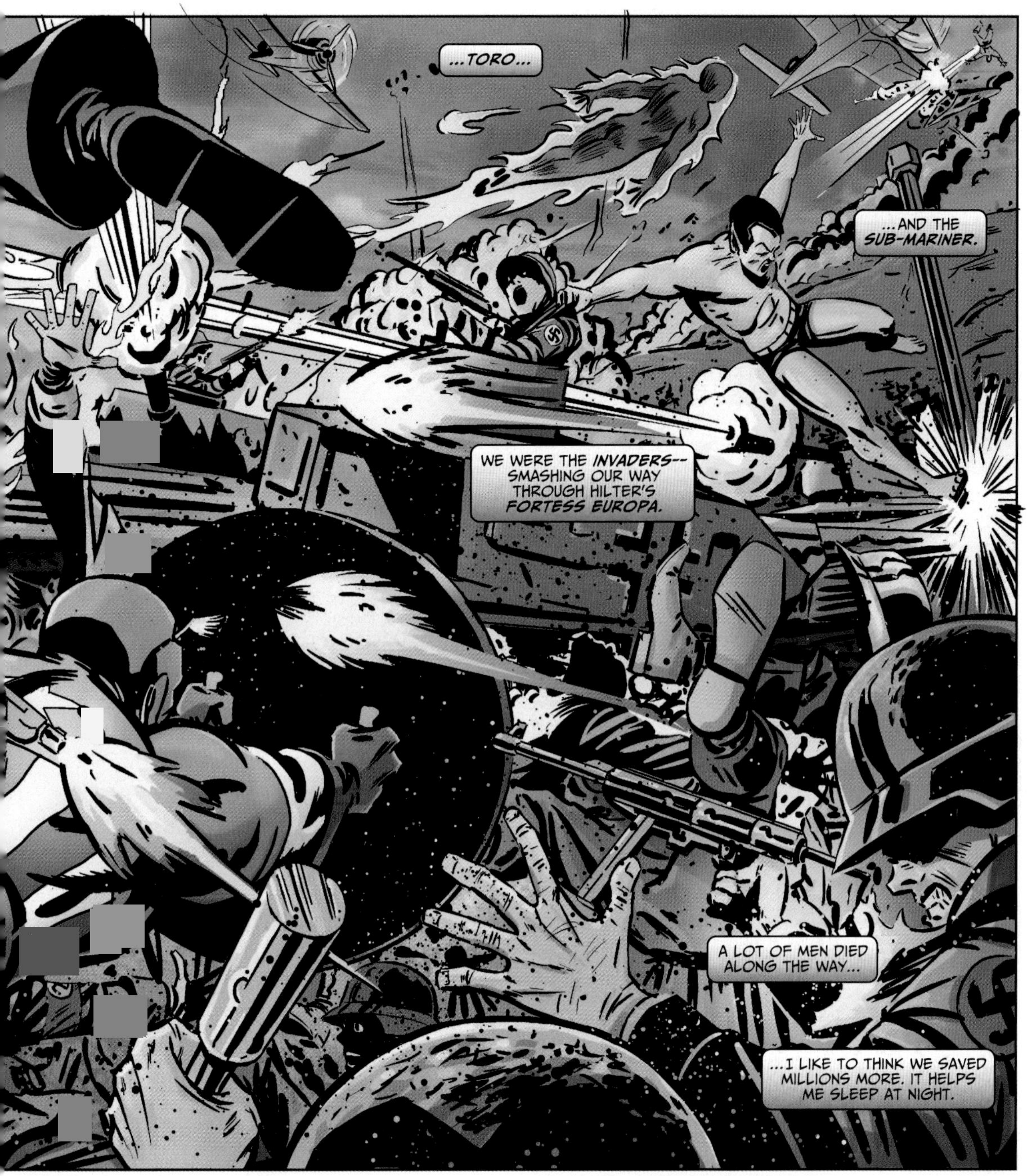
...TORO...
...AND THE SUB-MARINER.
WE WERE THE INVADERS-- SMASHING OUR WAY THROUGH HILTER'S FORTESS EUROPA.
A LOT OF MEN DIED ALONG THE WAY...
...I LIKE TO THINK WE SAVED MILLIONS MORE. IT HELPS ME SLEEP AT NIGHT.

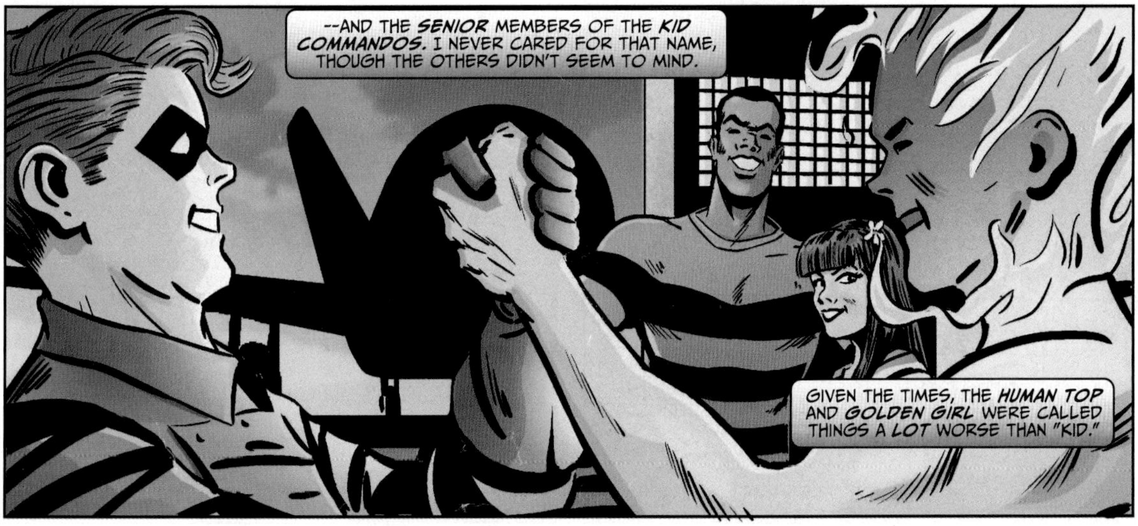
--AND THE SENIOR MEMBERS OF THE KID COMMANDOS. I NEVER CARED FOR THAT NAME, THOUGH THE OTHERS DIDN'T SEEM TO MIND.
GIVEN THE TIMES, THE HUMAN TOP AND GOLDEN GIRL WERE CALLED THINGS A LOT WORSE THAN "KID."

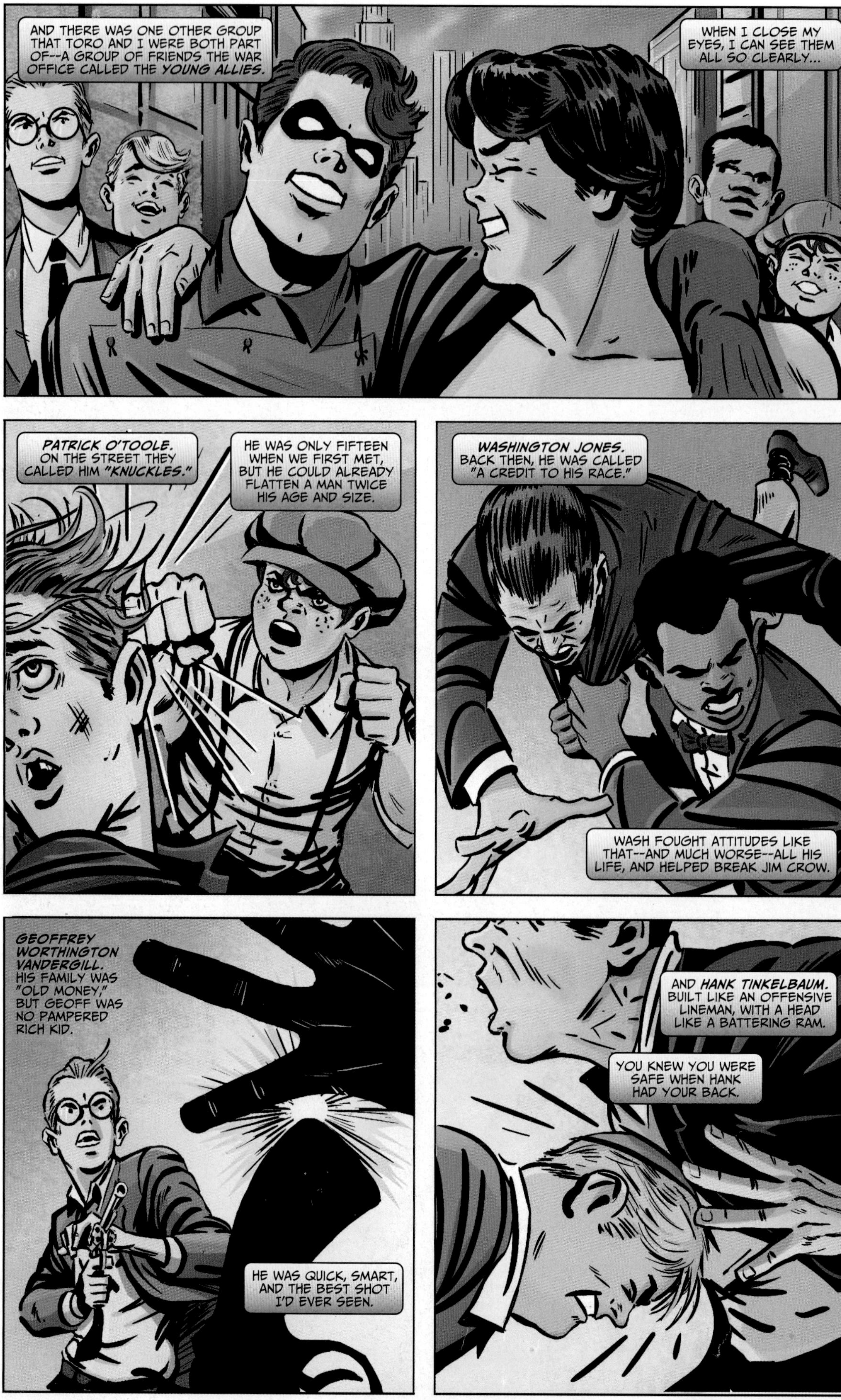
AND THERE WAS ONE OTHER GROUP THAT TORO AND I WERE BOTH PART OF--A GROUP OF FRIENDS THE WAR OFFICE CALLED THE *YOUNG ALLIES*.
WHEN I CLOSE MY EYES, I CAN SEE THEM ALL SO CLEARLY...
PATRICK O'TOOLE. ON THE STREET THEY CALLED HIM *"KNUCKLES."*
HE WAS ONLY FIFTEEN WHEN WE FIRST MET, BUT HE COULD ALREADY FLATTEN A MAN TWICE HIS AGE AND SIZE.
WASHINGTON JONES. BACK THEN, HE WAS CALLED "A CREDIT TO HIS RACE."
WASH FOUGHT ATTITUDES LIKE THAT--AND MUCH WORSE--ALL HIS LIFE, AND HELPED BREAK JIM CROW.
GEOFFREY WORTHINGTON VANDERGILL. HIS FAMILY WAS "OLD MONEY," BUT GEOFF WAS NO PAMPERED RICH KID.
HE WAS QUICK, SMART, AND THE BEST SHOT I'D EVER SEEN.
AND *HANK TINKELBAUM.* BUILT LIKE AN OFFENSIVE LINEMAN, WITH A HEAD LIKE A BATTERING RAM.
YOU KNEW YOU WERE SAFE WHEN HANK HAD YOUR BACK.

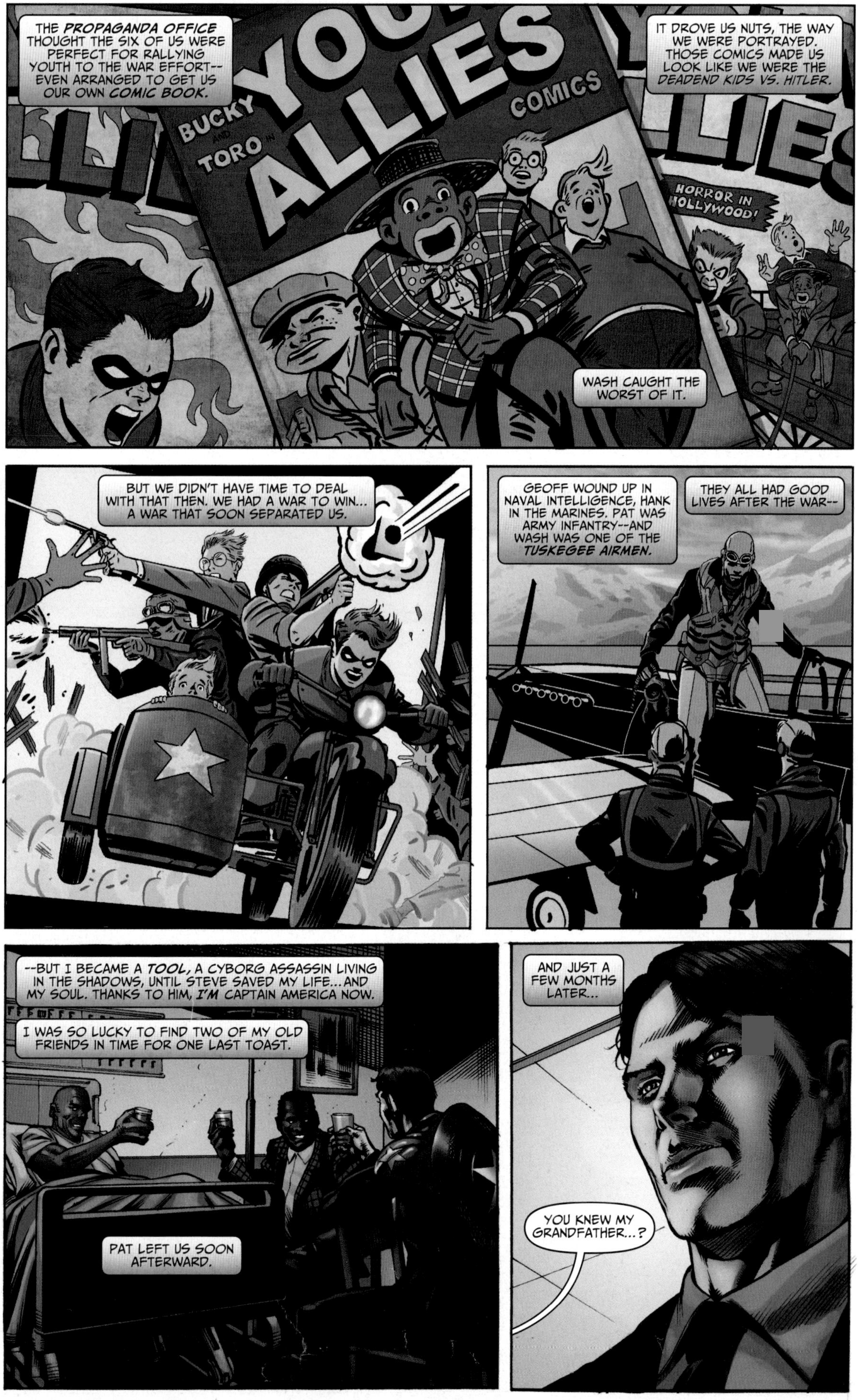
THE *PROPAGANDA OFFICE* THOUGHT THE SIX OF US WERE PERFECT FOR RALLYING YOUTH TO THE WAR EFFORT--EVEN ARRANGED TO GET US OUR OWN *COMIC BOOK.*
ALLIES
BUCKY AND TORO IN
COMICS
IT DROVE US NUTS, THE WAY WE WERE PORTRAYED. THOSE COMICS MADE US LOOK LIKE WE WERE THE *DEADEND KIDS VS. HITLER.*
HORROR IN HOLLYWOOD!
WASH CAUGHT THE WORST OF IT.
BUT WE DIDN'T HAVE TIME TO DEAL WITH THAT THEN. WE HAD A WAR TO WIN... A WAR THAT SOON SEPARATED US.
GEOFF WOUND UP IN NAVAL INTELLIGENCE, HANK IN THE MARINES. PAT WAS ARMY INFANTRY--AND WASH WAS ONE OF THE *TUSKEGEE AIRMEN.*
THEY ALL HAD GOOD LIVES AFTER THE WAR--
--BUT I BECAME A *TOOL,* A CYBORG ASSASSIN LIVING IN THE SHADOWS, UNTIL STEVE SAVED MY LIFE... AND MY SOUL. THANKS TO HIM, *I'M* CAPTAIN AMERICA NOW.
I WAS SO LUCKY TO FIND TWO OF MY OLD FRIENDS IN TIME FOR ONE LAST TOAST.
PAT LEFT US SOON AFTERWARD.
AND JUST A FEW MONTHS LATER...
YOU KNEW MY GRANDFATHER...?

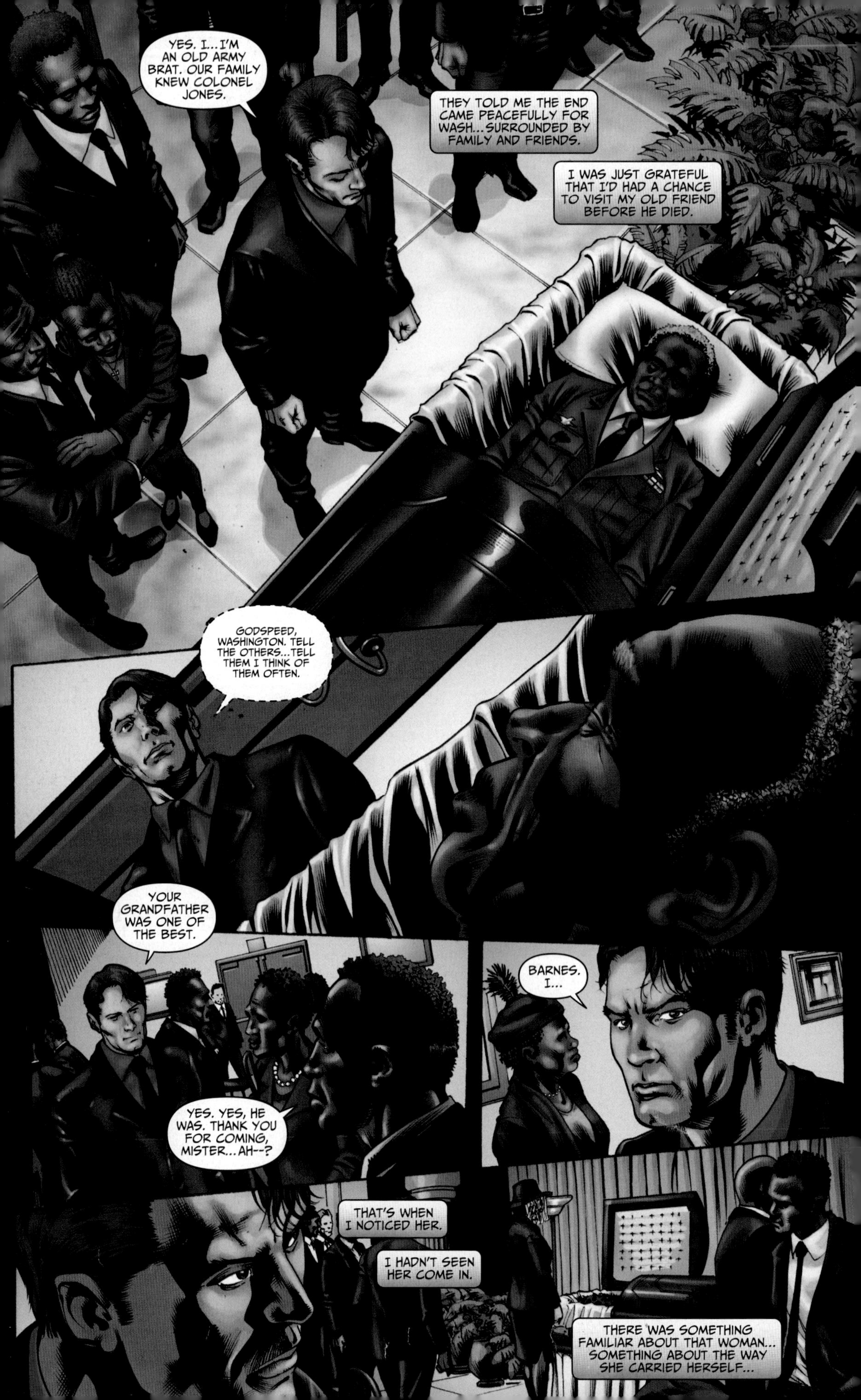
YES. I...I'M AN OLD ARMY BRAT. OUR FAMILY KNEW COLONEL JONES.
THEY TOLD ME THE END CAME PEACEFULLY FOR WASH...SURROUNDED BY FAMILY AND FRIENDS.
I WAS JUST GRATEFUL THAT I'D HAD A CHANCE TO VISIT MY OLD FRIEND BEFORE HE DIED.
GODSPEED, WASHINGTON. TELL THE OTHERS...TELL THEM I THINK OF THEM OFTEN.
YOUR GRANDFATHER WAS ONE OF THE BEST.
YES. YES, HE WAS. THANK YOU FOR COMING, MISTER...AH--?
BARNES. I...
THAT'S WHEN I NOTICED HER.
I HADN'T SEEN HER COME IN.
THERE WAS SOMETHING FAMILIAR ABOUT THAT WOMAN... SOMETHING ABOUT THE WAY SHE CARRIED HERSELF...

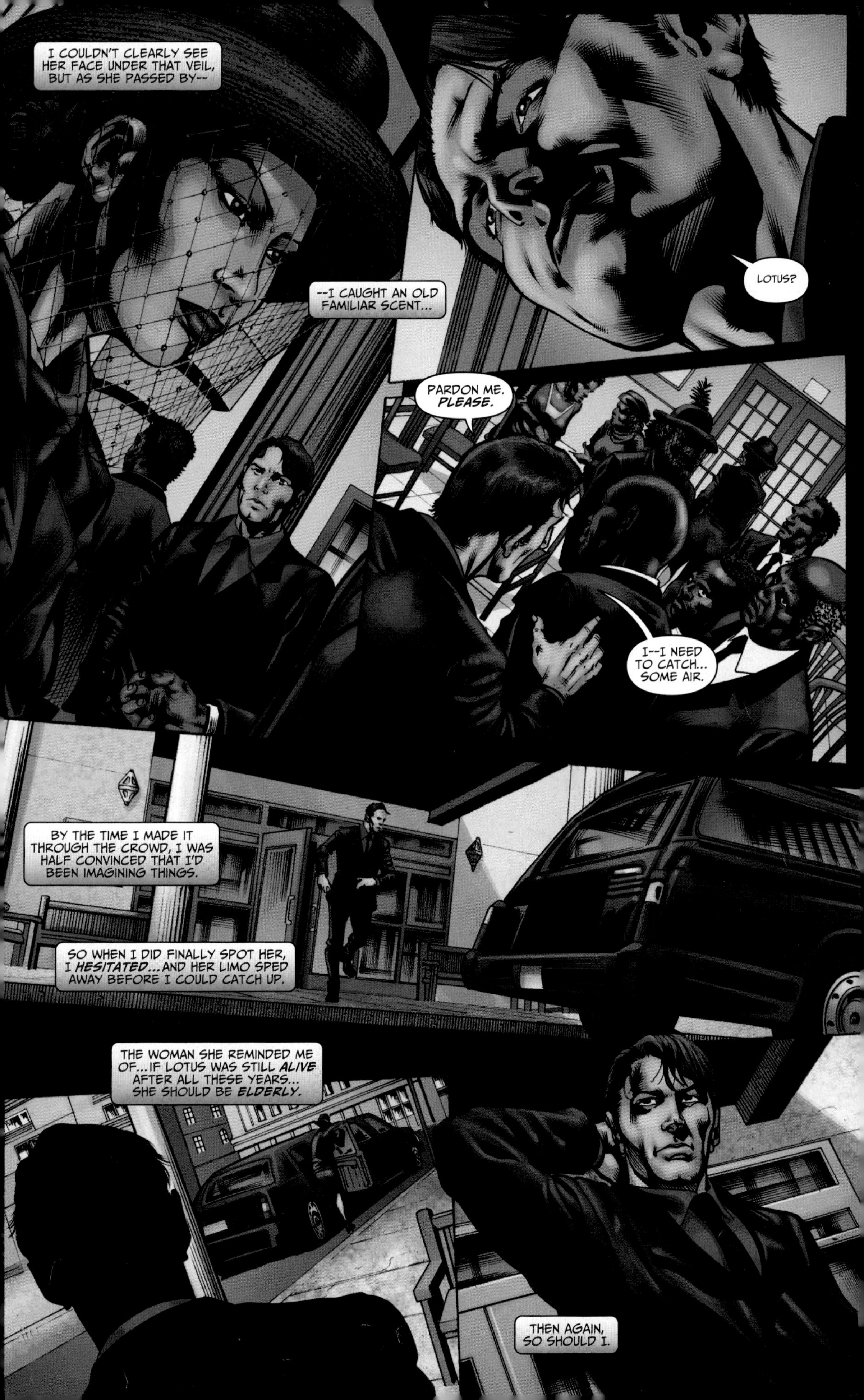
I COULDN'T CLEARLY SEE HER FACE UNDER THAT VEIL, BUT AS SHE PASSED BY--
--I CAUGHT AN OLD FAMILIAR SCENT...
LOTUS?
PARDON ME. *PLEASE.*
I--I NEED TO CATCH... SOME AIR.
BY THE TIME I MADE IT THROUGH THE CROWD, I WAS HALF CONVINCED THAT I'D BEEN IMAGINING THINGS.
SO WHEN I DID FINALLY SPOT HER, I *HESITATED...* AND HER LIMO SPED AWAY BEFORE I COULD CATCH UP.
THE WOMAN SHE REMINDED ME OF... IF LOTUS WAS STILL *ALIVE* AFTER ALL THESE YEARS... SHE SHOULD BE *ELDERLY.*
THEN AGAIN, SO SHOULD I.

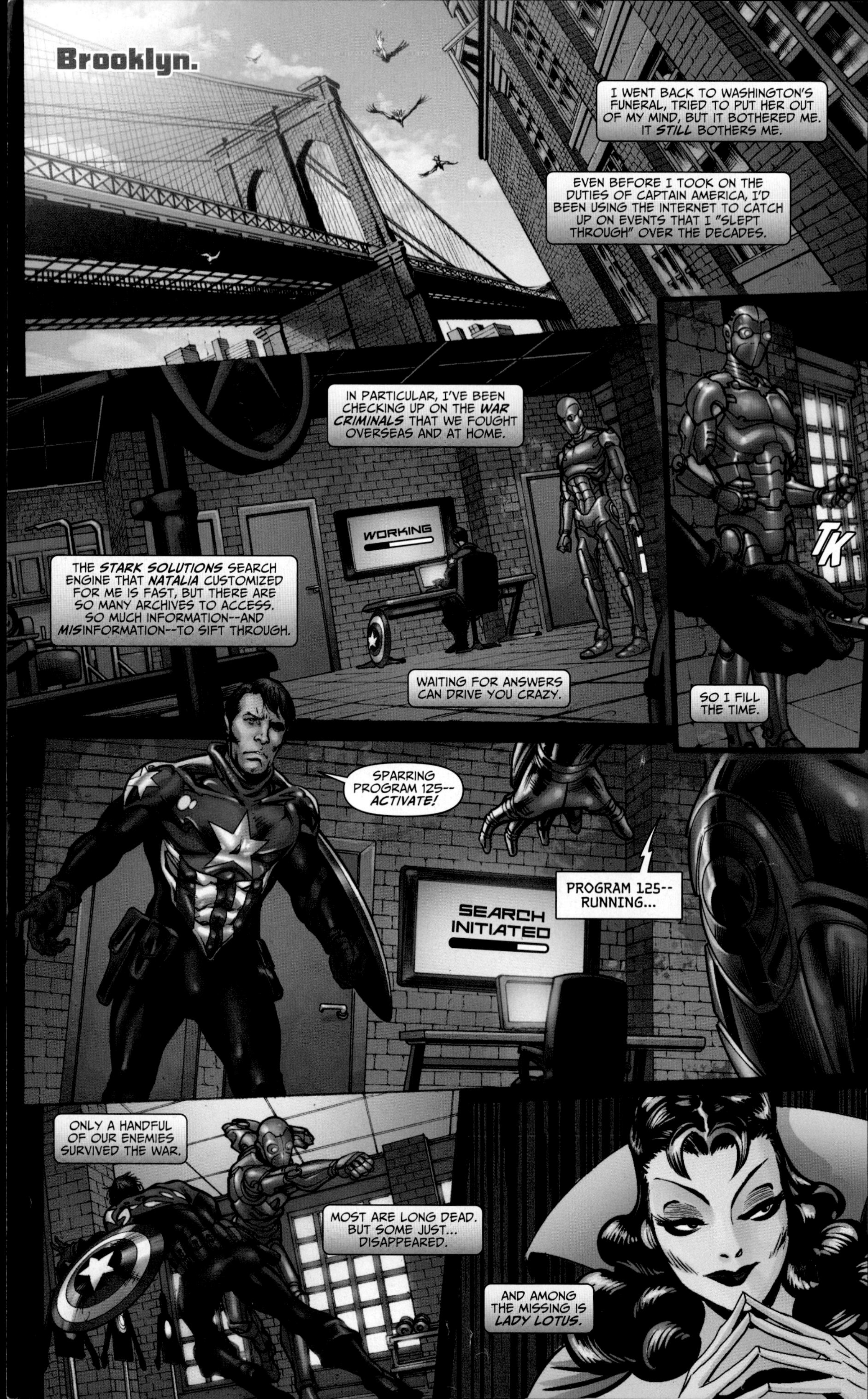
Brooklyn.
I WENT BACK TO WASHINGTON'S FUNERAL, TRIED TO PUT HER OUT OF MY MIND, BUT IT BOTHERED ME. IT STILL BOTHERS ME.
EVEN BEFORE I TOOK ON THE DUTIES OF CAPTAIN AMERICA, I'D BEEN USING THE INTERNET TO CATCH UP ON EVENTS THAT I "SLEPT THROUGH" OVER THE DECADES.
IN PARTICULAR, I'VE BEEN CHECKING UP ON THE WAR CRIMINALS THAT WE FOUGHT OVERSEAS AND AT HOME.
WORKING
THE STARK SOLUTIONS SEARCH ENGINE THAT NATALIA CUSTOMIZED FOR ME IS FAST, BUT THERE ARE SO MANY ARCHIVES TO ACCESS. SO MUCH INFORMATION--AND MISINFORMATION--TO SIFT THROUGH.
WAITING FOR ANSWERS CAN DRIVE YOU CRAZY.
TK
SO I FILL THE TIME.
SPARRING PROGRAM 125--ACTIVATE!
PROGRAM 125--RUNNING...
SEARCH INITIATED
ONLY A HANDFUL OF OUR ENEMIES SURVIVED THE WAR.
MOST ARE LONG DEAD. BUT SOME JUST... DISAPPEARED.
AND AMONG THE MISSING IS LADY LOTUS.

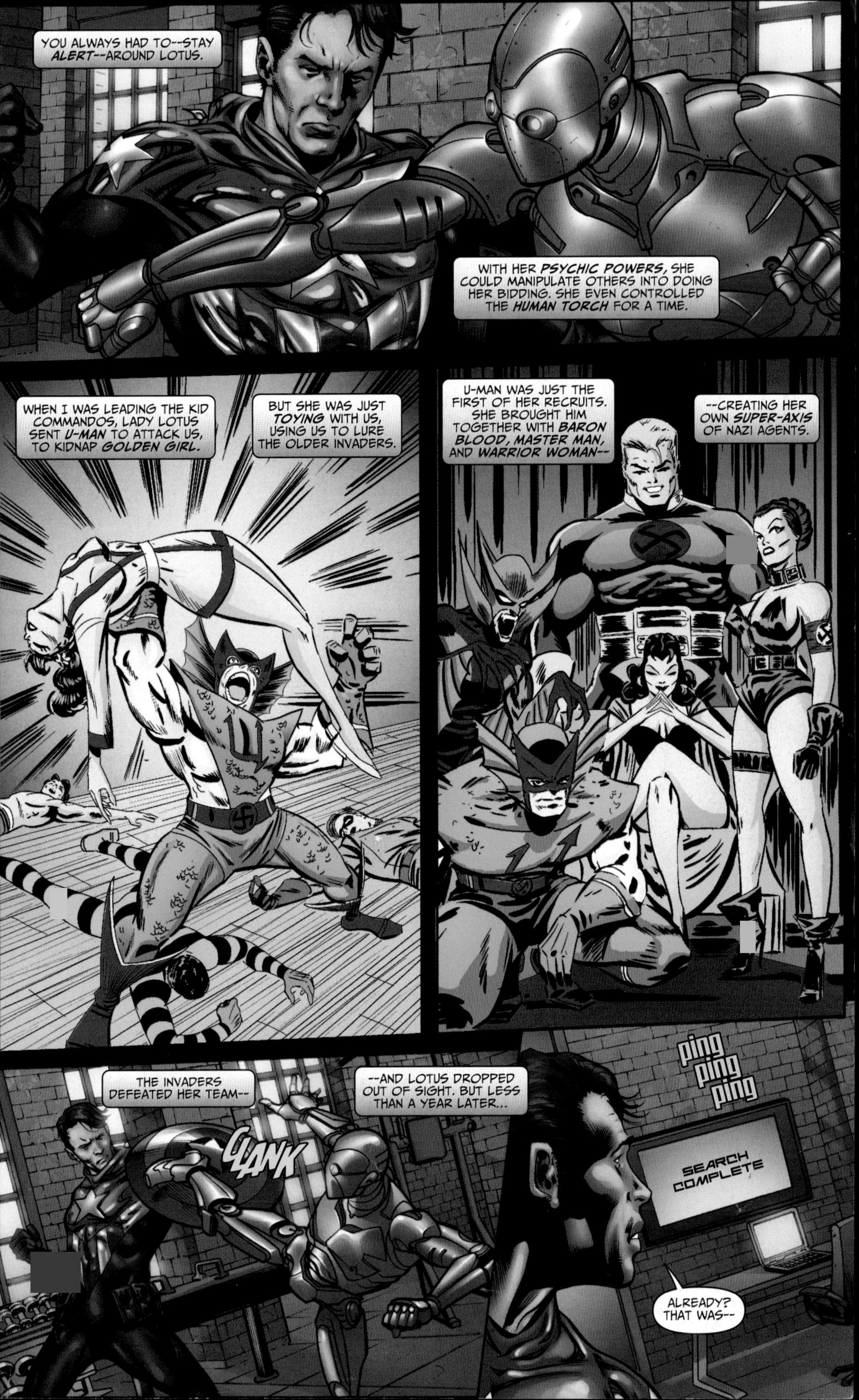
YOU ALWAYS HAD TO--STAY ALERT--AROUND LOTUS.
WITH HER PSYCHIC POWERS, SHE COULD MANIPULATE OTHERS INTO DOING HER BIDDING. SHE EVEN CONTROLLED THE HUMAN TORCH FOR A TIME.
WHEN I WAS LEADING THE KID COMMANDOS, LADY LOTUS SENT U-MAN TO ATTACK US, TO KIDNAP GOLDEN GIRL.
BUT SHE WAS JUST TOYING WITH US, USING US TO LURE THE OLDER INVADERS.
U-MAN WAS JUST THE FIRST OF HER RECRUITS. SHE BROUGHT HIM TOGETHER WITH BARON BLOOD, MASTER MAN, AND WARRIOR WOMAN--
--CREATING HER OWN SUPER-AXIS OF NAZI AGENTS.
THE INVADERS DEFEATED HER TEAM--
CLANK
--AND LOTUS DROPPED OUT OF SIGHT. BUT LESS THAN A YEAR LATER...
ping ping ping
SEARCH COMPLETE
ALREADY? THAT WAS--

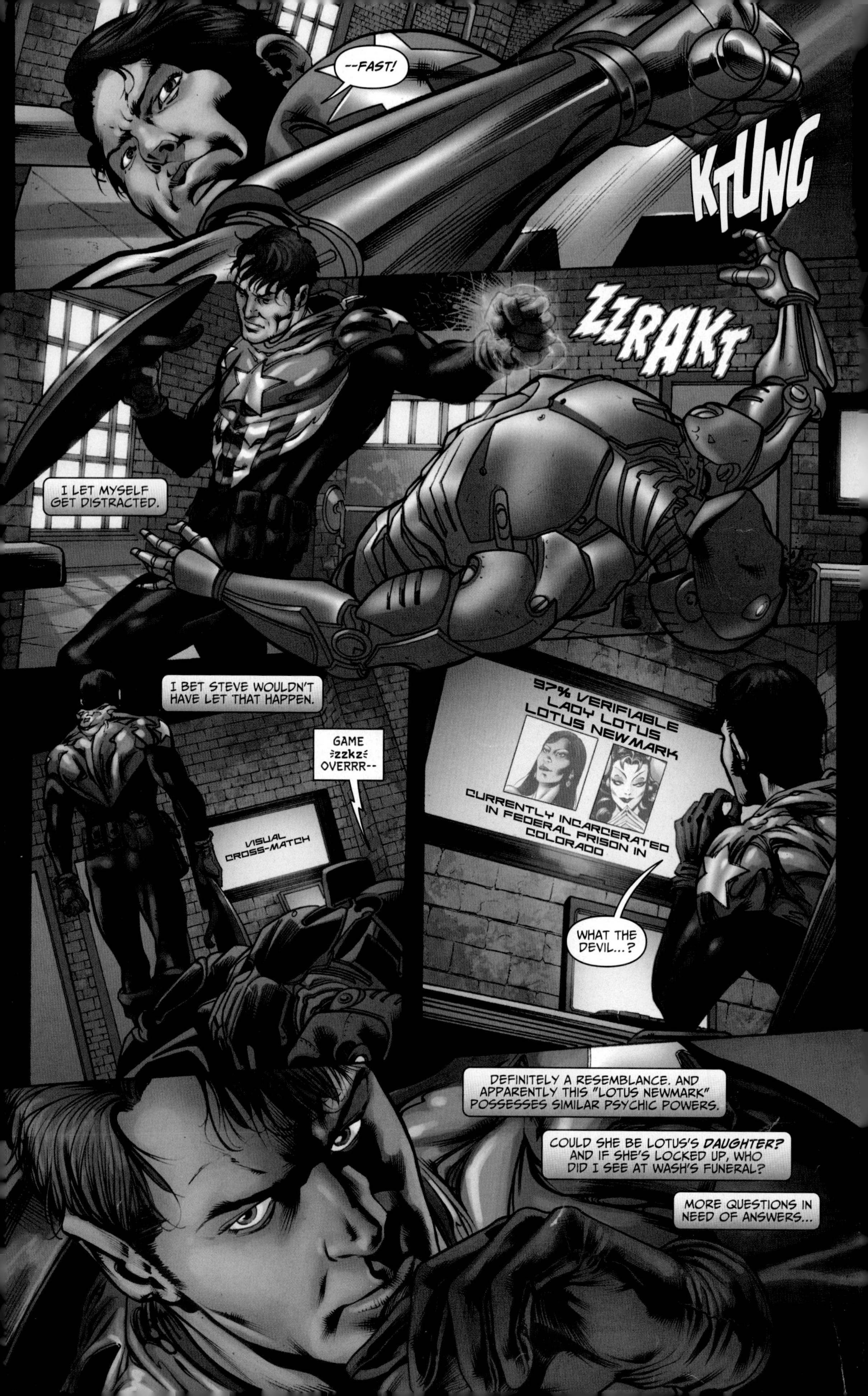
--FAST!
KTUNG
ZZRAKT
I LET MYSELF GET DISTRACTED.
I BET STEVE WOULDN'T HAVE LET THAT HAPPEN.
GAME zzkz OVERRR--
VISUAL CROSS-MATCH
97% VERIFIABLE
LADY LOTUS
LOTUS NEWMARK
CURRENTLY INCARCERATED IN FEDERAL PRISON IN COLORADO
WHAT THE DEVIL...?
DEFINITELY A RESEMBLANCE. AND APPARENTLY THIS "LOTUS NEWMARK" POSSESSES SIMILAR PSYCHIC POWERS.
COULD SHE BE LOTUS'S DAUGHTER? AND IF SHE'S LOCKED UP, WHO DID I SEE AT WASH'S FUNERAL?
MORE QUESTIONS IN NEED OF ANSWERS...

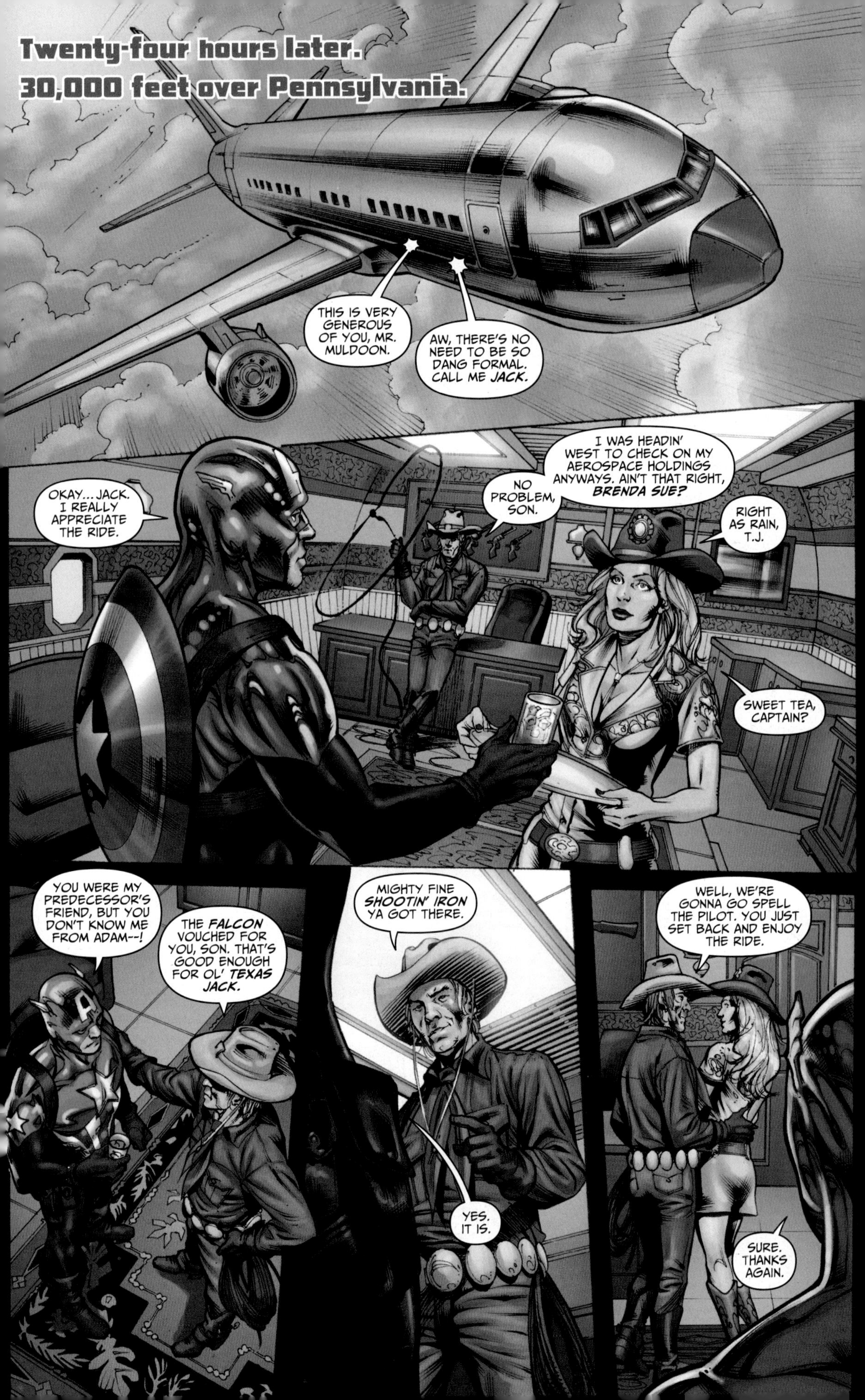
Twenty-four hours later.
30,000 feet over Pennsylvania.
THIS IS VERY GENEROUS OF YOU, MR. MULDOON.
AW, THERE'S NO NEED TO BE SO DANG FORMAL. CALL ME JACK.
OKAY... JACK. I REALLY APPRECIATE THE RIDE.
NO PROBLEM, SON.
I WAS HEADIN' WEST TO CHECK ON MY AEROSPACE HOLDINGS ANYWAYS. AIN'T THAT RIGHT, BRENDA SUE?
RIGHT AS RAIN, T.J.
SWEET TEA, CAPTAIN?
YOU WERE MY PREDECESSOR'S FRIEND, BUT YOU DON'T KNOW ME FROM ADAM--!
THE FALCON VOUCHED FOR YOU, SON. THAT'S GOOD ENOUGH FOR OL' TEXAS JACK.
MIGHTY FINE SHOOTIN' IRON YA GOT THERE.
YES. IT IS.
WELL, WE'RE GONNA GO SPELL THE PILOT. YOU JUST SET BACK AND ENJOY THE RIDE.
SURE. THANKS AGAIN.

I ALWAYS NEEDED A GUN MORE THAN STEVE DID. HE WAS THE BEST.

WE COULD HAVE USED HIS HELP BACK THEN...

Los Angeles. 1943.

PARAMOUNT

WAR BOND DRIVE FEATURING THE "YOUI G ALLIES"

YOU *MUST* BE JOKING!

DO I *LOOK* LIKE I'M JOKING, SEAMAN--?

THAT'S *ENSIGN* VANDERGILL, MR. FRAWLEY. AND WE DO NOT FIND THIS AT ALL ACCEPTABLE.

TYPICAL...

LEMME AT 'IM!

TAKE IT EASY, PRIVATE.

OUTTA MY WAY, TINKELBAUM. I DON'T CARE IF YOU *DO* OUTRANK ME, THERE'S NO WAY I'M STANDIN' FOR THIS!

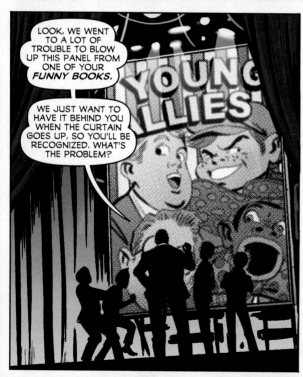

LOOK, WE WENT TO A LOT OF TROUBLE TO BLOW UP THIS PANEL FROM ONE OF YOUR *FUNNY BOOKS.*

WE JUST WANT TO HAVE IT BEHIND YOU WHEN THE CURTAIN GOES UP, SO YOU'LL BE RECOGNIZED. WHAT'S THE PROBLEM?

YOUNG ALLIES

HERE'S THE PROBLEM, MR. FRAWLEY--WE NEVER APPROVED THOSE COMICS.

AND THAT CARICATURE IS *INSULTING.*

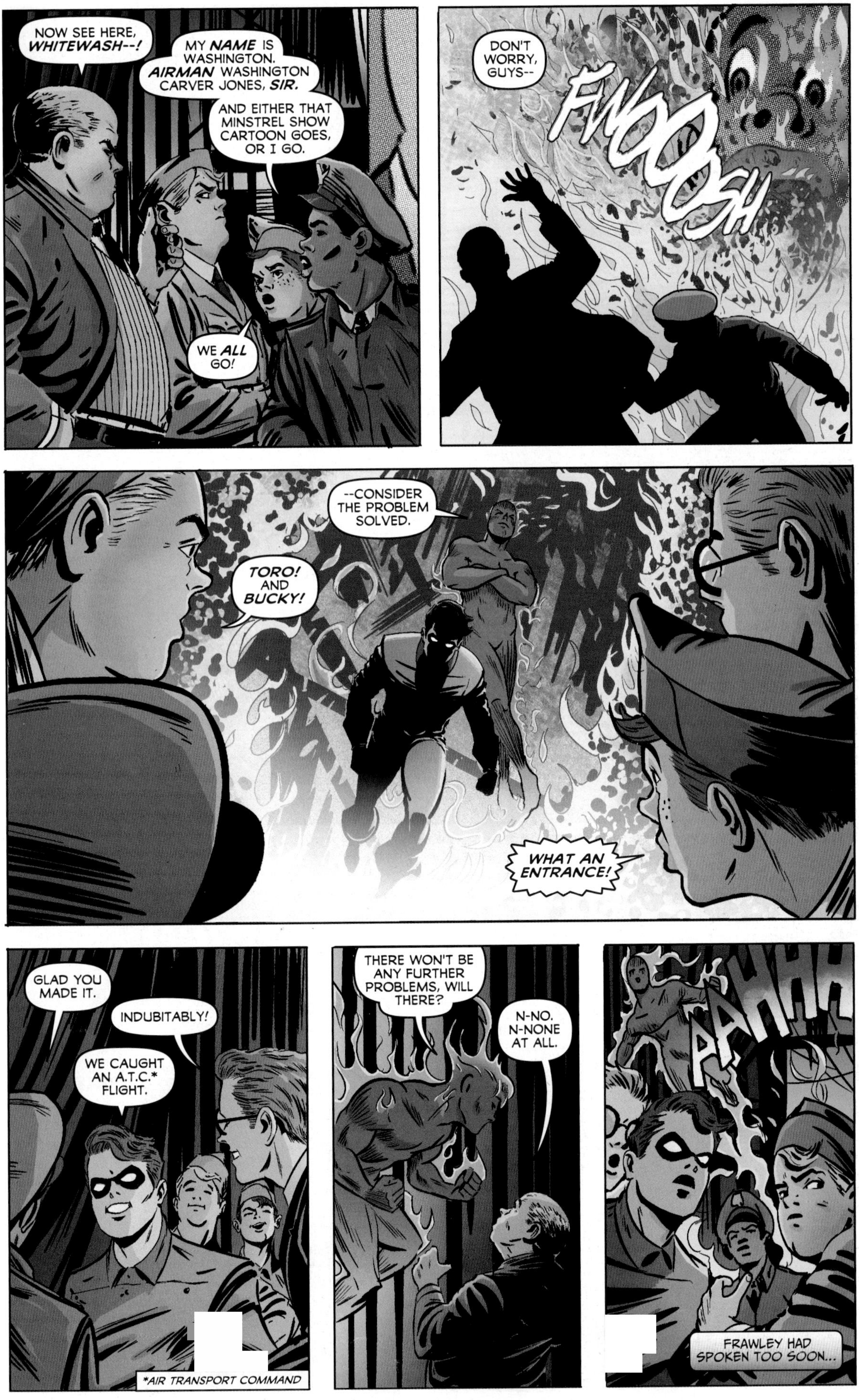
NOW SEE HERE, WHITEWASH--!
MY NAME IS WASHINGTON. AIRMAN WASHINGTON CARVER JONES, SIR.
AND EITHER THAT MINSTREL SHOW CARTOON GOES, OR I GO.
WE ALL GO!
DON'T WORRY, GUYS--
FWOOOSH
--CONSIDER THE PROBLEM SOLVED.
TORO! AND BUCKY!
WHAT AN ENTRANCE!
GLAD YOU MADE IT.
INDUBITABLY!
WE CAUGHT AN A.T.C.* FLIGHT.
*AIR TRANSPORT COMMAND
THERE WON'T BE ANY FURTHER PROBLEMS, WILL THERE?
N-NO. N-NONE AT ALL.
AAHHHH
FRAWLEY HAD SPOKEN TOO SOON...

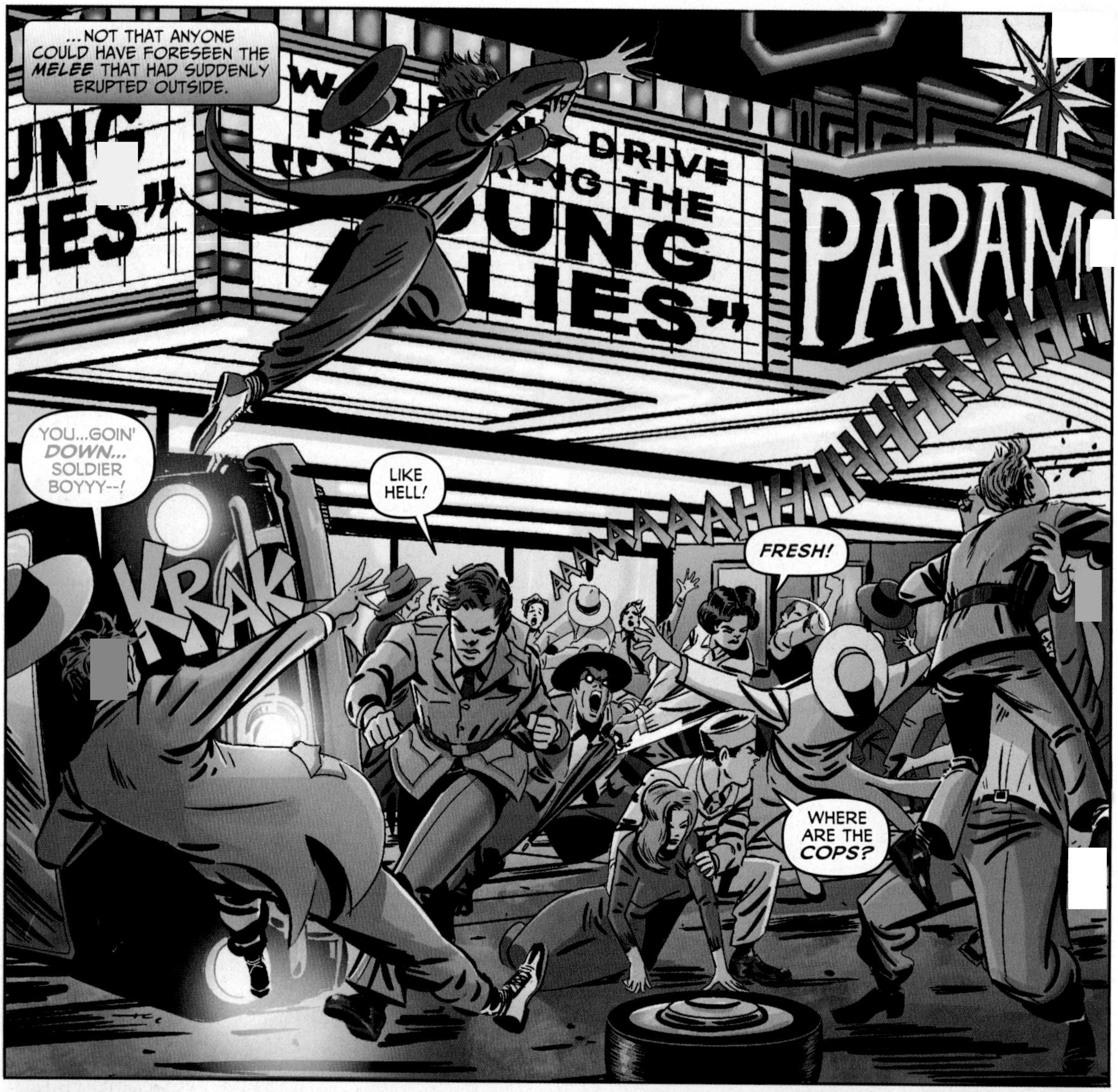
...NOT THAT ANYONE COULD HAVE FORESEEN THE *MELEE* THAT HAD SUDDENLY ERUPTED OUTSIDE.
YOU...GOIN' *DOWN...* SOLDIER BOYYY--!
KRAK
LIKE HELL!
AAAAAAAHHHHHHHHHHHHHH
FRESH!
WHERE ARE THE *COPS?*

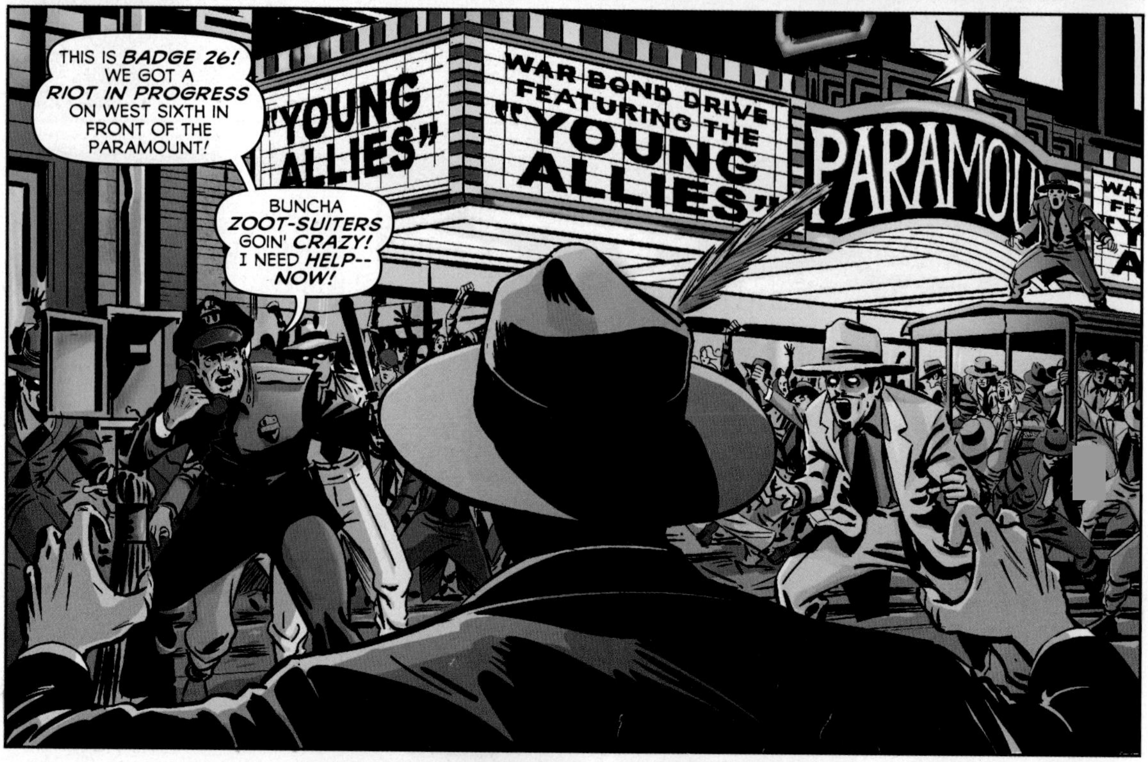
"YOUNG ALLIES"
WAR BOND DRIVE FEATURING THE "YOUNG ALLIES"
THIS IS *BADGE 26!* WE GOT A *RIOT IN PROGRESS* ON WEST SIXTH IN FRONT OF THE PARAMOUNT!
BUNCHA *ZOOT-SUITERS* GOIN' *CRAZY!* I NEED *HELP-- NOW!*

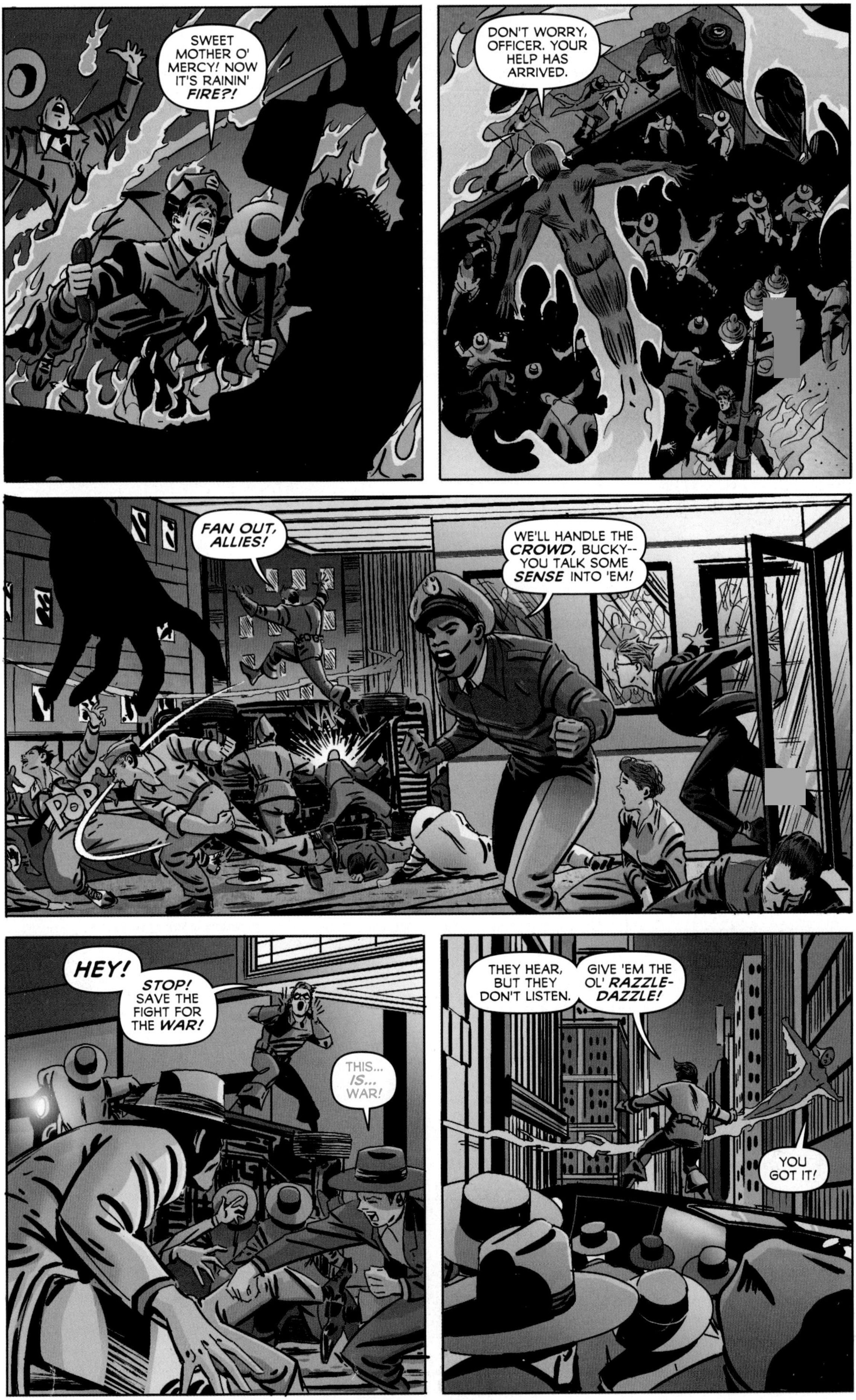
SWEET MOTHER O' MERCY! NOW IT'S RAININ' *FIRE?!*
DON'T WORRY, OFFICER. YOUR HELP HAS ARRIVED.
FAN OUT, ALLIES!
WE'LL HANDLE THE *CROWD,* BUCKY-- YOU TALK SOME *SENSE* INTO 'EM!
POP
HEY!
STOP! SAVE THE FIGHT FOR THE *WAR!*
THIS... *IS...* WAR!
THEY HEAR, BUT THEY DON'T LISTEN.
GIVE 'EM THE OL' *RAZZLE-DAZZLE!*
YOU GOT IT!

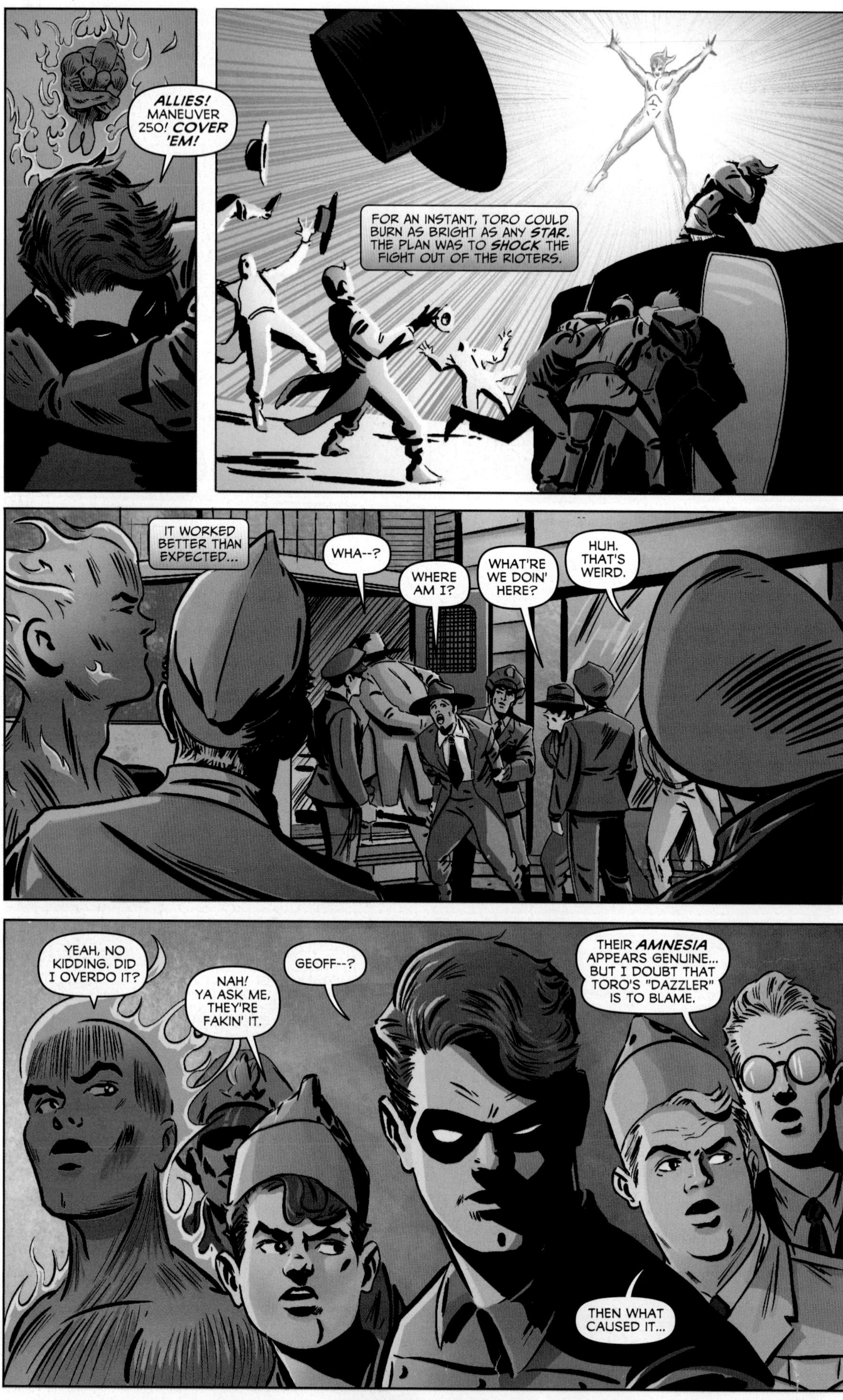

ALLIES! MANEUVER 250! COVER 'EM!
FOR AN INSTANT, TORO COULD BURN AS BRIGHT AS ANY STAR. THE PLAN WAS TO SHOCK THE FIGHT OUT OF THE RIOTERS.
IT WORKED BETTER THAN EXPECTED...
WHA--?
WHERE AM I?
WHAT'RE WE DOIN' HERE?
HUH. THAT'S WEIRD.
YEAH, NO KIDDING. DID I OVERDO IT?
NAH! YA ASK ME, THEY'RE FAKIN' IT.
GEOFF--?
THEIR AMNESIA APPEARS GENUINE... BUT I DOUBT THAT TORO'S "DAZZLER" IS TO BLAME.
THEN WHAT CAUSED IT...

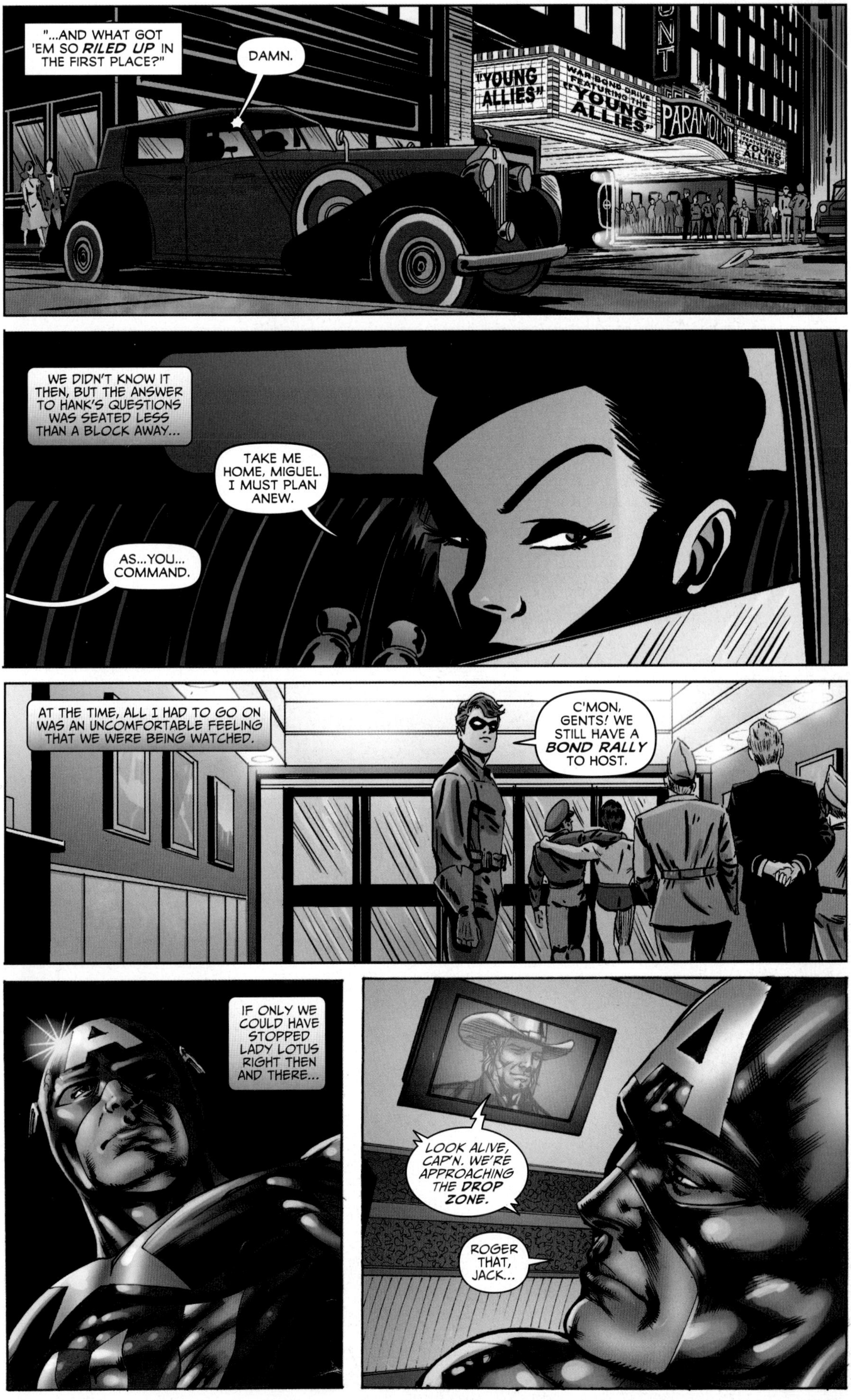
"...AND WHAT GOT 'EM SO **RILED UP** IN THE FIRST PLACE?"
DAMN.
"YOUNG ALLIES"
WAR BOND DRIVE FEATURING THE "YOUNG ALLIES"
PARAMOUNT
WE DIDN'T KNOW IT THEN, BUT THE ANSWER TO HANK'S QUESTIONS WAS SEATED LESS THAN A BLOCK AWAY...
TAKE ME HOME, MIGUEL. I MUST PLAN ANEW.
AS...YOU... COMMAND.
AT THE TIME, ALL I HAD TO GO ON WAS AN UNCOMFORTABLE FEELING THAT WE WERE BEING WATCHED.
C'MON, GENTS! WE STILL HAVE A **BOND RALLY** TO HOST.
IF ONLY WE COULD HAVE STOPPED LADY LOTUS RIGHT THEN AND THERE...
*LOOK ALIVE, CAP'N. WE'RE APPROACHING THE **DROP ZONE**.*
ROGER THAT, JACK...

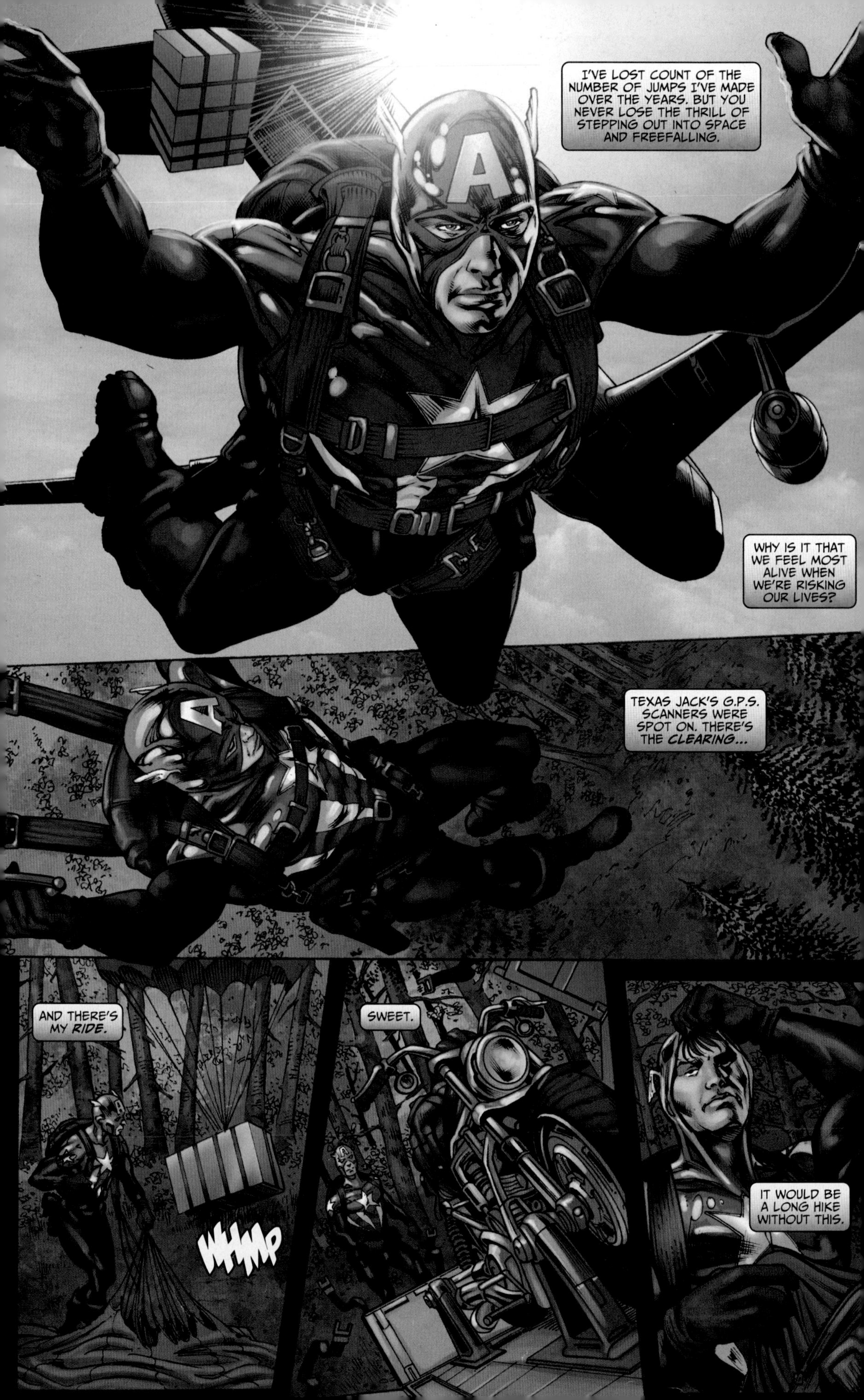
I'VE LOST COUNT OF THE NUMBER OF JUMPS I'VE MADE OVER THE YEARS. BUT YOU NEVER LOSE THE THRILL OF STEPPING OUT INTO SPACE AND FREEFALLING.
WHY IS IT THAT WE FEEL MOST ALIVE WHEN WE'RE RISKING OUR LIVES?
TEXAS JACK'S G.P.S. SCANNERS WERE SPOT ON. THERE'S THE *CLEARING*...
AND THERE'S MY *RIDE*.
WHMP
SWEET.
IT WOULD BE A LONG HIKE WITHOUT THIS.

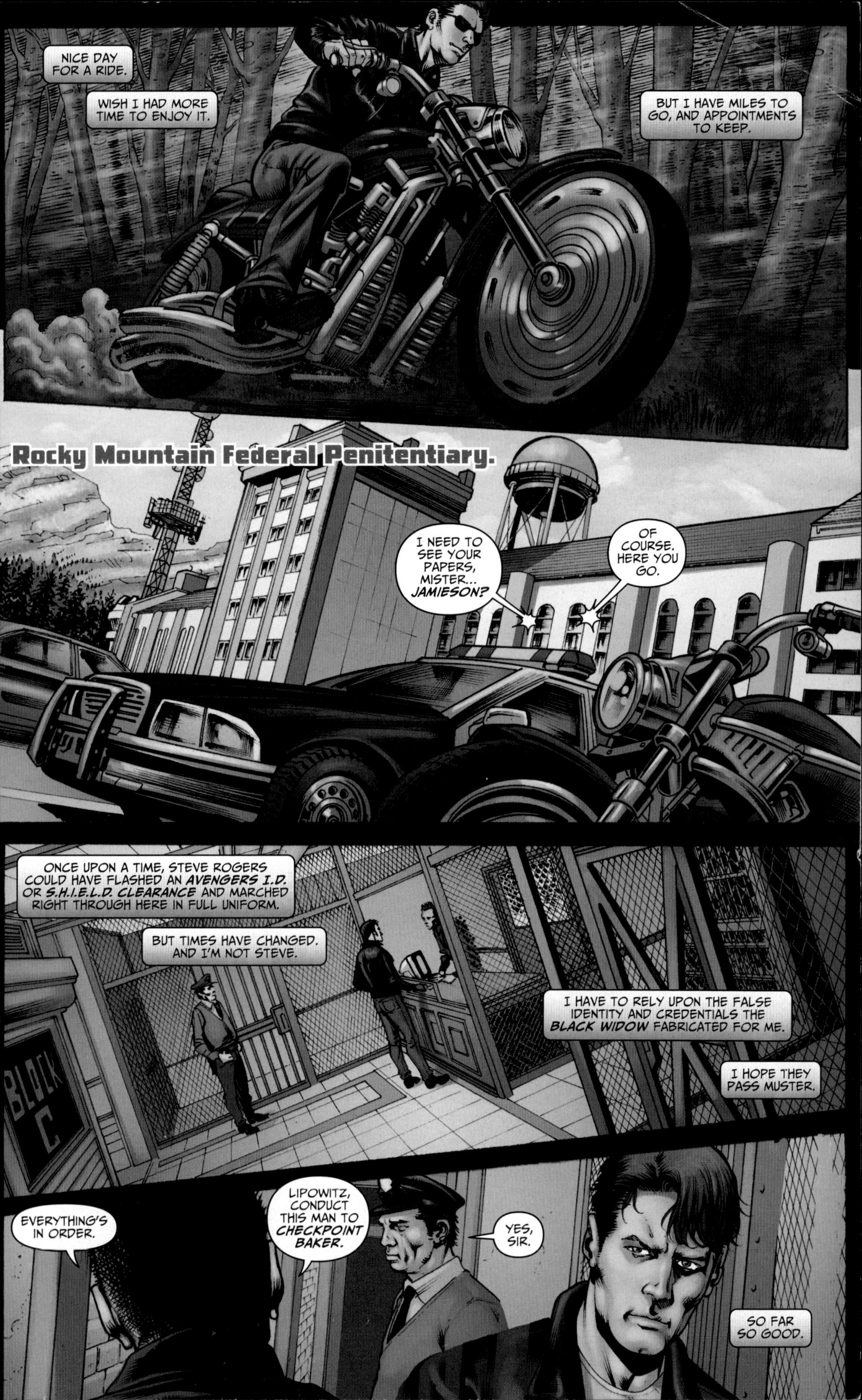
NICE DAY FOR A RIDE.
WISH I HAD MORE TIME TO ENJOY IT.
BUT I HAVE MILES TO GO, AND APPOINTMENTS TO KEEP.
Rocky Mountain Federal Penitentiary.
I NEED TO SEE YOUR PAPERS, MISTER... JAMIESON?
OF COURSE. HERE YOU GO.
ONCE UPON A TIME, STEVE ROGERS COULD HAVE FLASHED AN AVENGERS I.D. OR S.H.I.E.L.D. CLEARANCE AND MARCHED RIGHT THROUGH HERE IN FULL UNIFORM.
BUT TIMES HAVE CHANGED. AND I'M NOT STEVE.
I HAVE TO RELY UPON THE FALSE IDENTITY AND CREDENTIALS THE BLACK WIDOW FABRICATED FOR ME.
I HOPE THEY PASS MUSTER.
BLOCK C
EVERYTHING'S IN ORDER.
LIPOWITZ, CONDUCT THIS MAN TO CHECKPOINT BAKER.
YES, SIR.
SO FAR SO GOOD.

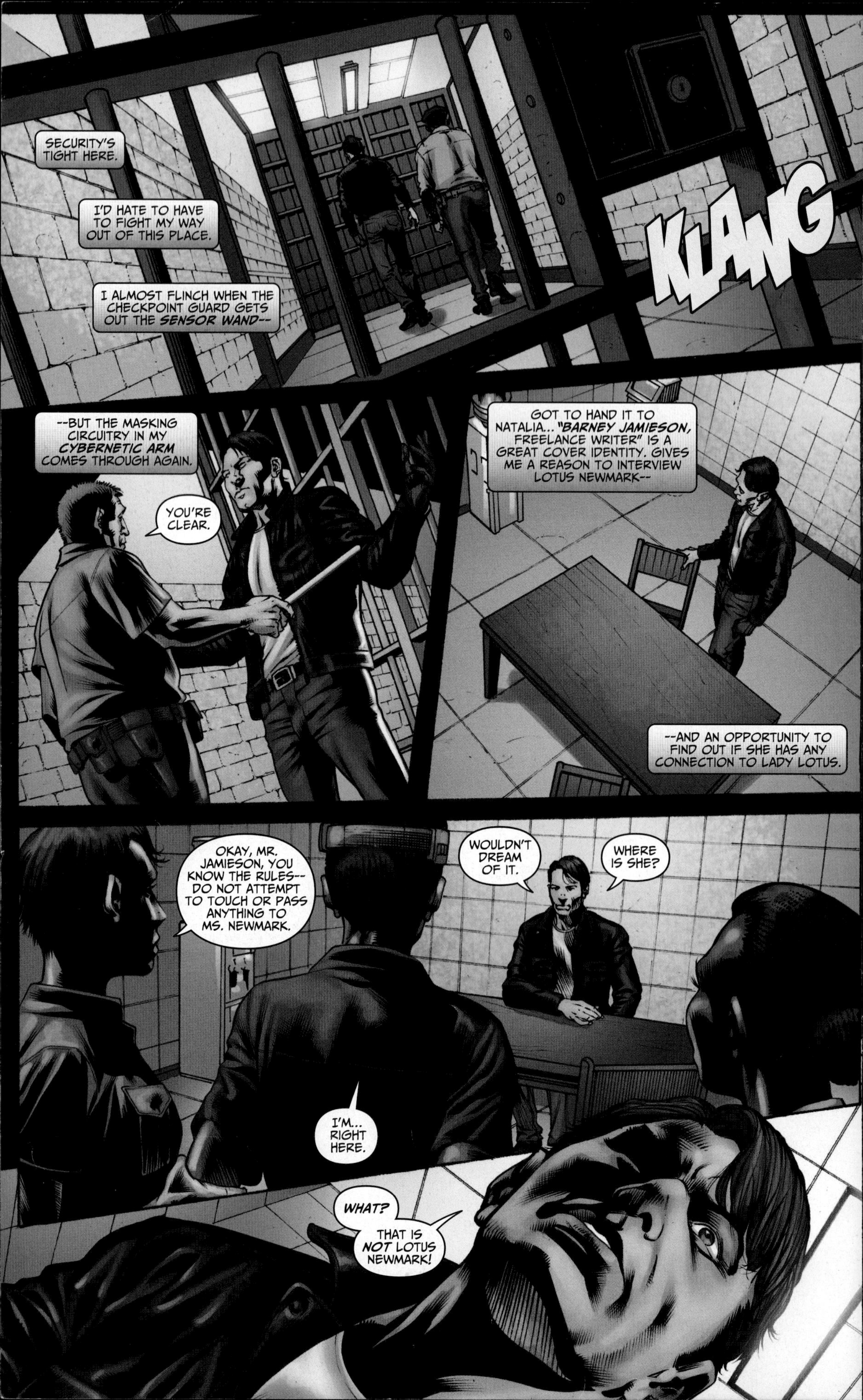
SECURITY'S TIGHT HERE.
I'D HATE TO HAVE TO FIGHT MY WAY OUT OF THIS PLACE.
I ALMOST FLINCH WHEN THE CHECKPOINT GUARD GETS OUT THE SENSOR WAND--
KLANG
--BUT THE MASKING CIRCUITRY IN MY CYBERNETIC ARM COMES THROUGH AGAIN.
YOU'RE CLEAR.
GOT TO HAND IT TO NATALIA... "BARNEY JAMIESON, FREELANCE WRITER" IS A GREAT COVER IDENTITY. GIVES ME A REASON TO INTERVIEW LOTUS NEWMARK--
--AND AN OPPORTUNITY TO FIND OUT IF SHE HAS ANY CONNECTION TO LADY LOTUS.
OKAY, MR. JAMIESON, YOU KNOW THE RULES-- DO NOT ATTEMPT TO TOUCH OR PASS ANYTHING TO MS. NEWMARK.
WOULDN'T DREAM OF IT.
WHERE IS SHE?
I'M... RIGHT HERE.
WHAT?
THAT IS NOT LOTUS NEWMARK!

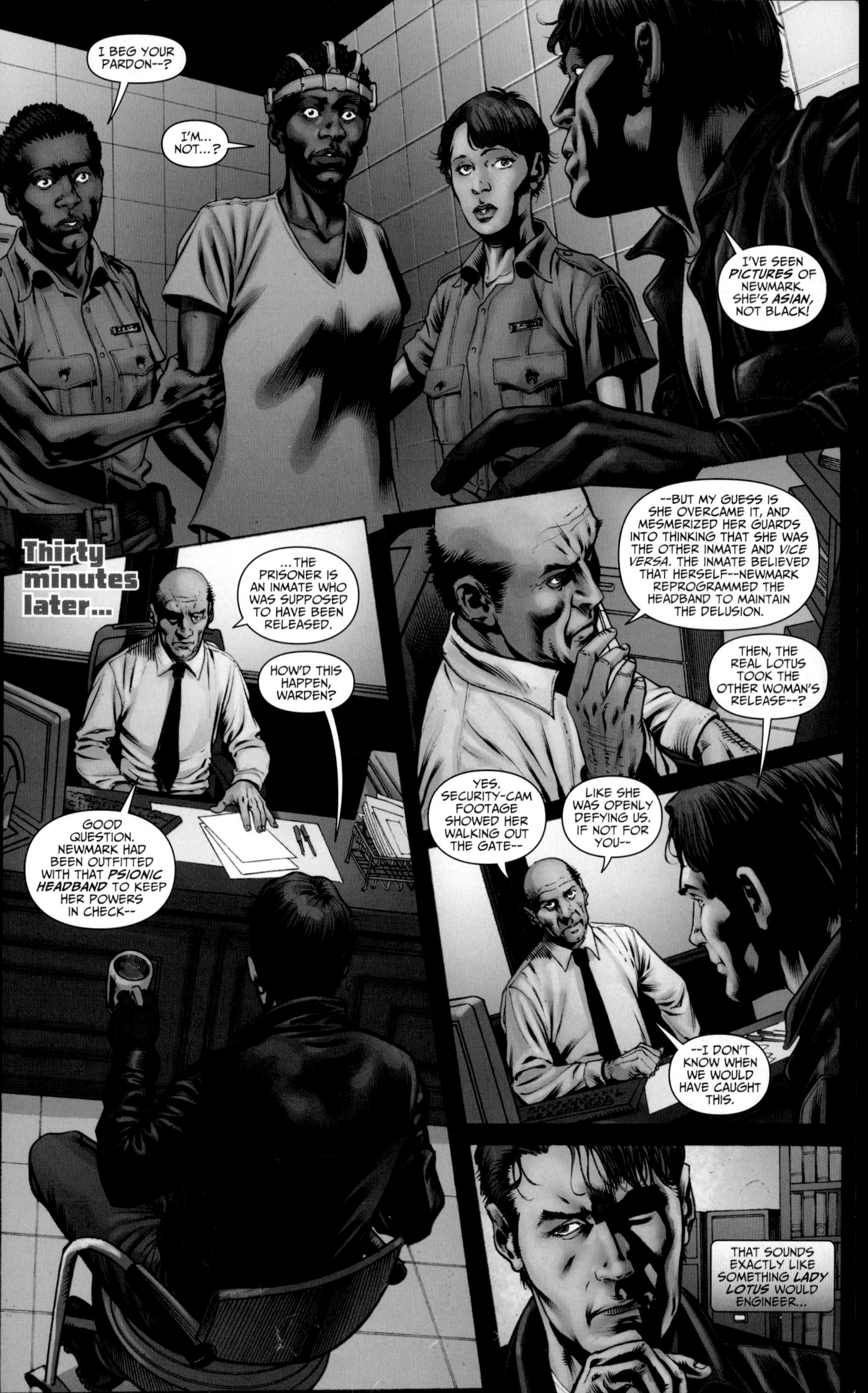
I BEG YOUR PARDON--?
I'M... NOT...?
I'VE SEEN *PICTURES* OF NEWMARK. SHE'S *ASIAN*, NOT BLACK!
Thirty minutes later...
...THE PRISONER IS AN INMATE WHO WAS SUPPOSED TO HAVE BEEN RELEASED.
HOW'D THIS HAPPEN, WARDEN?
GOOD QUESTION. NEWMARK HAD BEEN OUTFITTED WITH THAT *PSIONIC HEADBAND* TO KEEP HER POWERS IN CHECK--
--BUT MY GUESS IS SHE OVERCAME IT, AND MESMERIZED HER GUARDS INTO THINKING THAT SHE WAS THE OTHER INMATE AND *VICE VERSA*. THE INMATE BELIEVED THAT HERSELF--NEWMARK REPROGRAMMED THE HEADBAND TO MAINTAIN THE DELUSION.
THEN, THE REAL LOTUS TOOK THE OTHER WOMAN'S RELEASE--?
YES. SECURITY-CAM FOOTAGE SHOWED HER WALKING OUT THE GATE--
LIKE SHE WAS OPENLY DEFYING US. IF NOT FOR YOU--
--I DON'T KNOW WHEN WE WOULD HAVE CAUGHT THIS.
THAT SOUNDS EXACTLY LIKE SOMETHING *LADY LOTUS* WOULD ENGINEER...

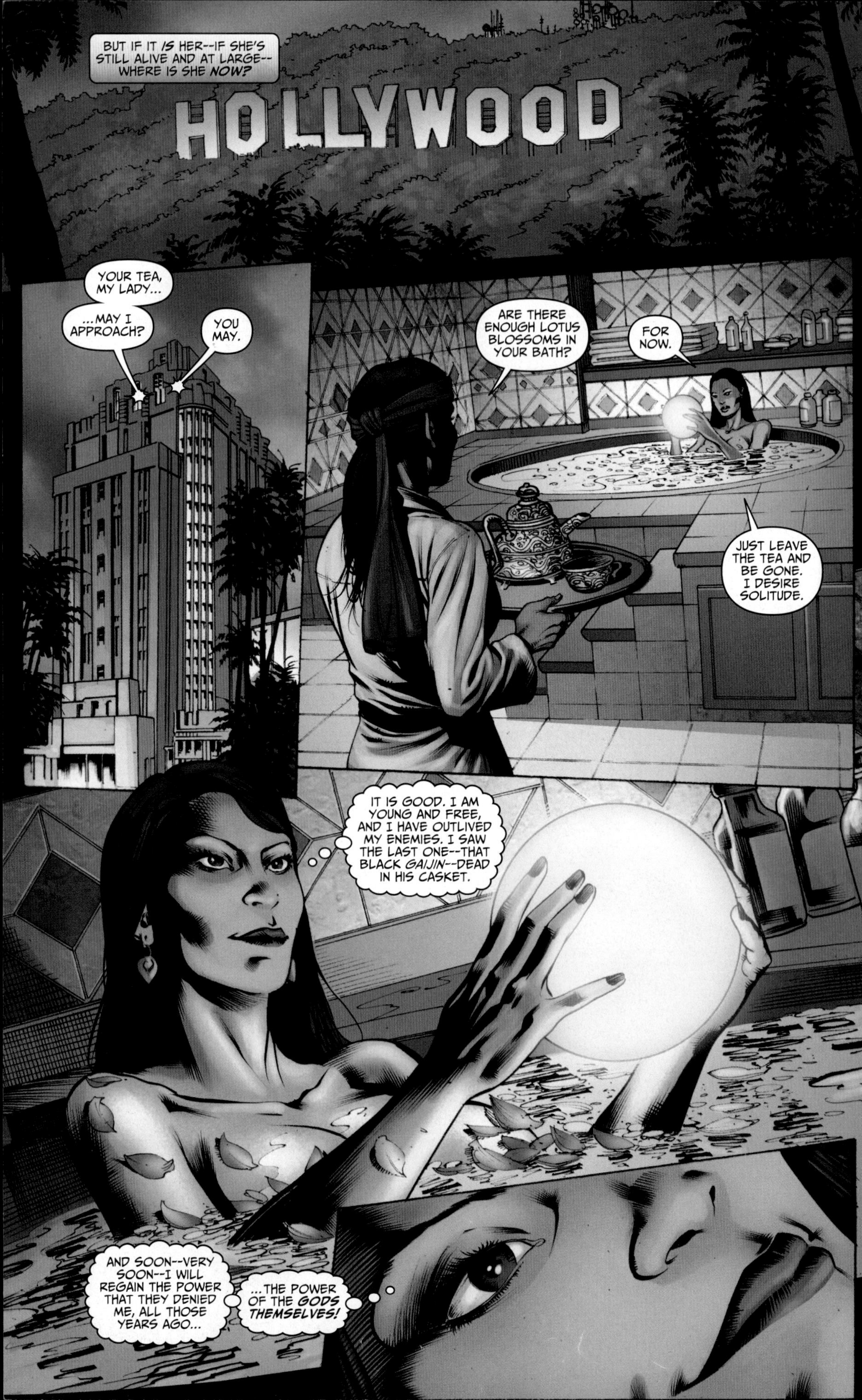
BUT IF IT IS HER--IF SHE'S STILL ALIVE AND AT LARGE-- WHERE IS SHE NOW?
HOLLYWOOD
YOUR TEA, MY LADY...
...MAY I APPROACH?
YOU MAY.
ARE THERE ENOUGH LOTUS BLOSSOMS IN YOUR BATH?
FOR NOW.
JUST LEAVE THE TEA AND BE GONE. I DESIRE SOLITUDE.
IT IS GOOD. I AM YOUNG AND FREE, AND I HAVE OUTLIVED MY ENEMIES. I SAW THE LAST ONE--THAT BLACK GAIJIN--DEAD IN HIS CASKET.
AND SOON--VERY SOON--I WILL REGAIN THE POWER THAT THEY DENIED ME, ALL THOSE YEARS AGO...
...THE POWER OF THE GODS THEMSELVES!

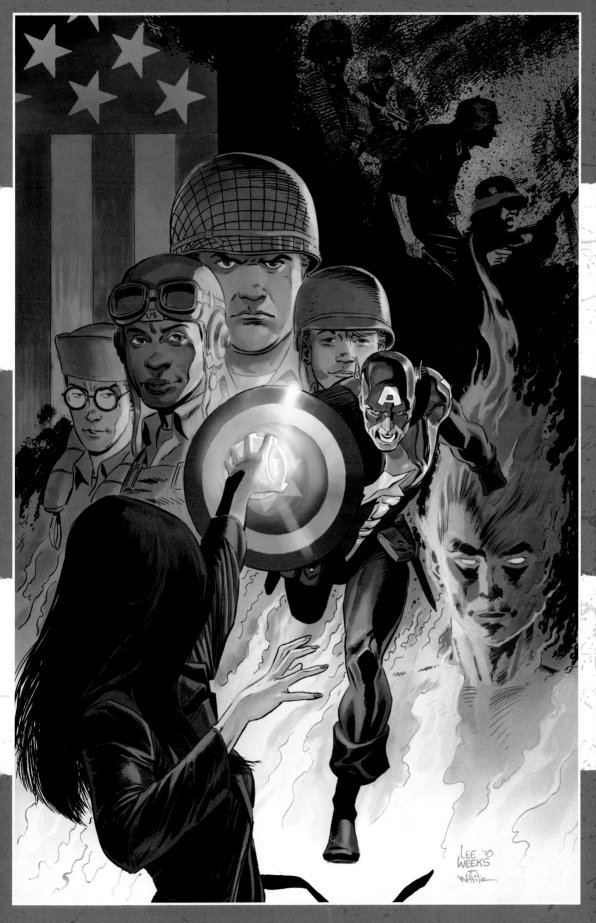

CAPTAIN AMERICA: FOREVER ALLIES #2

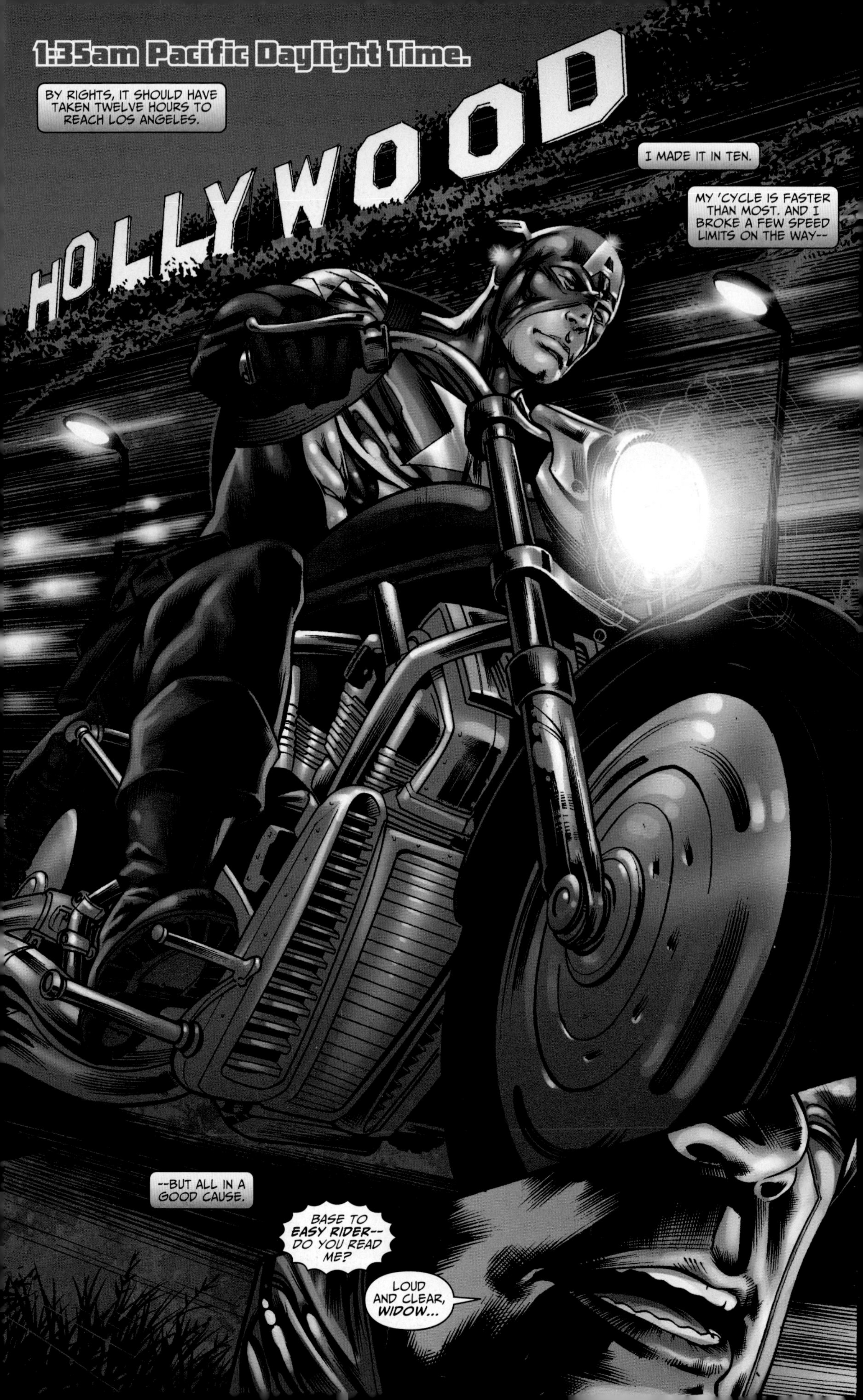
1:35am Pacific Daylight Time.
BY RIGHTS, IT SHOULD HAVE TAKEN TWELVE HOURS TO REACH LOS ANGELES.
HOLLYWOOD
I MADE IT IN TEN.
MY 'CYCLE IS FASTER THAN MOST. AND I BROKE A FEW SPEED LIMITS ON THE WAY--
--BUT ALL IN A GOOD CAUSE.
BASE TO EASY RIDER-- DO YOU READ ME?
LOUD AND CLEAR, WIDOW...

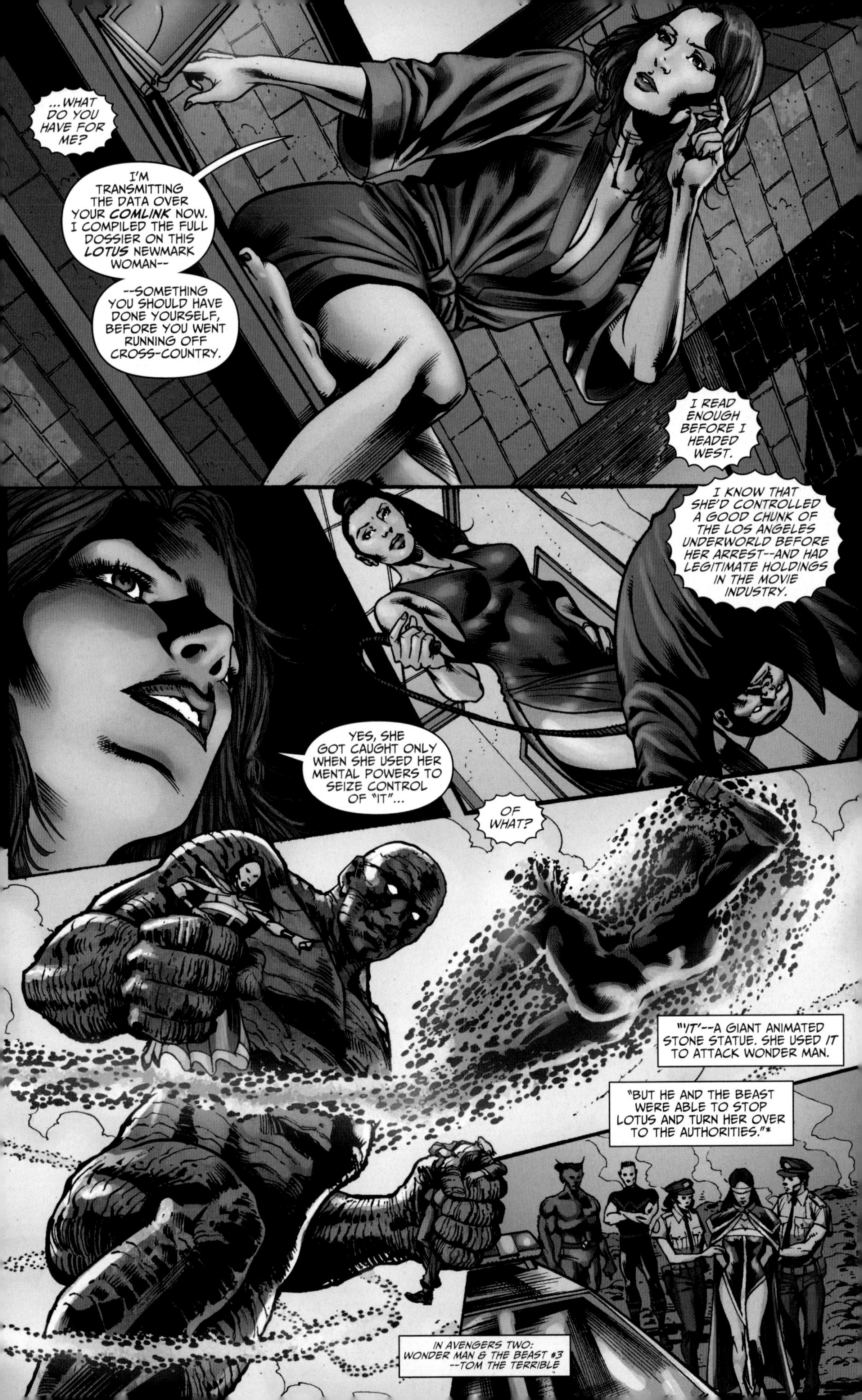
...WHAT DO YOU HAVE FOR ME?
I'M TRANSMITTING THE DATA OVER YOUR COMLINK NOW. I COMPILED THE FULL DOSSIER ON THIS LOTUS NEWMARK WOMAN--
--SOMETHING YOU SHOULD HAVE DONE YOURSELF, BEFORE YOU WENT RUNNING OFF CROSS-COUNTRY.
I READ ENOUGH BEFORE I HEADED WEST.
I KNOW THAT SHE'D CONTROLLED A GOOD CHUNK OF THE LOS ANGELES UNDERWORLD BEFORE HER ARREST--AND HAD LEGITIMATE HOLDINGS IN THE MOVIE INDUSTRY.
YES, SHE GOT CAUGHT ONLY WHEN SHE USED HER MENTAL POWERS TO SEIZE CONTROL OF "IT"...
OF WHAT?
"'IT'--A GIANT ANIMATED STONE STATUE. SHE USED IT TO ATTACK WONDER MAN.
"BUT HE AND THE BEAST WERE ABLE TO STOP LOTUS AND TURN HER OVER TO THE AUTHORITIES."*
IN AVENGERS TWO: WONDER MAN & THE BEAST #3 --TOM THE TERRIBLE

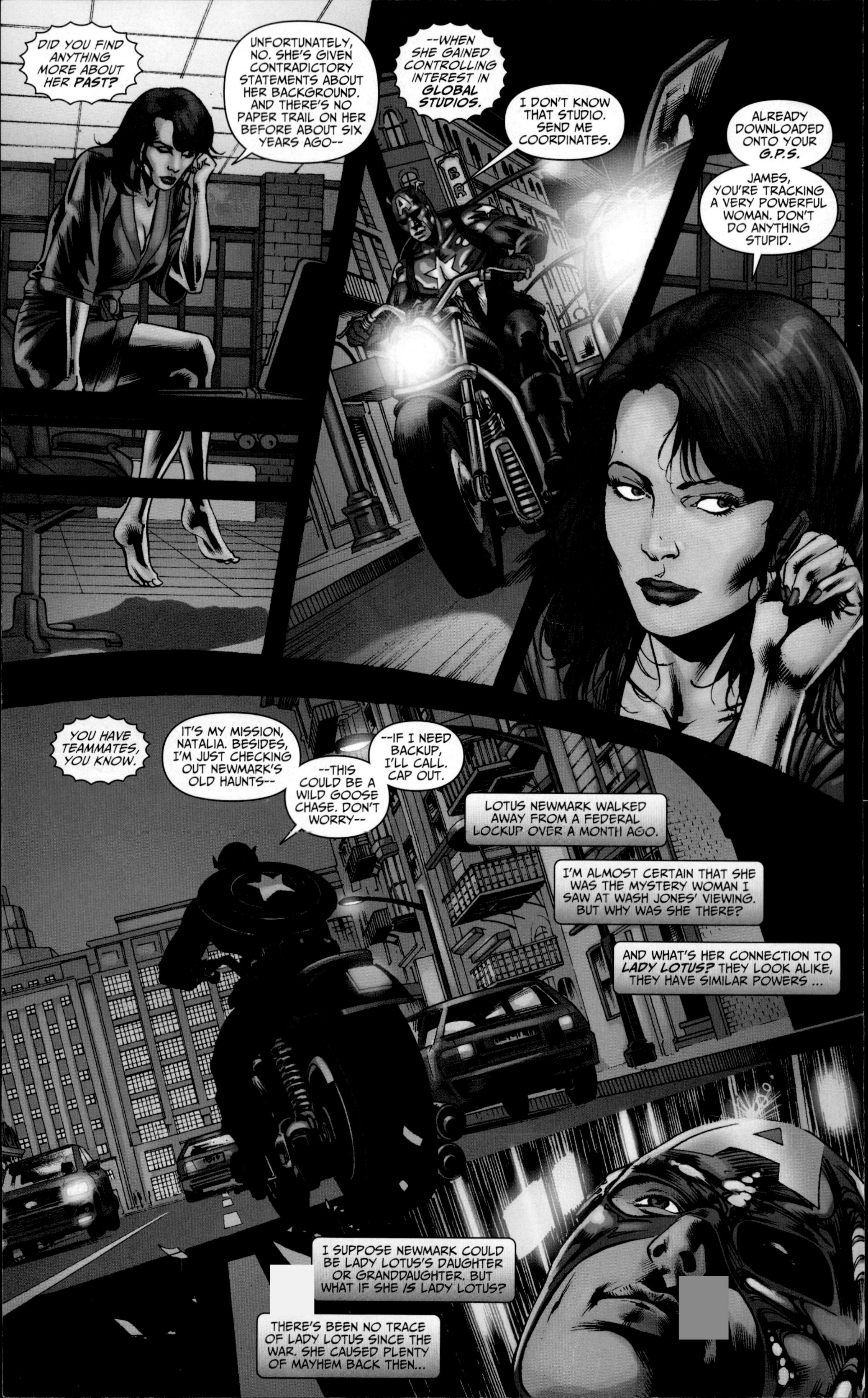
DID YOU FIND ANYTHING MORE ABOUT HER *PAST?*
UNFORTUNATELY, NO. SHE'S GIVEN CONTRADICTORY STATEMENTS ABOUT HER BACKGROUND. AND THERE'S NO PAPER TRAIL ON HER BEFORE ABOUT SIX YEARS AGO--
--WHEN SHE GAINED CONTROLLING INTEREST IN *GLOBAL STUDIOS.*
I DON'T KNOW THAT STUDIO. SEND ME COORDINATES.
ALREADY DOWNLOADED ONTO YOUR *G.P.S.*
JAMES, YOU'RE TRACKING A VERY POWERFUL WOMAN. DON'T DO ANYTHING STUPID.
YOU HAVE TEAMMATES, YOU KNOW.
IT'S MY MISSION, NATALIA. BESIDES, I'M JUST CHECKING OUT NEWMARK'S OLD HAUNTS--
--THIS COULD BE A WILD GOOSE CHASE. DON'T WORRY--
--IF I NEED BACKUP, I'LL CALL. CAP OUT.
LOTUS NEWMARK WALKED AWAY FROM A FEDERAL LOCKUP OVER A MONTH AGO.
I'M ALMOST CERTAIN THAT SHE WAS THE MYSTERY WOMAN I SAW AT WASH JONES' VIEWING. BUT WHY WAS SHE THERE?
AND WHAT'S HER CONNECTION TO *LADY LOTUS?* THEY LOOK ALIKE, THEY HAVE SIMILAR POWERS ...
I SUPPOSE NEWMARK COULD BE LADY LOTUS'S DAUGHTER OR GRANDDAUGHTER. BUT WHAT IF SHE *IS* LADY LOTUS?
THERE'S BEEN NO TRACE OF LADY LOTUS SINCE THE WAR. SHE CAUSED PLENTY OF MAYHEM BACK THEN...

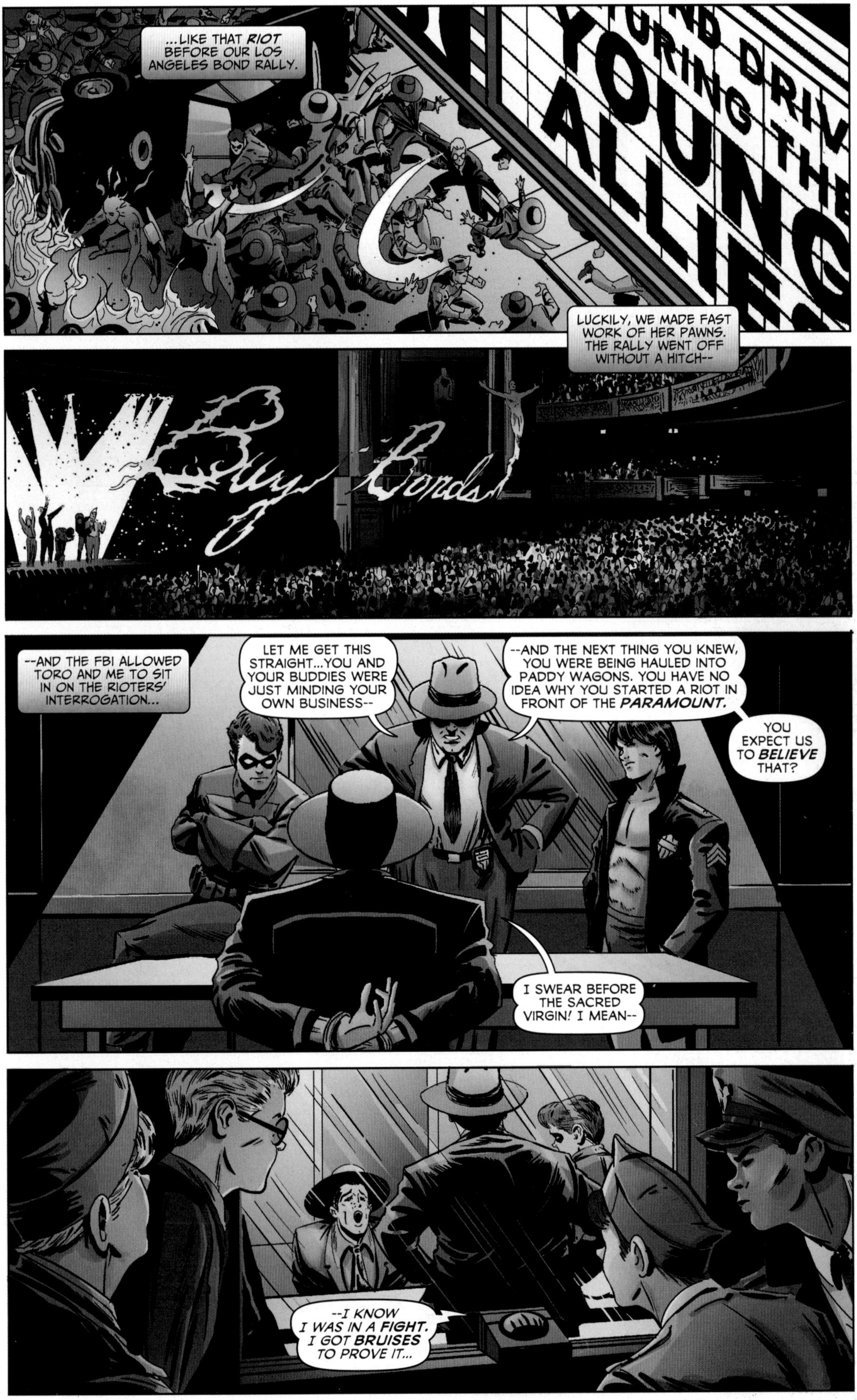

...LIKE THAT RIOT BEFORE OUR LOS ANGELES BOND RALLY.
YOUNG THE ALLIES
LUCKILY, WE MADE FAST WORK OF HER PAWNS. THE RALLY WENT OFF WITHOUT A HITCH--
Buy Bonds
--AND THE FBI ALLOWED TORO AND ME TO SIT IN ON THE RIOTERS' INTERROGATION...
LET ME GET THIS STRAIGHT...YOU AND YOUR BUDDIES WERE JUST MINDING YOUR OWN BUSINESS--
--AND THE NEXT THING YOU KNEW, YOU WERE BEING HAULED INTO PADDY WAGONS. YOU HAVE NO IDEA WHY YOU STARTED A RIOT IN FRONT OF THE PARAMOUNT.
YOU EXPECT US TO BELIEVE THAT?
I SWEAR BEFORE THE SACRED VIRGIN! I MEAN--
--I KNOW I WAS IN A FIGHT. I GOT BRUISES TO PROVE IT...

...BUT **WHY?** I DUNNO. LAST THING I REMEMBER--

--WAS BUMPING INTO SOME **DRAGON LADY,** DOWN IN CHINATOWN.

SHE GIMME A DIRTY LOOK-- AN' THE NEXT THING I KNEW, THE COPS WAS HAULIN' ME AWAY.

A "DRAGON LADY"...?

YOU'RE SURE OF THAT?

SURE AS I'M SITTING HERE. WHAT HAPPENED TO ME?

WHAT'S GONNA HAPPEN NOW?

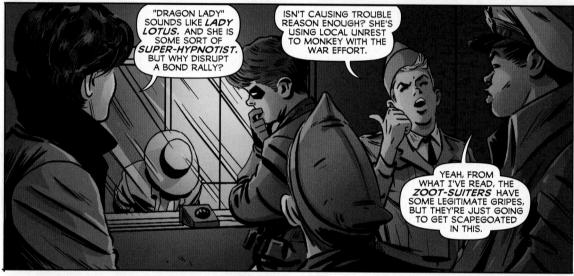

"DRAGON LADY" SOUNDS LIKE **LADY LOTUS.** AND SHE IS SOME SORT OF **SUPER-HYPNOTIST.** BUT WHY DISRUPT A BOND RALLY?

ISN'T CAUSING TROUBLE REASON ENOUGH? SHE'S USING LOCAL UNREST TO MONKEY WITH THE WAR EFFORT.

YEAH, FROM WHAT I'VE READ, THE **ZOOT-SUITERS** HAVE SOME LEGITIMATE GRIPES, BUT THEY'RE JUST GOING TO GET SCAPEGOATED IN THIS.

THAT STINKS OUT LOUD! WE GOTTA TRACK THIS LOTUS DAME DOWN!

NO, YOU DON'T. THIS IS A BUREAU CASE NOW.

AND YOU GENTLEMEN HAVE OTHER RESPONSIBILITIES.

REGRETTABLY, THE AGENT IS CORRECT. WE WERE SENT HERE TO RALLY THE HOME FRONT.

IF LADY LOTUS IS BEHIND THIS, WE WON'T BE SIDE-LINED FOR LONG. JUDGING BY HER TRACK RECORD--

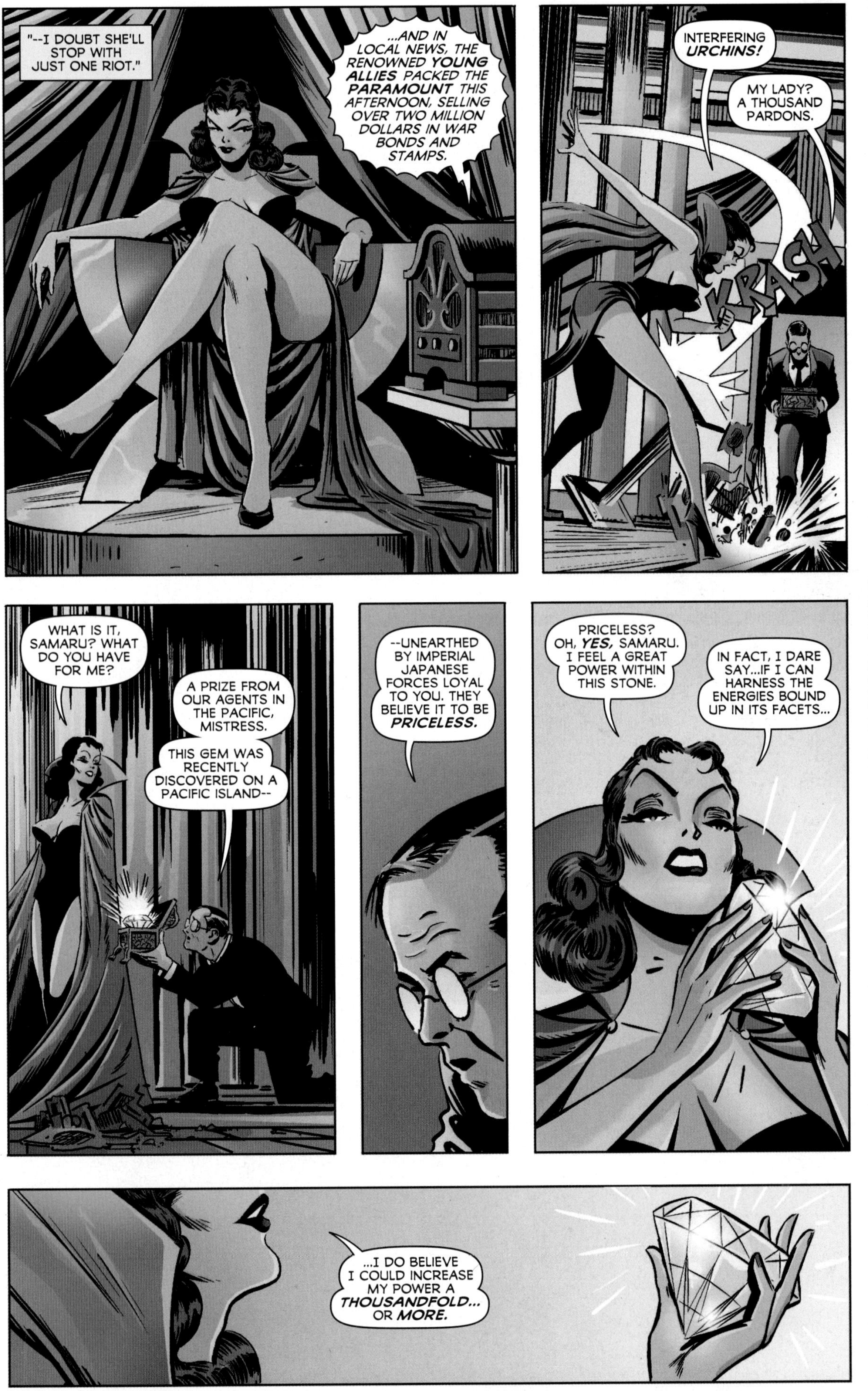
"--I DOUBT SHE'LL STOP WITH JUST ONE RIOT."
...AND IN LOCAL NEWS, THE RENOWNED **YOUNG ALLIES** PACKED THE **PARAMOUNT** THIS AFTERNOON, SELLING OVER TWO MILLION DOLLARS IN WAR BONDS AND STAMPS.
INTERFERING ***URCHINS!***
MY LADY? A THOUSAND PARDONS.
KRASH
WHAT IS IT, SAMARU? WHAT DO YOU HAVE FOR ME?
A PRIZE FROM OUR AGENTS IN THE PACIFIC, MISTRESS.
THIS GEM WAS RECENTLY DISCOVERED ON A PACIFIC ISLAND--
--UNEARTHED BY IMPERIAL JAPANESE FORCES LOYAL TO YOU. THEY BELIEVE IT TO BE ***PRICELESS.***
PRICELESS? OH, ***YES,*** SAMARU. I FEEL A GREAT POWER WITHIN THIS STONE.
IN FACT, I DARE SAY...IF I CAN HARNESS THE ENERGIES BOUND UP IN ITS FACETS...
...I DO BELIEVE I COULD INCREASE MY POWER A ***THOUSANDFOLD...*** OR ***MORE.***

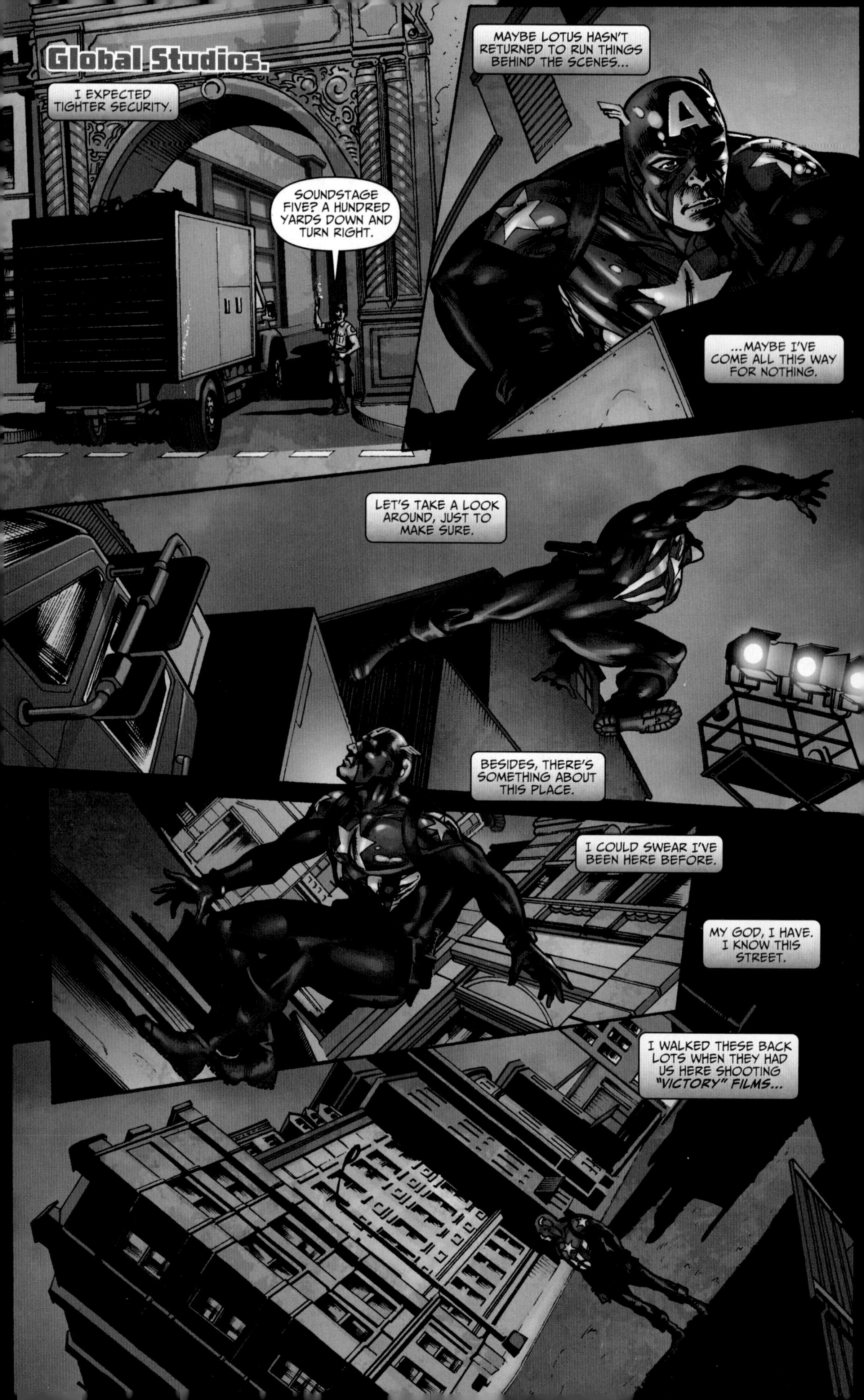
Global Studios.
I EXPECTED TIGHTER SECURITY.
SOUNDSTAGE FIVE? A HUNDRED YARDS DOWN AND TURN RIGHT.
MAYBE LOTUS HASN'T RETURNED TO RUN THINGS BEHIND THE SCENES...
...MAYBE I'VE COME ALL THIS WAY FOR NOTHING.
LET'S TAKE A LOOK AROUND, JUST TO MAKE SURE.
BESIDES, THERE'S SOMETHING ABOUT THIS PLACE.
I COULD SWEAR I'VE BEEN HERE BEFORE.
MY GOD, I HAVE. I KNOW THIS STREET.
I WALKED THESE BACK LOTS WHEN THEY HAD US HERE SHOOTING "VICTORY" FILMS...

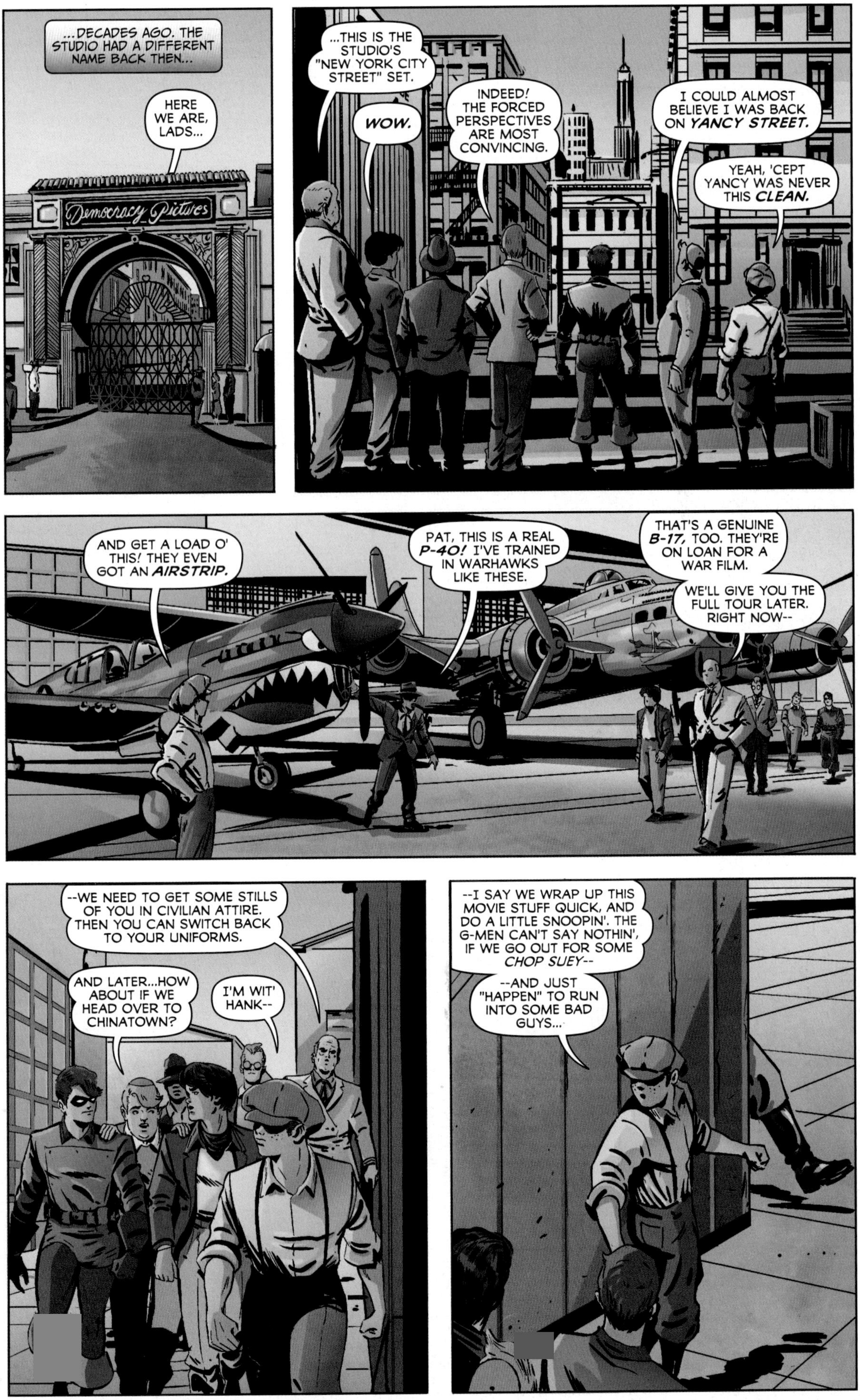
...DECADES AGO. THE STUDIO HAD A DIFFERENT NAME BACK THEN...
HERE WE ARE, LADS...
Democracy Pictures
...THIS IS THE STUDIO'S "NEW YORK CITY STREET" SET.
WOW.
INDEED! THE FORCED PERSPECTIVES ARE MOST CONVINCING.
I COULD ALMOST BELIEVE I WAS BACK ON YANCY STREET.
YEAH, 'CEPT YANCY WAS NEVER THIS CLEAN.
AND GET A LOAD O' THIS! THEY EVEN GOT AN AIRSTRIP.
PAT, THIS IS A REAL P-40! I'VE TRAINED IN WARHAWKS LIKE THESE.
THAT'S A GENUINE B-17, TOO. THEY'RE ON LOAN FOR A WAR FILM.
WE'LL GIVE YOU THE FULL TOUR LATER. RIGHT NOW--
--WE NEED TO GET SOME STILLS OF YOU IN CIVILIAN ATTIRE. THEN YOU CAN SWITCH BACK TO YOUR UNIFORMS.
AND LATER...HOW ABOUT IF WE HEAD OVER TO CHINATOWN?
I'M WIT' HANK--
--I SAY WE WRAP UP THIS MOVIE STUFF QUICK, AND DO A LITTLE SNOOPIN'. THE G-MEN CAN'T SAY NOTHIN', IF WE GO OUT FOR SOME CHOP SUEY--
--AND JUST "HAPPEN" TO RUN INTO SOME BAD GUYS...

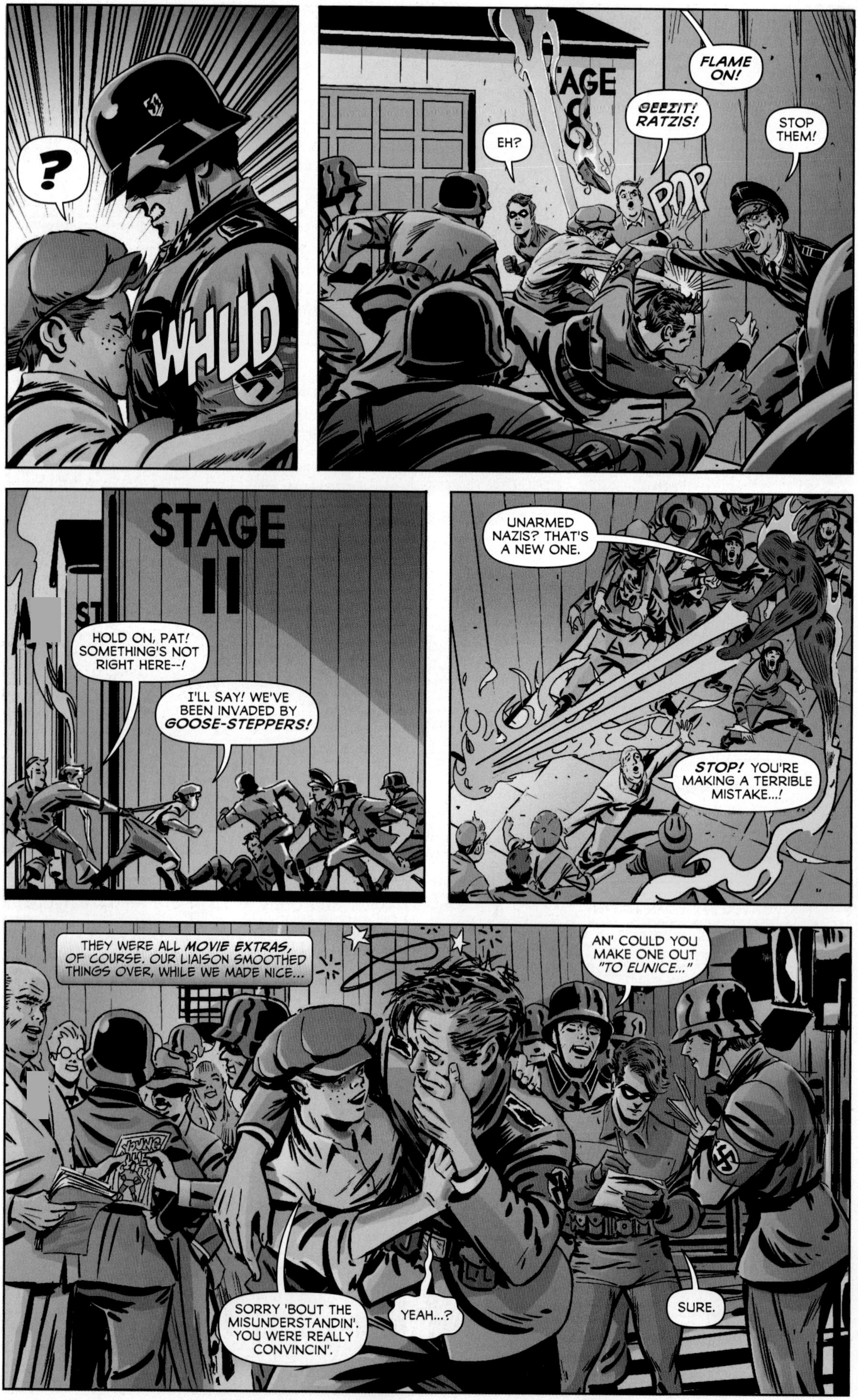
?
WHUD
STAGE 8
FLAME ON!
GEEZIT! RATZIS!
EH?
STOP THEM!
POP
STAGE 11
HOLD ON, PAT! SOMETHING'S NOT RIGHT HERE--!
I'LL SAY! WE'VE BEEN INVADED BY *GOOSE-STEPPERS!*
UNARMED NAZIS? THAT'S A NEW ONE.
STOP! YOU'RE MAKING A TERRIBLE MISTAKE...!
THEY WERE ALL *MOVIE EXTRAS*, OF COURSE. OUR LIAISON SMOOTHED THINGS OVER, WHILE WE MADE NICE...
AN' COULD YOU MAKE ONE OUT *"TO EUNICE..."*
SORRY 'BOUT THE MISUNDERSTANDIN'. YOU WERE REALLY CONVINCIN'.
YEAH...?
SURE.

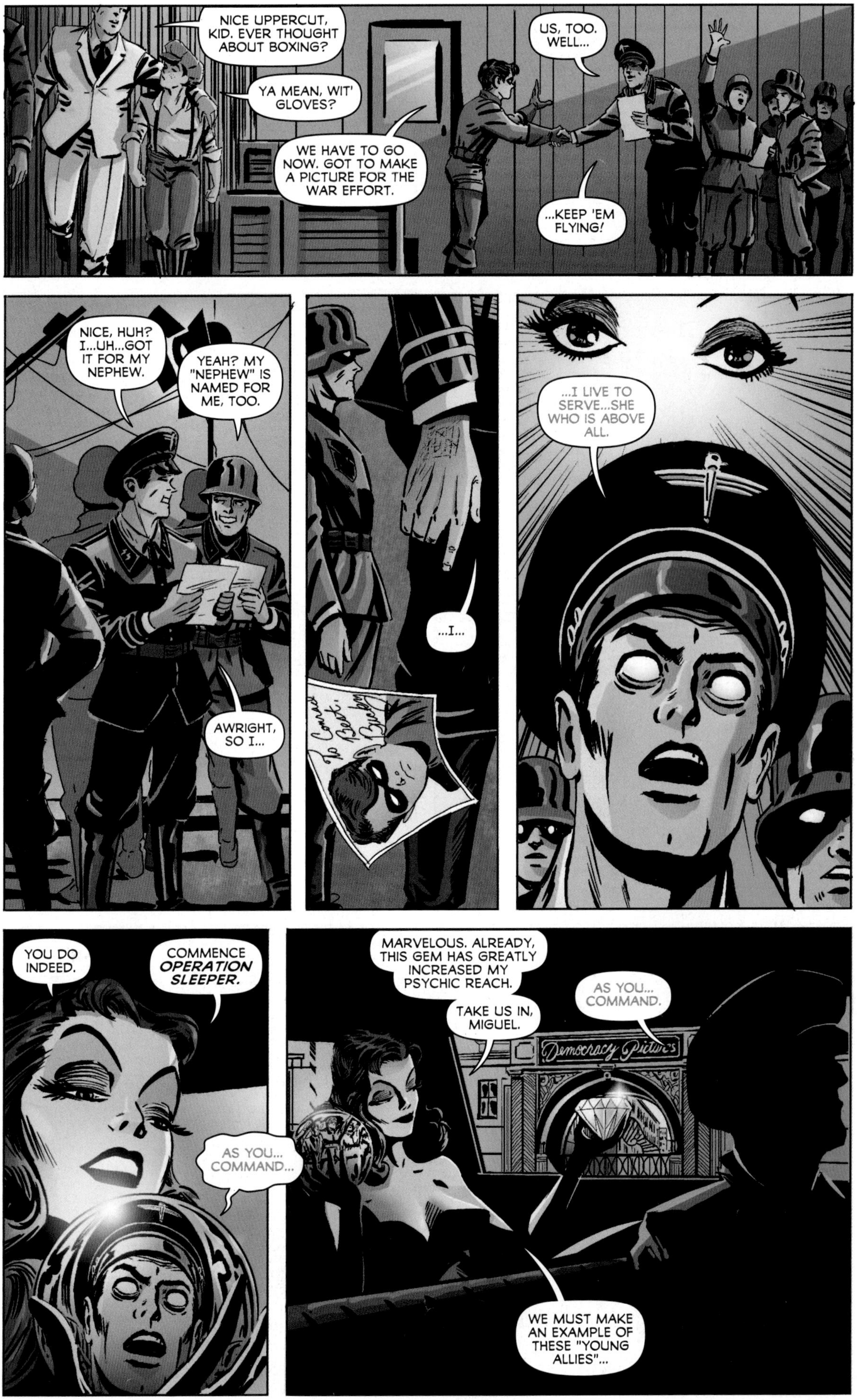
NICE UPPERCUT, KID. EVER THOUGHT ABOUT BOXING?
YA MEAN, WIT' GLOVES?
WE HAVE TO GO NOW. GOT TO MAKE A PICTURE FOR THE WAR EFFORT.
US, TOO. WELL...
...KEEP 'EM FLYING!
NICE, HUH? I...UH...GOT IT FOR MY NEPHEW.
YEAH? MY "NEPHEW" IS NAMED FOR ME, TOO.
AWRIGHT, SO I...
...I...
...I LIVE TO SERVE...SHE WHO IS ABOVE ALL.
YOU DO INDEED.
COMMENCE *OPERATION SLEEPER.*
AS YOU... COMMAND...
MARVELOUS. ALREADY, THIS GEM HAS GREATLY INCREASED MY PSYCHIC REACH.
TAKE US IN, MIGUEL.
AS YOU... COMMAND.
Democracy Pictures
WE MUST MAKE AN EXAMPLE OF THESE "YOUNG ALLIES"...

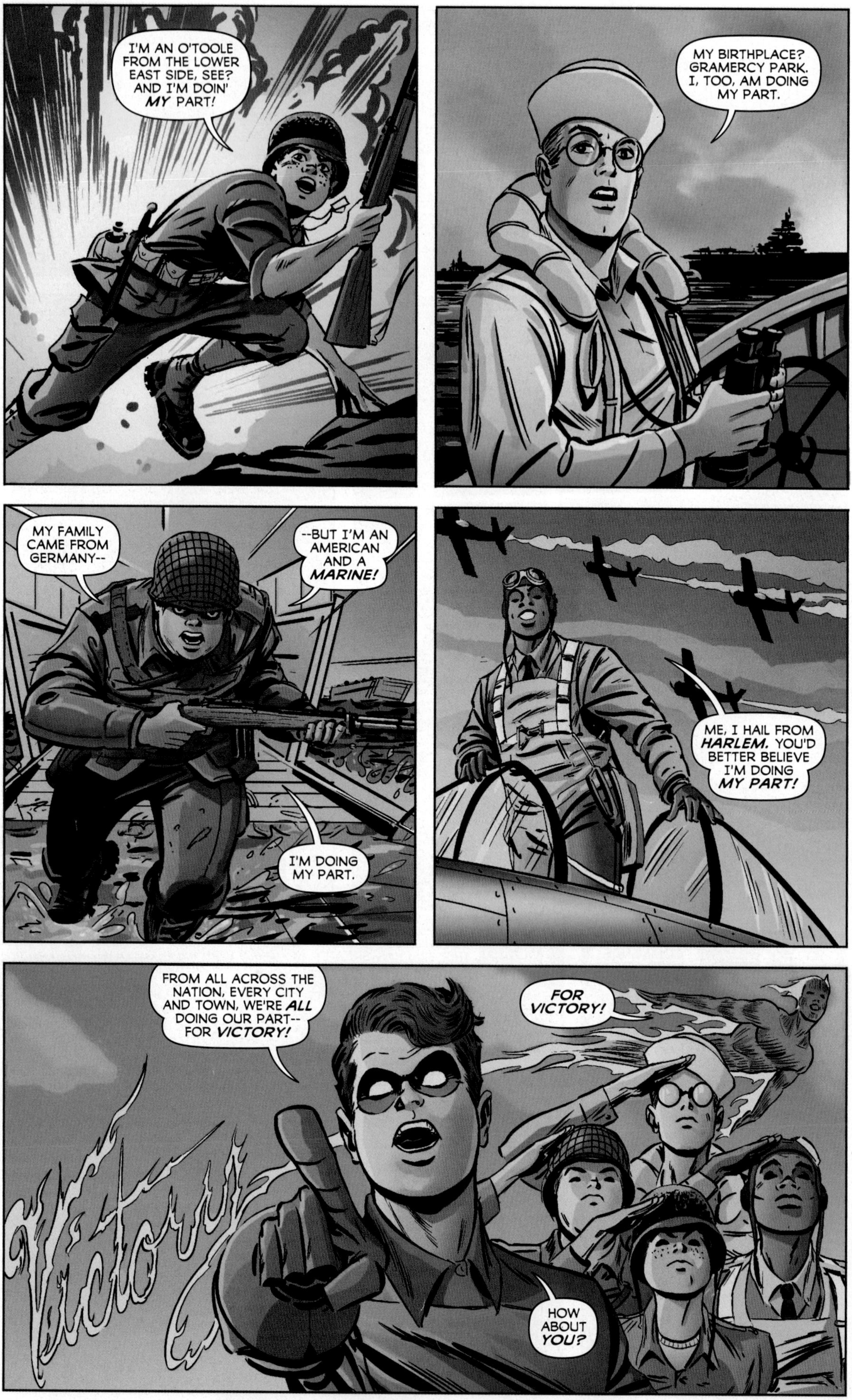
I'M AN O'TOOLE FROM THE LOWER EAST SIDE, SEE? AND I'M DOIN' *MY* PART!
MY BIRTHPLACE? GRAMERCY PARK. I, TOO, AM DOING MY PART.
MY FAMILY CAME FROM GERMANY--
--BUT I'M AN AMERICAN AND A *MARINE!*
I'M DOING MY PART.
ME, I HAIL FROM *HARLEM.* YOU'D BETTER BELIEVE I'M DOING *MY PART!*
FROM ALL ACROSS THE NATION, EVERY CITY AND TOWN, WE'RE *ALL* DOING OUR PART-- FOR *VICTORY!*
FOR VICTORY!
Victory
HOW ABOUT *YOU?*

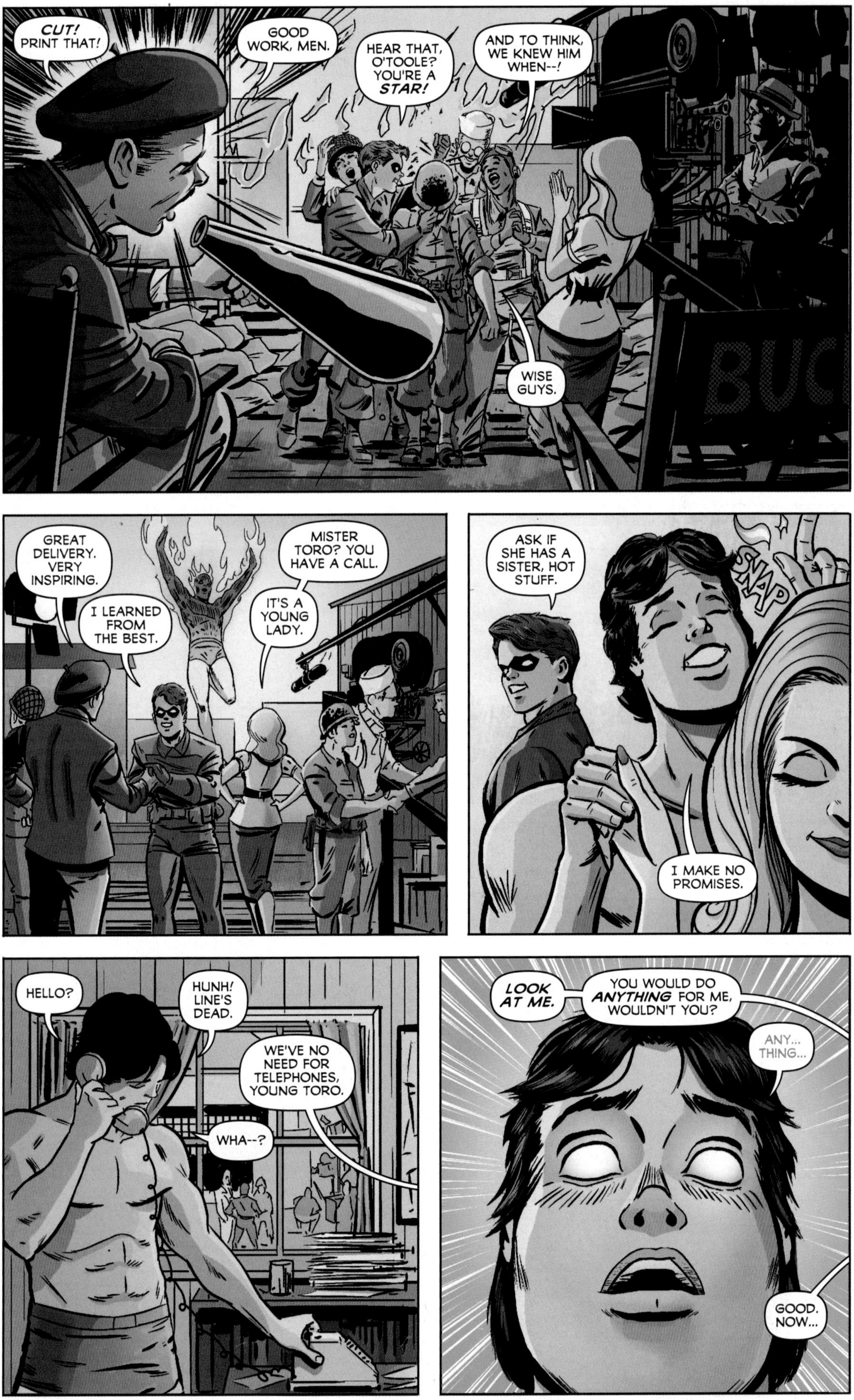
CUT! PRINT THAT!
GOOD WORK, MEN.
HEAR THAT, O'TOOLE? YOU'RE A STAR!
AND TO THINK, WE KNEW HIM WHEN--!
WISE GUYS.
BUC
GREAT DELIVERY. VERY INSPIRING.
I LEARNED FROM THE BEST.
MISTER TORO? YOU HAVE A CALL.
IT'S A YOUNG LADY.
ASK IF SHE HAS A SISTER, HOT STUFF.
SNAP
I MAKE NO PROMISES.
HELLO?
HUNH! LINE'S DEAD.
WE'VE NO NEED FOR TELEPHONES, YOUNG TORO.
WHA--?
LOOK AT ME.
YOU WOULD DO ANYTHING FOR ME, WOULDN'T YOU?
ANY... THING...
GOOD. NOW...

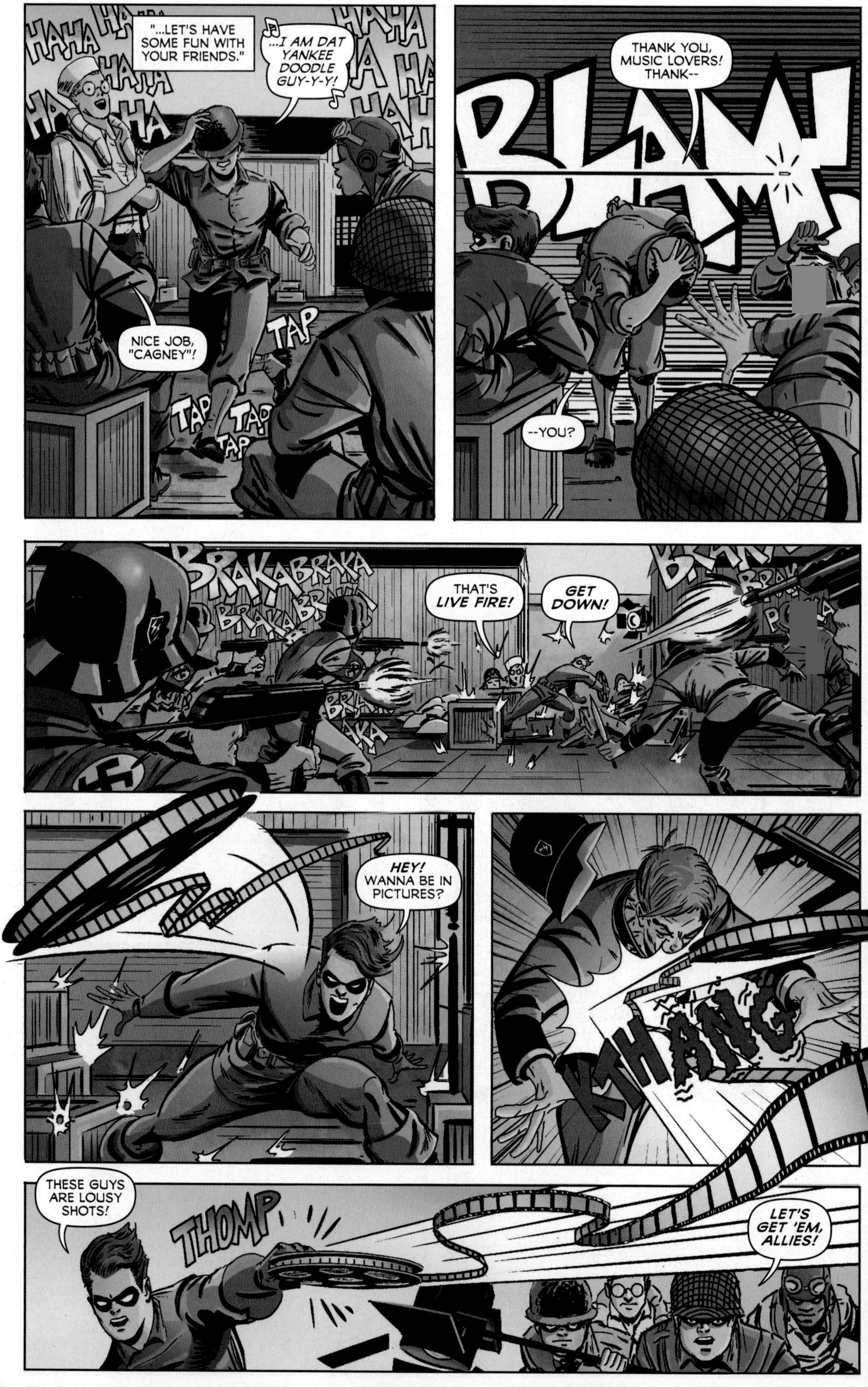
HAHA HAHA HAHA HAHA
"...LET'S HAVE SOME FUN WITH YOUR FRIENDS."
...I AM DAT YANKEE DOODLE GUY-Y-Y!
HAHA HA HA HAHA
NICE JOB, "CAGNEY"!
TAP
TAP TAP TAP
THANK YOU, MUSIC LOVERS! THANK--
BLAM
--YOU?
BRAKABRAKA
THAT'S LIVE FIRE!
GET DOWN!
HEY! WANNA BE IN PICTURES?
KTHANG
THESE GUYS ARE LOUSY SHOTS!
THOMP
LET'S GET 'EM, ALLIES!

WE WERE OUTNUMBERED AT LEAST FIVE TO ONE. BUT EVEN SO, WE TORE THROUGH THEM LIKE THEY WERE HALF-ASLEEP.

WASH WAS THE FIRST TO NOTICE WHY...

WHAM

BRAKA BRAKA

BRAKA BRAKA

BRAKA BRAKA

BRAKA

BONK

POP

WAK

THESE GUYS ARE ENTRANCED-- JUST LIKE THE ZOOT-SUITERS WERE!

BE THAT AS IT MAY--

--THEIR STATE OF MIND DOES NOT NEGATE THEIR FIREPOWER!

BLAM

KRAK

'BOUT TIME YOU GOT BACK, HOTHEAD!

WE NEED ANOTHER DOSE OF THE OLD RAZZLE-DAZZLE!

PCHOW

THUD

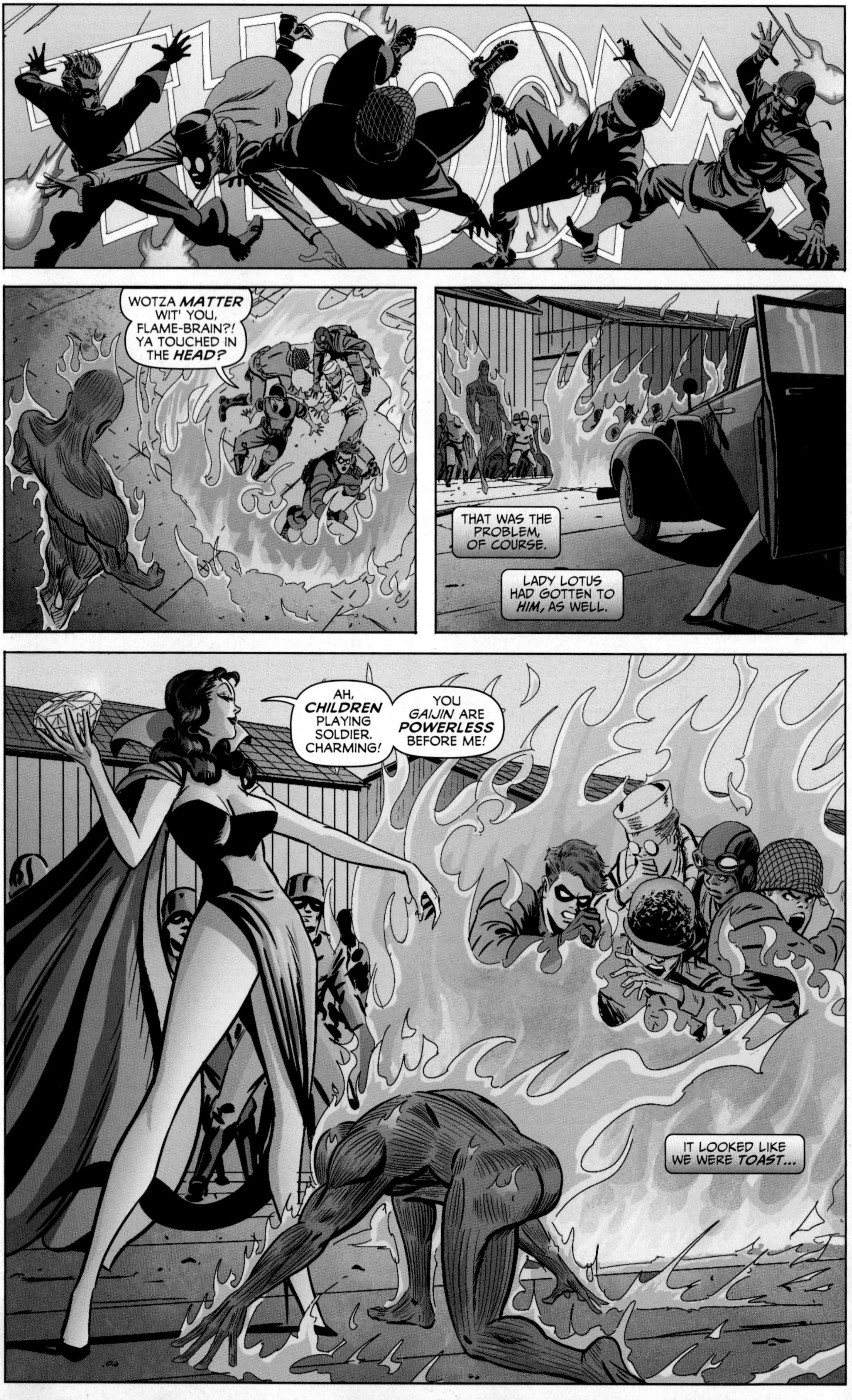
WOTZA MATTER WIT' YOU, FLAME-BRAIN?! YA TOUCHED IN THE HEAD?
THAT WAS THE PROBLEM, OF COURSE.
LADY LOTUS HAD GOTTEN TO HIM, AS WELL.
AH, CHILDREN PLAYING SOLDIER. CHARMING!
YOU GAIJIN ARE POWERLESS BEFORE ME!
IT LOOKED LIKE WE WERE TOAST...

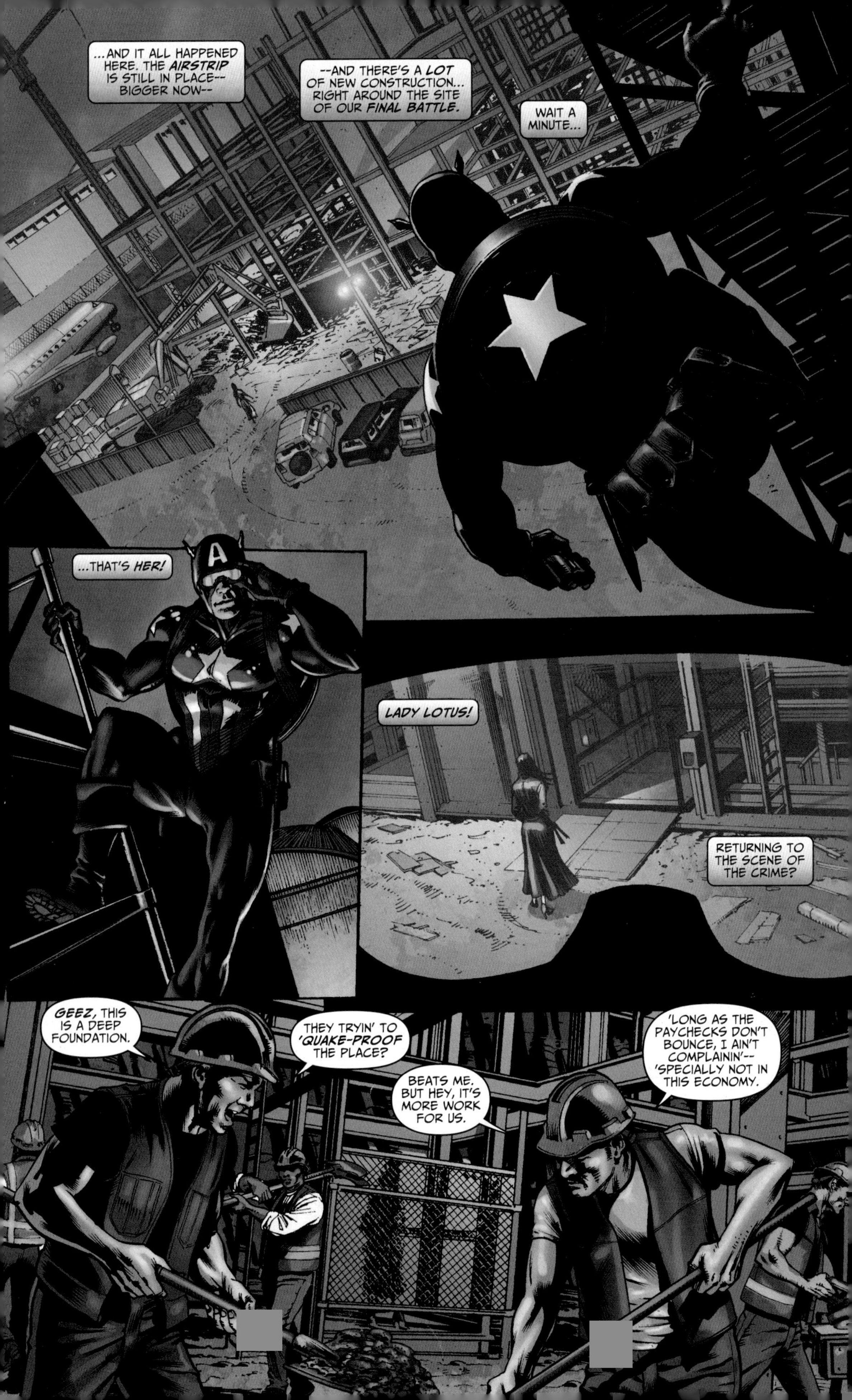
...AND IT ALL HAPPENED HERE. THE AIRSTRIP IS STILL IN PLACE-- BIGGER NOW--
--AND THERE'S A LOT OF NEW CONSTRUCTION... RIGHT AROUND THE SITE OF OUR FINAL BATTLE.
WAIT A MINUTE...
...THAT'S HER!
LADY LOTUS!
RETURNING TO THE SCENE OF THE CRIME?
GEEZ, THIS IS A DEEP FOUNDATION.
THEY TRYIN' TO 'QUAKE-PROOF THE PLACE?
BEATS ME. BUT HEY, IT'S MORE WORK FOR US.
'LONG AS THE PAYCHECKS DON'T BOUNCE, I AIN'T COMPLAININ'-- 'SPECIALLY NOT IN THIS ECONOMY.

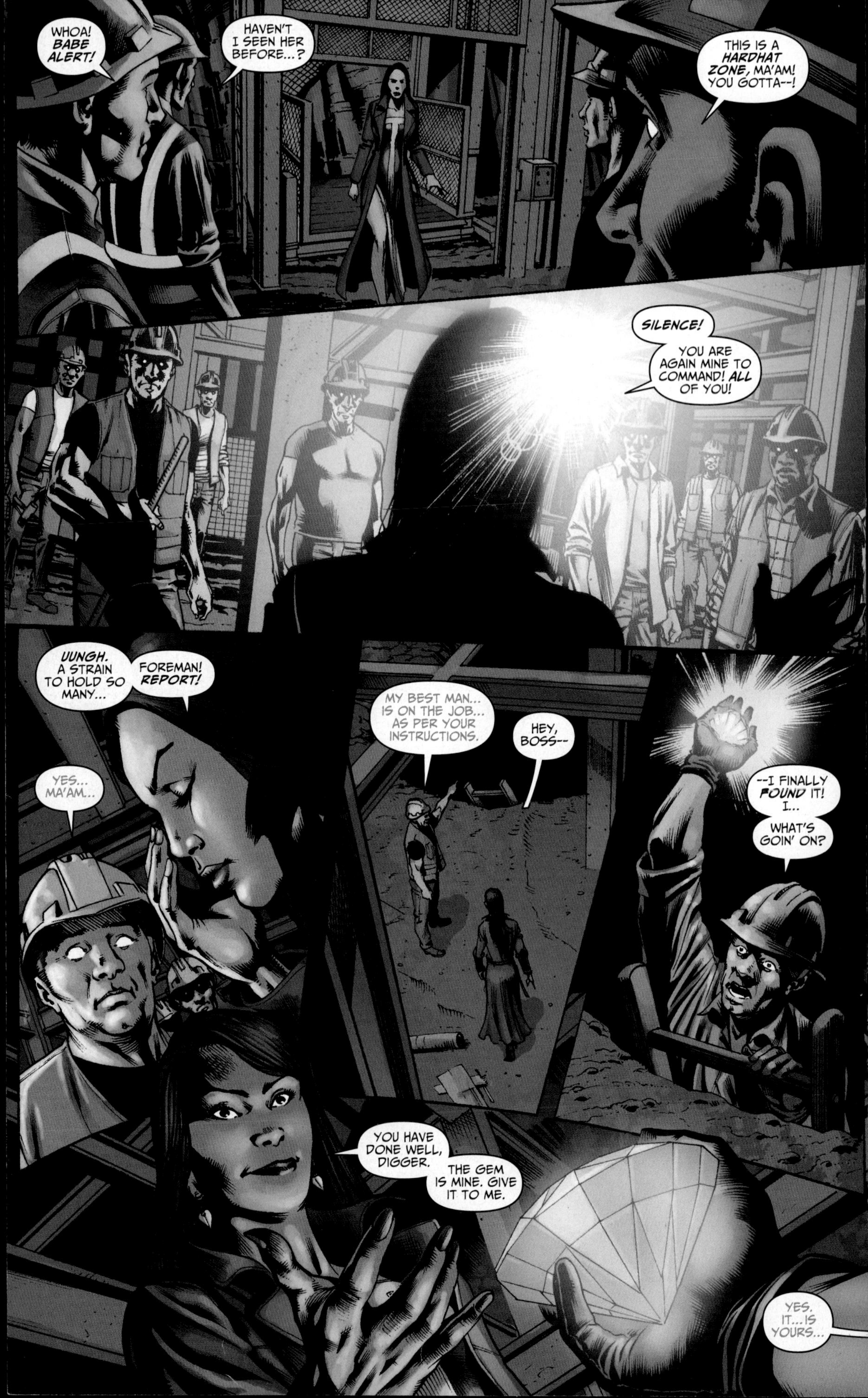

WHOA! BABE ALERT!
HAVEN'T I SEEN HER BEFORE...?
THIS IS A HARDHAT ZONE, MA'AM! YOU GOTTA--!
SILENCE!
YOU ARE AGAIN MINE TO COMMAND! ALL OF YOU!
UUNGH. A STRAIN TO HOLD SO MANY...
FOREMAN! REPORT!
YES... MA'AM...
MY BEST MAN... IS ON THE JOB... AS PER YOUR INSTRUCTIONS.
HEY, BOSS--
--I FINALLY FOUND IT! I...
WHAT'S GOIN' ON?
YOU HAVE DONE WELL, DIGGER.
THE GEM IS MINE. GIVE IT TO ME.
YES. IT... IS YOURS...

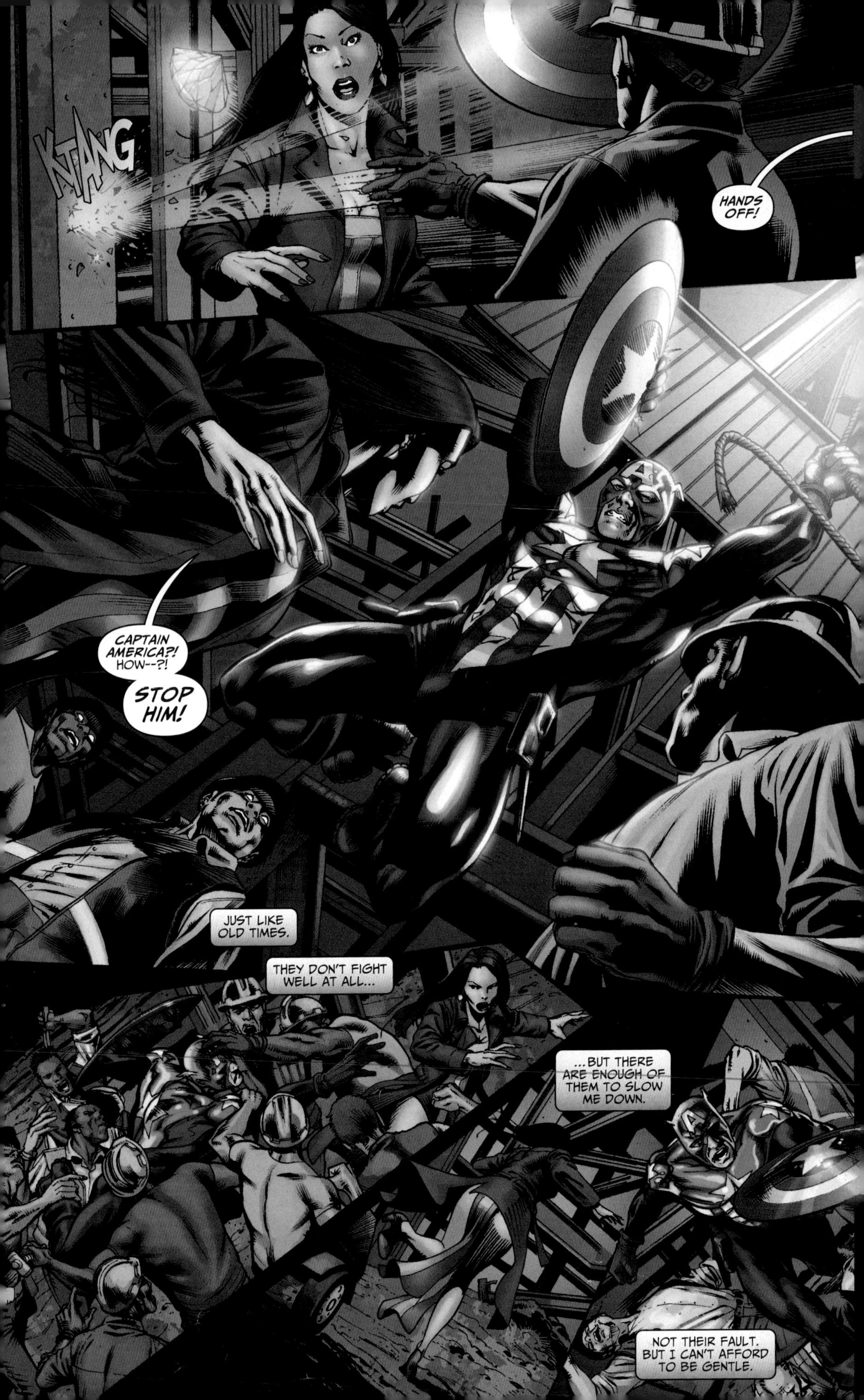
KTANG
HANDS OFF!
CAPTAIN AMERICA?! HOW--?!
STOP HIM!
JUST LIKE OLD TIMES.
THEY DON'T FIGHT WELL AT ALL...
...BUT THERE ARE ENOUGH OF THEM TO SLOW ME DOWN.
NOT THEIR FAULT. BUT I CAN'T AFFORD TO BE GENTLE.

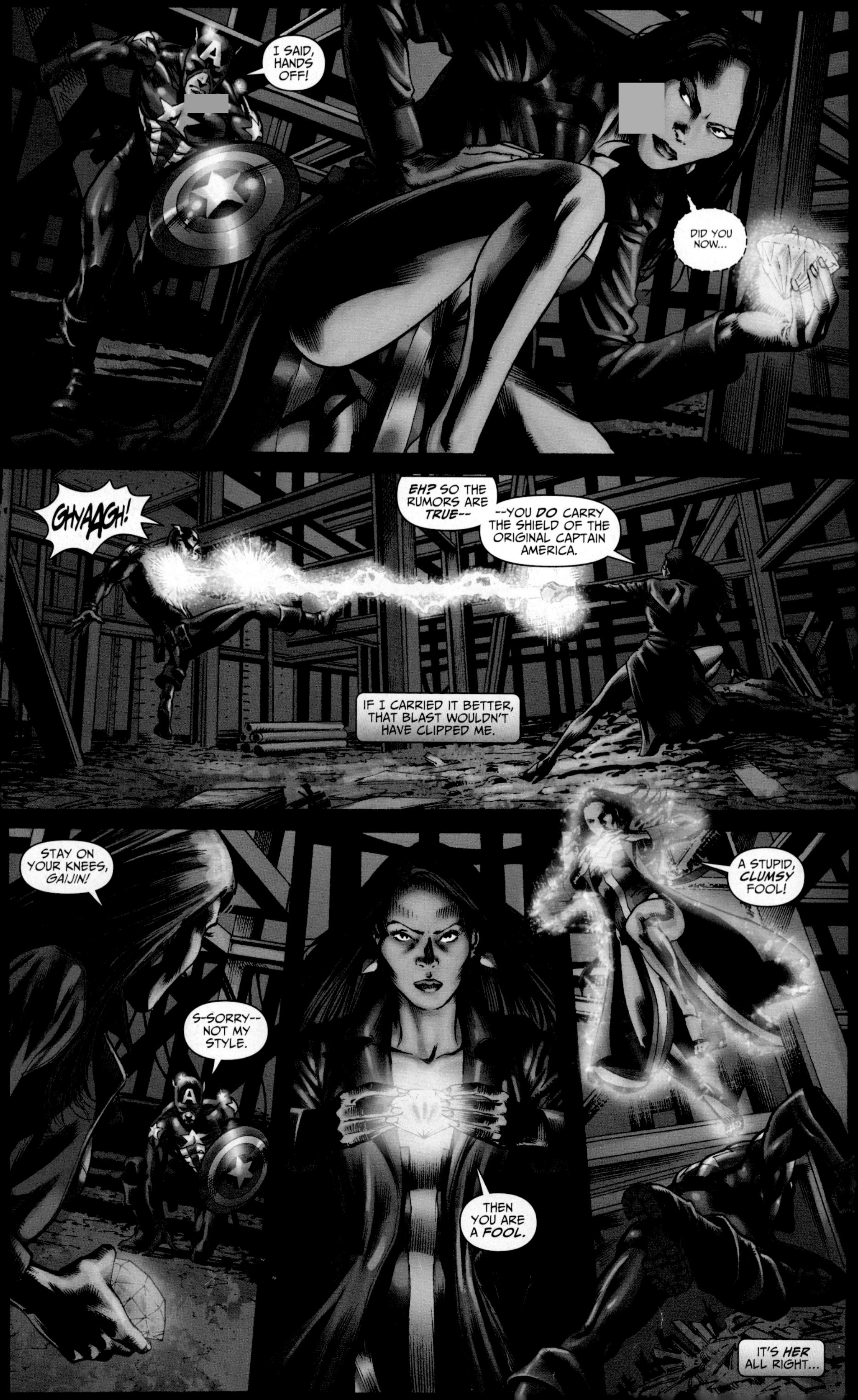
I SAID, HANDS OFF!
DID YOU NOW...
GHYAAGH!
EH? SO THE RUMORS ARE TRUE--
--YOU DO CARRY THE SHIELD OF THE ORIGINAL CAPTAIN AMERICA.
IF I CARRIED IT BETTER, THAT BLAST WOULDN'T HAVE CLIPPED ME.
STAY ON YOUR KNEES, GAIJIN!
S-SORRY-- NOT MY STYLE.
A STUPID, CLUMSY FOOL!
THEN YOU ARE A FOOL.
IT'S HER ALL RIGHT...

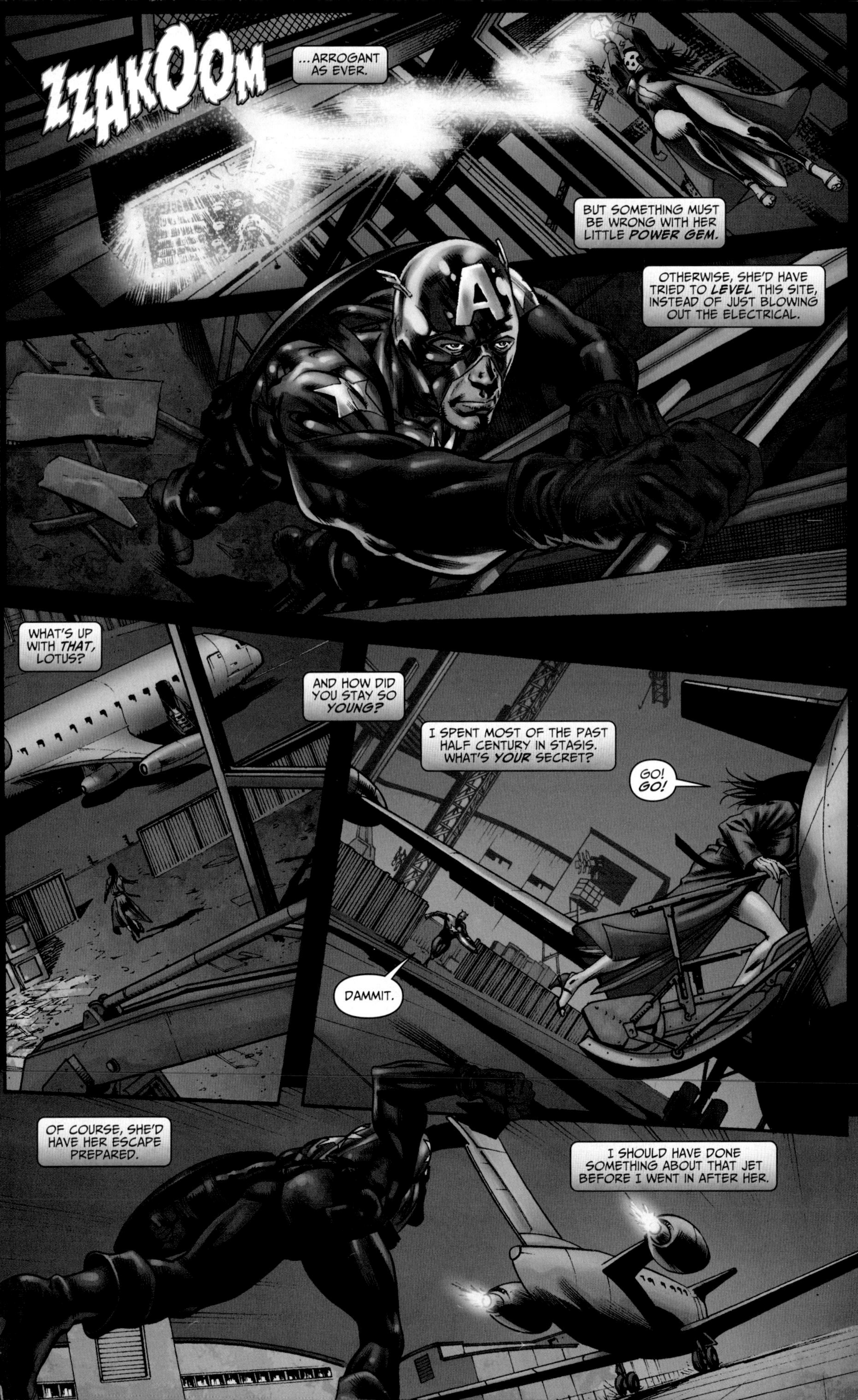
ZZAKOOM
...ARROGANT AS EVER.
BUT SOMETHING MUST BE WRONG WITH HER LITTLE POWER GEM.
OTHERWISE, SHE'D HAVE TRIED TO LEVEL THIS SITE, INSTEAD OF JUST BLOWING OUT THE ELECTRICAL.
WHAT'S UP WITH THAT, LOTUS?
AND HOW DID YOU STAY SO YOUNG?
I SPENT MOST OF THE PAST HALF CENTURY IN STASIS. WHAT'S YOUR SECRET?
GO! GO!
DAMMIT.
OF COURSE, SHE'D HAVE HER ESCAPE PREPARED.
I SHOULD HAVE DONE SOMETHING ABOUT THAT JET BEFORE I WENT IN AFTER HER.

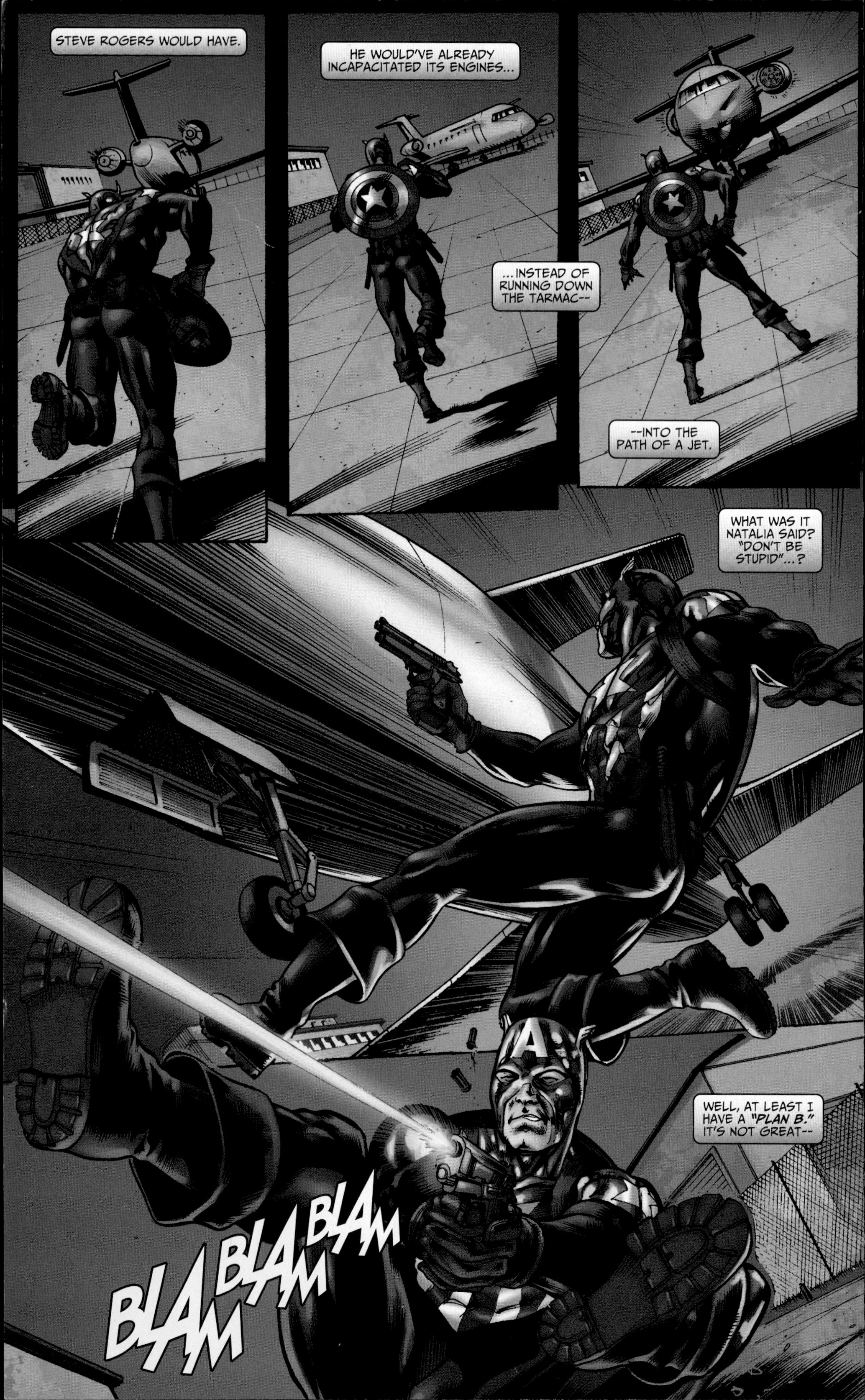
STEVE ROGERS WOULD HAVE.
HE WOULD'VE ALREADY INCAPACITATED ITS ENGINES...
...INSTEAD OF RUNNING DOWN THE TARMAC--
--INTO THE PATH OF A JET.
WHAT WAS IT NATALIA SAID? "DON'T BE STUPID"...?
WELL, AT LEAST I HAVE A "PLAN B." IT'S NOT GREAT--
BLAM BLAM BLAM BLAM

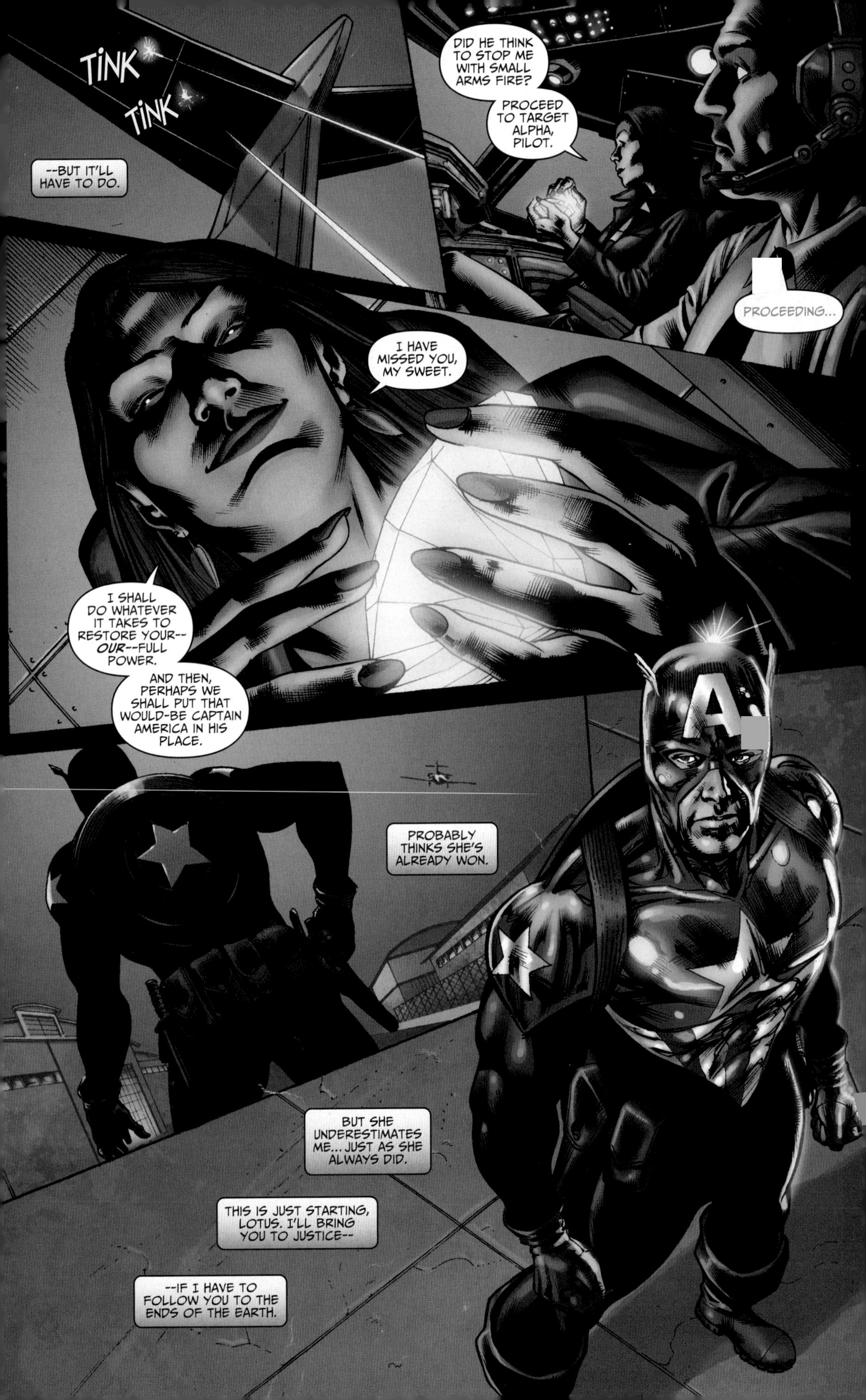
TINK
TINK
--BUT IT'LL HAVE TO DO.
DID HE THINK TO STOP ME WITH SMALL ARMS FIRE?
PROCEED TO TARGET ALPHA, PILOT.
PROCEEDING...
I HAVE MISSED YOU, MY SWEET.
I SHALL DO WHATEVER IT TAKES TO RESTORE YOUR--OUR--FULL POWER.
AND THEN, PERHAPS WE SHALL PUT THAT WOULD-BE CAPTAIN AMERICA IN HIS PLACE.
PROBABLY THINKS SHE'S ALREADY WON.
BUT SHE UNDERESTIMATES ME... JUST AS SHE ALWAYS DID.
THIS IS JUST STARTING, LOTUS. I'LL BRING YOU TO JUSTICE--
--IF I HAVE TO FOLLOW YOU TO THE ENDS OF THE EARTH.

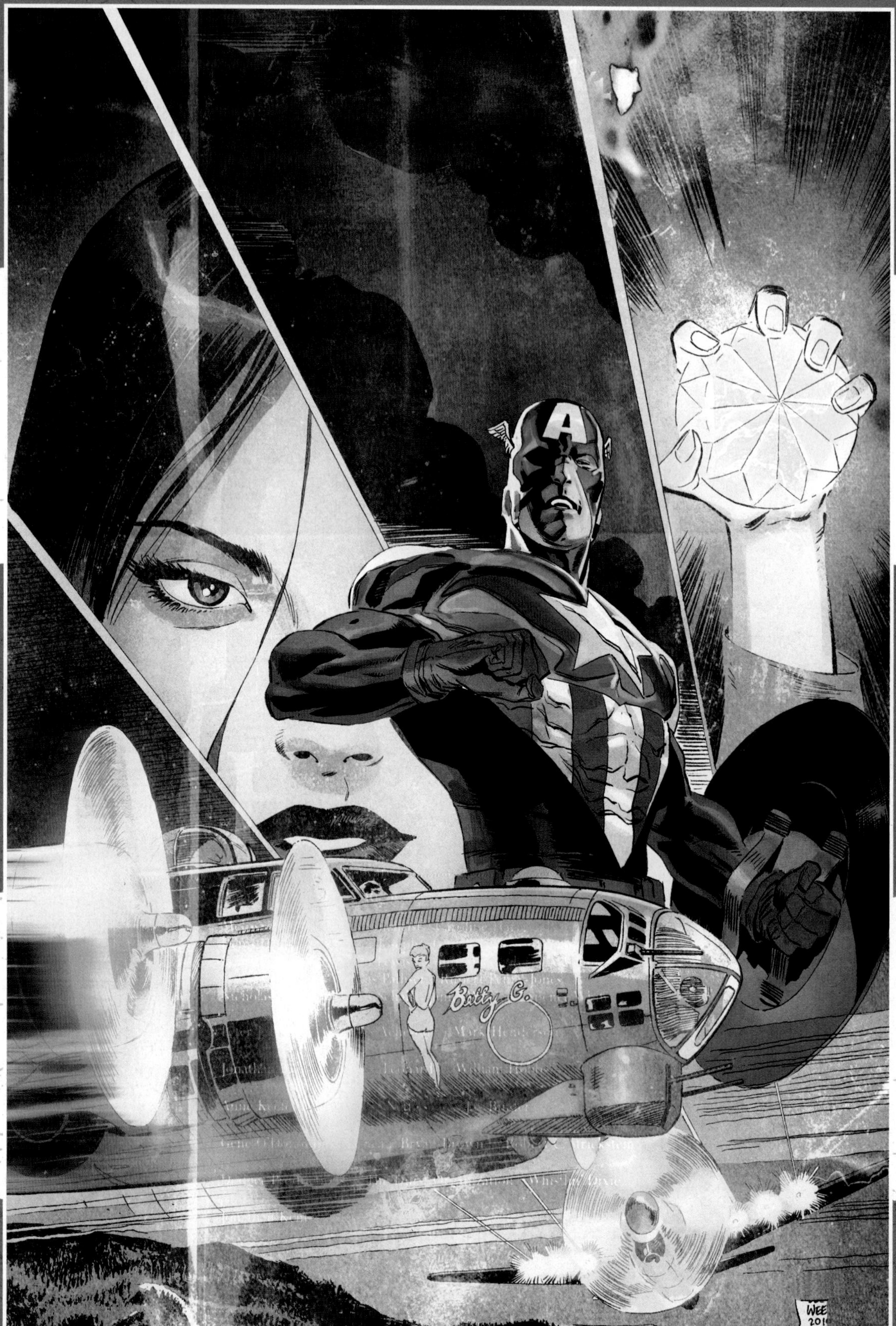
3 OF 4

CAPTAIN AMERICA: FOREVER ALLIES #3

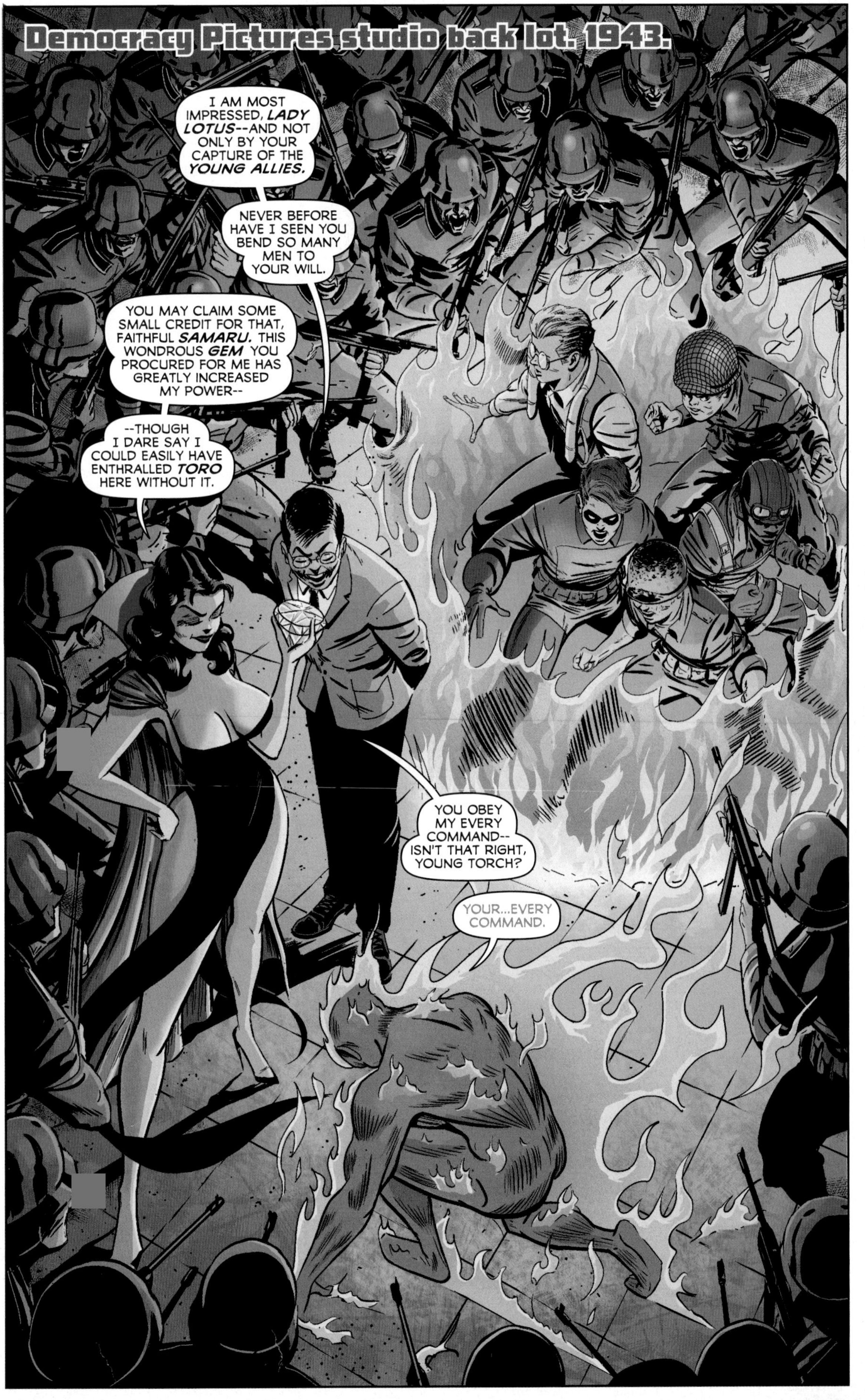
Democracy Pictures studio back lot. 1943.
I AM MOST IMPRESSED, LADY LOTUS--AND NOT ONLY BY YOUR CAPTURE OF THE YOUNG ALLIES.
NEVER BEFORE HAVE I SEEN YOU BEND SO MANY MEN TO YOUR WILL.
YOU MAY CLAIM SOME SMALL CREDIT FOR THAT, FAITHFUL SAMARU. THIS WONDROUS GEM YOU PROCURED FOR ME HAS GREATLY INCREASED MY POWER--
--THOUGH I DARE SAY I COULD EASILY HAVE ENTHRALLED TORO HERE WITHOUT IT.
YOU OBEY MY EVERY COMMAND-- ISN'T THAT RIGHT, YOUNG TORCH?
YOUR...EVERY COMMAND.

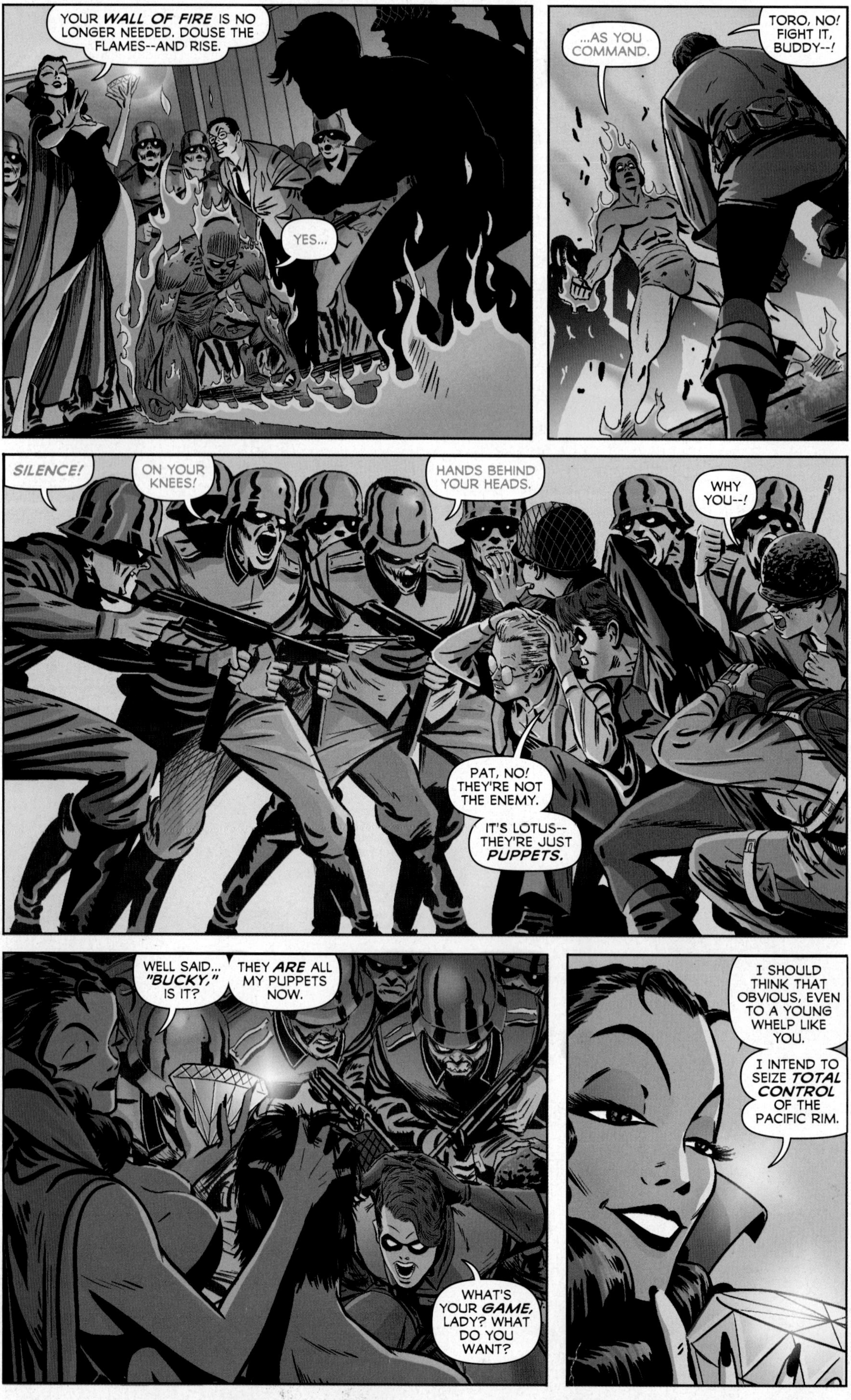
YOUR ***WALL OF FIRE*** IS NO LONGER NEEDED. DOUSE THE FLAMES--AND RISE.
YES...
...AS YOU COMMAND.
TORO, NO! FIGHT IT, BUDDY--!
SILENCE!
ON YOUR KNEES!
HANDS BEHIND YOUR HEADS.
WHY YOU--!
PAT, NO! THEY'RE NOT THE ENEMY.
IT'S LOTUS-- THEY'RE JUST ***PUPPETS.***
WELL SAID... ***"BUCKY,"*** IS IT?
THEY ***ARE*** ALL MY PUPPETS NOW.
WHAT'S YOUR ***GAME,*** LADY? WHAT DO YOU WANT?
I SHOULD THINK THAT OBVIOUS, EVEN TO A YOUNG WHELP LIKE YOU.
I INTEND TO SEIZE ***TOTAL CONTROL*** OF THE PACIFIC RIM.

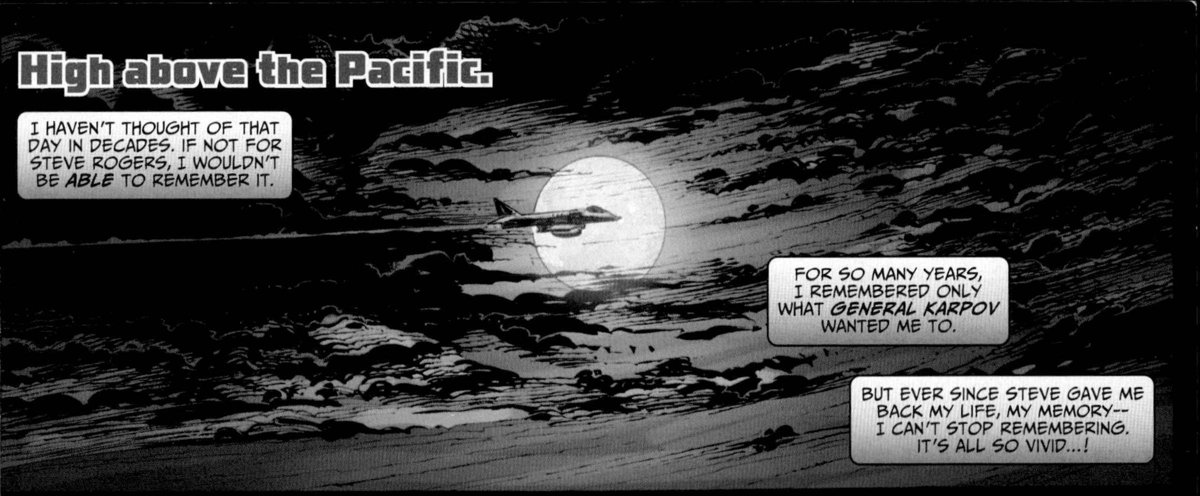
High above the Pacific.
I HAVEN'T THOUGHT OF THAT DAY IN DECADES. IF NOT FOR STEVE ROGERS, I WOULDN'T BE ABLE TO REMEMBER IT.
FOR SO MANY YEARS, I REMEMBERED ONLY WHAT GENERAL KARPOV WANTED ME TO.
BUT EVER SINCE STEVE GAVE ME BACK MY LIFE, MY MEMORY-- I CAN'T STOP REMEMBERING. IT'S ALL SO VIVID...!

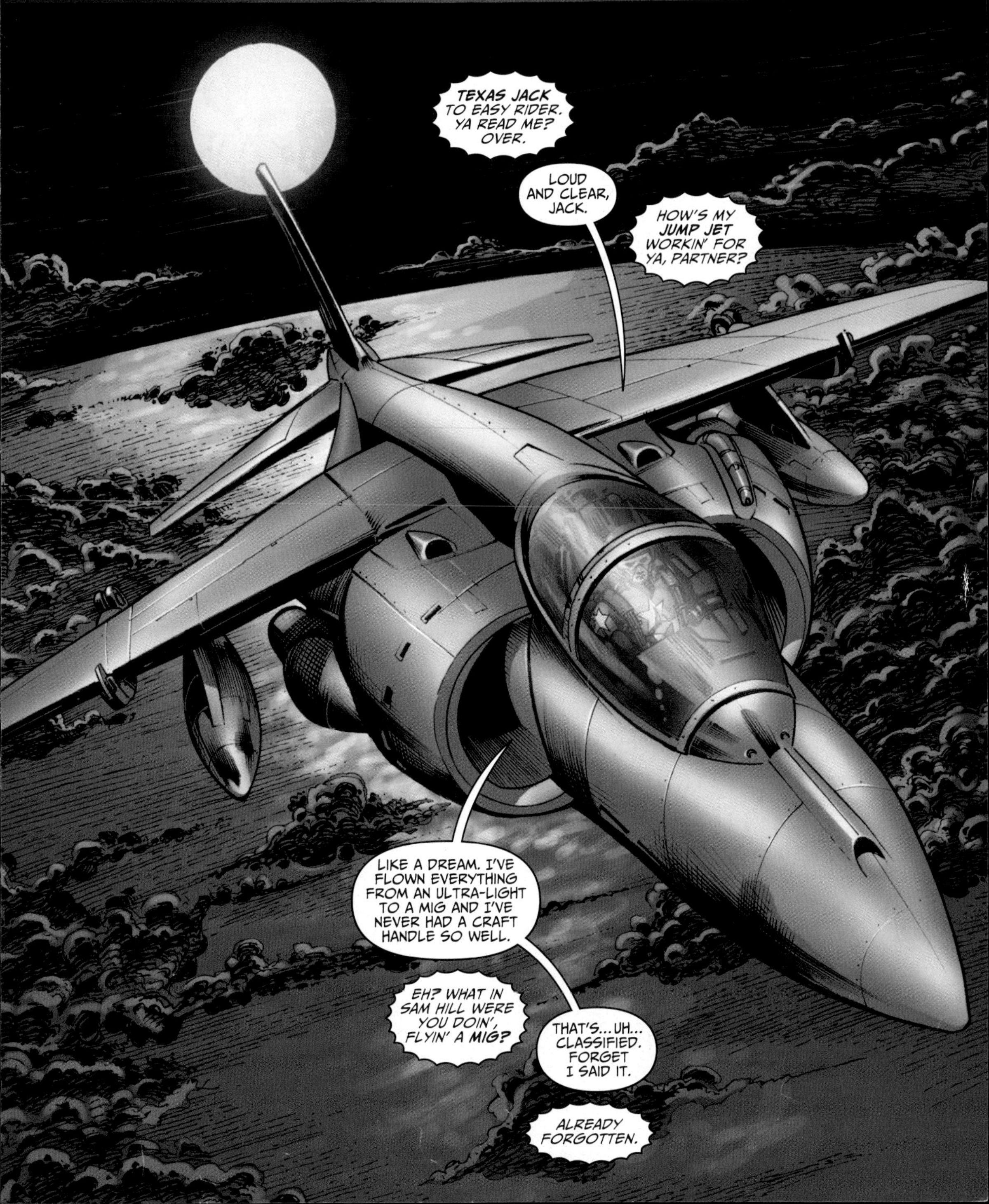
TEXAS JACK TO EASY RIDER. YA READ ME? OVER.
LOUD AND CLEAR, JACK.
HOW'S MY JUMP JET WORKIN' FOR YA, PARTNER?
LIKE A DREAM. I'VE FLOWN EVERYTHING FROM AN ULTRA-LIGHT TO A MIG AND I'VE NEVER HAD A CRAFT HANDLE SO WELL.
EH? WHAT IN SAM HILL WERE YOU DOIN', FLYIN' A MIG?
THAT'S...UH... CLASSIFIED. FORGET I SAID IT.
ALREADY FORGOTTEN.

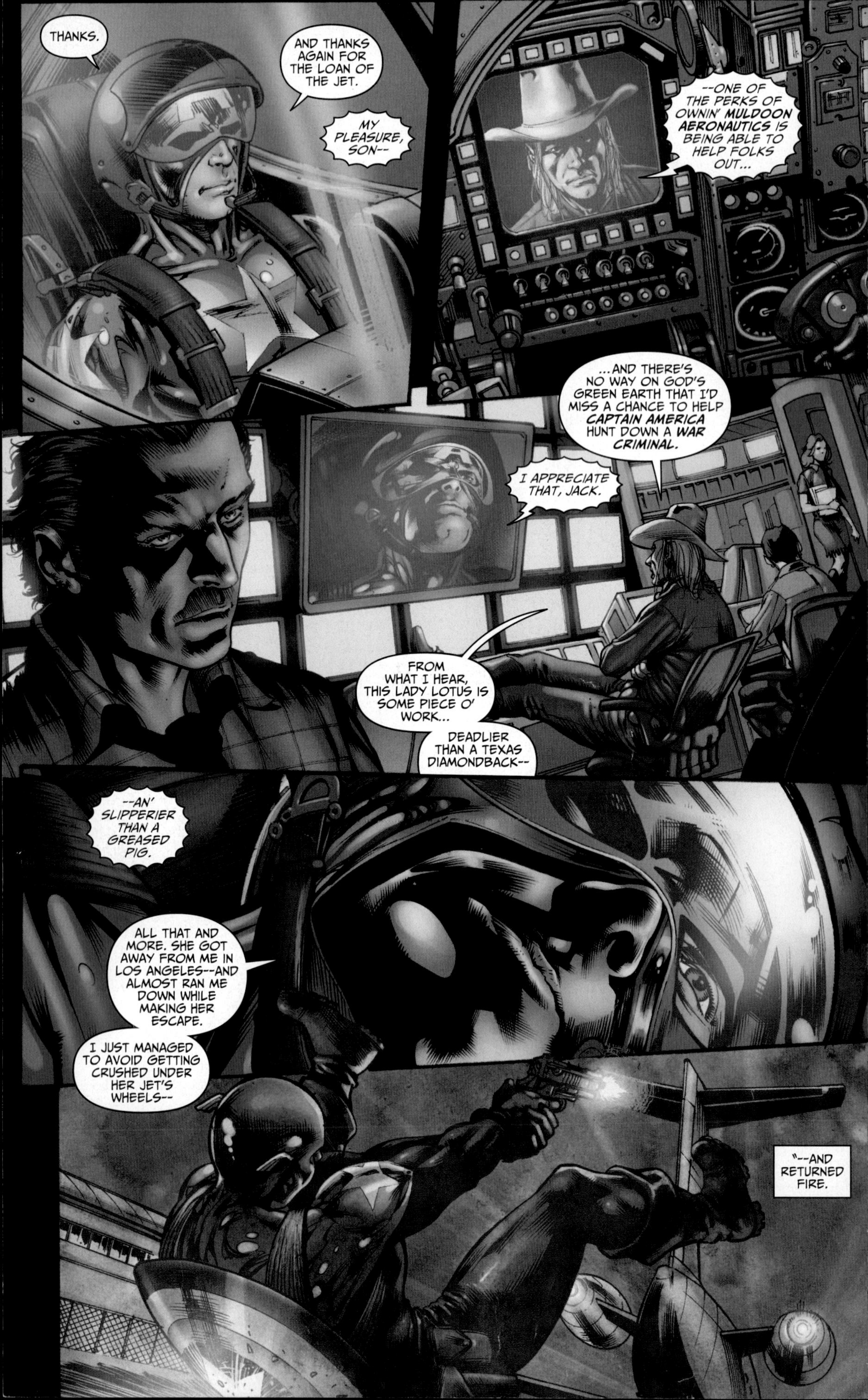
THANKS.
AND THANKS AGAIN FOR THE LOAN OF THE JET.
MY PLEASURE, SON--
--ONE OF THE PERKS OF OWNIN' MULDOON AERONAUTICS IS BEING ABLE TO HELP FOLKS OUT...
...AND THERE'S NO WAY ON GOD'S GREEN EARTH THAT I'D MISS A CHANCE TO HELP CAPTAIN AMERICA HUNT DOWN A WAR CRIMINAL.
I APPRECIATE THAT, JACK.
FROM WHAT I HEAR, THIS LADY LOTUS IS SOME PIECE O' WORK...
DEADLIER THAN A TEXAS DIAMONDBACK--
--AN' SLIPPERIER THAN A GREASED PIG.
ALL THAT AND MORE. SHE GOT AWAY FROM ME IN LOS ANGELES--AND ALMOST RAN ME DOWN WHILE MAKING HER ESCAPE.
I JUST MANAGED TO AVOID GETTING CRUSHED UNDER HER JET'S WHEELS--
"--AND RETURNED FIRE.

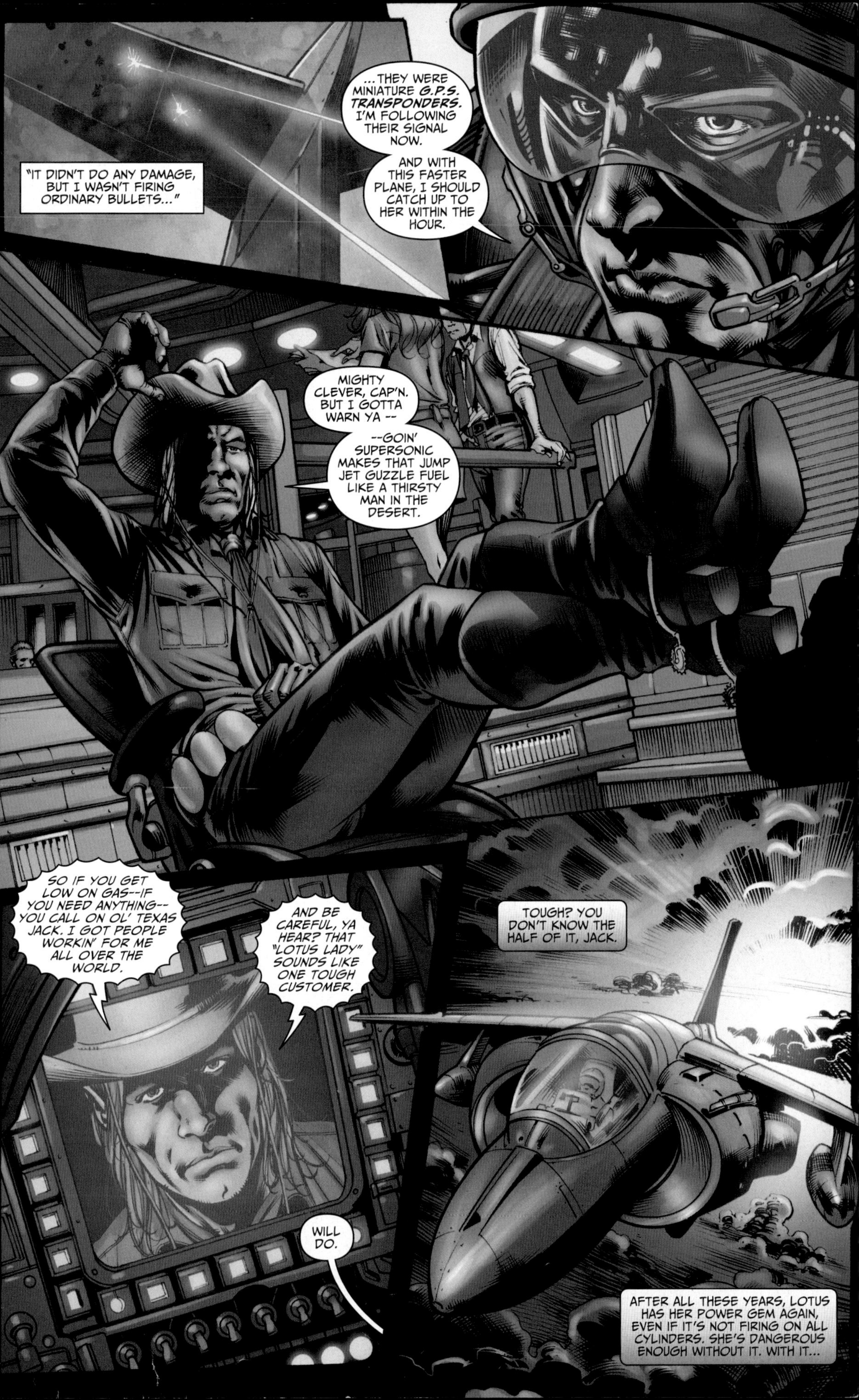
"IT DIDN'T DO ANY DAMAGE, BUT I WASN'T FIRING ORDINARY BULLETS..."
...THEY WERE MINIATURE G.P.S. TRANSPONDERS. I'M FOLLOWING THEIR SIGNAL NOW.
AND WITH THIS FASTER PLANE, I SHOULD CATCH UP TO HER WITHIN THE HOUR.
MIGHTY CLEVER, CAP'N. BUT I GOTTA WARN YA --
--GOIN' SUPERSONIC MAKES THAT JUMP JET GUZZLE FUEL LIKE A THIRSTY MAN IN THE DESERT.
SO IF YOU GET LOW ON GAS--IF YOU NEED ANYTHING--YOU CALL ON OL' TEXAS JACK. I GOT PEOPLE WORKIN' FOR ME ALL OVER THE WORLD.
AND BE CAREFUL, YA HEAR? THAT "LOTUS LADY" SOUNDS LIKE ONE TOUGH CUSTOMER.
WILL DO.
TOUGH? YOU DON'T KNOW THE HALF OF IT, JACK.
AFTER ALL THESE YEARS, LOTUS HAS HER POWER GEM AGAIN, EVEN IF IT'S NOT FIRING ON ALL CYLINDERS. SHE'S DANGEROUS ENOUGH WITHOUT IT. WITH IT...

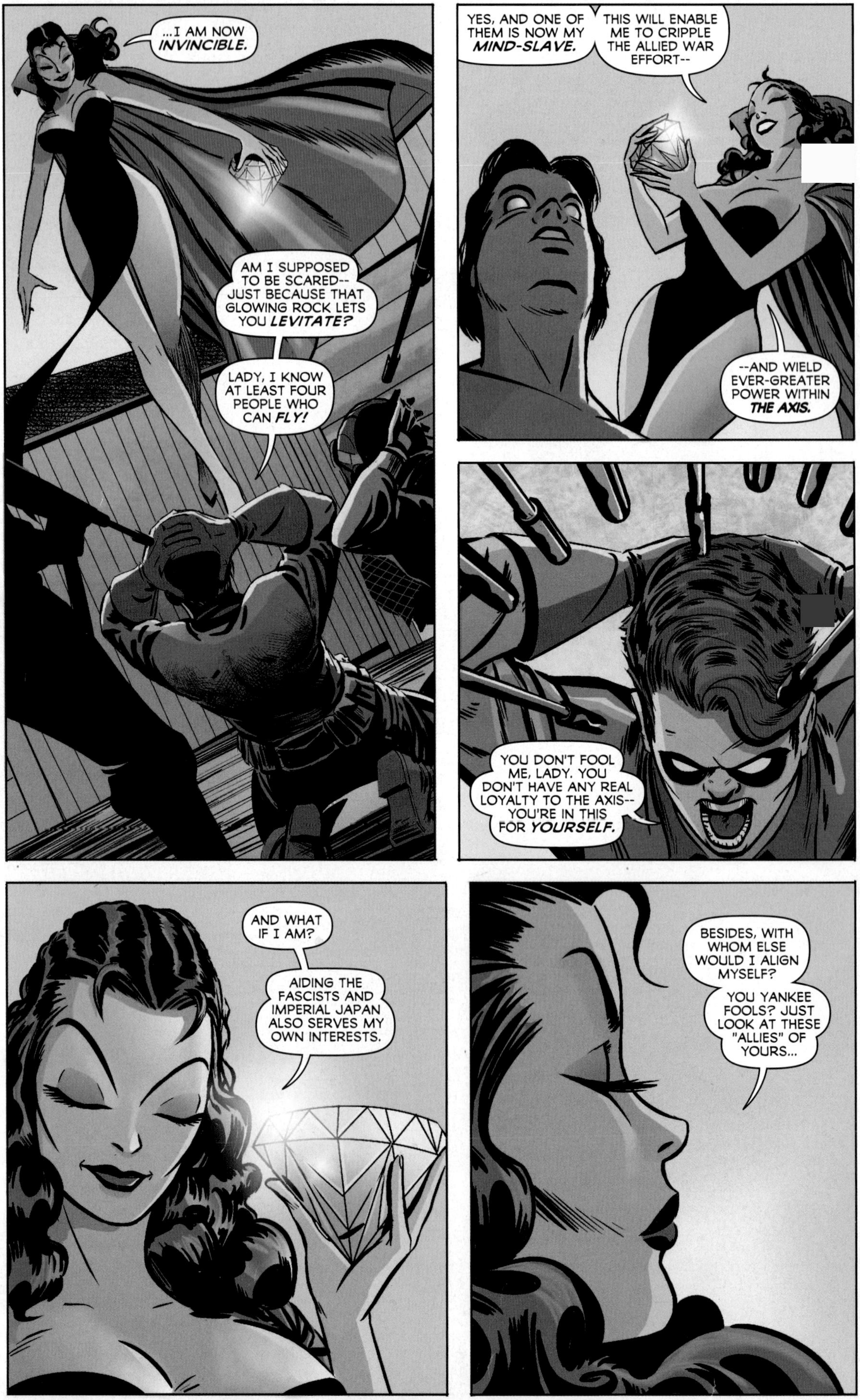
...I AM NOW INVINCIBLE.
AM I SUPPOSED TO BE SCARED-- JUST BECAUSE THAT GLOWING ROCK LETS YOU LEVITATE?
LADY, I KNOW AT LEAST FOUR PEOPLE WHO CAN FLY!
YES, AND ONE OF THEM IS NOW MY MIND-SLAVE.
THIS WILL ENABLE ME TO CRIPPLE THE ALLIED WAR EFFORT--
--AND WIELD EVER-GREATER POWER WITHIN THE AXIS.
YOU DON'T FOOL ME, LADY. YOU DON'T HAVE ANY REAL LOYALTY TO THE AXIS-- YOU'RE IN THIS FOR YOURSELF.
AND WHAT IF I AM?
AIDING THE FASCISTS AND IMPERIAL JAPAN ALSO SERVES MY OWN INTERESTS.
BESIDES, WITH WHOM ELSE WOULD I ALIGN MYSELF?
YOU YANKEE FOOLS? JUST LOOK AT THESE "ALLIES" OF YOURS...

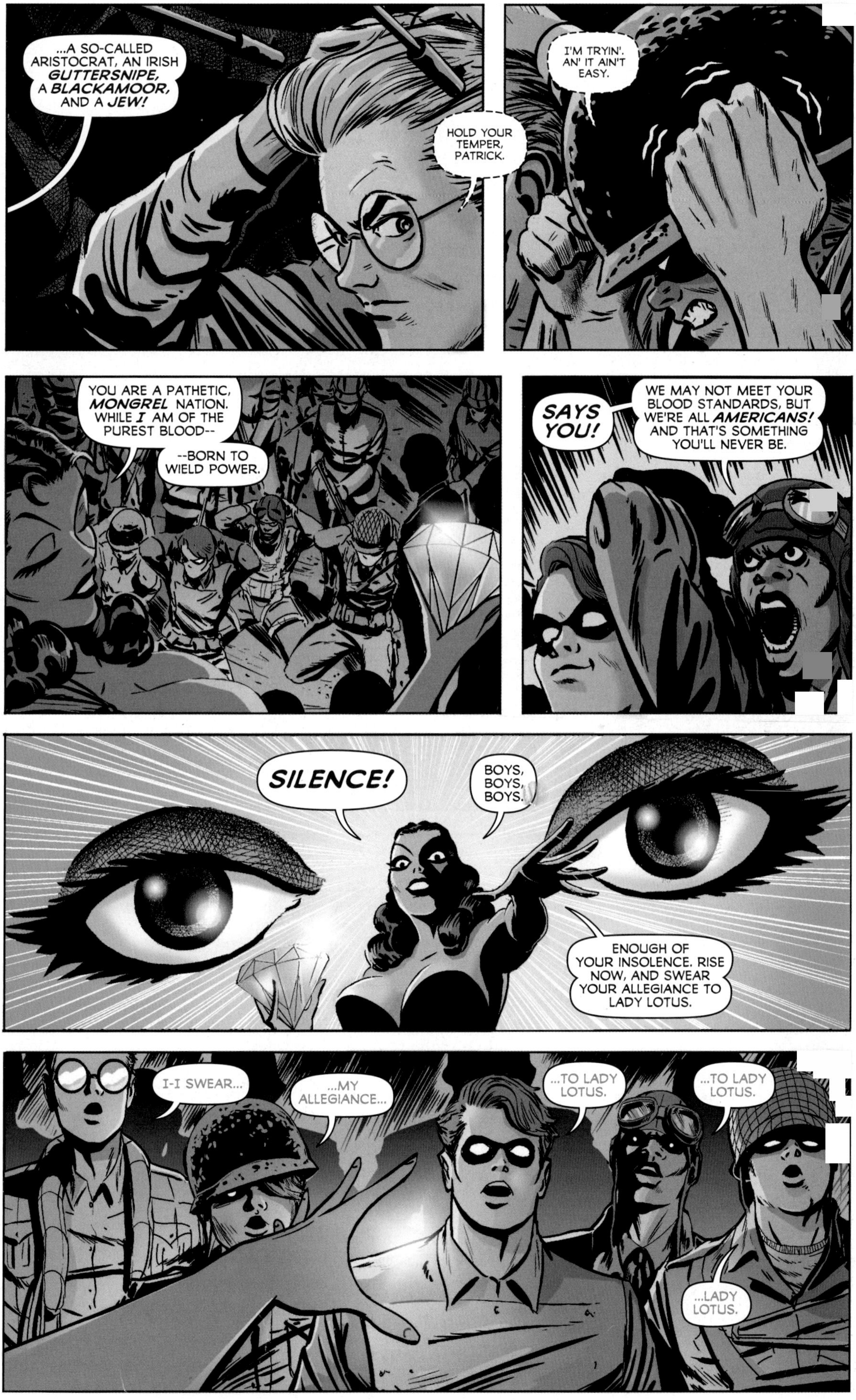
...A SO-CALLED ARISTOCRAT, AN IRISH GUTTERSNIPE, A BLACKAMOOR, AND A JEW!
HOLD YOUR TEMPER, PATRICK.
I'M TRYIN'. AN' IT AIN'T EASY.
YOU ARE A PATHETIC, MONGREL NATION. WHILE I AM OF THE PUREST BLOOD--
--BORN TO WIELD POWER.
SAYS YOU!
WE MAY NOT MEET YOUR BLOOD STANDARDS, BUT WE'RE ALL AMERICANS! AND THAT'S SOMETHING YOU'LL NEVER BE.
SILENCE!
BOYS, BOYS, BOYS.
ENOUGH OF YOUR INSOLENCE. RISE NOW, AND SWEAR YOUR ALLEGIANCE TO LADY LOTUS.
I-I SWEAR...
...MY ALLEGIANCE...
...TO LADY LOTUS.
...TO LADY LOTUS.
...LADY LOTUS.

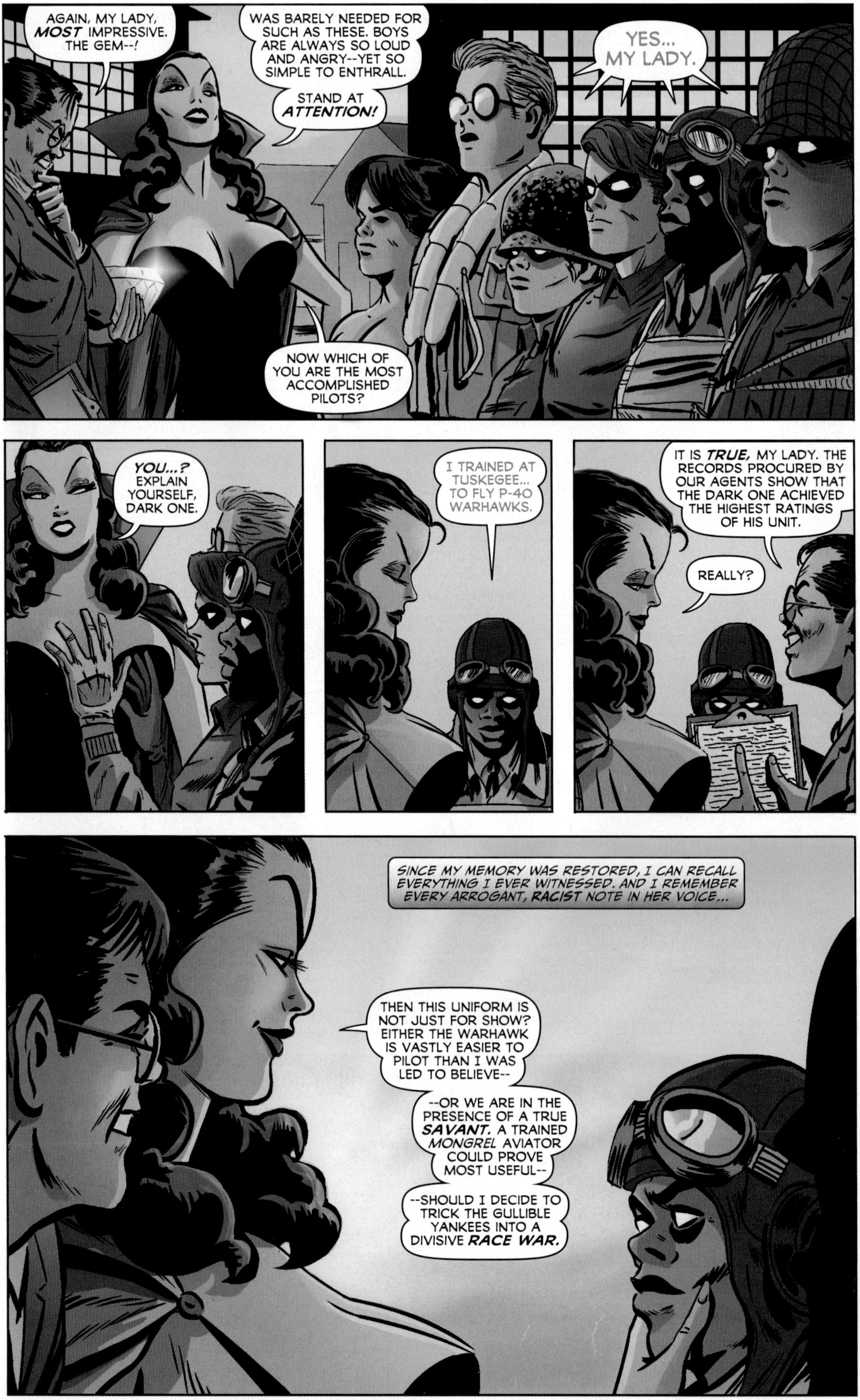
AGAIN, MY LADY, MOST IMPRESSIVE. THE GEM--!
WAS BARELY NEEDED FOR SUCH AS THESE. BOYS ARE ALWAYS SO LOUD AND ANGRY--YET SO SIMPLE TO ENTHRALL.
STAND AT ATTENTION!
YES... MY LADY.
NOW WHICH OF YOU ARE THE MOST ACCOMPLISHED PILOTS?
YOU...? EXPLAIN YOURSELF, DARK ONE.
I TRAINED AT TUSKEGEE... TO FLY P-40 WARHAWKS.
IT IS TRUE, MY LADY. THE RECORDS PROCURED BY OUR AGENTS SHOW THAT THE DARK ONE ACHIEVED THE HIGHEST RATINGS OF HIS UNIT.
REALLY?
SINCE MY MEMORY WAS RESTORED, I CAN RECALL EVERYTHING I EVER WITNESSED. AND I REMEMBER EVERY ARROGANT, RACIST NOTE IN HER VOICE...
THEN THIS UNIFORM IS NOT JUST FOR SHOW? EITHER THE WARHAWK IS VASTLY EASIER TO PILOT THAN I WAS LED TO BELIEVE--
--OR WE ARE IN THE PRESENCE OF A TRUE SAVANT. A TRAINED MONGREL AVIATOR COULD PROVE MOST USEFUL--
--SHOULD I DECIDE TO TRICK THE GULLIBLE YANKEES INTO A DIVISIVE RACE WAR.

LOTUS MARCHED US ALL TO THE *AIRSTRIP* AT THE FAR END OF THE BACK LOT--WHERE TWO PLANES ON LOAN TO THE STUDIO WERE BEING LOADED WITH *LIVE MUNITIONS* BY THE STUNTMEN THAT SHE'D ENTRANCED.

THE ONLY OTHER ONE THERE IN HIS RIGHT MIND--IF YOU CAN CALL IT THAT--WAS HER RIGHT-HAND MAN, *SAMARU*...

HAVE THE MISTRESS'S ORDERS BEEN CARRIED OUT?

YES, SIR... PLANES ARE READY FOR TAKE-OFF.

SAMARU-- THE MAPS?

HERE, MY LADY.

STUDY THEM WELL, YOUNG PILOTS. SUCCEED IN YOUR MISSION.

YES, MY LADY.

WE WERE AIRBORNE WITHIN MINUTES--ME AT THE STICK OF THE B-17, WITH WASH IN THE P-40 AND TORO AS MY WINGMEN.

OUR TARGET: *MUROC ARMY AIR FIELD.*

MY LADY, WE ARE SENDING THEM OFF... UNCHAPERONED?

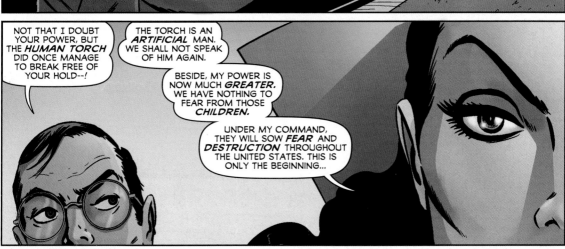

NOT THAT I DOUBT YOUR POWER, BUT THE *HUMAN TORCH* DID ONCE MANAGE TO BREAK FREE OF YOUR HOLD--!

THE TORCH IS AN *ARTIFICIAL* MAN. WE SHALL NOT SPEAK OF HIM AGAIN.

BESIDE, MY POWER IS NOW MUCH *GREATER.* WE HAVE NOTHING TO FEAR FROM THOSE *CHILDREN.*

UNDER MY COMMAND, THEY WILL SOW *FEAR* AND *DESTRUCTION* THROUGHOUT THE UNITED STATES. THIS IS ONLY THE BEGINNING...

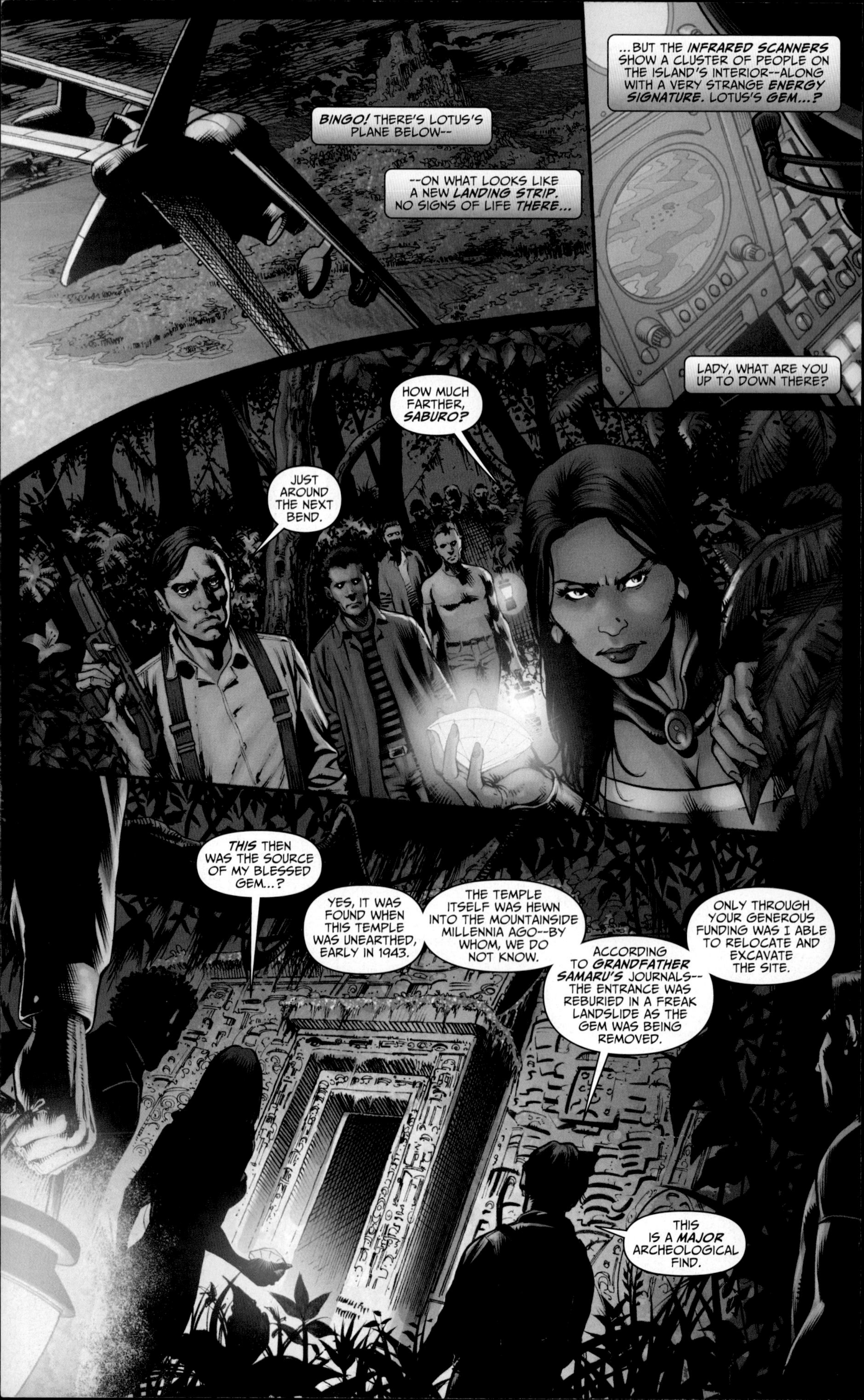
BINGO! THERE'S LOTUS'S PLANE BELOW--
--ON WHAT LOOKS LIKE A NEW LANDING STRIP. NO SIGNS OF LIFE THERE...
...BUT THE INFRARED SCANNERS SHOW A CLUSTER OF PEOPLE ON THE ISLAND'S INTERIOR--ALONG WITH A VERY STRANGE ENERGY SIGNATURE. LOTUS'S GEM...?
LADY, WHAT ARE YOU UP TO DOWN THERE?
HOW MUCH FARTHER, SABURO?
JUST AROUND THE NEXT BEND.
THIS THEN WAS THE SOURCE OF MY BLESSED GEM...?
YES, IT WAS FOUND WHEN THIS TEMPLE WAS UNEARTHED, EARLY IN 1943.
THE TEMPLE ITSELF WAS HEWN INTO THE MOUNTAINSIDE MILLENNIA AGO--BY WHOM, WE DO NOT KNOW.
ACCORDING TO GRANDFATHER SAMARU'S JOURNALS--THE ENTRANCE WAS REBURIED IN A FREAK LANDSLIDE AS THE GEM WAS BEING REMOVED.
ONLY THROUGH YOUR GENEROUS FUNDING WAS I ABLE TO RELOCATE AND EXCAVATE THE SITE.
THIS IS A MAJOR ARCHEOLOGICAL FIND.

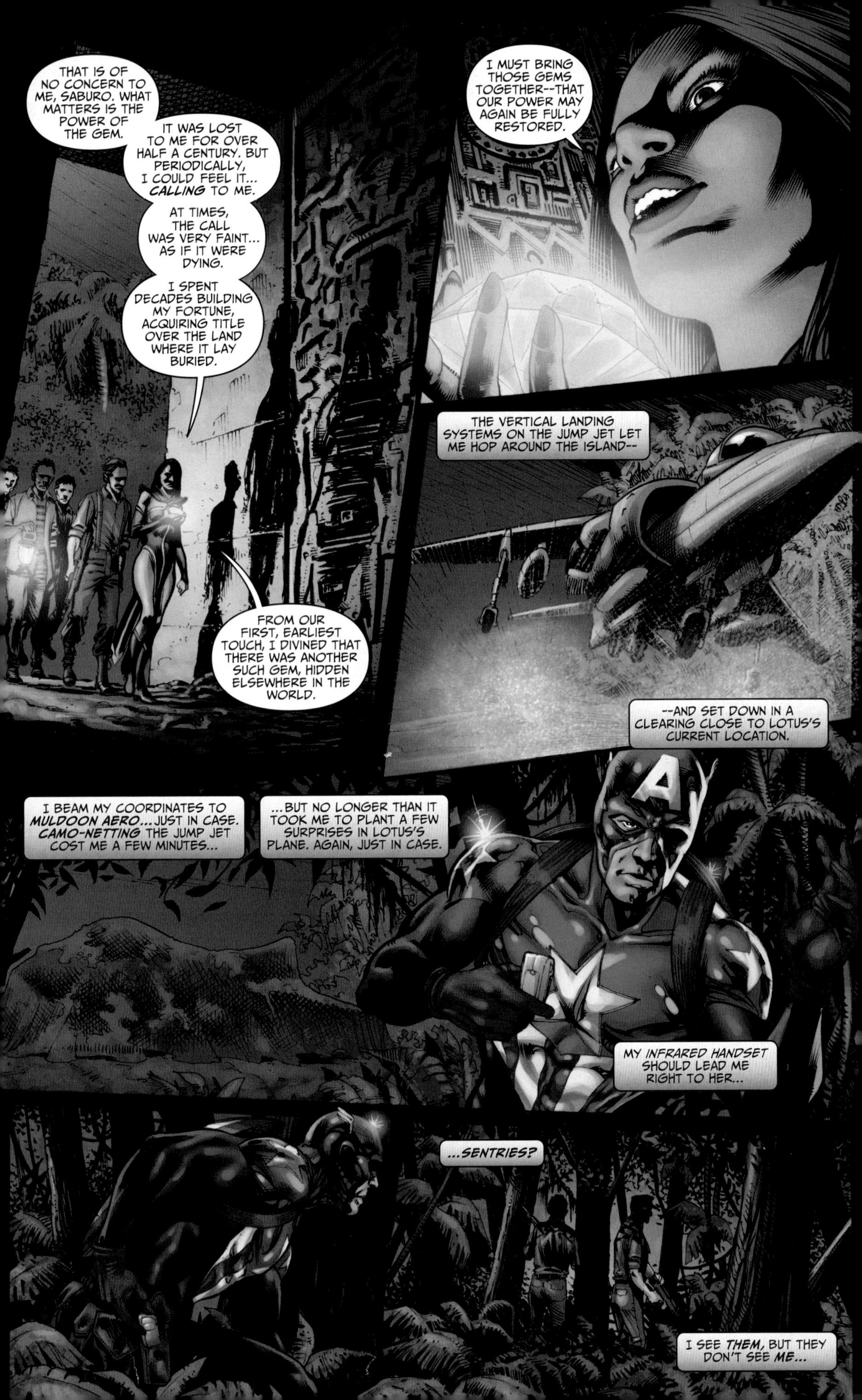
THAT IS OF NO CONCERN TO ME, SABURO. WHAT MATTERS IS THE POWER OF THE GEM.
IT WAS LOST TO ME FOR OVER HALF A CENTURY. BUT PERIODICALLY, I COULD FEEL IT... CALLING TO ME.
AT TIMES, THE CALL WAS VERY FAINT... AS IF IT WERE DYING.
I SPENT DECADES BUILDING MY FORTUNE, ACQUIRING TITLE OVER THE LAND WHERE IT LAY BURIED.
FROM OUR FIRST, EARLIEST TOUCH, I DIVINED THAT THERE WAS ANOTHER SUCH GEM, HIDDEN ELSEWHERE IN THE WORLD.
I MUST BRING THOSE GEMS TOGETHER--THAT OUR POWER MAY AGAIN BE FULLY RESTORED.
THE VERTICAL LANDING SYSTEMS ON THE JUMP JET LET ME HOP AROUND THE ISLAND--
--AND SET DOWN IN A CLEARING CLOSE TO LOTUS'S CURRENT LOCATION.
I BEAM MY COORDINATES TO MULDOON AERO... JUST IN CASE. CAMO-NETTING THE JUMP JET COST ME A FEW MINUTES...
...BUT NO LONGER THAN IT TOOK ME TO PLANT A FEW SURPRISES IN LOTUS'S PLANE. AGAIN, JUST IN CASE.
MY INFRARED HANDSET SHOULD LEAD ME RIGHT TO HER...
...SENTRIES?
I SEE THEM, BUT THEY DON'T SEE ME...

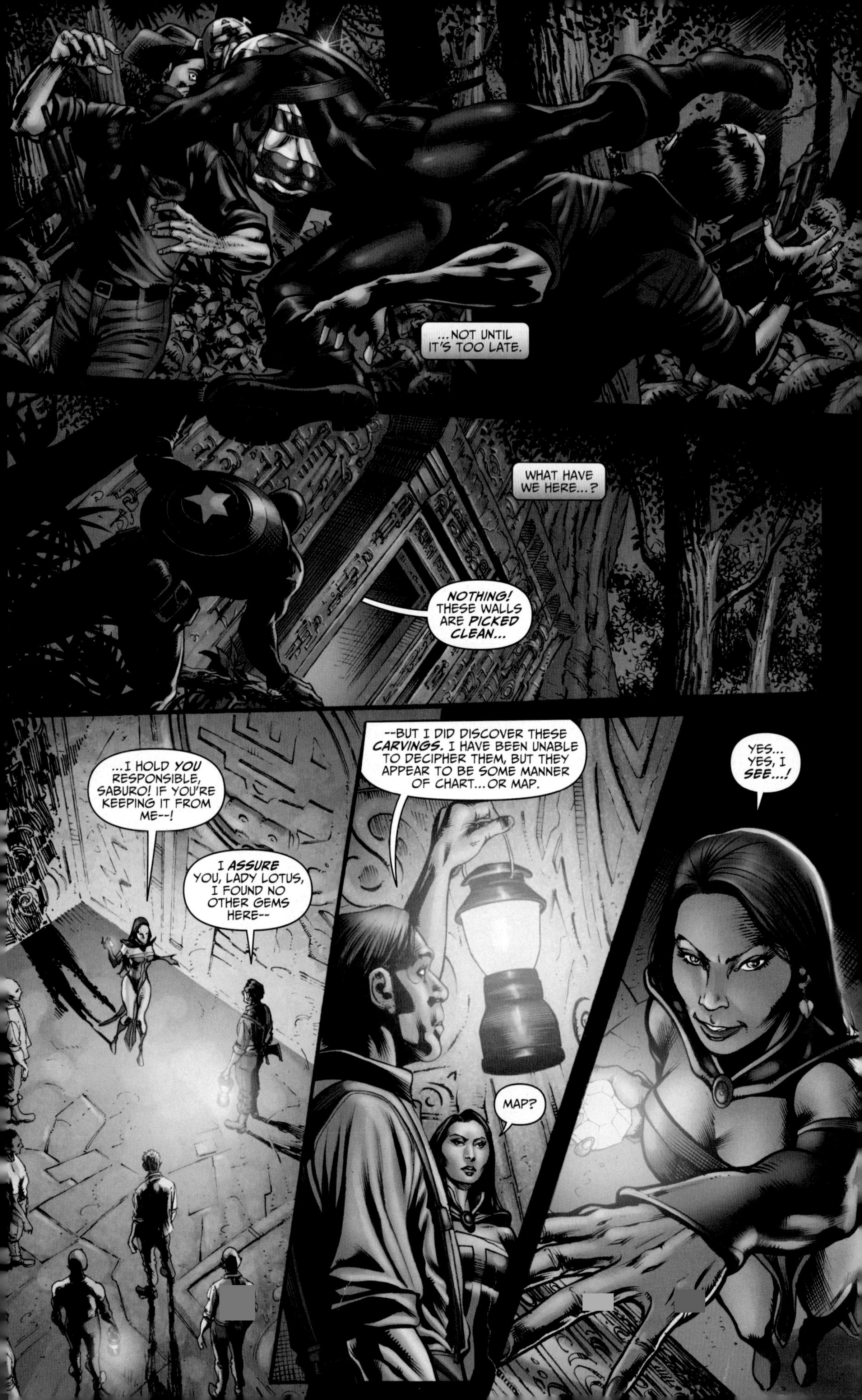
...NOT UNTIL IT'S TOO LATE.
WHAT HAVE WE HERE...?
NOTHING! THESE WALLS ARE PICKED CLEAN...
...I HOLD YOU RESPONSIBLE, SABURO! IF YOU'RE KEEPING IT FROM ME--!
I ASSURE YOU, LADY LOTUS, I FOUND NO OTHER GEMS HERE--
--BUT I DID DISCOVER THESE CARVINGS. I HAVE BEEN UNABLE TO DECIPHER THEM, BUT THEY APPEAR TO BE SOME MANNER OF CHART...OR MAP.
MAP?
YES... YES, I SEE...!

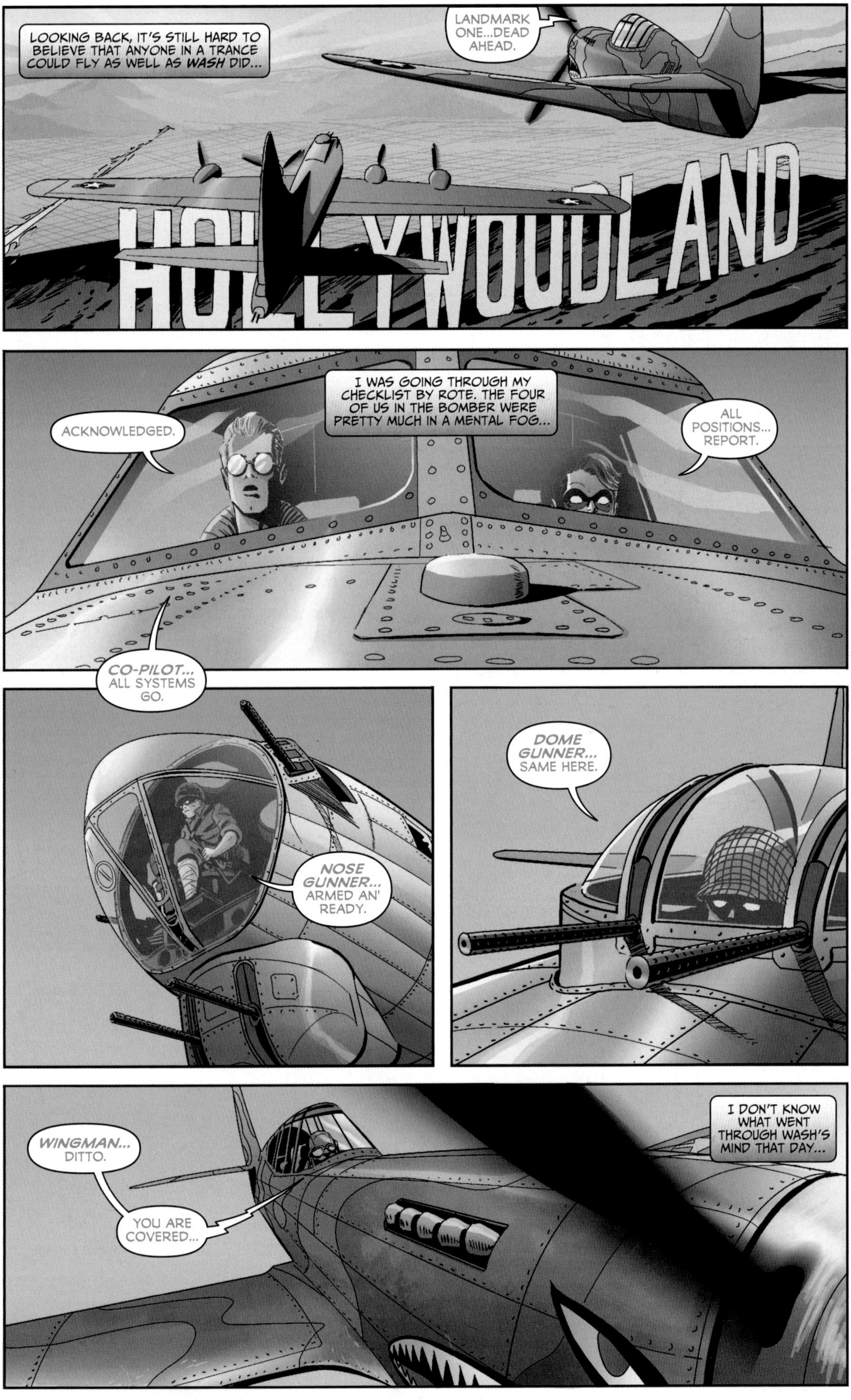
LOOKING BACK, IT'S STILL HARD TO BELIEVE THAT ANYONE IN A TRANCE COULD FLY AS WELL AS WASH DID...
LANDMARK ONE...DEAD AHEAD.
HOLLYWOODLAND
I WAS GOING THROUGH MY CHECKLIST BY ROTE. THE FOUR OF US IN THE BOMBER WERE PRETTY MUCH IN A MENTAL FOG...
ALL POSITIONS... REPORT.
ACKNOWLEDGED.
CO-PILOT... ALL SYSTEMS GO.
NOSE GUNNER... ARMED AN' READY.
DOME GUNNER... SAME HERE.
WINGMAN... DITTO.
YOU ARE COVERED...
I DON'T KNOW WHAT WENT THROUGH WASH'S MIND THAT DAY...

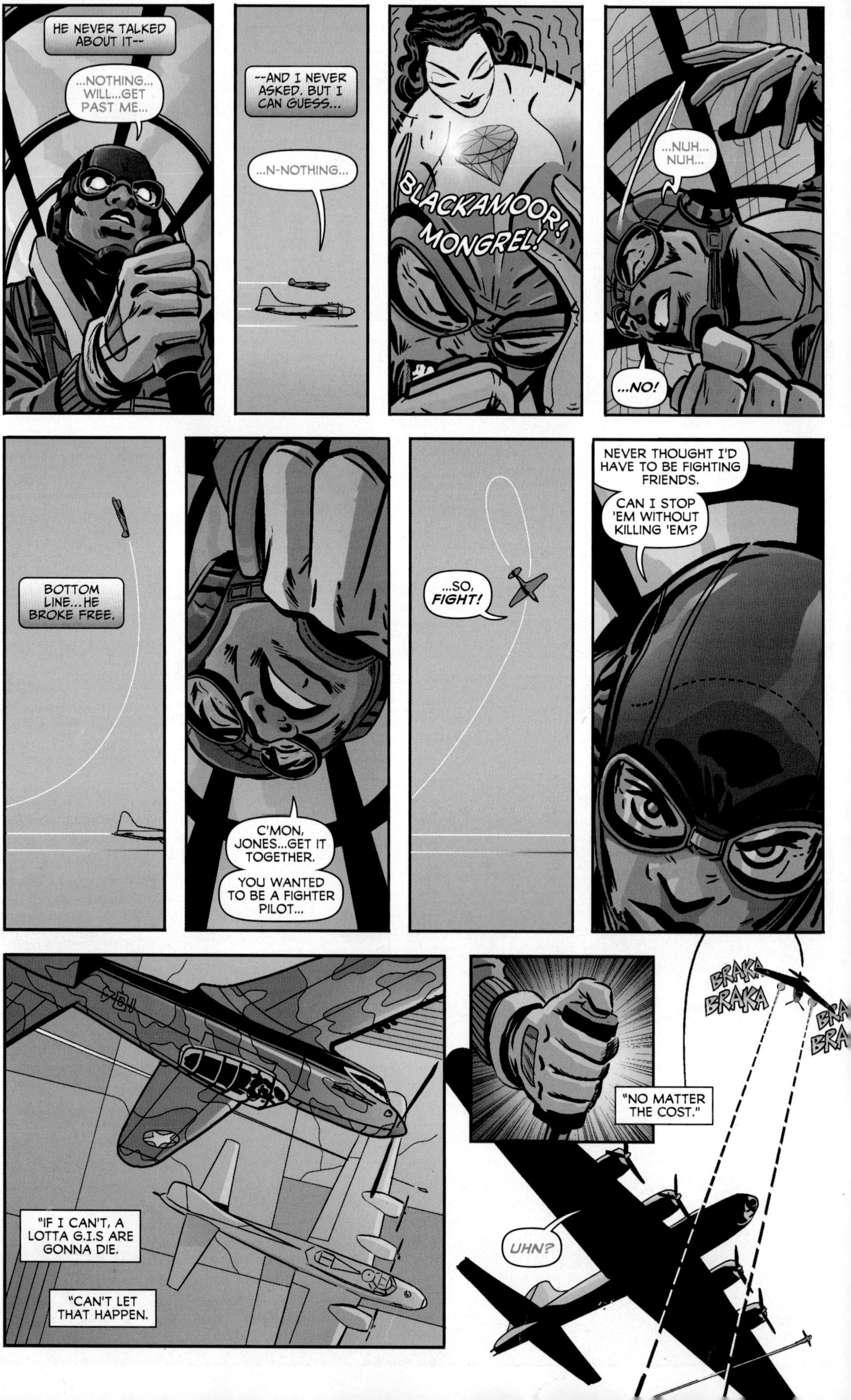

HE NEVER TALKED ABOUT IT--
...NOTHING... WILL...GET PAST ME...
--AND I NEVER ASKED. BUT I CAN GUESS...
...N-NOTHING...
BLACKAMOOR! MONGREL!
...NUH... NUH...
...NO!
BOTTOM LINE...HE BROKE FREE.
C'MON, JONES...GET IT TOGETHER.
YOU WANTED TO BE A FIGHTER PILOT...
...SO, FIGHT!
NEVER THOUGHT I'D HAVE TO BE FIGHTING FRIENDS.
CAN I STOP 'EM WITHOUT KILLING 'EM?
"IF I CAN'T, A LOTTA G.I.S ARE GONNA DIE.
"CAN'T LET THAT HAPPEN.
"NO MATTER THE COST."
BRAKA BRAKA
BRA BRA
UHN?

WHA--?

UNDER *ATTACK!*

RETURN FIRE!

THAT'S WHEN OUR *OTHER* WINGMAN FLEW INTO ACTION.

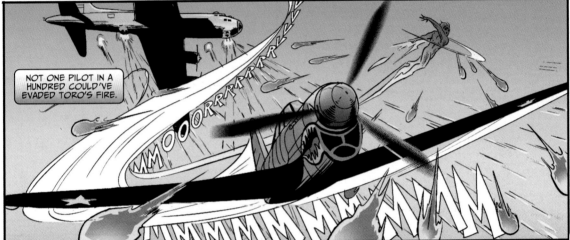

NOT ONE PILOT IN A HUNDRED COULD'VE EVADED TORO'S FIRE.

BUT WASH DID.

HEY, *HOT SHOT--*

THOMP

--HAVE SOME *FLARE!*

PCHOOM

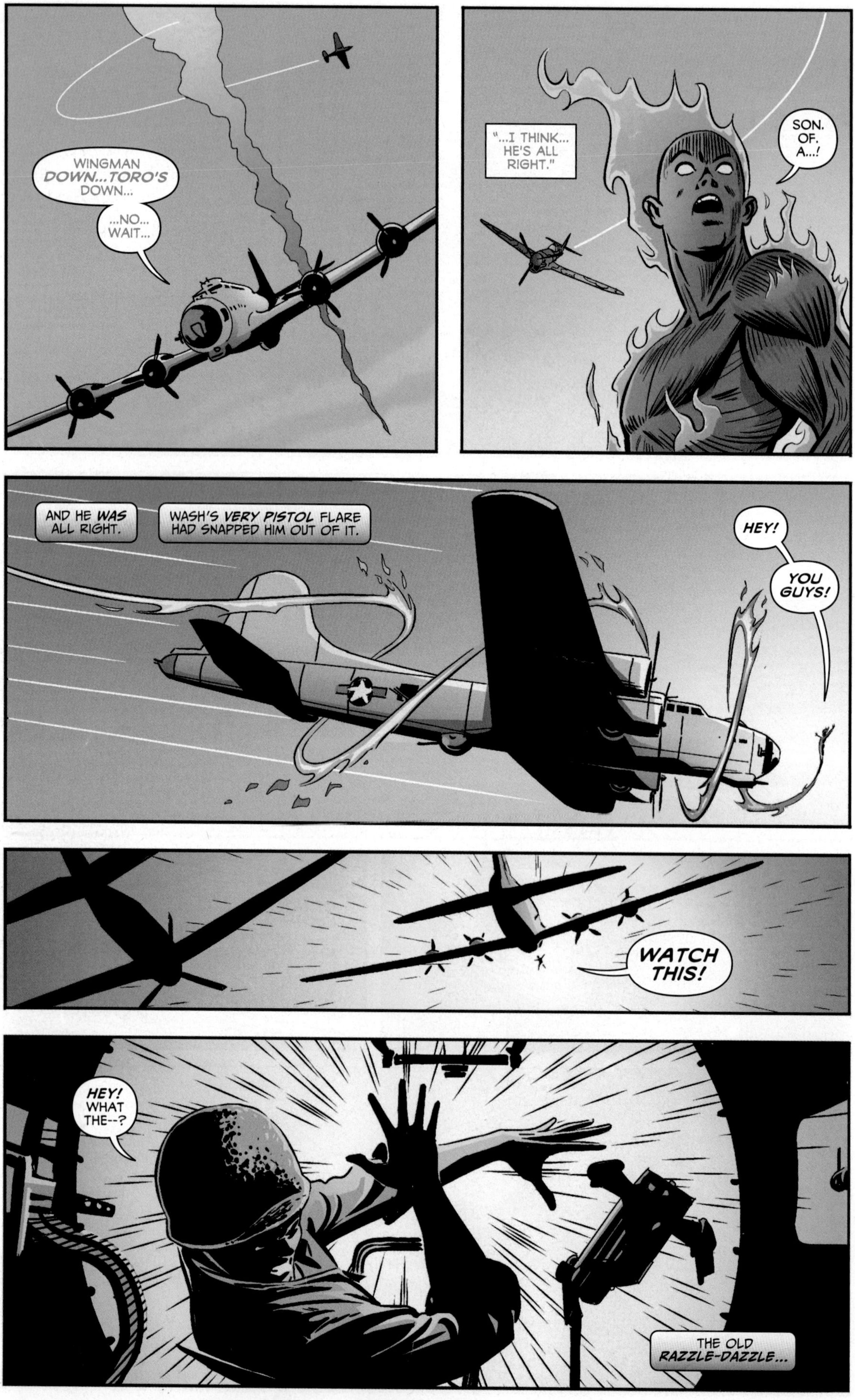
WINGMAN DOWN...TORO'S DOWN...
...NO... WAIT...
"...I THINK... HE'S ALL RIGHT."
SON. OF. A...!
AND HE WAS ALL RIGHT.
WASH'S VERY PISTOL FLARE HAD SNAPPED HIM OUT OF IT.
HEY!
YOU GUYS!
WATCH THIS!
HEY! WHAT THE--?
THE OLD RAZZLE-DAZZLE...

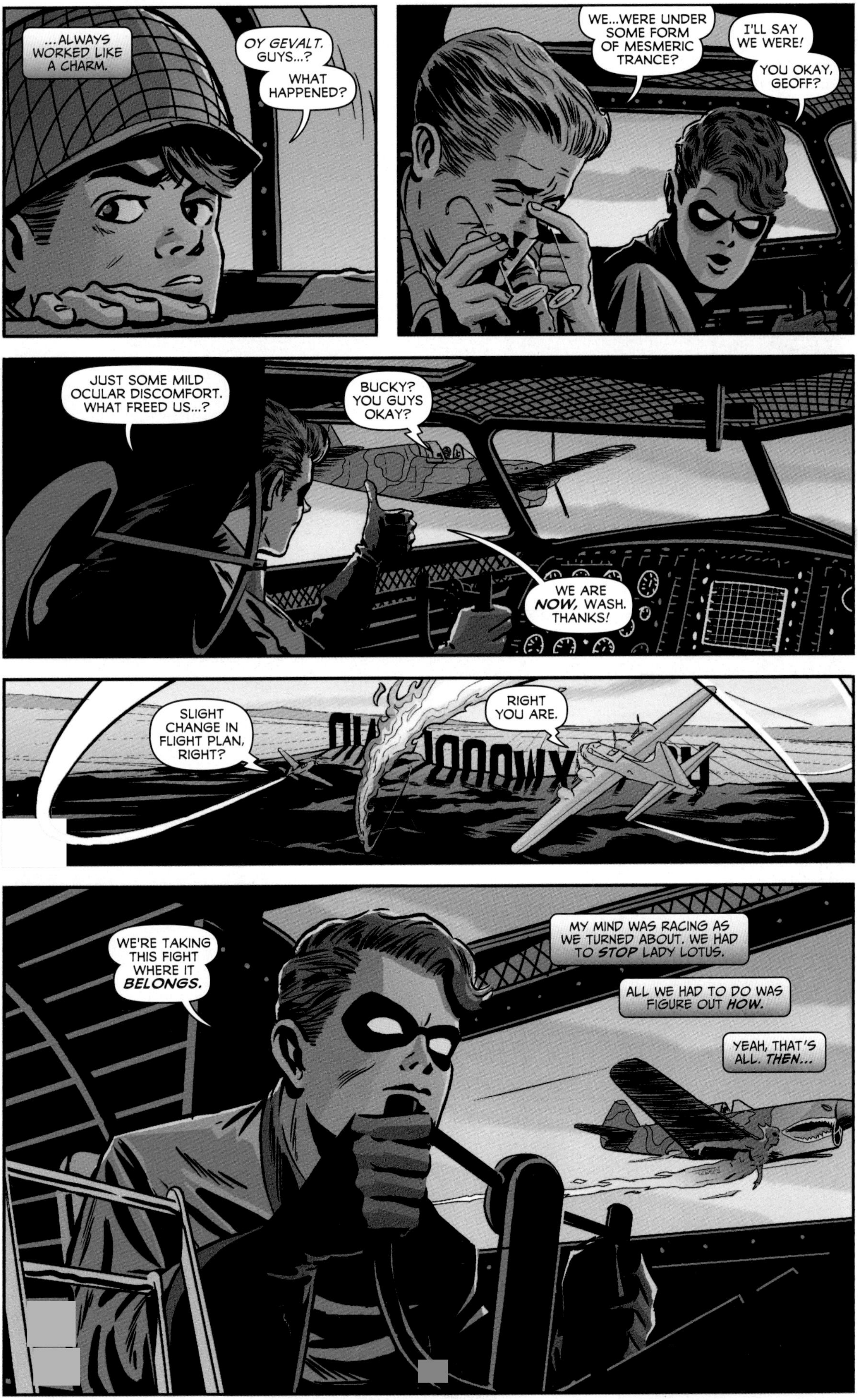
...ALWAYS WORKED LIKE A CHARM.
OY GEVALT. GUYS...?
WHAT HAPPENED?
WE...WERE UNDER SOME FORM OF MESMERIC TRANCE?
I'LL SAY WE WERE!
YOU OKAY, GEOFF?
JUST SOME MILD OCULAR DISCOMFORT. WHAT FREED US...?
BUCKY? YOU GUYS OKAY?
WE ARE NOW, WASH. THANKS!
SLIGHT CHANGE IN FLIGHT PLAN, RIGHT?
RIGHT YOU ARE.
WE'RE TAKING THIS FIGHT WHERE IT BELONGS.
MY MIND WAS RACING AS WE TURNED ABOUT. WE HAD TO STOP LADY LOTUS.
ALL WE HAD TO DO WAS FIGURE OUT HOW.
YEAH, THAT'S ALL. THEN...

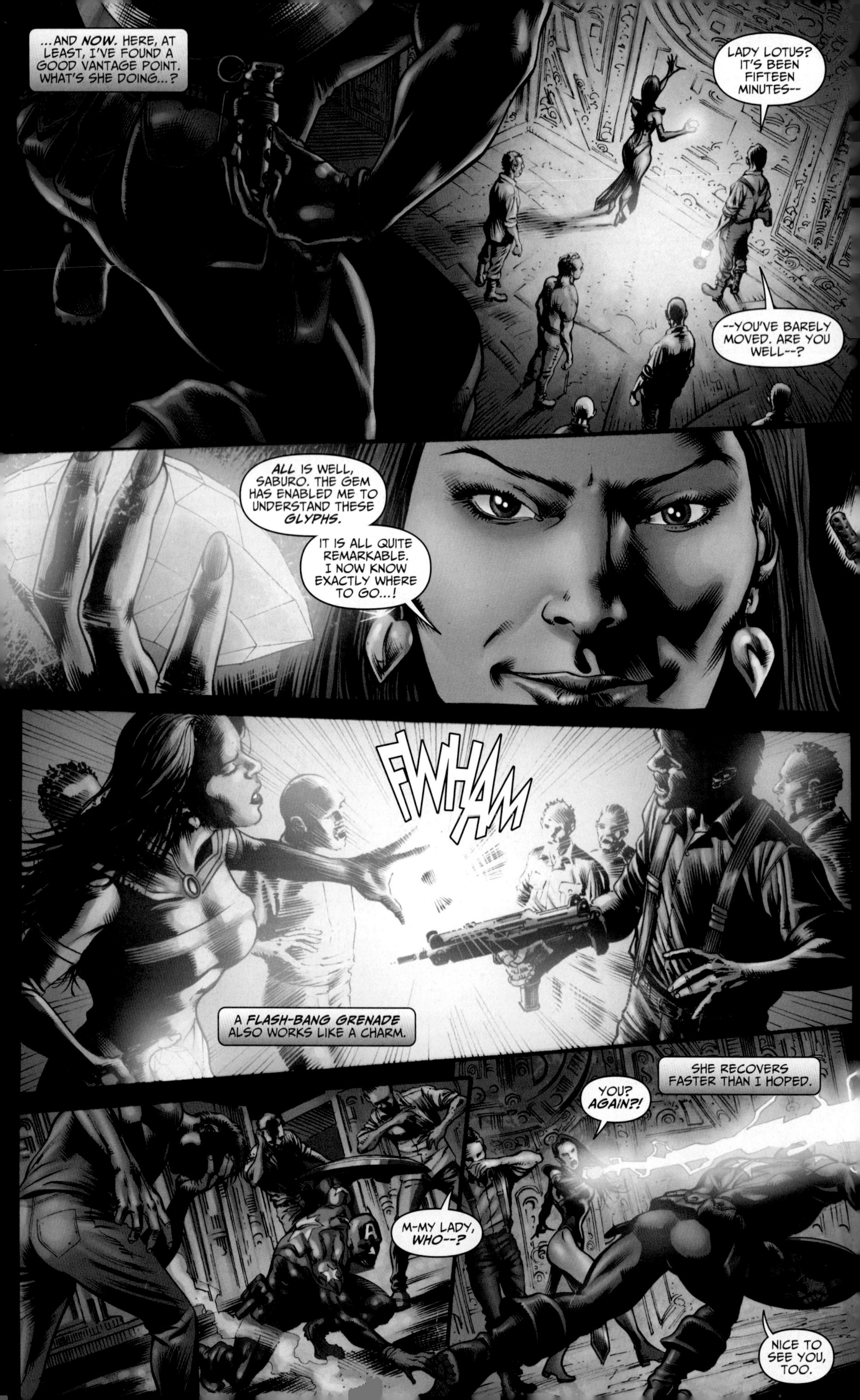

...AND NOW. HERE, AT LEAST, I'VE FOUND A GOOD VANTAGE POINT. WHAT'S SHE DOING...?
LADY LOTUS? IT'S BEEN FIFTEEN MINUTES--
--YOU'VE BARELY MOVED. ARE YOU WELL--?
ALL IS WELL, SABURO. THE GEM HAS ENABLED ME TO UNDERSTAND THESE GLYPHS.
IT IS ALL QUITE REMARKABLE. I NOW KNOW EXACTLY WHERE TO GO...!
FWHAM
A FLASH-BANG GRENADE ALSO WORKS LIKE A CHARM.
SHE RECOVERS FASTER THAN I HOPED.
YOU? AGAIN?!
M-MY LADY, WHO--?
NICE TO SEE YOU, TOO.

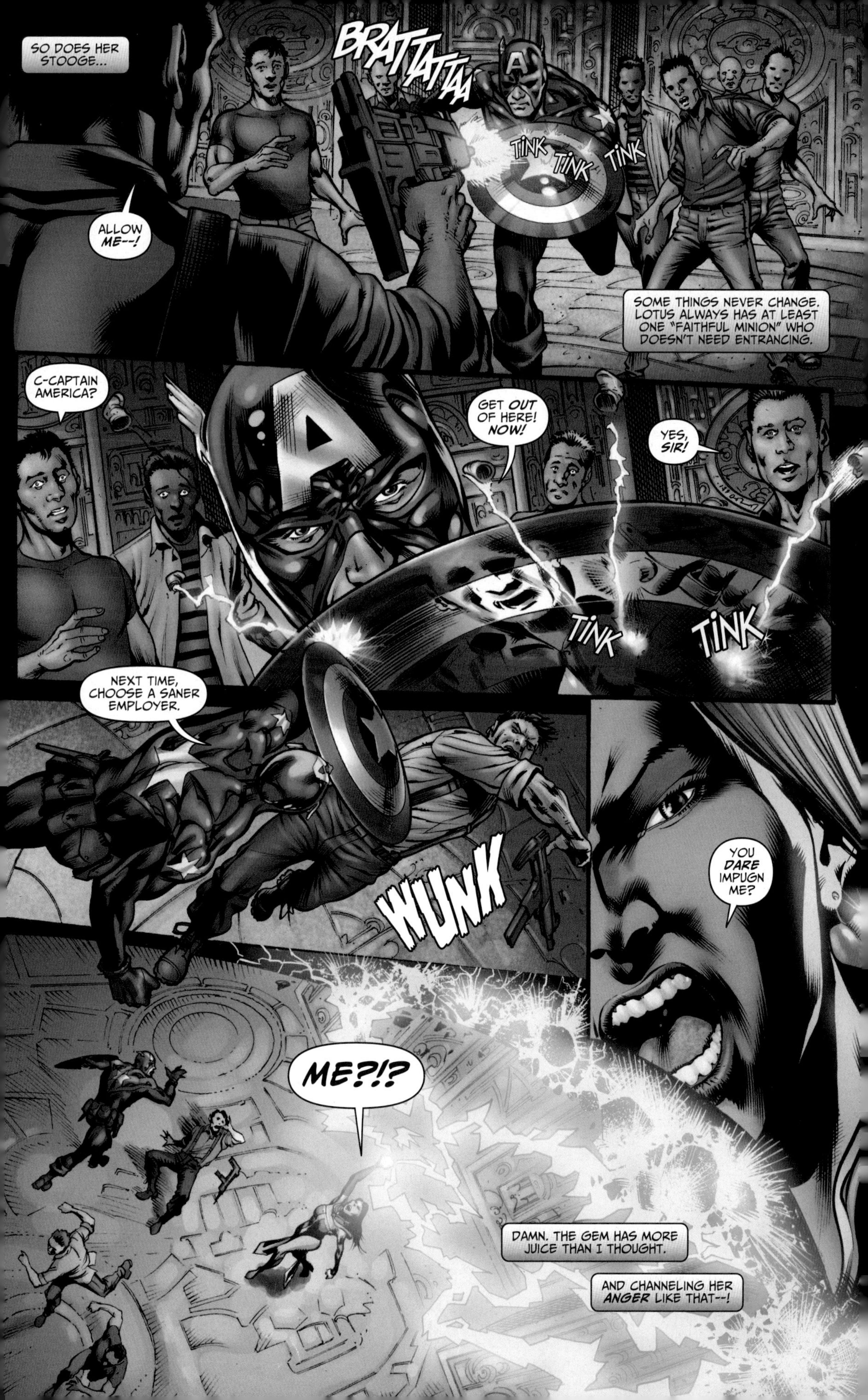
SO DOES HER STOOGE...
BRATTATTAA
ALLOW ME--!
TINK
TINK
TINK
SOME THINGS NEVER CHANGE. LOTUS ALWAYS HAS AT LEAST ONE "FAITHFUL MINION" WHO DOESN'T NEED ENTRANCING.
C-CAPTAIN AMERICA?
GET OUT OF HERE! NOW!
YES, SIR!
TINK
TINK
NEXT TIME, CHOOSE A SANER EMPLOYER.
WUNK
YOU DARE IMPUGN ME?
ME?!?
DAMN. THE GEM HAS MORE JUICE THAN I THOUGHT.
AND CHANNELING HER ANGER LIKE THAT--!

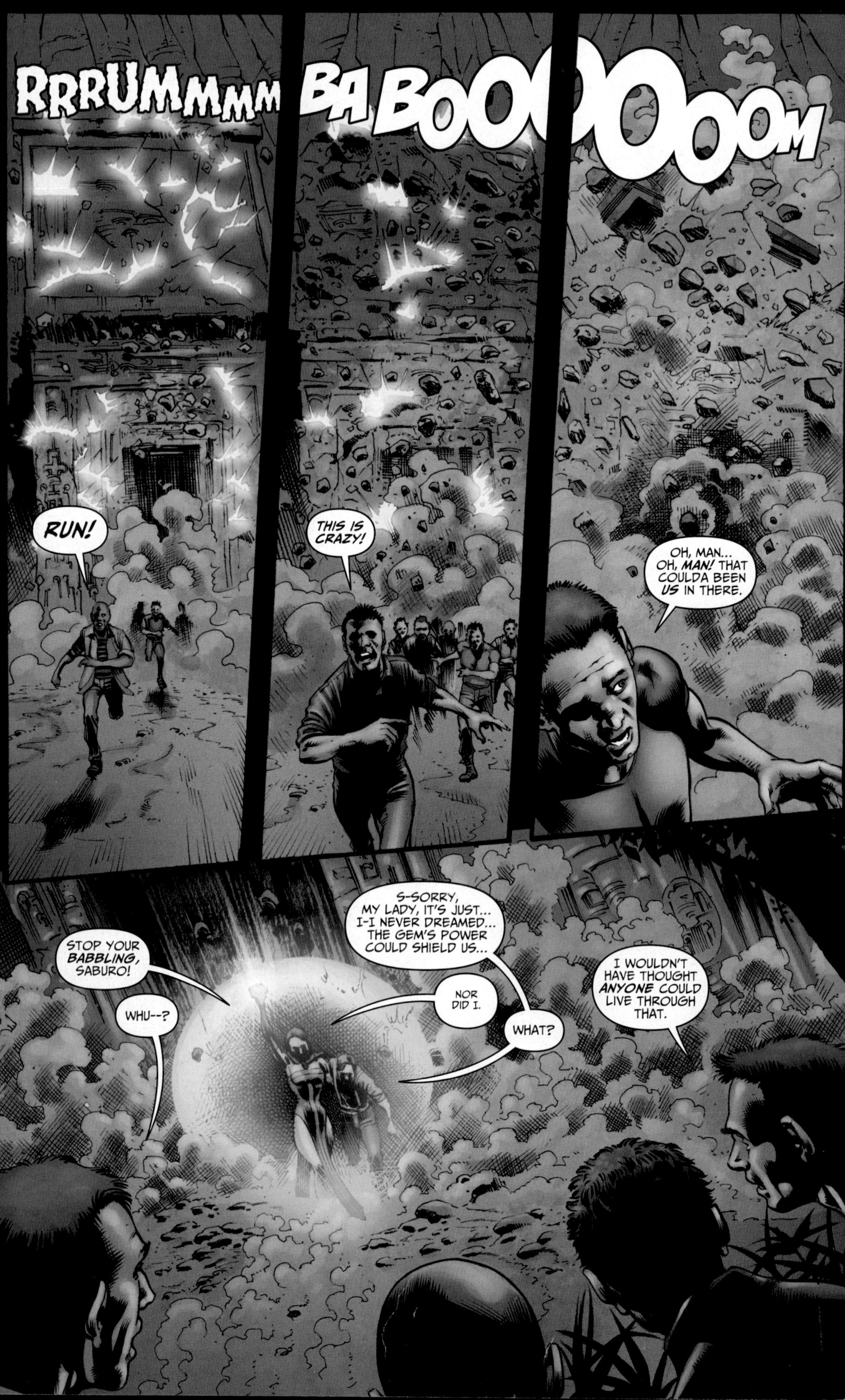
RRRUMMMMM BA BOOOOOoom
RUN!
THIS IS CRAZY!
OH, MAN... OH, MAN! THAT COULDA BEEN US IN THERE.
S-SORRY, MY LADY, IT'S JUST... I-I NEVER DREAMED... THE GEM'S POWER COULD SHIELD US...
STOP YOUR BABBLING, SABURO!
WHU--?
NOR DID I.
WHAT?
I WOULDN'T HAVE THOUGHT ANYONE COULD LIVE THROUGH THAT.

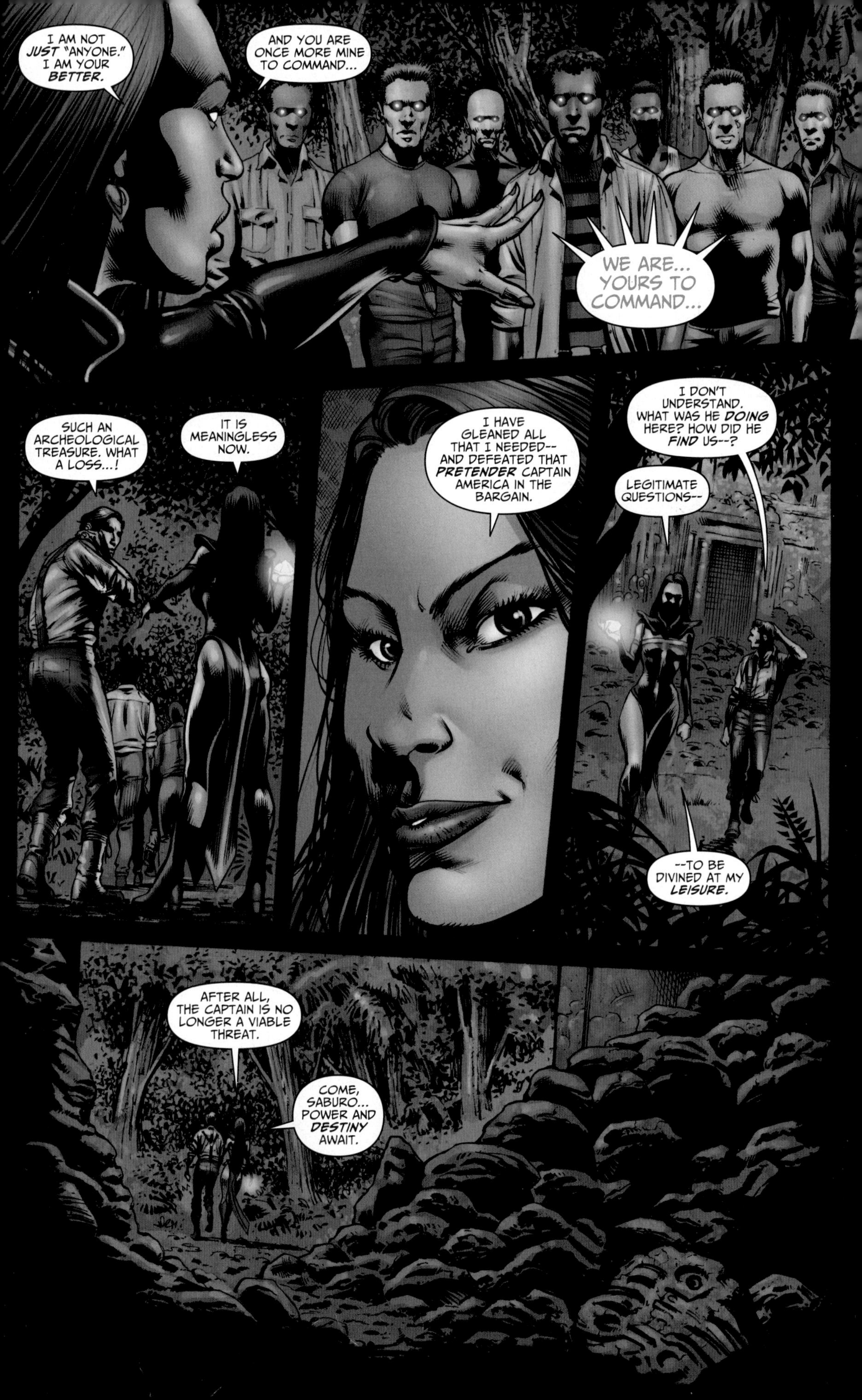

I AM NOT JUST "ANYONE." I AM YOUR BETTER.
AND YOU ARE ONCE MORE MINE TO COMMAND...
WE ARE... YOURS TO COMMAND...
SUCH AN ARCHEOLOGICAL TREASURE. WHAT A LOSS...!
IT IS MEANINGLESS NOW.
I HAVE GLEANED ALL THAT I NEEDED-- AND DEFEATED THAT PRETENDER CAPTAIN AMERICA IN THE BARGAIN.
I DON'T UNDERSTAND. WHAT WAS HE DOING HERE? HOW DID HE FIND US--?
LEGITIMATE QUESTIONS--
--TO BE DIVINED AT MY LEISURE.
AFTER ALL, THE CAPTAIN IS NO LONGER A VIABLE THREAT.
COME, SABURO... POWER AND DESTINY AWAIT.

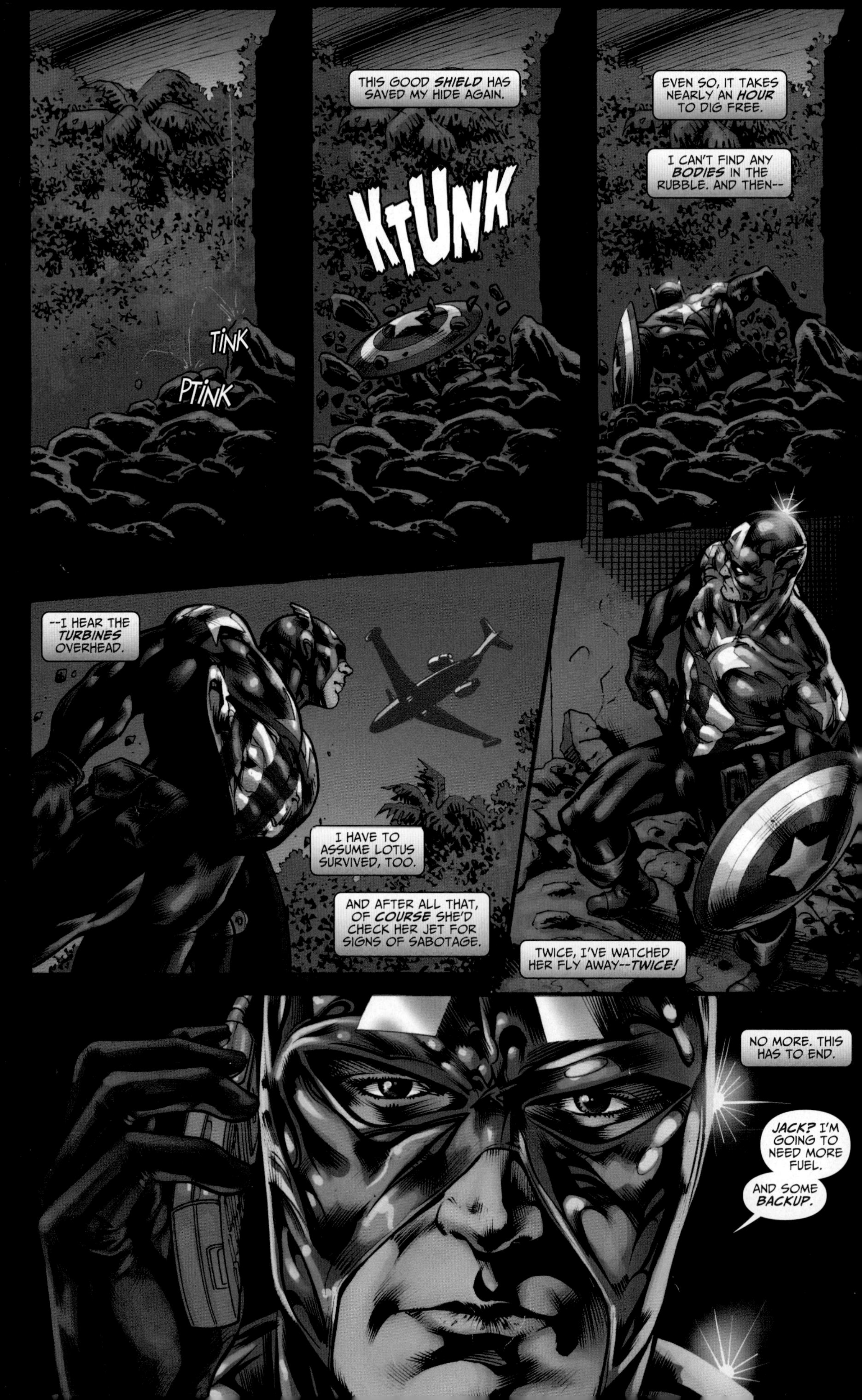
TINK
PTINK
THIS GOOD SHIELD HAS SAVED MY HIDE AGAIN.
KTUNK
EVEN SO, IT TAKES NEARLY AN HOUR TO DIG FREE.
I CAN'T FIND ANY BODIES IN THE RUBBLE. AND THEN--
--I HEAR THE TURBINES OVERHEAD.
I HAVE TO ASSUME LOTUS SURVIVED, TOO.
AND AFTER ALL THAT, OF COURSE SHE'D CHECK HER JET FOR SIGNS OF SABOTAGE.
TWICE, I'VE WATCHED HER FLY AWAY--TWICE!
NO MORE. THIS HAS TO END.
JACK? I'M GOING TO NEED MORE FUEL.
AND SOME BACKUP.

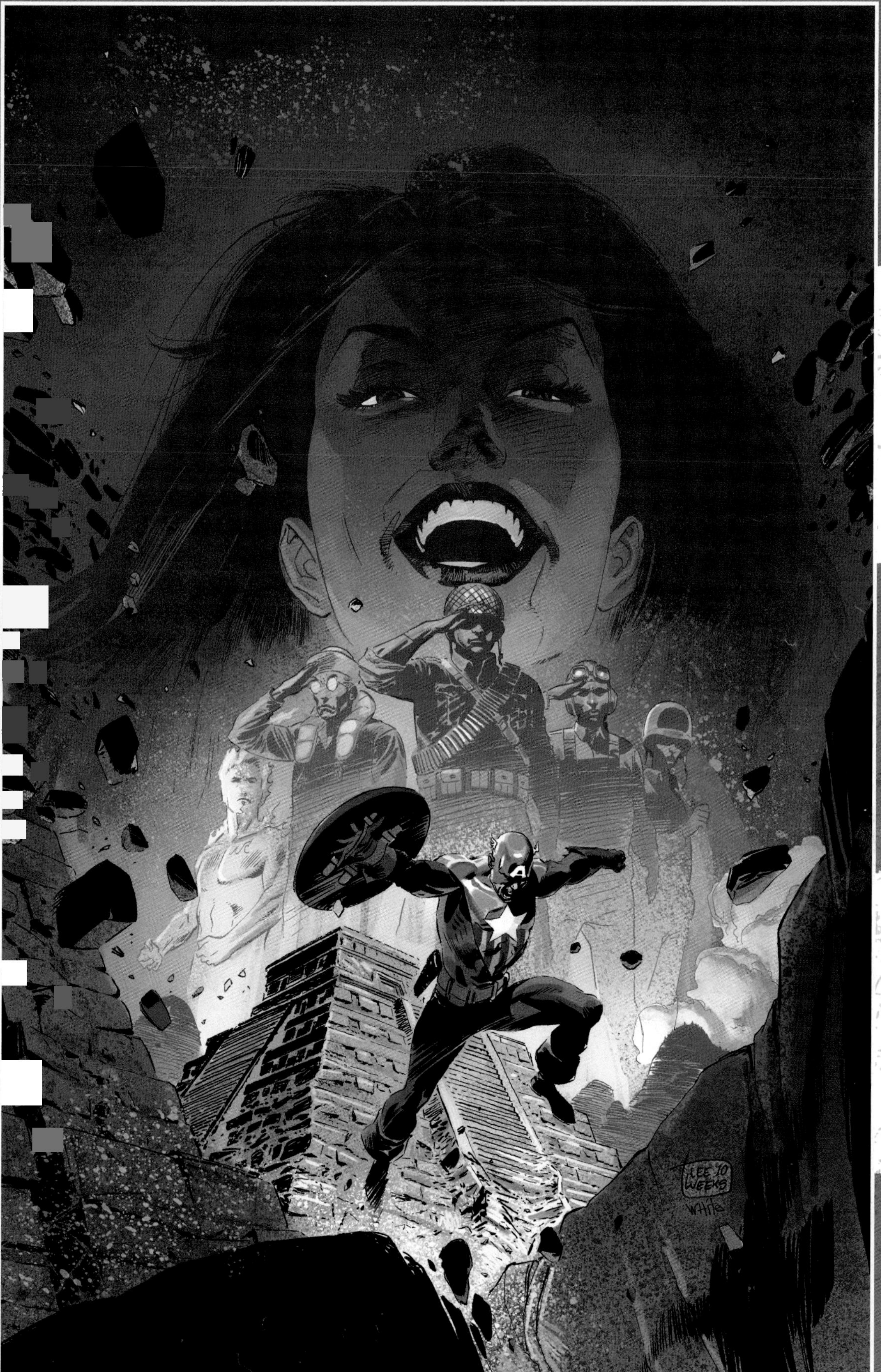

CAPTAIN AMERICA: FOREVER ALLIES #4

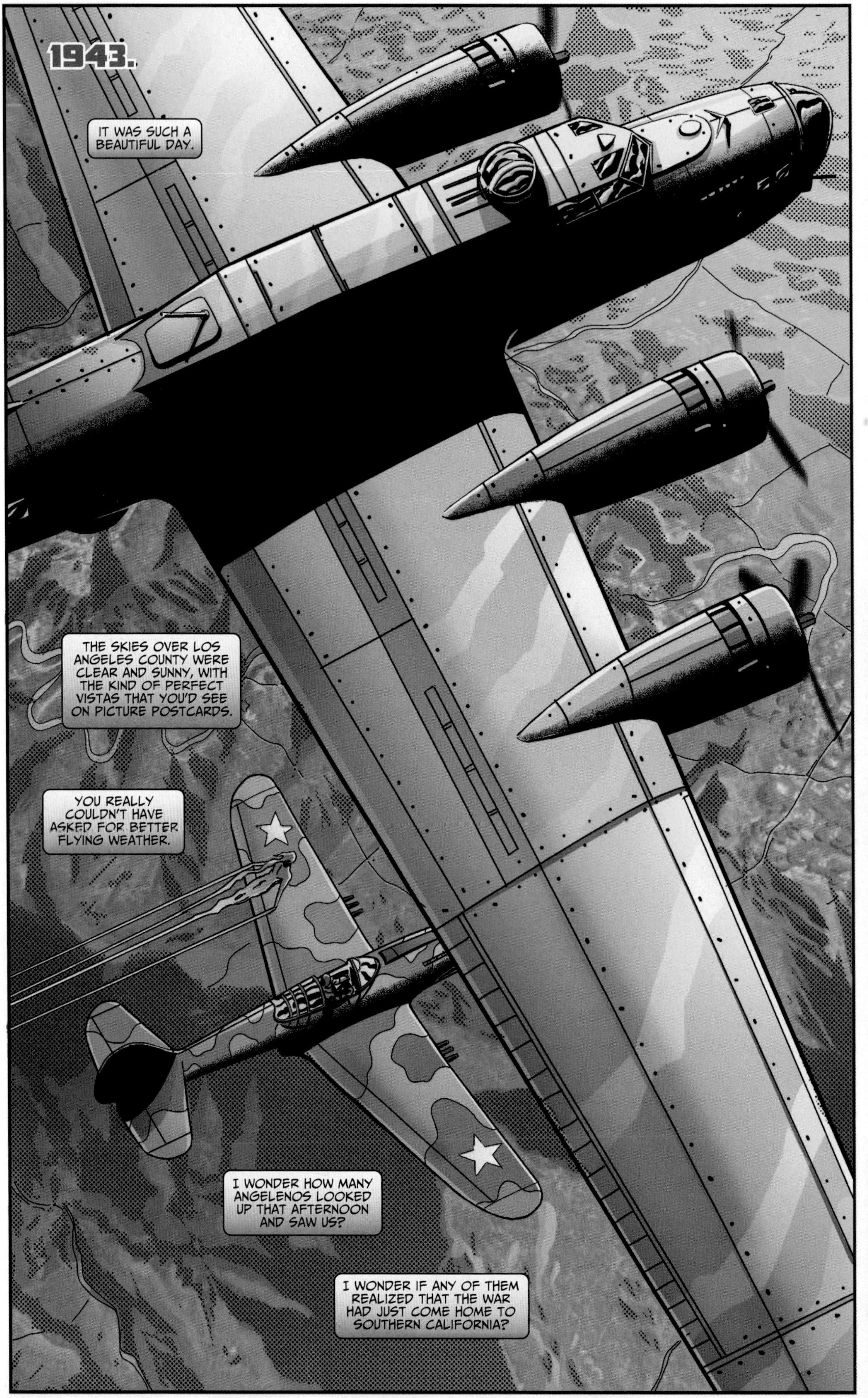
1943.
IT WAS SUCH A BEAUTIFUL DAY.
THE SKIES OVER LOS ANGELES COUNTY WERE CLEAR AND SUNNY, WITH THE KIND OF PERFECT VISTAS THAT YOU'D SEE ON PICTURE POSTCARDS.
YOU REALLY COULDN'T HAVE ASKED FOR BETTER FLYING WEATHER.
I WONDER HOW MANY ANGELENOS LOOKED UP THAT AFTERNOON AND SAW US?
I WONDER IF ANY OF THEM REALIZED THAT THE WAR HAD JUST COME HOME TO SOUTHERN CALIFORNIA?

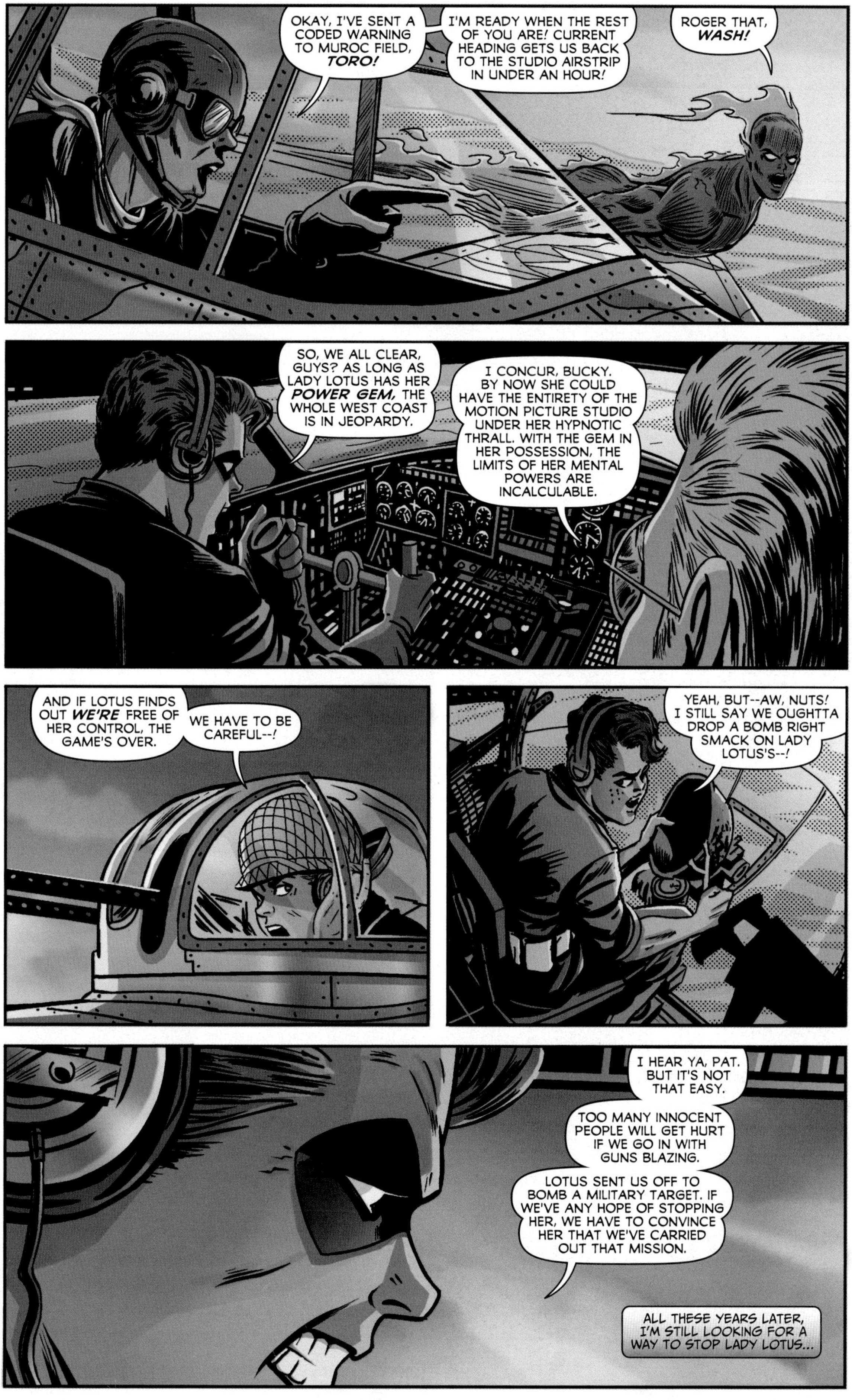
OKAY, I'VE SENT A CODED WARNING TO MUROC FIELD, TORO!
I'M READY WHEN THE REST OF YOU ARE! CURRENT HEADING GETS US BACK TO THE STUDIO AIRSTRIP IN UNDER AN HOUR!
ROGER THAT, WASH!
SO, WE ALL CLEAR, GUYS? AS LONG AS LADY LOTUS HAS HER POWER GEM, THE WHOLE WEST COAST IS IN JEOPARDY.
I CONCUR, BUCKY. BY NOW SHE COULD HAVE THE ENTIRETY OF THE MOTION PICTURE STUDIO UNDER HER HYPNOTIC THRALL. WITH THE GEM IN HER POSSESSION, THE LIMITS OF HER MENTAL POWERS ARE INCALCULABLE.
AND IF LOTUS FINDS OUT WE'RE FREE OF HER CONTROL, THE GAME'S OVER.
WE HAVE TO BE CAREFUL--!
YEAH, BUT--AW, NUTS! I STILL SAY WE OUGHTTA DROP A BOMB RIGHT SMACK ON LADY LOTUS'S--!
I HEAR YA, PAT. BUT IT'S NOT THAT EASY.
TOO MANY INNOCENT PEOPLE WILL GET HURT IF WE GO IN WITH GUNS BLAZING.
LOTUS SENT US OFF TO BOMB A MILITARY TARGET. IF WE'VE ANY HOPE OF STOPPING HER, WE HAVE TO CONVINCE HER THAT WE'VE CARRIED OUT THAT MISSION.
ALL THESE YEARS LATER, I'M STILL LOOKING FOR A WAY TO STOP LADY LOTUS...

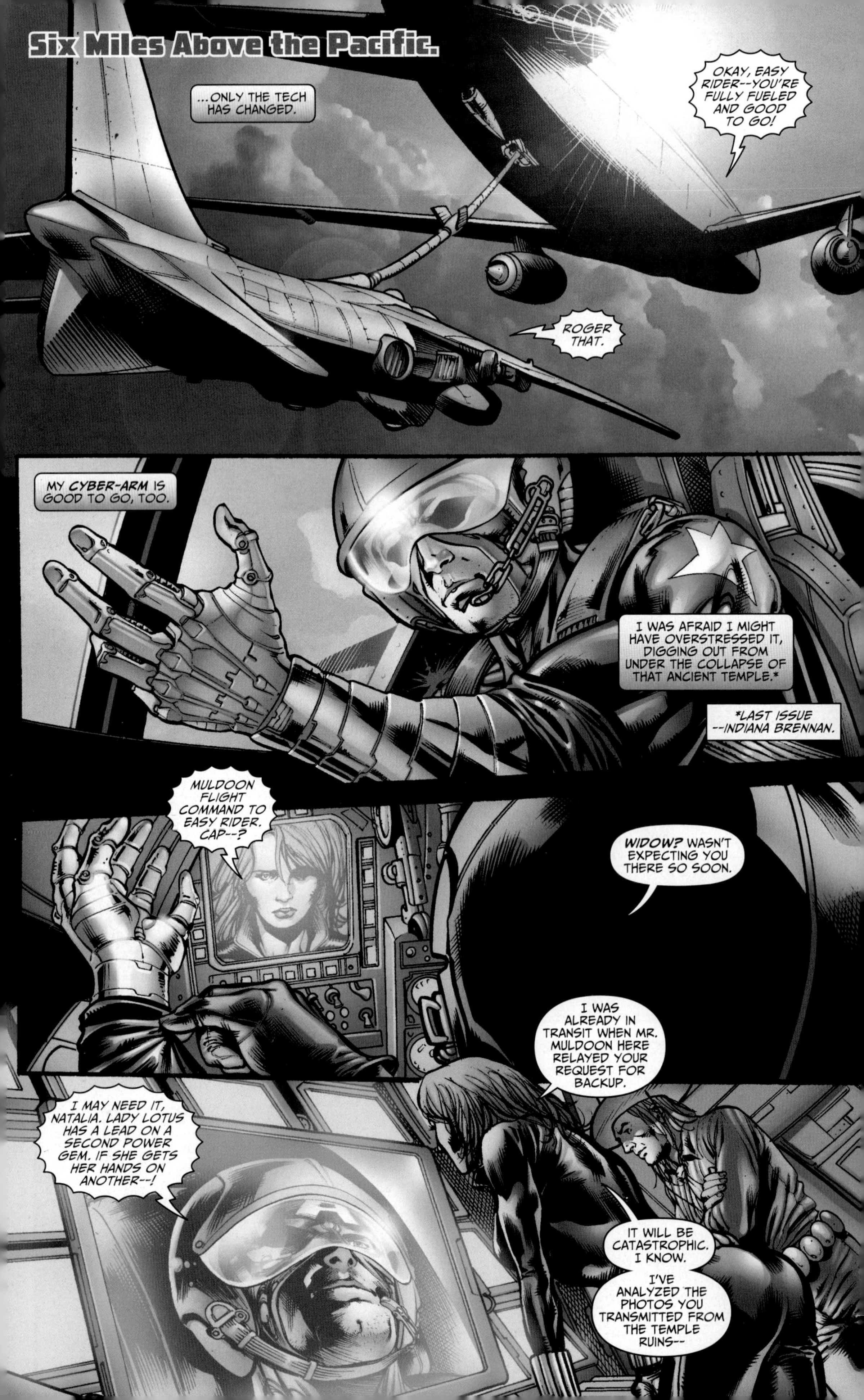
Six Miles Above the Pacific.
...ONLY THE TECH HAS CHANGED.
OKAY, EASY RIDER--YOU'RE FULLY FUELED AND GOOD TO GO!
ROGER THAT.
MY CYBER-ARM IS GOOD TO GO, TOO.
I WAS AFRAID I MIGHT HAVE OVERSTRESSED IT, DIGGING OUT FROM UNDER THE COLLAPSE OF THAT ANCIENT TEMPLE.*
*LAST ISSUE --INDIANA BRENNAN.
MULDOON FLIGHT COMMAND TO EASY RIDER. CAP--?
WIDOW? WASN'T EXPECTING YOU THERE SO SOON.
I WAS ALREADY IN TRANSIT WHEN MR. MULDOON HERE RELAYED YOUR REQUEST FOR BACKUP.
I MAY NEED IT, NATALIA. LADY LOTUS HAS A LEAD ON A SECOND POWER GEM. IF SHE GETS HER HANDS ON ANOTHER--!
IT WILL BE CATASTROPHIC. I KNOW.
I'VE ANALYZED THE PHOTOS YOU TRANSMITTED FROM THE TEMPLE RUINS--

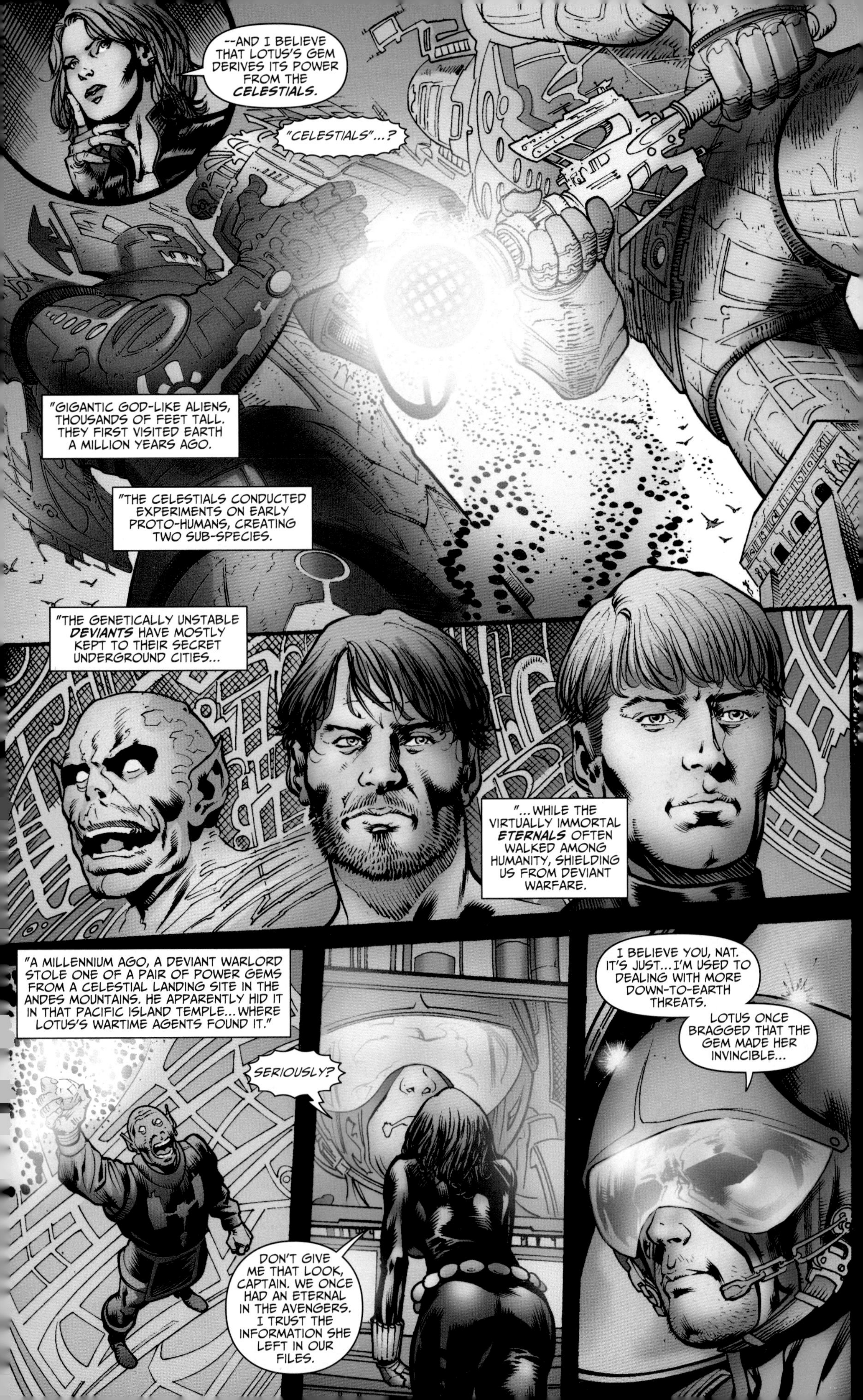
--AND I BELIEVE THAT LOTUS'S GEM DERIVES ITS POWER FROM THE CELESTIALS.
"CELESTIALS"...?
"GIGANTIC GOD-LIKE ALIENS, THOUSANDS OF FEET TALL. THEY FIRST VISITED EARTH A MILLION YEARS AGO.
"THE CELESTIALS CONDUCTED EXPERIMENTS ON EARLY PROTO-HUMANS, CREATING TWO SUB-SPECIES.
"THE GENETICALLY UNSTABLE DEVIANTS HAVE MOSTLY KEPT TO THEIR SECRET UNDERGROUND CITIES...
"...WHILE THE VIRTUALLY IMMORTAL ETERNALS OFTEN WALKED AMONG HUMANITY, SHIELDING US FROM DEVIANT WARFARE.
"A MILLENNIUM AGO, A DEVIANT WARLORD STOLE ONE OF A PAIR OF POWER GEMS FROM A CELESTIAL LANDING SITE IN THE ANDES MOUNTAINS. HE APPARENTLY HID IT IN THAT PACIFIC ISLAND TEMPLE... WHERE LOTUS'S WARTIME AGENTS FOUND IT."
SERIOUSLY?
DON'T GIVE ME THAT LOOK, CAPTAIN. WE ONCE HAD AN ETERNAL IN THE AVENGERS. I TRUST THE INFORMATION SHE LEFT IN OUR FILES.
I BELIEVE YOU, NAT. IT'S JUST... I'M USED TO DEALING WITH MORE DOWN-TO-EARTH THREATS.
LOTUS ONCE BRAGGED THAT THE GEM MADE HER INVINCIBLE...

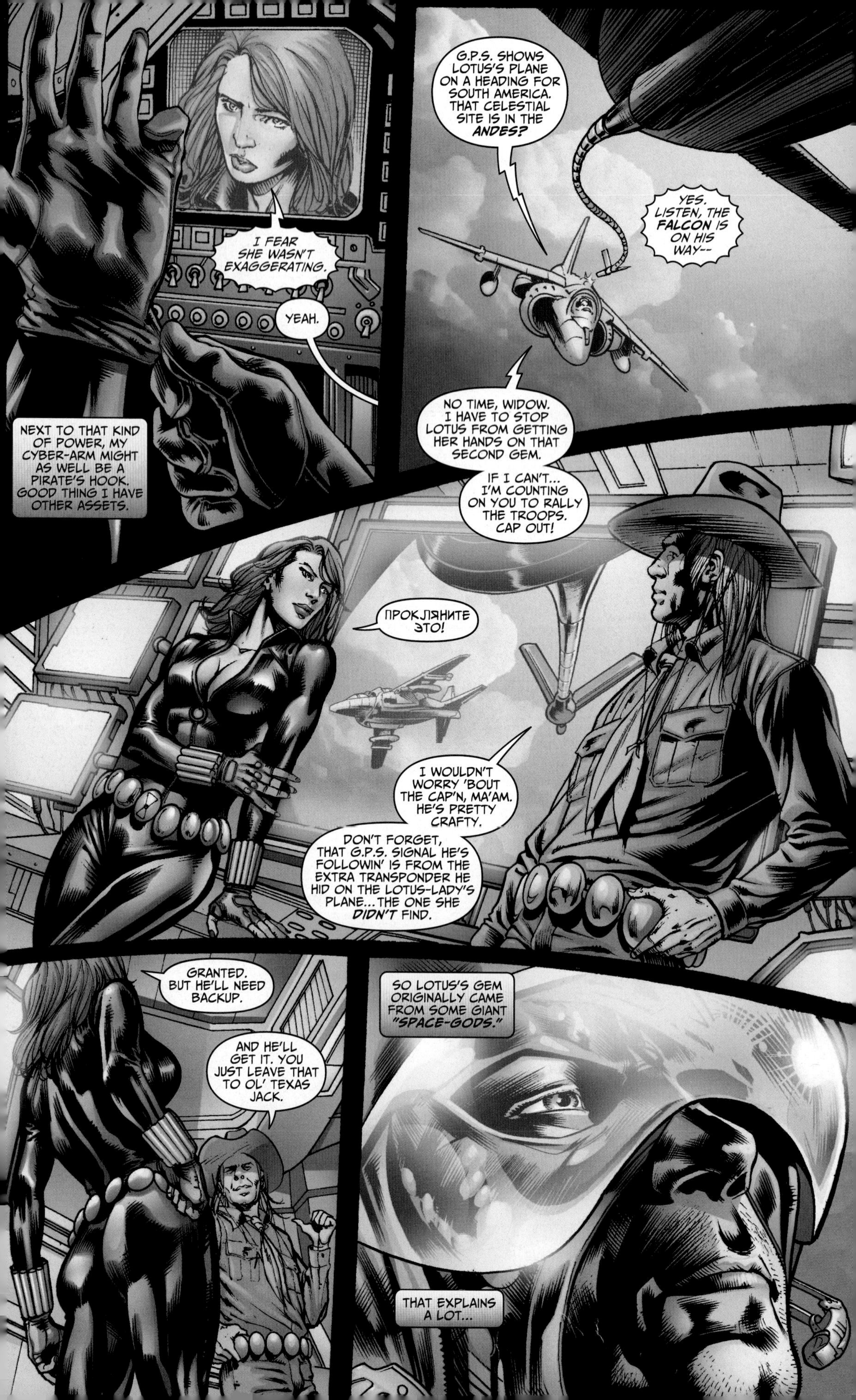
I FEAR SHE WASN'T EXAGGERATING.
YEAH.
NEXT TO THAT KIND OF POWER, MY CYBER-ARM MIGHT AS WELL BE A PIRATE'S HOOK. GOOD THING I HAVE OTHER ASSETS.
G.P.S. SHOWS LOTUS'S PLANE ON A HEADING FOR SOUTH AMERICA. THAT CELESTIAL SITE IS IN THE ANDES?
YES. LISTEN, THE FALCON IS ON HIS WAY--
NO TIME, WIDOW. I HAVE TO STOP LOTUS FROM GETTING HER HANDS ON THAT SECOND GEM.
IF I CAN'T... I'M COUNTING ON YOU TO RALLY THE TROOPS. CAP OUT!
ПРОКЛЯНИТЕ ЭТО!
I WOULDN'T WORRY 'BOUT THE CAP'N, MA'AM. HE'S PRETTY CRAFTY.
DON'T FORGET, THAT G.P.S. SIGNAL HE'S FOLLOWIN' IS FROM THE EXTRA TRANSPONDER HE HID ON THE LOTUS-LADY'S PLANE... THE ONE SHE DIDN'T FIND.
GRANTED. BUT HE'LL NEED BACKUP.
AND HE'LL GET IT. YOU JUST LEAVE THAT TO OL' TEXAS JACK.
SO LOTUS'S GEM ORIGINALLY CAME FROM SOME GIANT "SPACE-GODS."
THAT EXPLAINS A LOT...

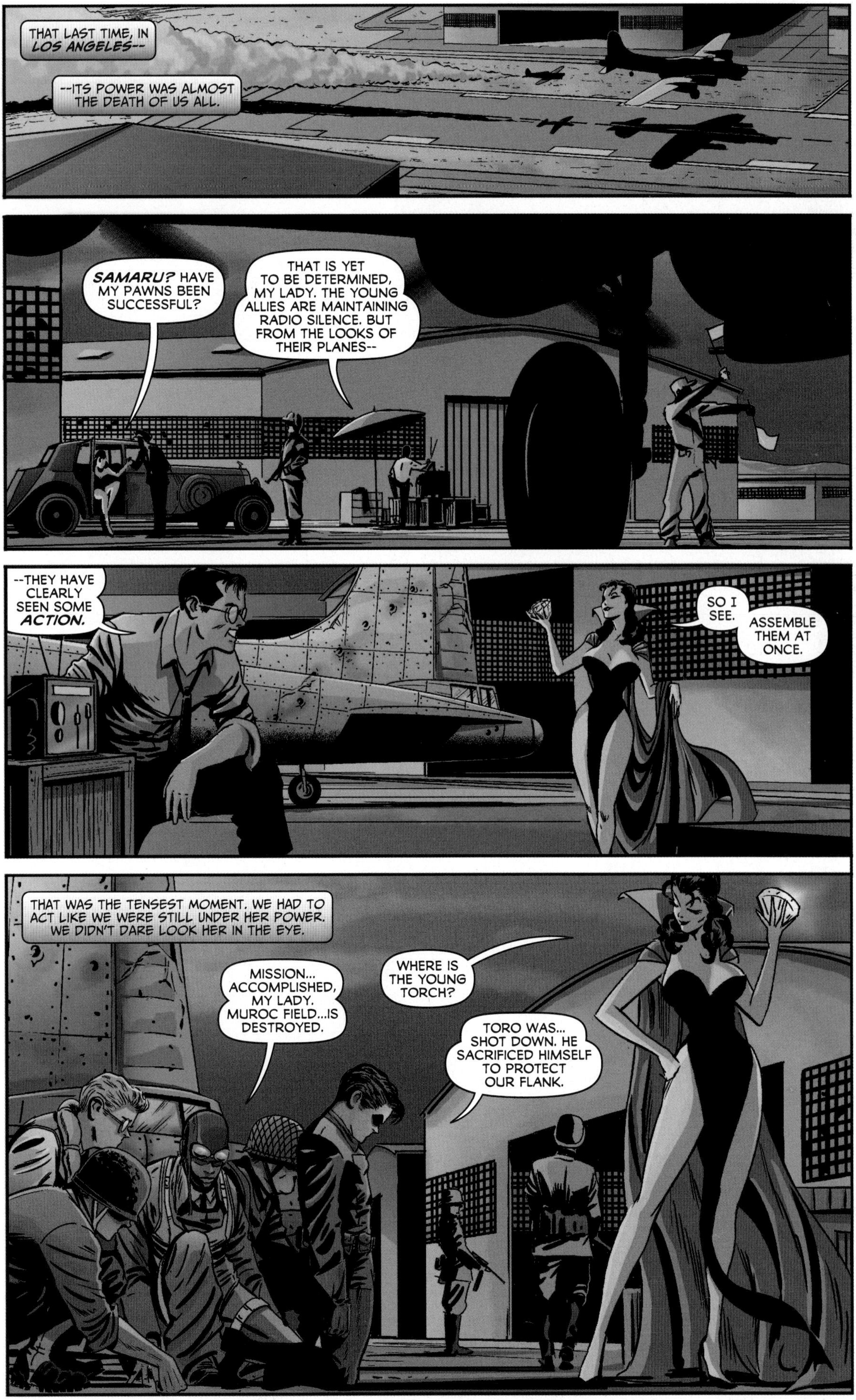
THAT LAST TIME, IN LOS ANGELES--
--ITS POWER WAS ALMOST THE DEATH OF US ALL.
SAMARU? HAVE MY PAWNS BEEN SUCCESSFUL?
THAT IS YET TO BE DETERMINED, MY LADY. THE YOUNG ALLIES ARE MAINTAINING RADIO SILENCE. BUT FROM THE LOOKS OF THEIR PLANES--
--THEY HAVE CLEARLY SEEN SOME ACTION.
SO I SEE.
ASSEMBLE THEM AT ONCE.
THAT WAS THE TENSEST MOMENT. WE HAD TO ACT LIKE WE WERE STILL UNDER HER POWER. WE DIDN'T DARE LOOK HER IN THE EYE.
MISSION... ACCOMPLISHED, MY LADY. MUROC FIELD...IS DESTROYED.
WHERE IS THE YOUNG TORCH?
TORO WAS... SHOT DOWN. HE SACRIFICED HIMSELF TO PROTECT OUR FLANK.

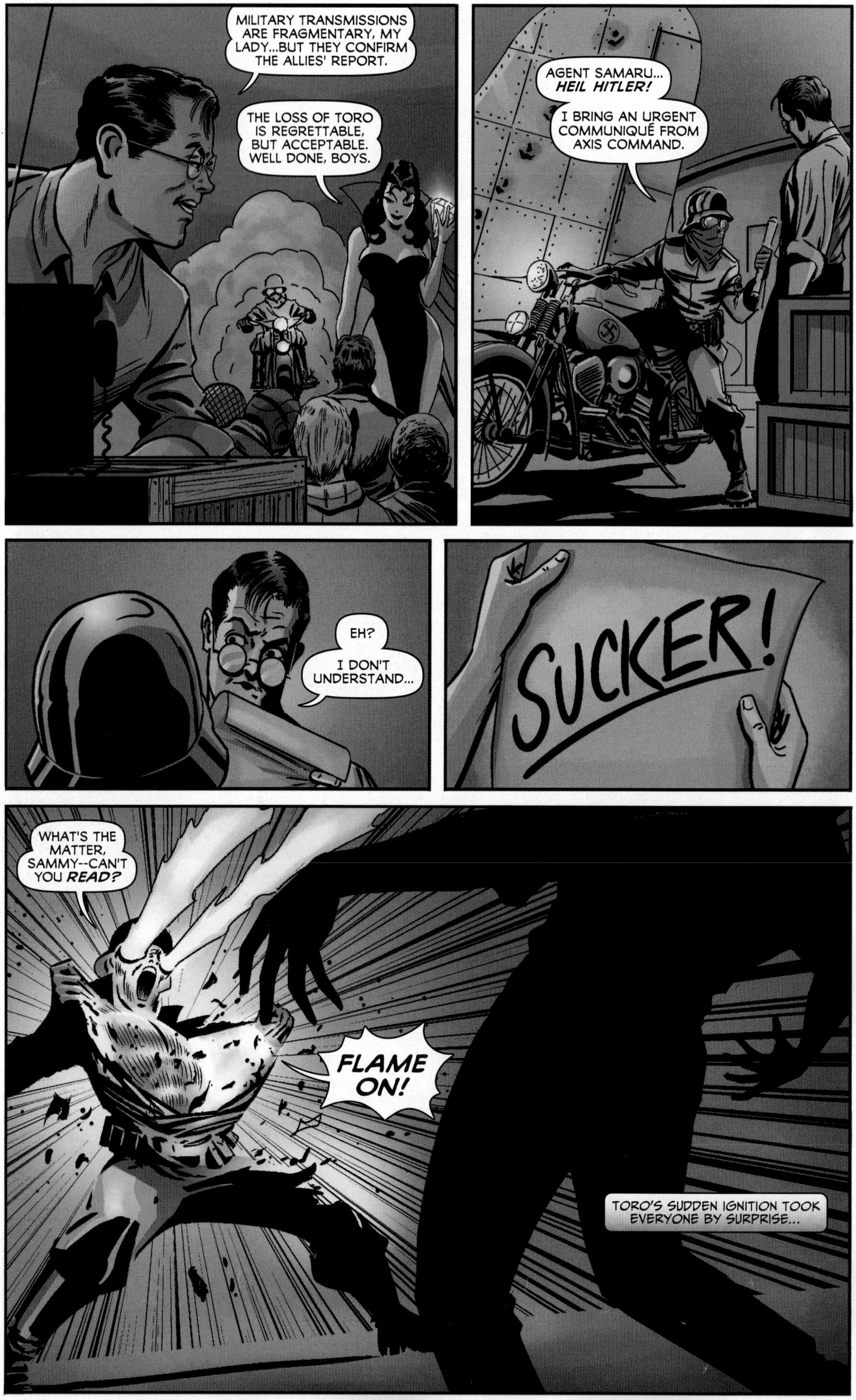
MILITARY TRANSMISSIONS ARE FRAGMENTARY, MY LADY...BUT THEY CONFIRM THE ALLIES' REPORT.
THE LOSS OF TORO IS REGRETTABLE, BUT ACCEPTABLE. WELL DONE, BOYS.
AGENT SAMARU... HEIL HITLER!
I BRING AN URGENT COMMUNIQUÉ FROM AXIS COMMAND.
EH?
I DON'T UNDERSTAND...
SUCKER!
WHAT'S THE MATTER, SAMMY--CAN'T YOU READ?
FLAME ON!
TORO'S SUDDEN IGNITION TOOK EVERYONE BY SURPRISE...

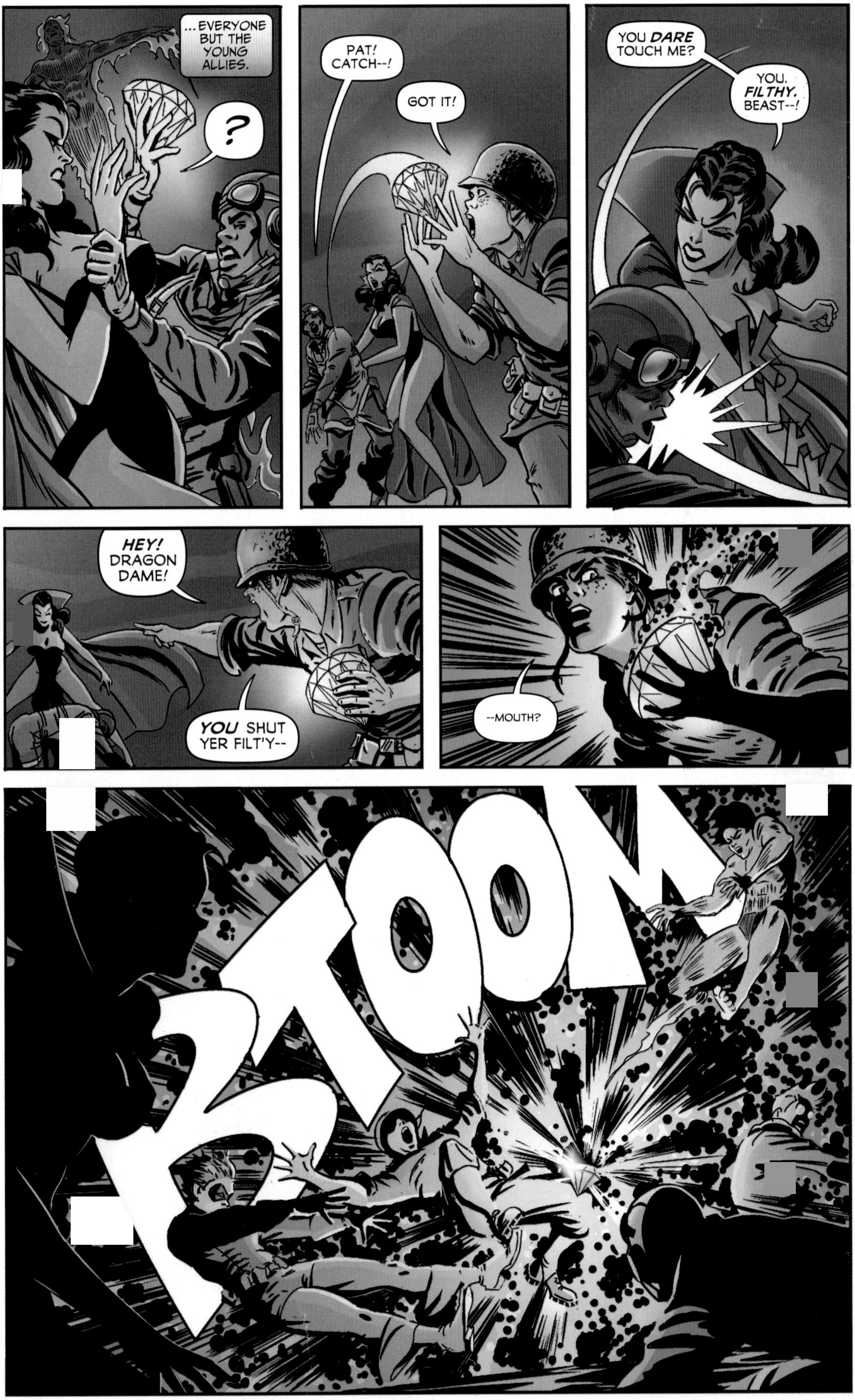
...EVERYONE BUT THE YOUNG ALLIES.
?
PAT! CATCH--!
GOT IT!
YOU DARE TOUCH ME?
YOU. FILTHY. BEAST--!
KRAKKK
HEY! DRAGON DAME!
YOU SHUT YER FILT'Y--
--MOUTH?
BTOOM

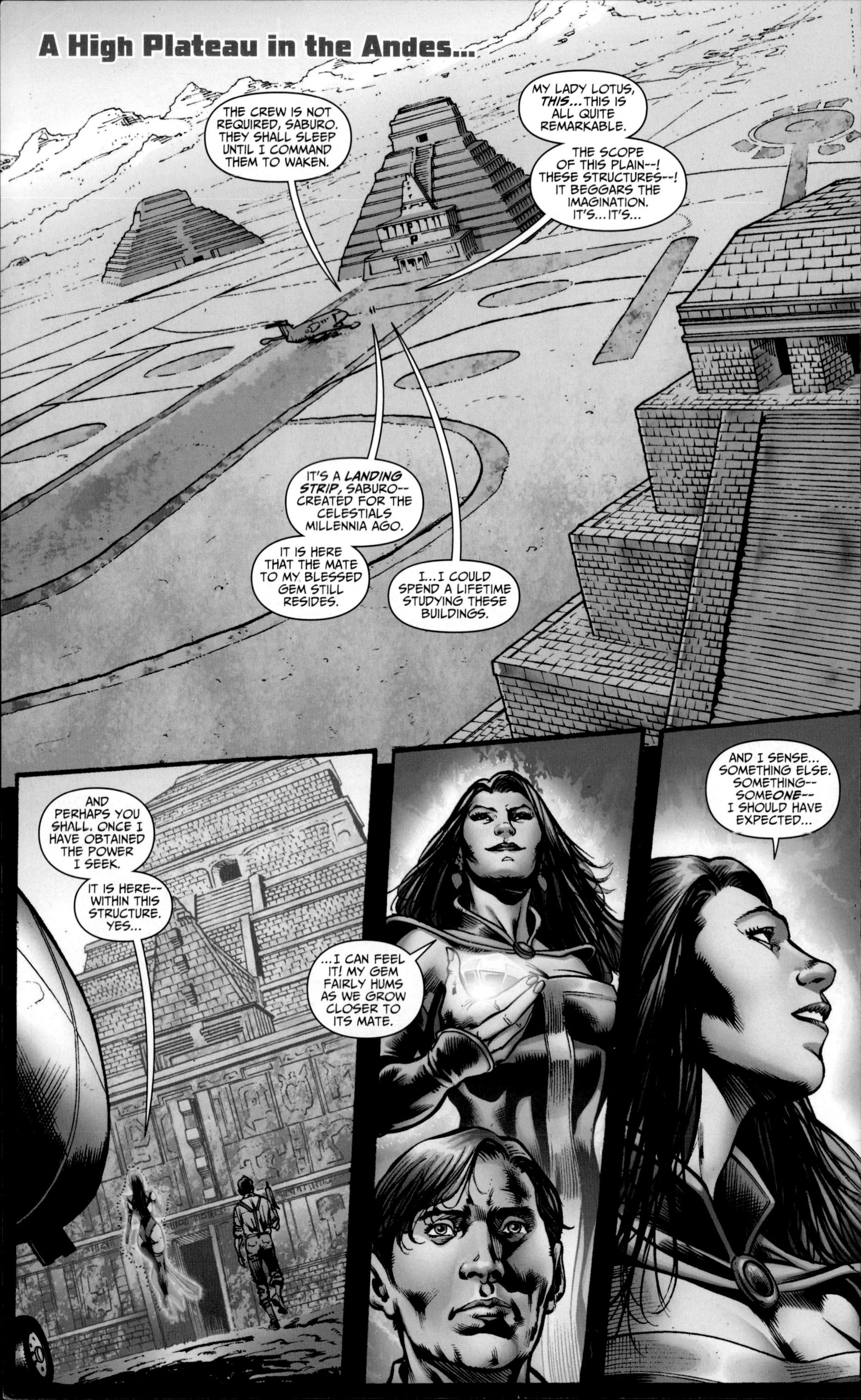
A High Plateau in the Andes...
THE CREW IS NOT REQUIRED, SABURO. THEY SHALL SLEEP UNTIL I COMMAND THEM TO WAKEN.
MY LADY LOTUS, THIS... THIS IS ALL QUITE REMARKABLE.
THE SCOPE OF THIS PLAIN--! THESE STRUCTURES--! IT BEGGARS THE IMAGINATION. IT'S... IT'S...
IT'S A LANDING STRIP, SABURO-- CREATED FOR THE CELESTIALS MILLENNIA AGO.
IT IS HERE THAT THE MATE TO MY BLESSED GEM STILL RESIDES.
I... I COULD SPEND A LIFETIME STUDYING THESE BUILDINGS.
AND PERHAPS YOU SHALL. ONCE I HAVE OBTAINED THE POWER I SEEK.
IT IS HERE-- WITHIN THIS STRUCTURE. YES...
...I CAN FEEL IT! MY GEM FAIRLY HUMS AS WE GROW CLOSER TO ITS MATE.
AND I SENSE... SOMETHING ELSE. SOMETHING-- SOMEONE-- I SHOULD HAVE EXPECTED...

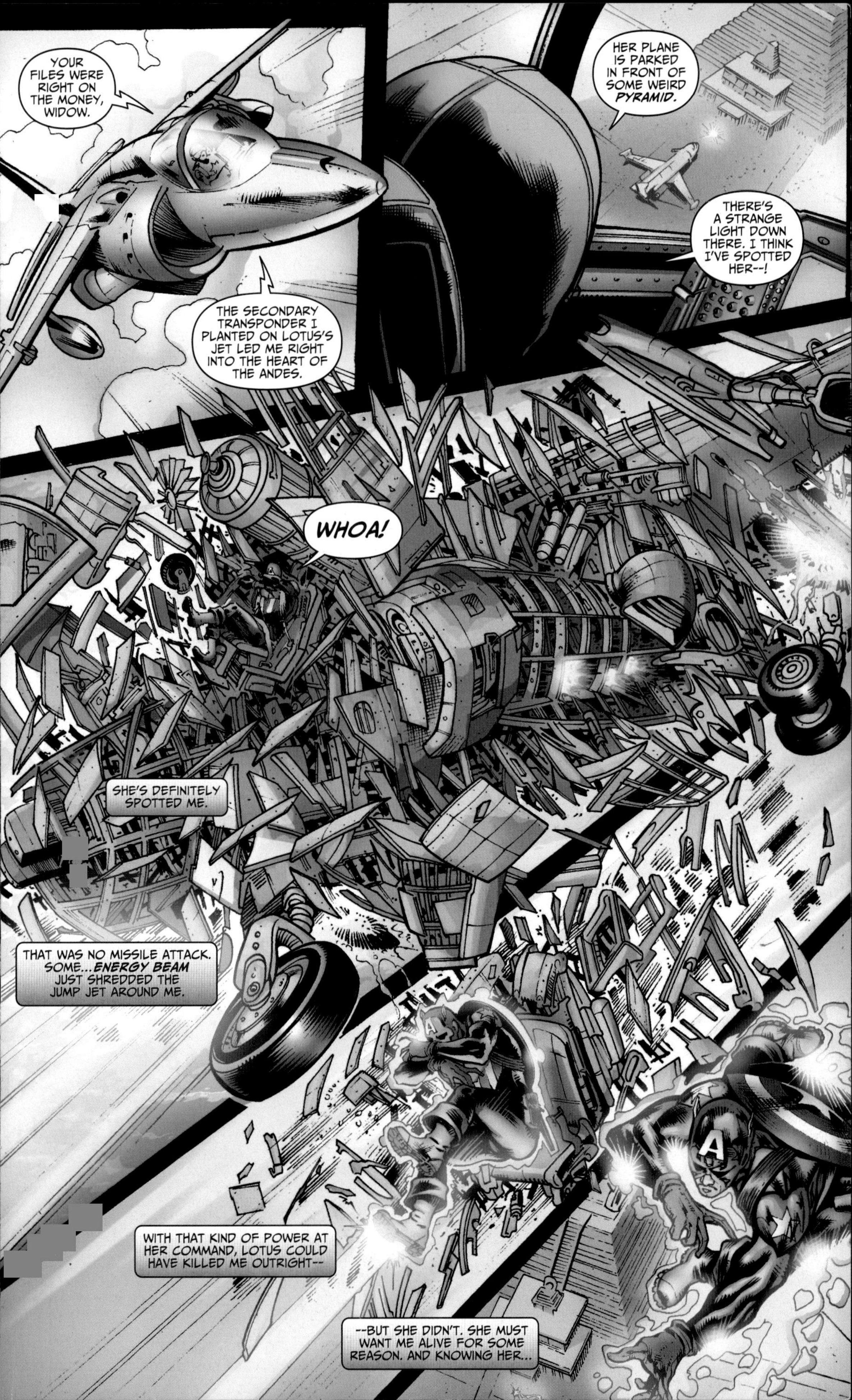
YOUR FILES WERE RIGHT ON THE MONEY, WIDOW.
HER PLANE IS PARKED IN FRONT OF SOME WEIRD PYRAMID.
THERE'S A STRANGE LIGHT DOWN THERE. I THINK I'VE SPOTTED HER--!
THE SECONDARY TRANSPONDER I PLANTED ON LOTUS'S JET LED ME RIGHT INTO THE HEART OF THE ANDES.
WHOA!
SHE'S DEFINITELY SPOTTED ME.
THAT WAS NO MISSILE ATTACK. SOME...ENERGY BEAM JUST SHREDDED THE JUMP JET AROUND ME.
WITH THAT KIND OF POWER AT HER COMMAND, LOTUS COULD HAVE KILLED ME OUTRIGHT--
--BUT SHE DIDN'T. SHE MUST WANT ME ALIVE FOR SOME REASON. AND KNOWING HER...

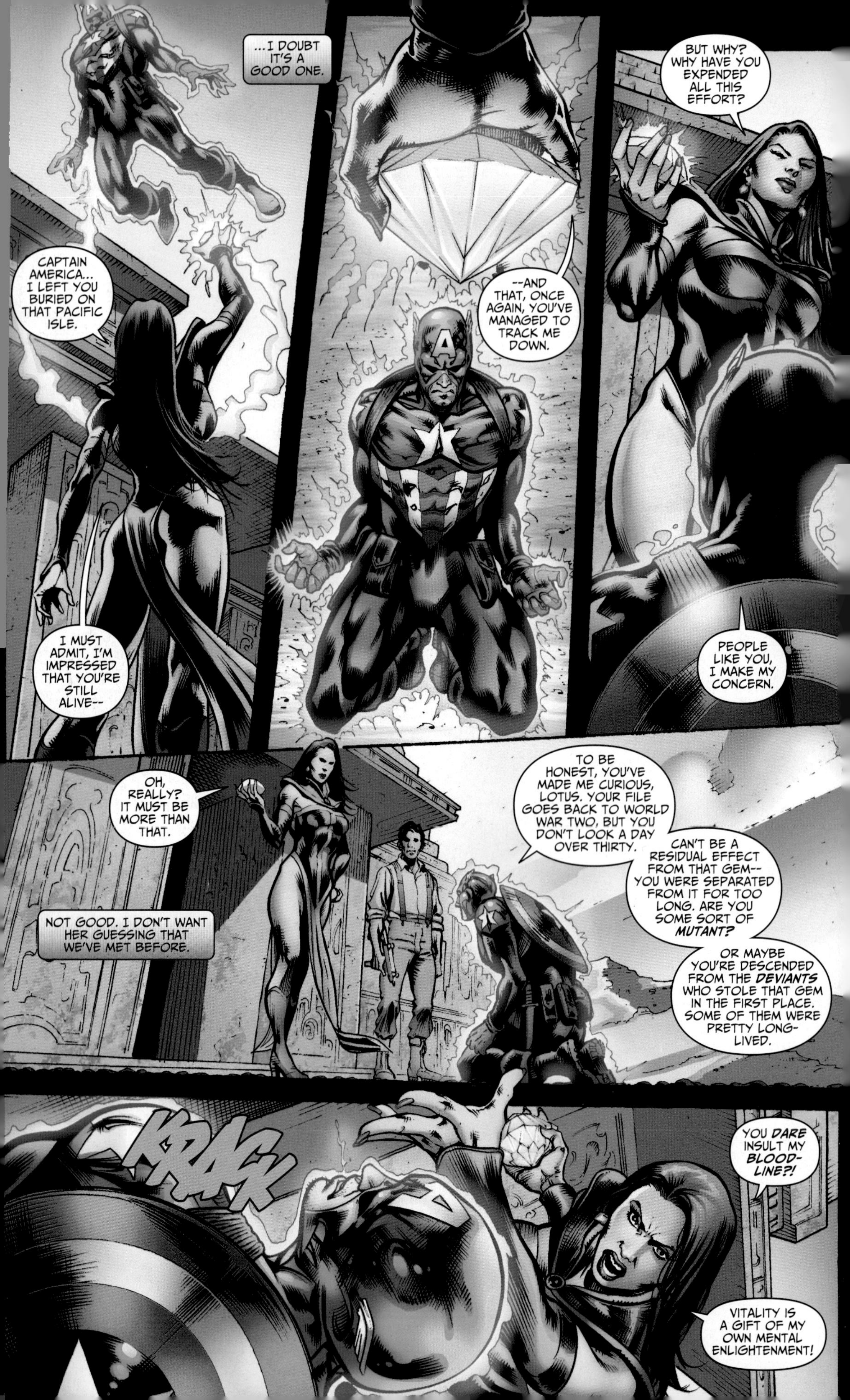
...I DOUBT IT'S A GOOD ONE.
CAPTAIN AMERICA... I LEFT YOU BURIED ON THAT PACIFIC ISLE.
I MUST ADMIT, I'M IMPRESSED THAT YOU'RE STILL ALIVE--
--AND THAT, ONCE AGAIN, YOU'VE MANAGED TO TRACK ME DOWN.
BUT WHY? WHY HAVE YOU EXPENDED ALL THIS EFFORT?
PEOPLE LIKE YOU, I MAKE MY CONCERN.
OH, REALLY? IT MUST BE MORE THAN THAT.
NOT GOOD. I DON'T WANT HER GUESSING THAT WE'VE MET BEFORE.
TO BE HONEST, YOU'VE MADE ME CURIOUS, LOTUS. YOUR FILE GOES BACK TO WORLD WAR TWO, BUT YOU DON'T LOOK A DAY OVER THIRTY.
CAN'T BE A RESIDUAL EFFECT FROM THAT GEM-- YOU WERE SEPARATED FROM IT FOR TOO LONG. ARE YOU SOME SORT OF *MUTANT?*
OR MAYBE YOU'RE DESCENDED FROM THE *DEVIANTS* WHO STOLE THAT GEM IN THE FIRST PLACE. SOME OF THEM WERE PRETTY LONG-LIVED.
KRACK
YOU *DARE* INSULT MY *BLOOD-LINE?!*
VITALITY IS A GIFT OF MY OWN MENTAL ENLIGHTENMENT!

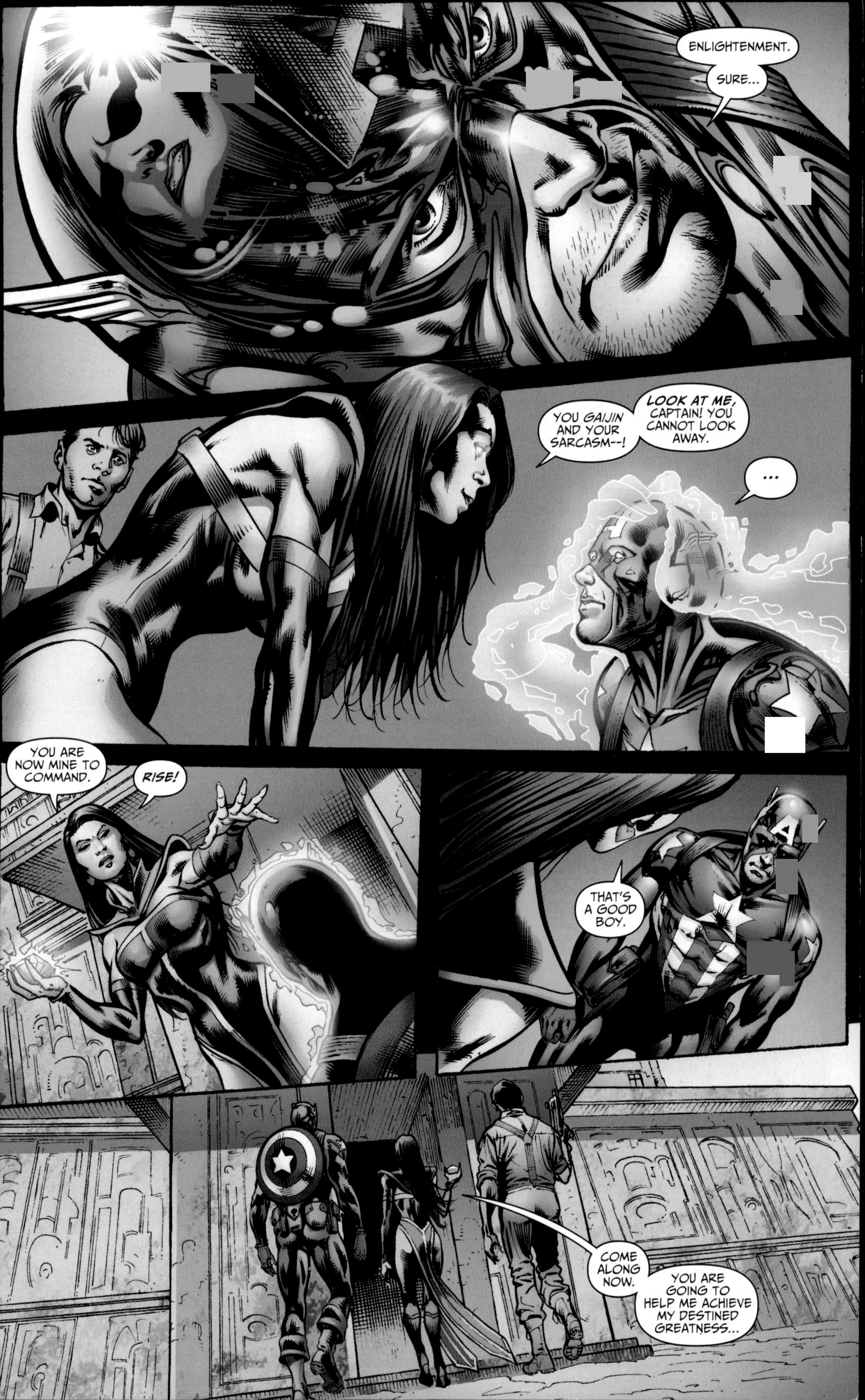
ENLIGHTENMENT.
SURE...
YOU GAIJIN AND YOUR SARCASM--!
LOOK AT ME, CAPTAIN! YOU CANNOT LOOK AWAY.
...
YOU ARE NOW MINE TO COMMAND.
RISE!
THAT'S A GOOD BOY.
COME ALONG NOW.
YOU ARE GOING TO HELP ME ACHIEVE MY DESTINED GREATNESS...

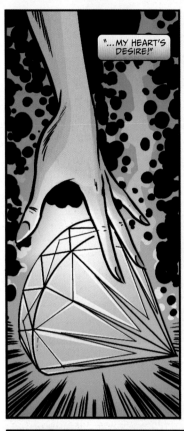

"...MY HEART'S DESIRE!"

YOU YOUNG FOOLS! THE GEM REACTS TO *EMOTION.* YOU ARE INCAPABLE OF HANDLING ITS MIGHT!

YOUR COMMON ANGER MIGHT HAVE KILLED YOU ALL. BUT NOW--

--*I* SHALL HAVE THAT PLEASURE!

YOU HAVE SULLIED THIS GEM WITH YOUR VULGAR TOUCH! YOU ARE UNWORTHY!

POWER IS MEANT FOR THE PUREST OF BLOOD--THE KEENEST OF MIND!

AND THIS POWER SHALL BE *MINE!*

MINE!

AND SHE SAID *PAT* COULDN'T HANDLE IT?

EGADS, SHE'S TRIGGERED AN--!

EARTHQUAKE!

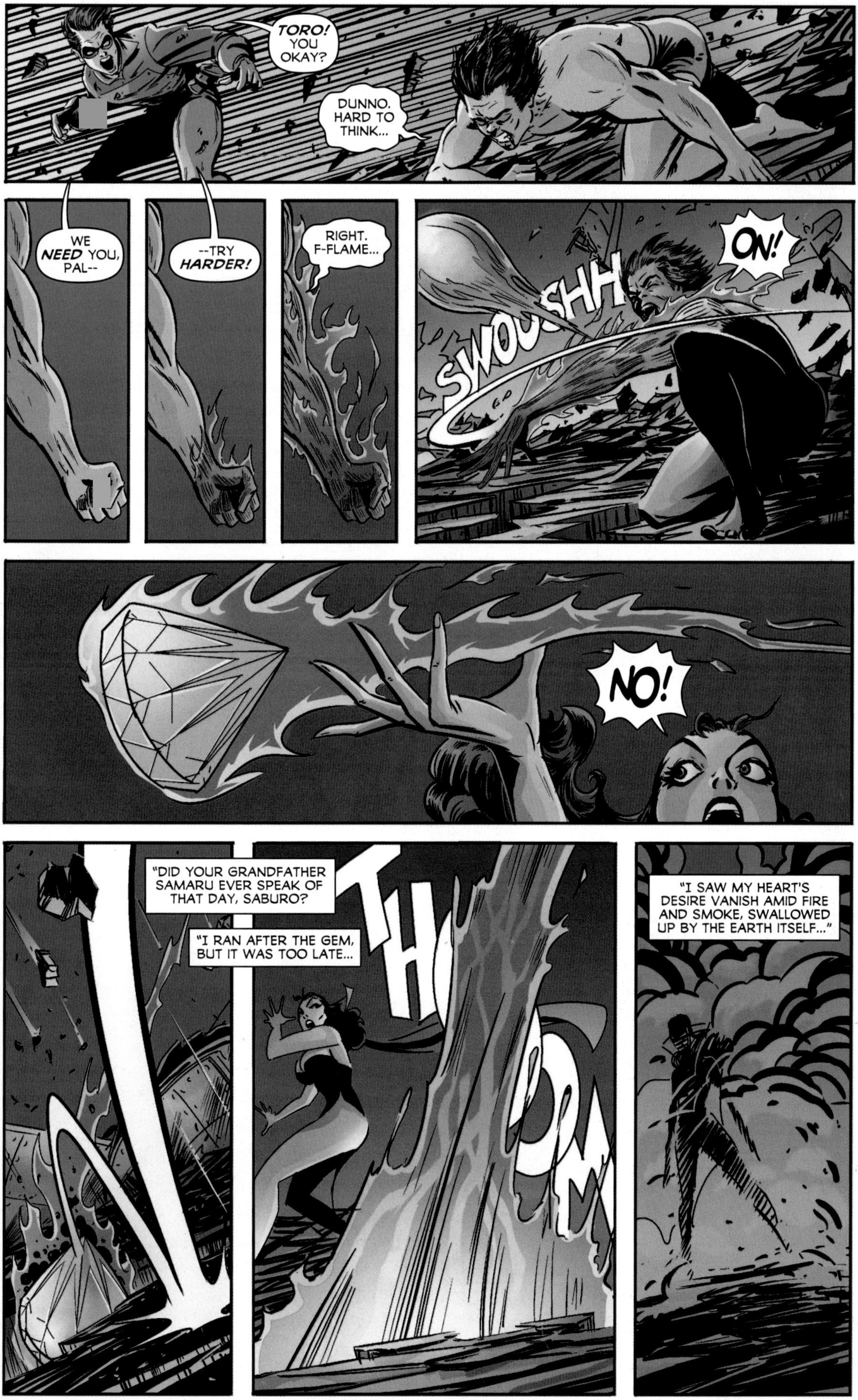

TORO! YOU OKAY?
DUNNO. HARD TO THINK...
WE NEED YOU, PAL--
--TRY HARDER!
RIGHT. F-FLAME...
SWOUSHH
ON!
NO!
"DID YOUR GRANDFATHER SAMARU EVER SPEAK OF THAT DAY, SABURO?
"I RAN AFTER THE GEM, BUT IT WAS TOO LATE...
"I SAW MY HEART'S DESIRE VANISH AMID FIRE AND SMOKE, SWALLOWED UP BY THE EARTH ITSELF..."

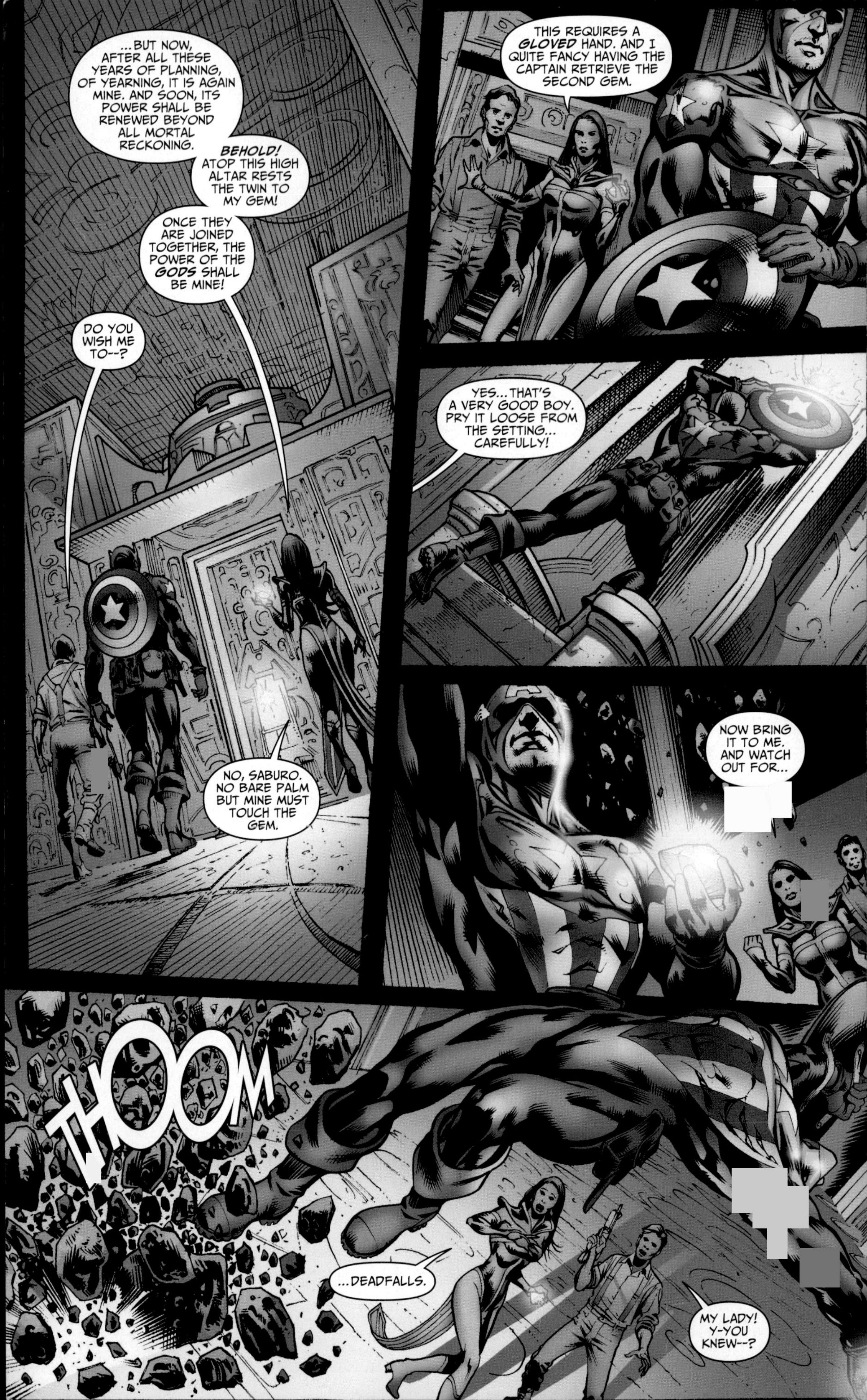
...BUT NOW, AFTER ALL THESE YEARS OF PLANNING, OF YEARNING, IT IS AGAIN MINE. AND SOON, ITS POWER SHALL BE RENEWED BEYOND ALL MORTAL RECKONING.
BEHOLD! ATOP THIS HIGH ALTAR RESTS THE TWIN TO MY GEM!
ONCE THEY ARE JOINED TOGETHER, THE POWER OF THE GODS SHALL BE MINE!
DO YOU WISH ME TO--?
NO, SABURO. NO BARE PALM BUT MINE MUST TOUCH THE GEM.
THIS REQUIRES A GLOVED HAND. AND I QUITE FANCY HAVING THE CAPTAIN RETRIEVE THE SECOND GEM.
YES... THAT'S A VERY GOOD BOY. PRY IT LOOSE FROM THE SETTING... CAREFULLY!
NOW BRING IT TO ME. AND WATCH OUT FOR...
THOOM
...DEADFALLS.
MY LADY! Y-YOU KNEW--?

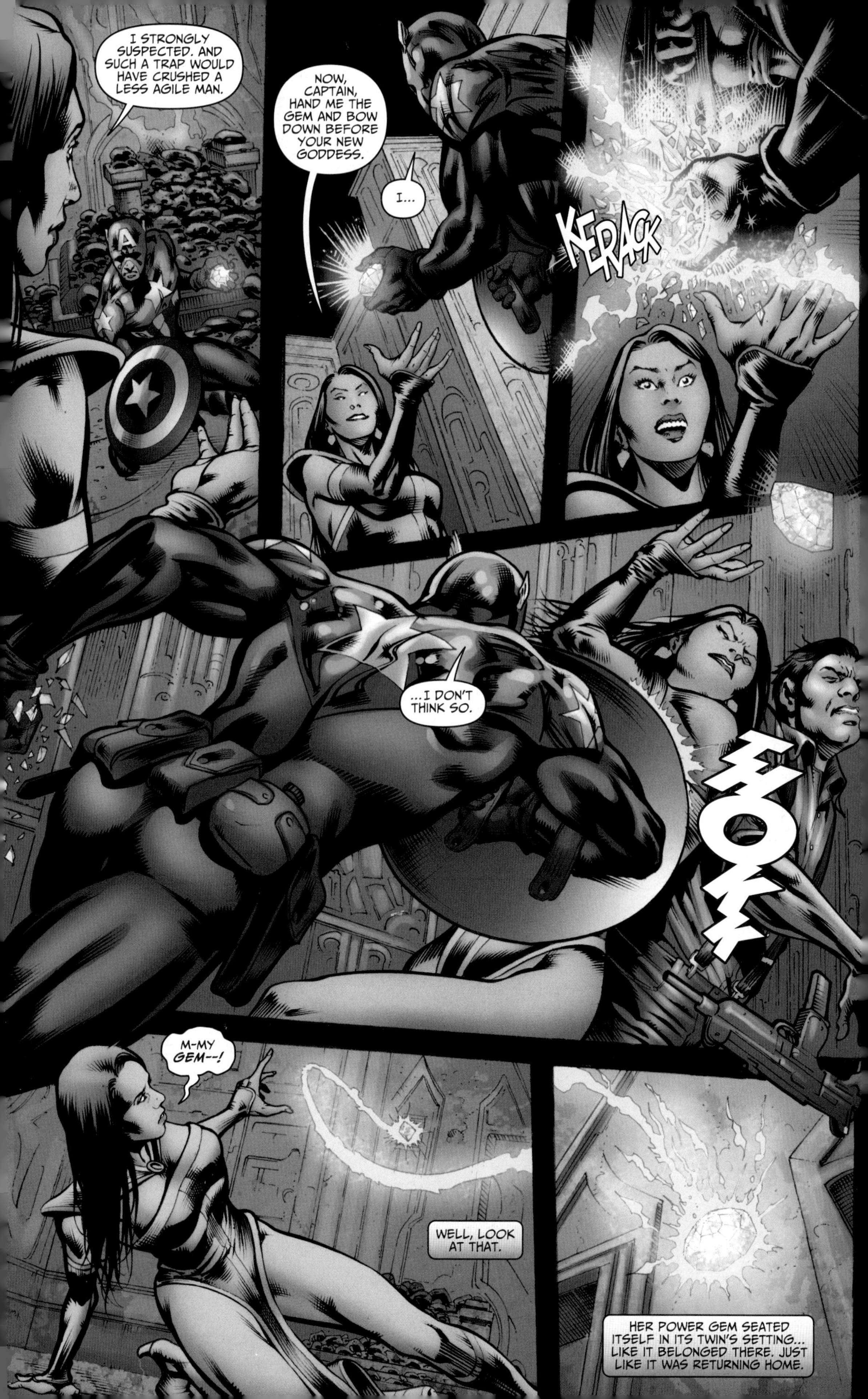
I STRONGLY SUSPECTED. AND SUCH A TRAP WOULD HAVE CRUSHED A LESS AGILE MAN.
NOW, CAPTAIN, HAND ME THE GEM AND BOW DOWN BEFORE YOUR NEW GODDESS.
I...
KERACK
...I DON'T THINK SO.
WOK
M-MY GEM--!
WELL, LOOK AT THAT.
HER POWER GEM SEATED ITSELF IN ITS TWIN'S SETTING... LIKE IT BELONGED THERE. JUST LIKE IT WAS RETURNING HOME.

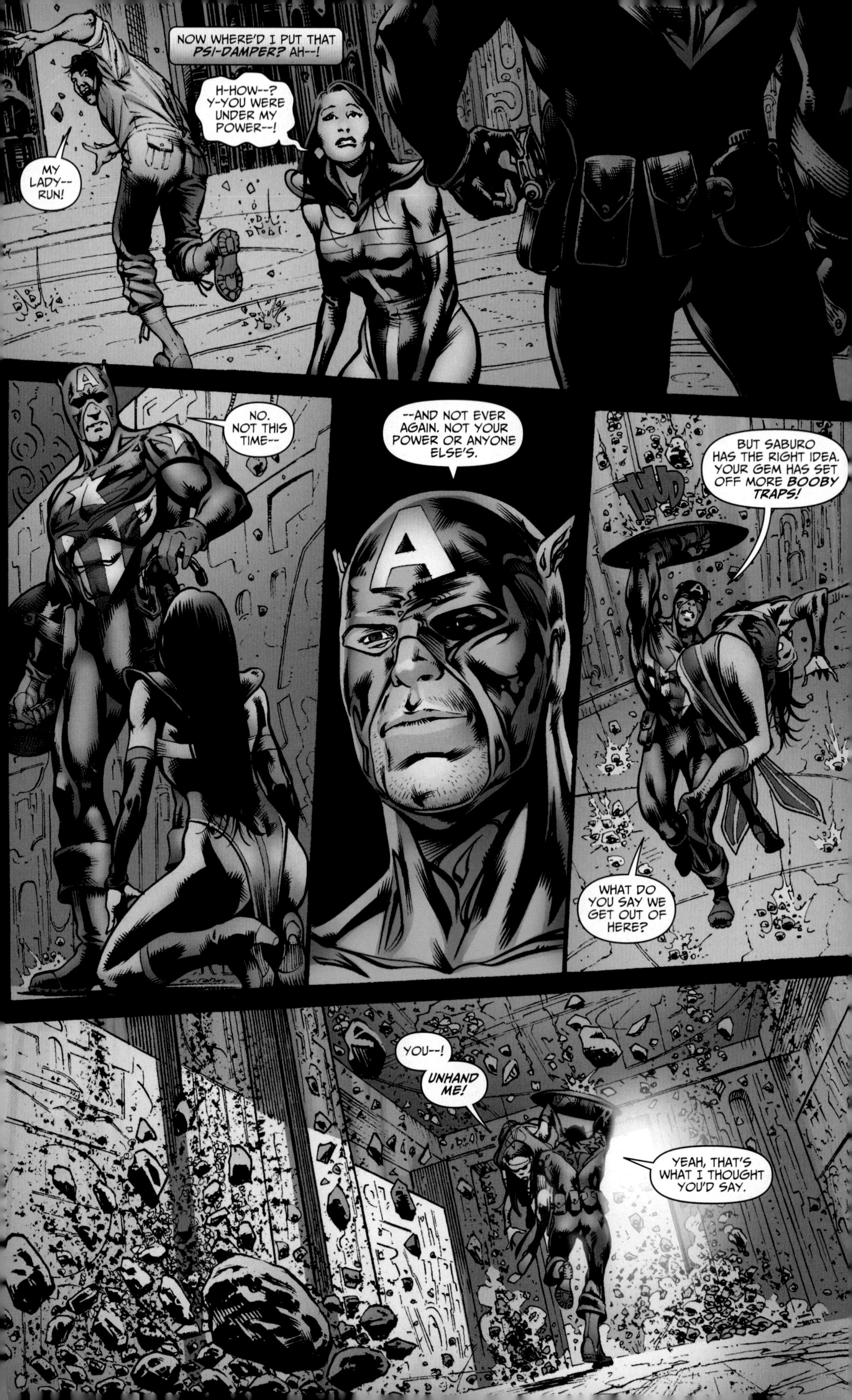
NOW WHERE'D I PUT THAT PSI-DAMPER? AH--!
H-HOW--? Y-YOU WERE UNDER MY POWER--!
MY LADY-- RUN!
NO. NOT THIS TIME--
--AND NOT EVER AGAIN. NOT YOUR POWER OR ANYONE ELSE'S.
THUD
BUT SABURO HAS THE RIGHT IDEA. YOUR GEM HAS SET OFF MORE BOOBY TRAPS!
WHAT DO YOU SAY WE GET OUT OF HERE?
YOU--! UNHAND ME!
YEAH, THAT'S WHAT I THOUGHT YOU'D SAY.

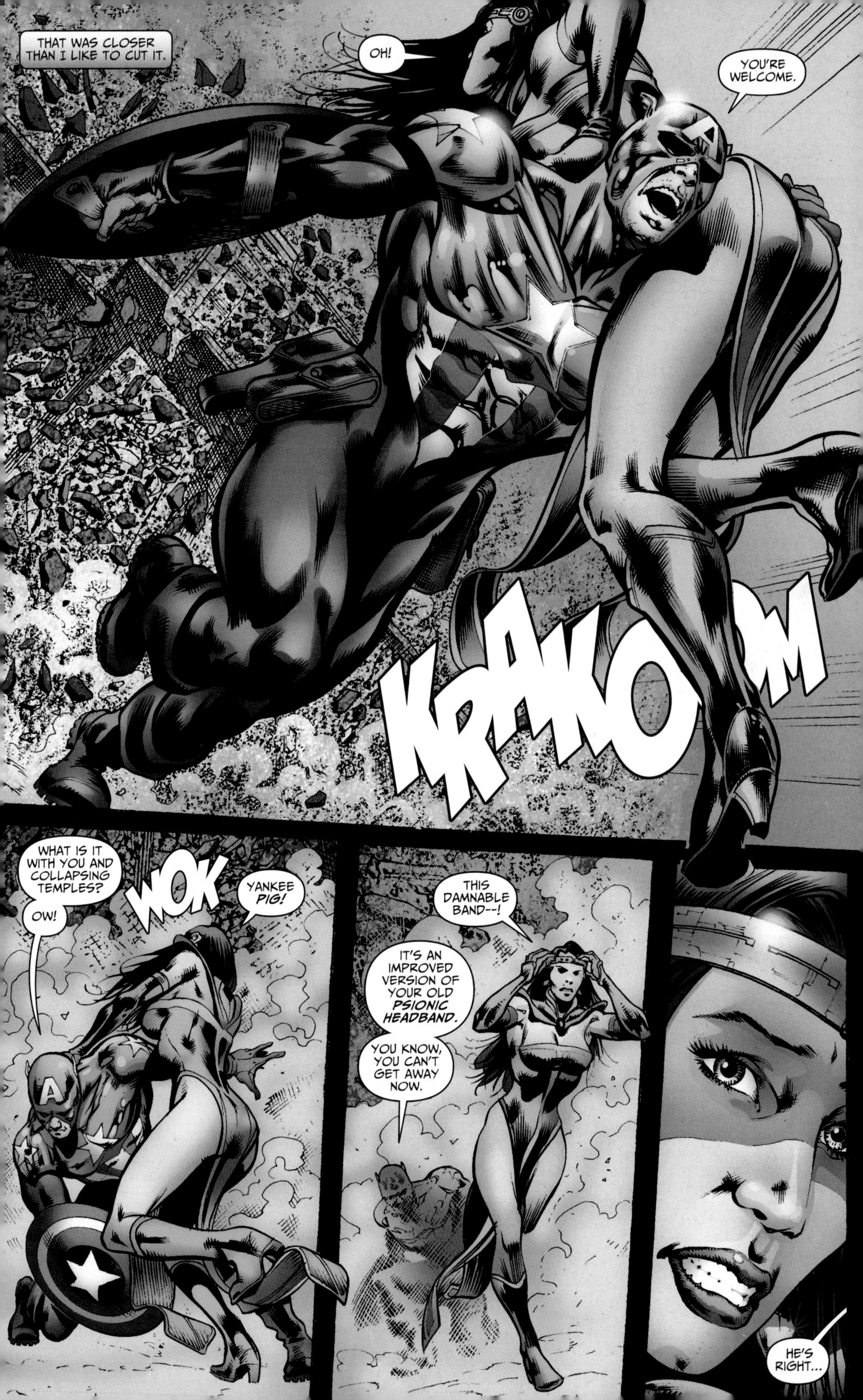
THAT WAS CLOSER THAN I LIKE TO CUT IT.
OH!
YOU'RE WELCOME.
KRAKOOM
WHAT IS IT WITH YOU AND COLLAPSING TEMPLES?
OW!
WOK
YANKEE PIG!
THIS DAMNABLE BAND--!
IT'S AN IMPROVED VERSION OF YOUR OLD PSIONIC HEADBAND.
YOU KNOW, YOU CAN'T GET AWAY NOW.
HE'S RIGHT...

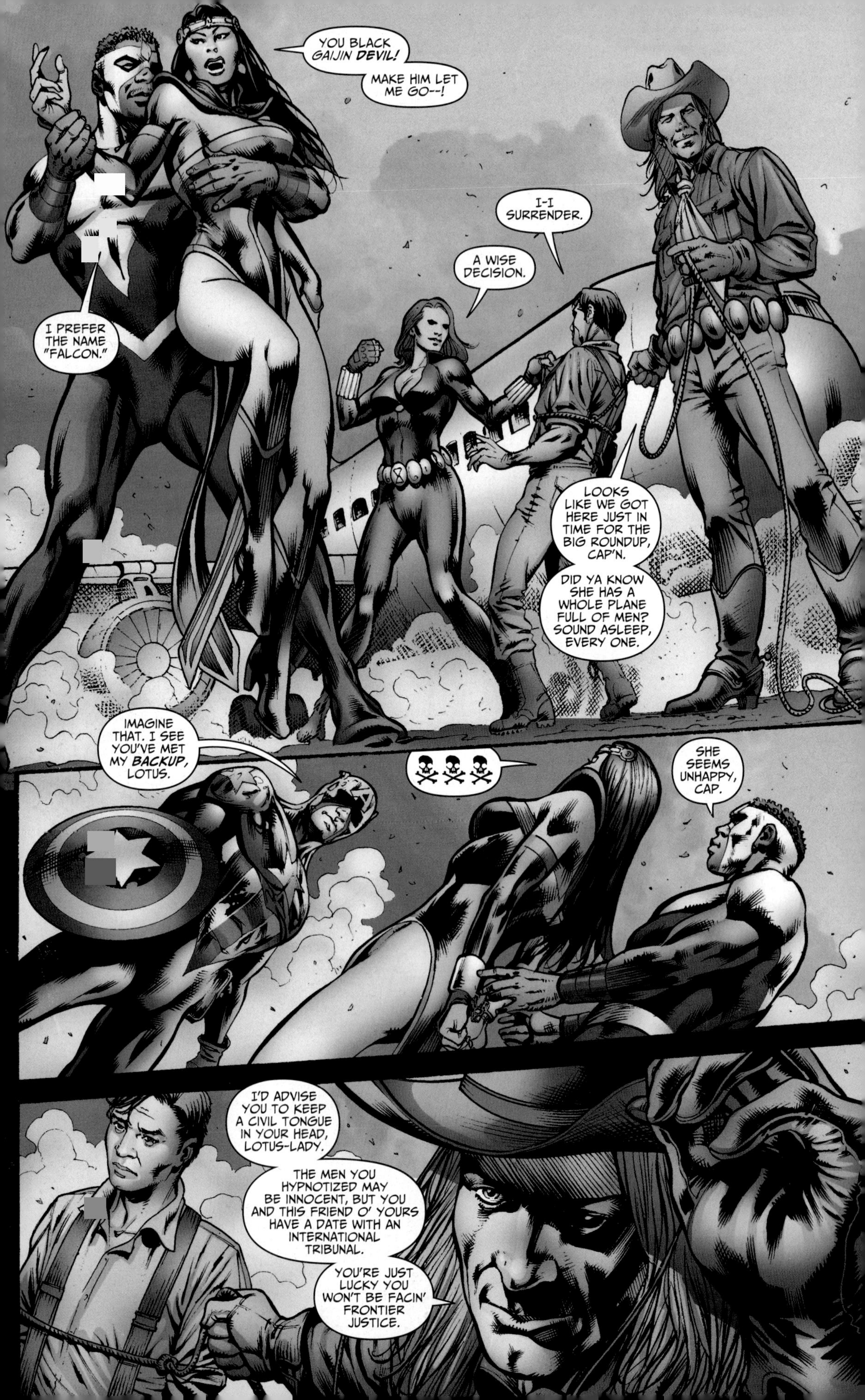
YOU BLACK GAIJIN DEVIL!
MAKE HIM LET ME GO--!
I PREFER THE NAME "FALCON."
I-I SURRENDER.
A WISE DECISION.
LOOKS LIKE WE GOT HERE JUST IN TIME FOR THE BIG ROUNDUP, CAP'N.
DID YA KNOW SHE HAS A WHOLE PLANE FULL OF MEN? SOUND ASLEEP, EVERY ONE.
IMAGINE THAT. I SEE YOU'VE MET MY BACKUP, LOTUS.
SHE SEEMS UNHAPPY, CAP.
I'D ADVISE YOU TO KEEP A CIVIL TONGUE IN YOUR HEAD, LOTUS-LADY.
THE MEN YOU HYPNOTIZED MAY BE INNOCENT, BUT YOU AND THIS FRIEND O' YOURS HAVE A DATE WITH AN INTERNATIONAL TRIBUNAL.
YOU'RE JUST LUCKY YOU WON'T BE FACIN' FRONTIER JUSTICE.

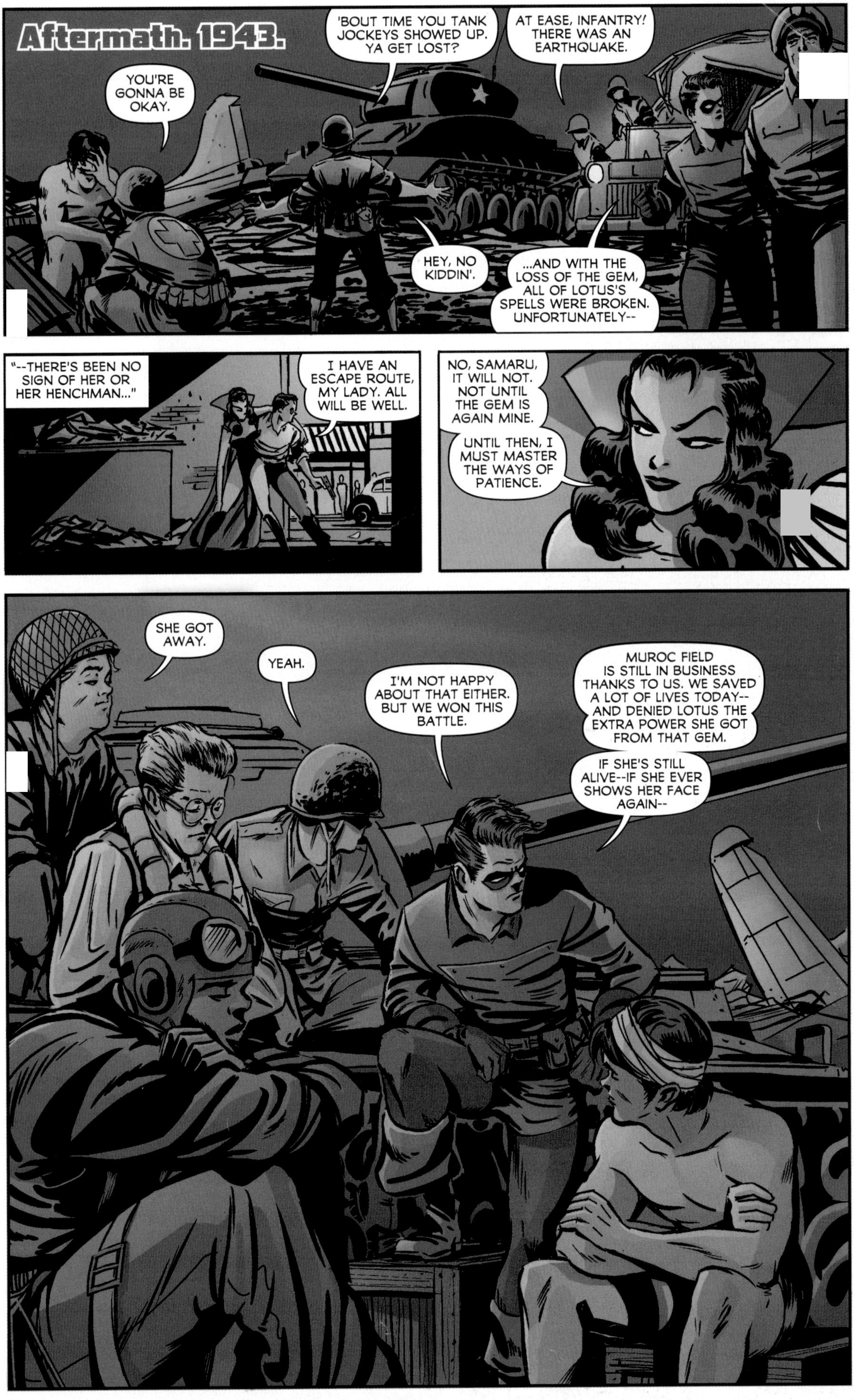
Aftermath. 1943.
YOU'RE GONNA BE OKAY.
'BOUT TIME YOU TANK JOCKEYS SHOWED UP. YA GET LOST?
AT EASE, INFANTRY! THERE WAS AN EARTHQUAKE.
HEY, NO KIDDIN'.
...AND WITH THE LOSS OF THE GEM, ALL OF LOTUS'S SPELLS WERE BROKEN. UNFORTUNATELY--
"--THERE'S BEEN NO SIGN OF HER OR HER HENCHMAN..."
I HAVE AN ESCAPE ROUTE, MY LADY. ALL WILL BE WELL.
NO, SAMARU, IT WILL NOT. NOT UNTIL THE GEM IS AGAIN MINE.
UNTIL THEN, I MUST MASTER THE WAYS OF PATIENCE.
SHE GOT AWAY.
YEAH.
I'M NOT HAPPY ABOUT THAT EITHER. BUT WE WON THIS BATTLE.
MUROC FIELD IS STILL IN BUSINESS THANKS TO US. WE SAVED A LOT OF LIVES TODAY-- AND DENIED LOTUS THE EXTRA POWER SHE GOT FROM THAT GEM.
IF SHE'S STILL ALIVE--IF SHE EVER SHOWS HER FACE AGAIN--

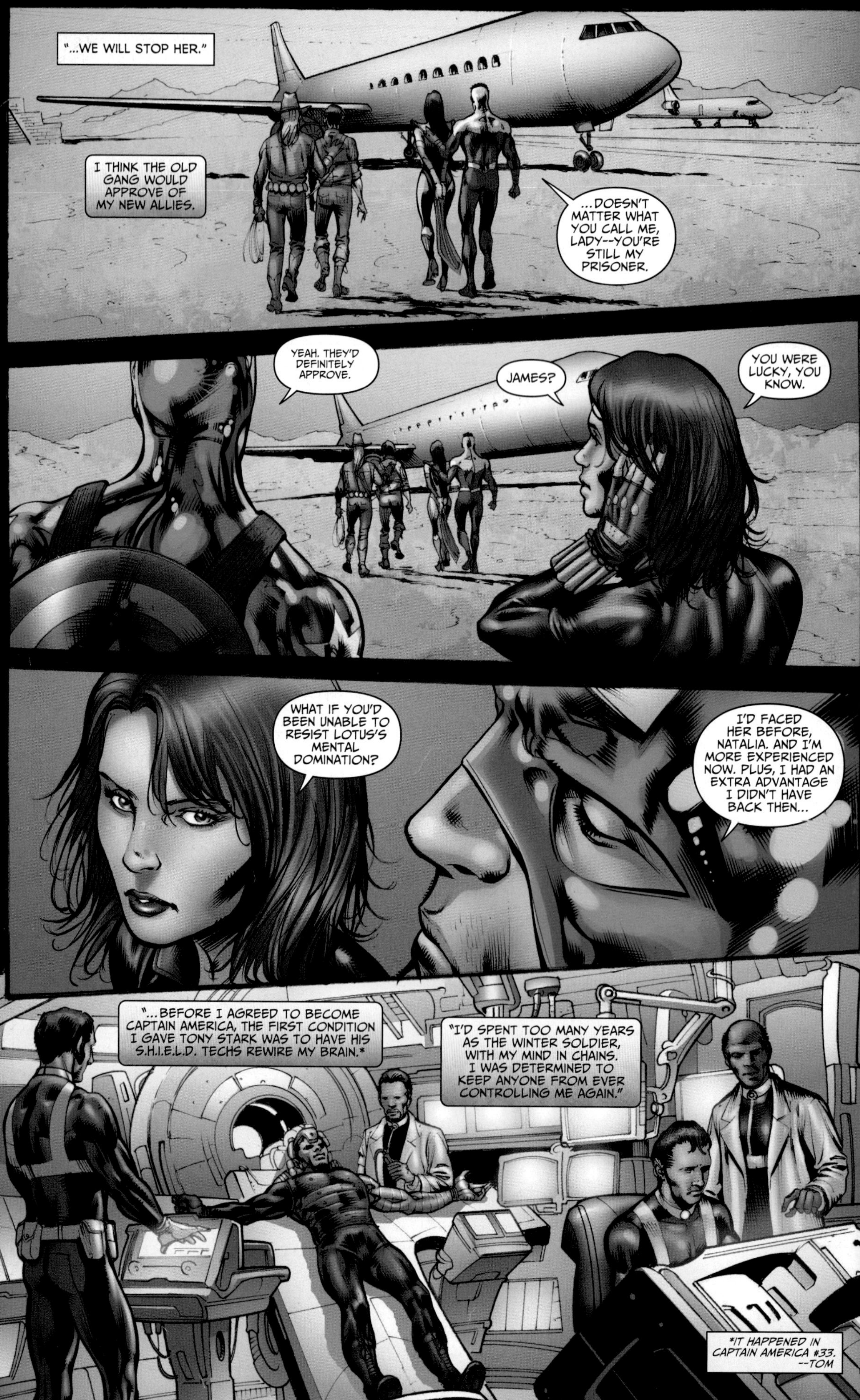
"...WE WILL STOP HER."
I THINK THE OLD GANG WOULD APPROVE OF MY NEW ALLIES.
...DOESN'T MATTER WHAT YOU CALL ME, LADY--YOU'RE STILL MY PRISONER.
YEAH. THEY'D DEFINITELY APPROVE.
JAMES?
YOU WERE LUCKY, YOU KNOW.
WHAT IF YOU'D BEEN UNABLE TO RESIST LOTUS'S MENTAL DOMINATION?
I'D FACED HER BEFORE, NATALIA. AND I'M MORE EXPERIENCED NOW. PLUS, I HAD AN EXTRA ADVANTAGE I DIDN'T HAVE BACK THEN...
"...BEFORE I AGREED TO BECOME CAPTAIN AMERICA, THE FIRST CONDITION I GAVE TONY STARK WAS TO HAVE HIS S.H.I.E.L.D. TECHS REWIRE MY BRAIN.*
"I'D SPENT TOO MANY YEARS AS THE WINTER SOLDIER, WITH MY MIND IN CHAINS. I WAS DETERMINED TO KEEP ANYONE FROM EVER CONTROLLING ME AGAIN."
*IT HAPPENED IN CAPTAIN AMERICA #33. --TOM

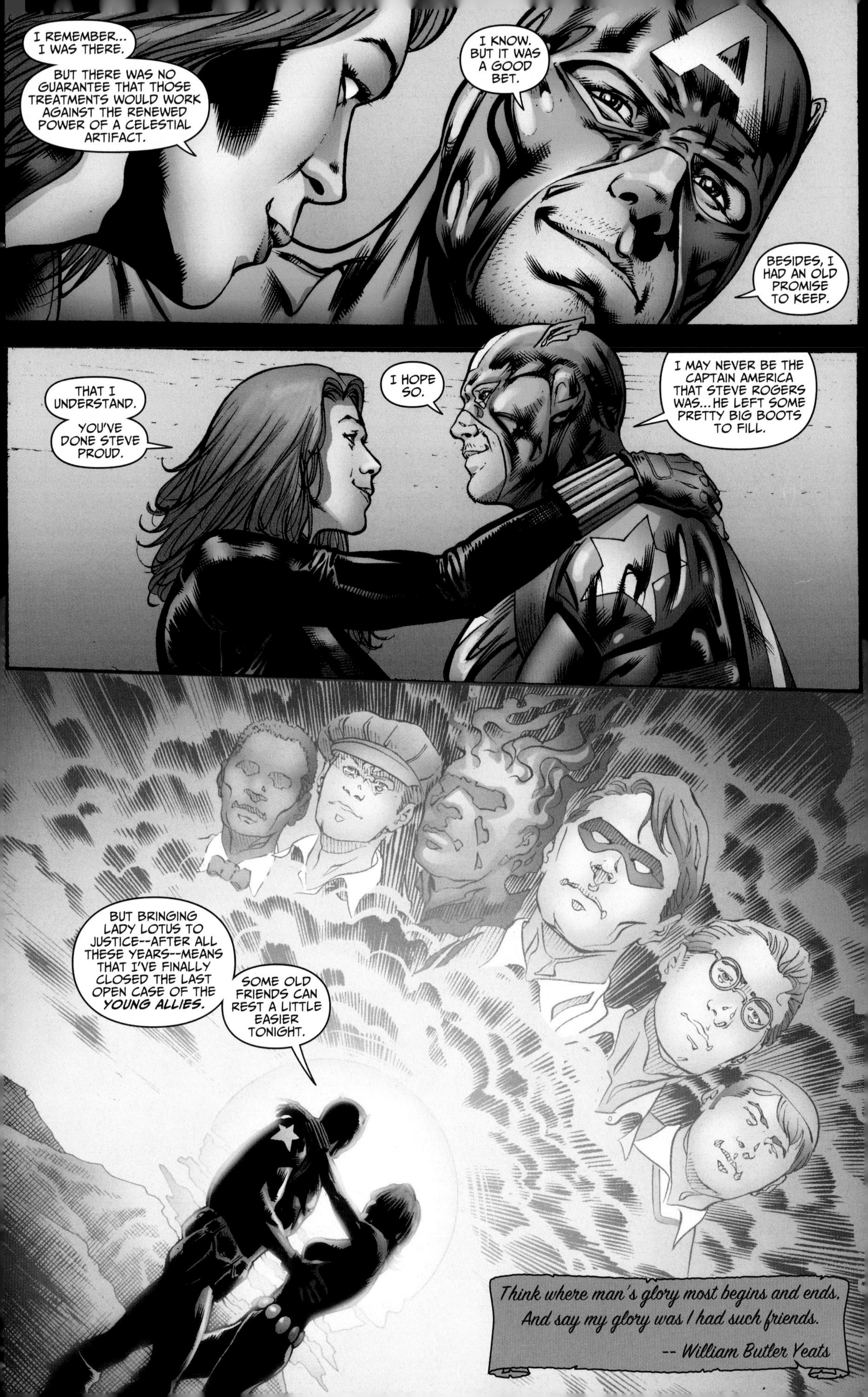
I REMEMBER... I WAS THERE.
BUT THERE WAS NO GUARANTEE THAT THOSE TREATMENTS WOULD WORK AGAINST THE RENEWED POWER OF A CELESTIAL ARTIFACT.
I KNOW. BUT IT WAS A GOOD BET.
BESIDES, I HAD AN OLD PROMISE TO KEEP.
THAT I UNDERSTAND.
YOU'VE DONE STEVE PROUD.
I HOPE SO.
I MAY NEVER BE THE CAPTAIN AMERICA THAT STEVE ROGERS WAS...HE LEFT SOME PRETTY BIG BOOTS TO FILL.
BUT BRINGING LADY LOTUS TO JUSTICE--AFTER ALL THESE YEARS--MEANS THAT I'VE FINALLY CLOSED THE LAST OPEN CASE OF THE *YOUNG ALLIES.*
SOME OLD FRIENDS CAN REST A LITTLE EASIER TONIGHT.
Think where man's glory most begins and ends,
And say my glory was I had such friends.
-- William Butler Yeats

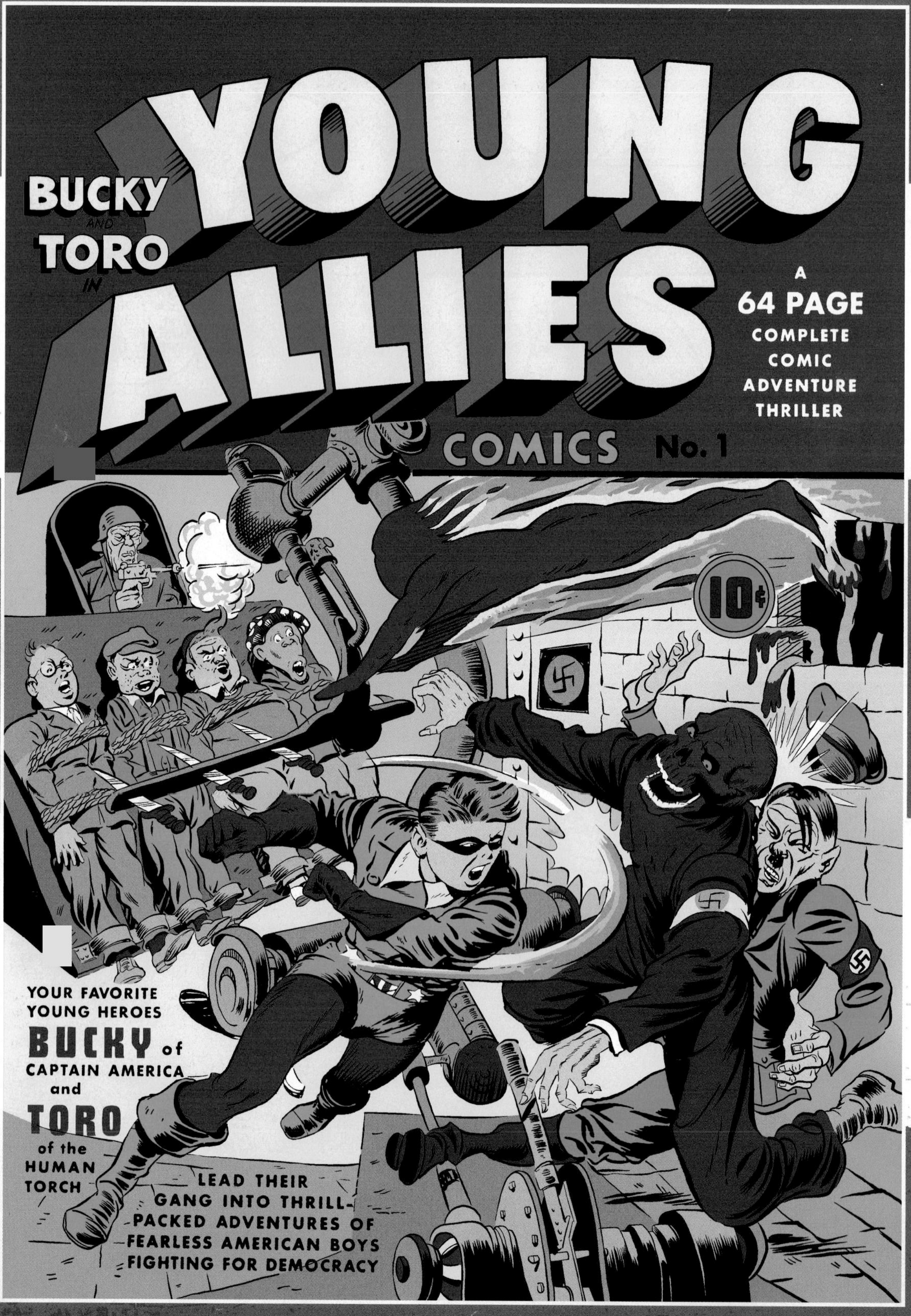
BUCKY AND TORO IN
YOUNG ALLIES
COMICS No. 1
A 64 PAGE COMPLETE COMIC ADVENTURE THRILLER
10¢
YOUR FAVORITE YOUNG HEROES
BUCKY of CAPTAIN AMERICA
and
TORO of the HUMAN TORCH
LEAD THEIR GANG INTO THRILL-PACKED ADVENTURES OF FEARLESS AMERICAN BOYS FIGHTING FOR DEMOCRACY

The YOUNG ALLIES

Vol. 1
No. 1
Summer Issue

JOE SIMON
Art editor

JACK KIRBY
Art director

The character TORO is from
the Human Torch.
By CARL BURGOS

TABLE OF CONTENTS

Have you read the new CAPTAIN AMERICA .. acclaimed by readers the greatest comic magazine in the world

YOUNG ALLIES is published quarterly by U. S. A. Comic Magazine Corp. at Meriden, Conn. Application for second class entry is pending at the Post Office, at Meriden, Conn., under act of March 3, 1879. Contents copyright 1941 by U. S. A. Comic Magazine Corp., 330 W. 42nd St., New York, N. Y. Single copies 10c. Yearly subscription 40c in the U. S. A. Summer, 1941 issue. Printed in the U.S.A.

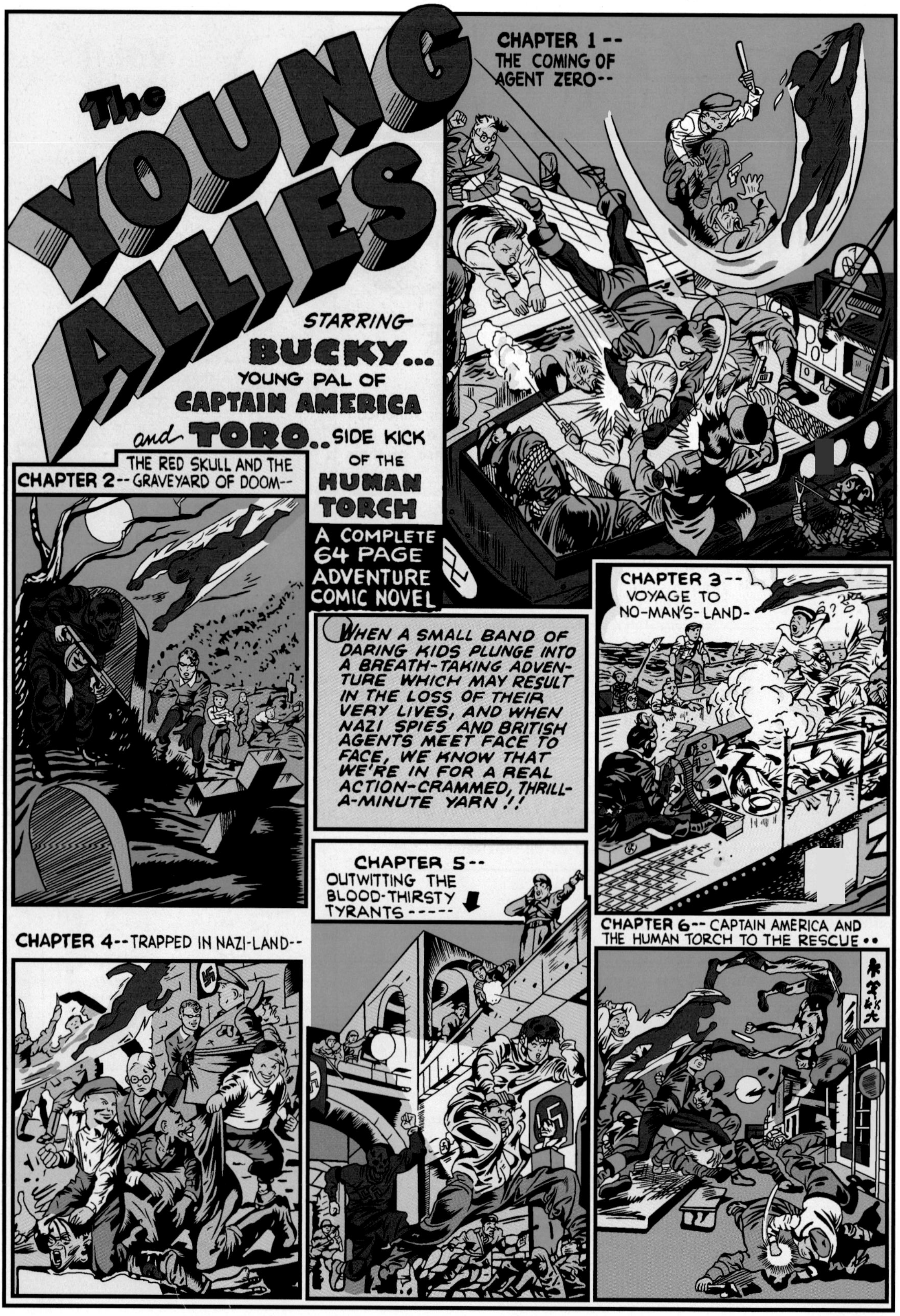

The YOUNG ALLIES
STARRING-
BUCKY...
YOUNG PAL OF
CAPTAIN AMERICA
and TORO.. SIDE KICK OF THE HUMAN TORCH
A COMPLETE 64 PAGE ADVENTURE COMIC NOVEL
CHAPTER 1 -- THE COMING OF AGENT ZERO--
CHAPTER 2-- THE RED SKULL AND THE GRAVEYARD OF DOOM--
WHEN A SMALL BAND OF DARING KIDS PLUNGE INTO A BREATH-TAKING ADVENTURE WHICH MAY RESULT IN THE LOSS OF THEIR VERY LIVES, AND WHEN NAZI SPIES AND BRITISH AGENTS MEET FACE TO FACE, WE KNOW THAT WE'RE IN FOR A REAL ACTION-CRAMMED, THRILL-A-MINUTE YARN !!
CHAPTER 3 -- VOYAGE TO NO-MAN'S-LAND-
CHAPTER 5 -- OUTWITTING THE BLOOD-THIRSTY TYRANTS -----
CHAPTER 4--TRAPPED IN NAZI-LAND--
CHAPTER 6-- CAPTAIN AMERICA AND THE HUMAN TORCH TO THE RESCUE ••

SUDDENLY -- THE STILL NIGHT AIR IS SHATTERED BY A SERIES OF SHOTS --

RAT-TAT-TAT-TAT-

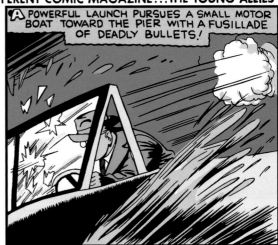

A POWERFUL LAUNCH PURSUES A SMALL MOTOR BOAT TOWARD THE PIER WITH A FUSILLADE OF DEADLY BULLETS!

Before THE FLEEING MOTOR BOAT CRASHES HEADLONG INTO THE PIER, ITS PILOT MAKES A DESPERATE LEAP TO THE DOCK AND SAFETY!

GOT TO GET AWAY FROM THOSE SPIES! GOT TO!

COME ON! DON'T LET HIM ESCAPE!

THE YOUNG MAN BEING PURSUED DESPERATELY DASHES INTO A SHACK ON THE DOCK!

HE CAN'T GET AWAY NOW! WE HAVE HIM TRAPPED!

2.

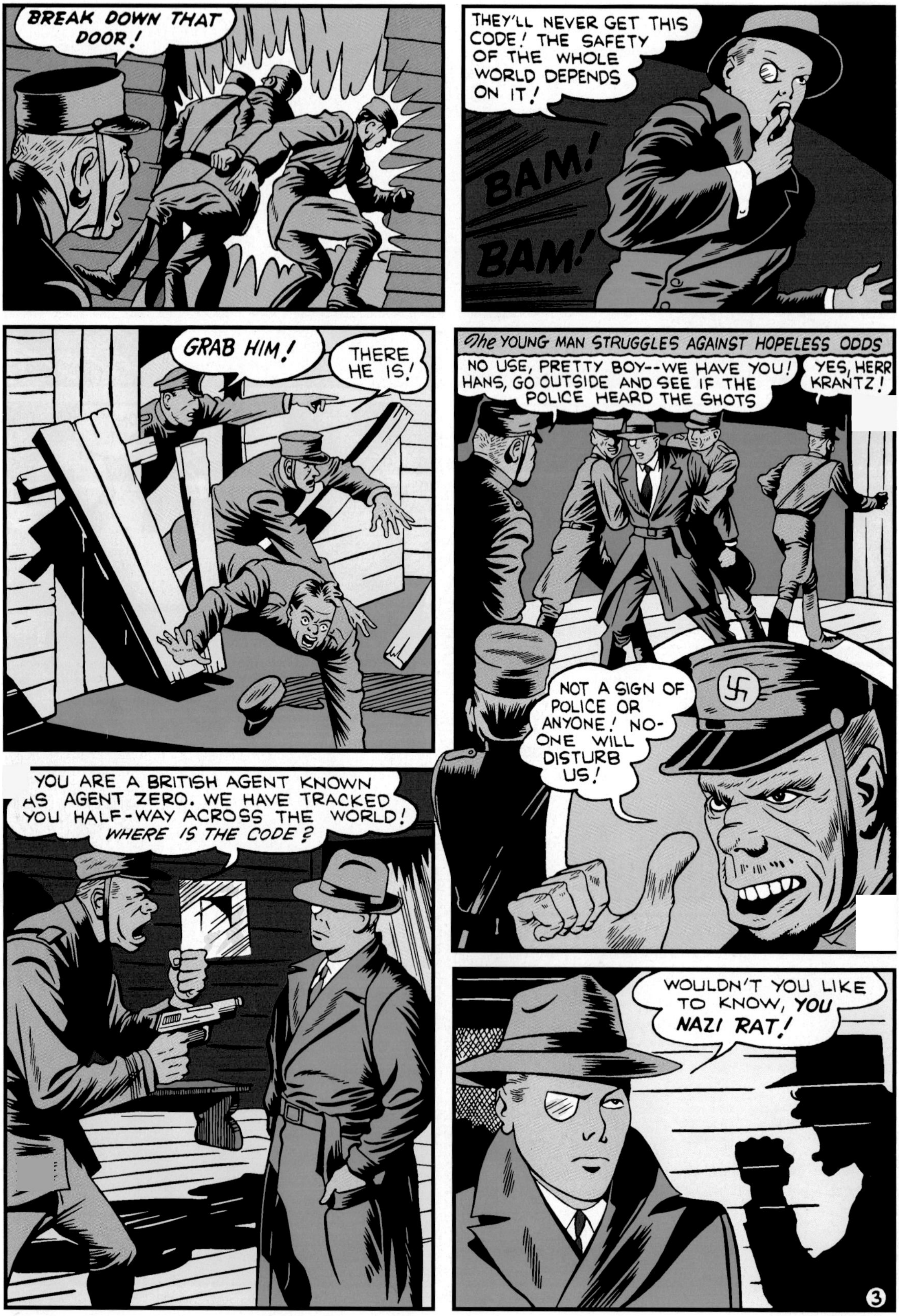
BREAK DOWN THAT DOOR!
THEY'LL NEVER GET THIS CODE! THE SAFETY OF THE WHOLE WORLD DEPENDS ON IT!
BAM!
BAM!
GRAB HIM!
THERE HE IS!
The YOUNG MAN STRUGGLES AGAINST HOPELESS ODDS
NO USE, PRETTY BOY--WE HAVE YOU! HANS, GO OUTSIDE AND SEE IF THE POLICE HEARD THE SHOTS
YES, HERR KRANTZ!
NOT A SIGN OF POLICE OR ANYONE! NO-ONE WILL DISTURB US!
YOU ARE A BRITISH AGENT KNOWN AS AGENT ZERO. WE HAVE TRACKED YOU HALF-WAY ACROSS THE WORLD! WHERE IS THE CODE?
WOULDN'T YOU LIKE TO KNOW, YOU NAZI RAT!
3

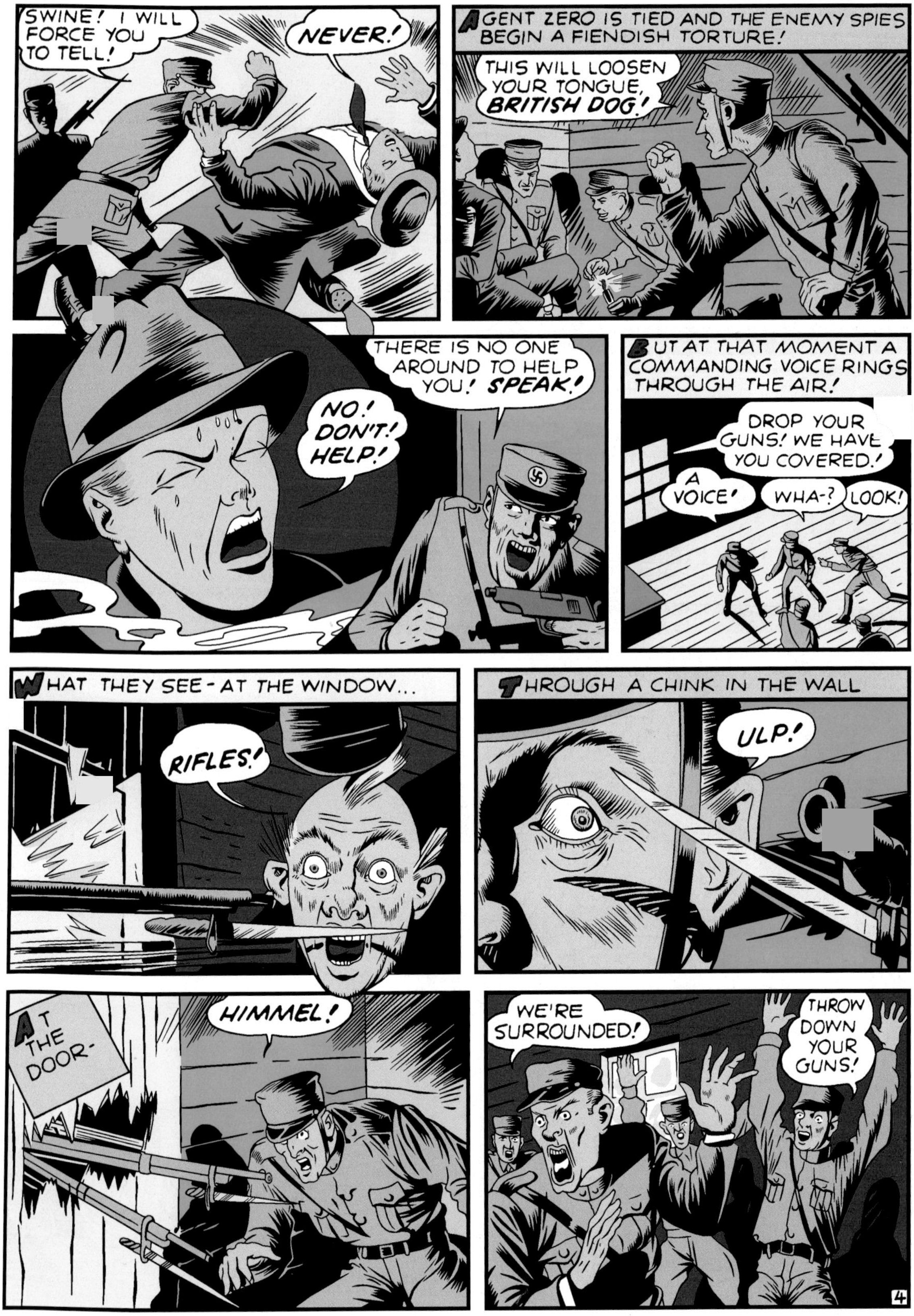
SWINE! I WILL FORCE YOU TO TELL!
NEVER!
AGENT ZERO IS TIED AND THE ENEMY SPIES BEGIN A FIENDISH TORTURE!
THIS WILL LOOSEN YOUR TONGUE, BRITISH DOG!
THERE IS NO ONE AROUND TO HELP YOU! SPEAK!
NO! DON'T! HELP!
BUT AT THAT MOMENT A COMMANDING VOICE RINGS THROUGH THE AIR!
DROP YOUR GUNS! WE HAVE YOU COVERED!
A VOICE!
WHA-?
LOOK!
WHAT THEY SEE - AT THE WINDOW...
RIFLES!
THROUGH A CHINK IN THE WALL
ULP!
AT THE DOOR-
HIMMEL!
WE'RE SURROUNDED!
THROW DOWN YOUR GUNS!
4

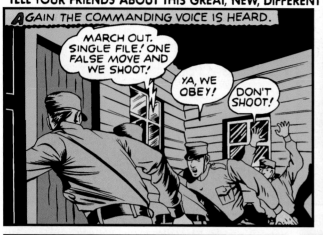

AGAIN THE COMMANDING VOICE IS HEARD.

MARCH OUT. SINGLE FILE! ONE FALSE MOVE AND WE SHOOT!

YA, WE OBEY!

DON'T SHOOT!

AS THE LAST OF THE SPY GANG LEAVES THE SHACK...

DON'T TURN AROUND - GET IN YOUR LAUNCH AND LEAVE!

WE'LL LET YOU GO THIS TIME BUT IF WE EVER SEE YOU AGAIN--

YA, WE GO!

YOU ARE KIND!

THE STUPID, SENTIMENTAL AMERICANS LET US GO! HAD THEY BEEN IN OUR PLACE, WE WOULD HAVE SHOT THEM!

WHEW! THEY FELL FOR IT. IF THEY FOUND OUT THESE GUNS ARE WOODEN, WE MIGHT HAVE BEEN AT THE END OF THEIR REAL GUNS!

SHUCKS! I COULDA LICKED 'EM WIT' ME BARE FISTS!

IS EVERYTHING OKAY, BUCKY?

HA, HA, DID WE TRICK 'EM!

IT'S EASY TO TALK, KNUCKLES. BUT THEY HAD *REAL* GUNS!

SO WHAT?

5

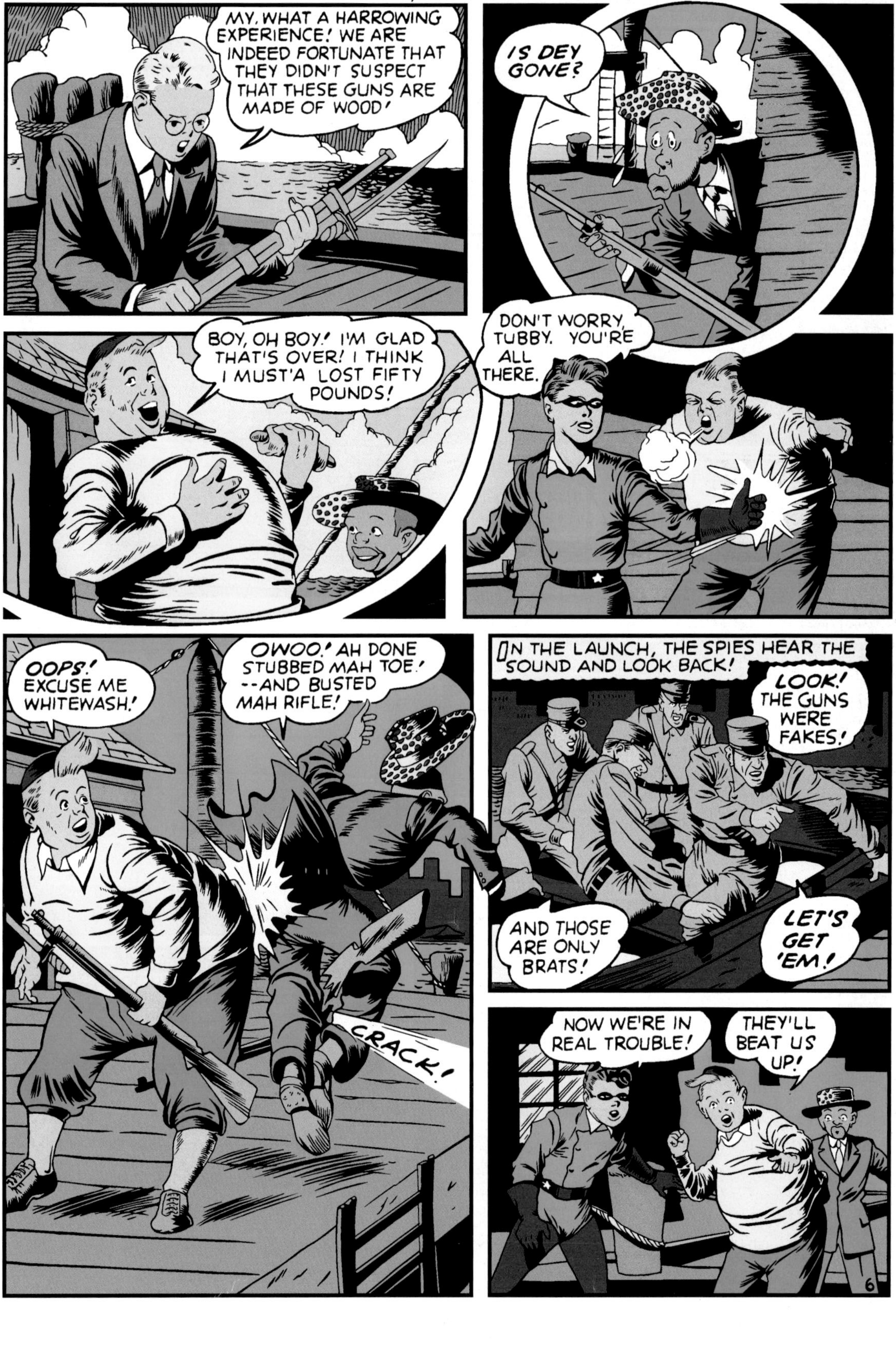
MY, WHAT A HARROWING EXPERIENCE! WE ARE INDEED FORTUNATE THAT THEY DIDN'T SUSPECT THAT THESE GUNS ARE MADE OF WOOD!
IS DEY GONE?
BOY, OH BOY! I'M GLAD THAT'S OVER! I THINK I MUST'A LOST FIFTY POUNDS!
DON'T WORRY, TUBBY. YOU'RE ALL THERE.
OOPS! EXCUSE ME WHITEWASH!
OWOO! AH DONE STUBBED MAH TOE! --AND BUSTED MAH RIFLE!
CRACK!
ON THE LAUNCH, THE SPIES HEAR THE SOUND AND LOOK BACK!
LOOK! THE GUNS WERE FAKES!
AND THOSE ARE ONLY BRATS!
LET'S GET 'EM!
NOW WE'RE IN REAL TROUBLE!
THEY'LL BEAT US UP!

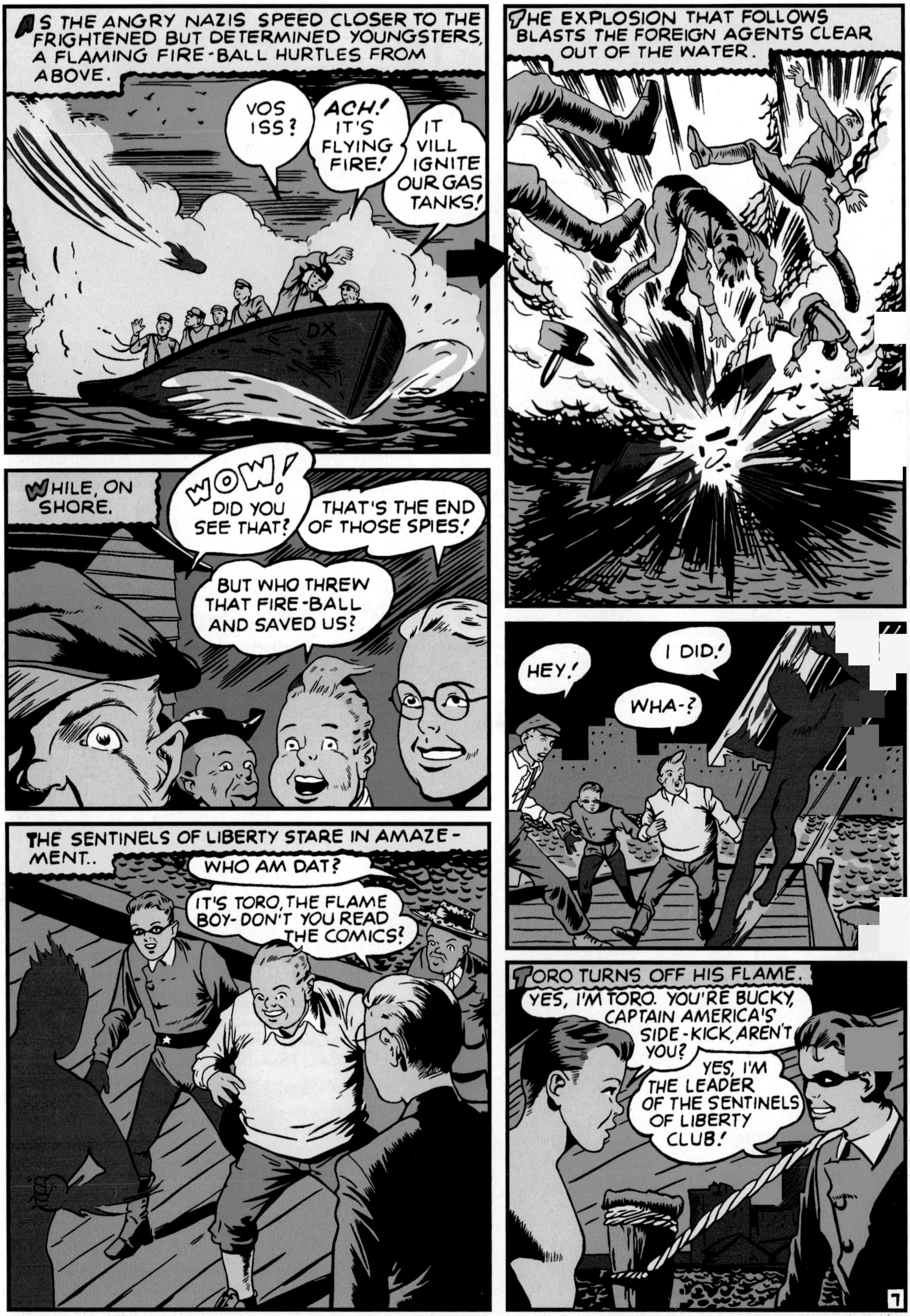

AS THE ANGRY NAZIS SPEED CLOSER TO THE FRIGHTENED BUT DETERMINED YOUNGSTERS, A FLAMING FIRE-BALL HURTLES FROM ABOVE.
VOS ISS?
ACH! IT'S FLYING FIRE!
IT VILL IGNITE OUR GAS TANKS!
DX
THE EXPLOSION THAT FOLLOWS BLASTS THE FOREIGN AGENTS CLEAR OUT OF THE WATER.
WHILE, ON SHORE.
WOW! DID YOU SEE THAT?
THAT'S THE END OF THOSE SPIES!
BUT WHO THREW THAT FIRE-BALL AND SAVED US?
HEY!
I DID!
WHA-?
THE SENTINELS OF LIBERTY STARE IN AMAZE-MENT..
WHO AM DAT?
IT'S TORO, THE FLAME BOY- DON'T YOU READ THE COMICS?
TORO TURNS OFF HIS FLAME.
YES, I'M TORO. YOU'RE BUCKY, CAPTAIN AMERICA'S SIDE-KICK, AREN'T YOU?
YES, I'M THE LEADER OF THE SENTINELS OF LIBERTY CLUB!
7

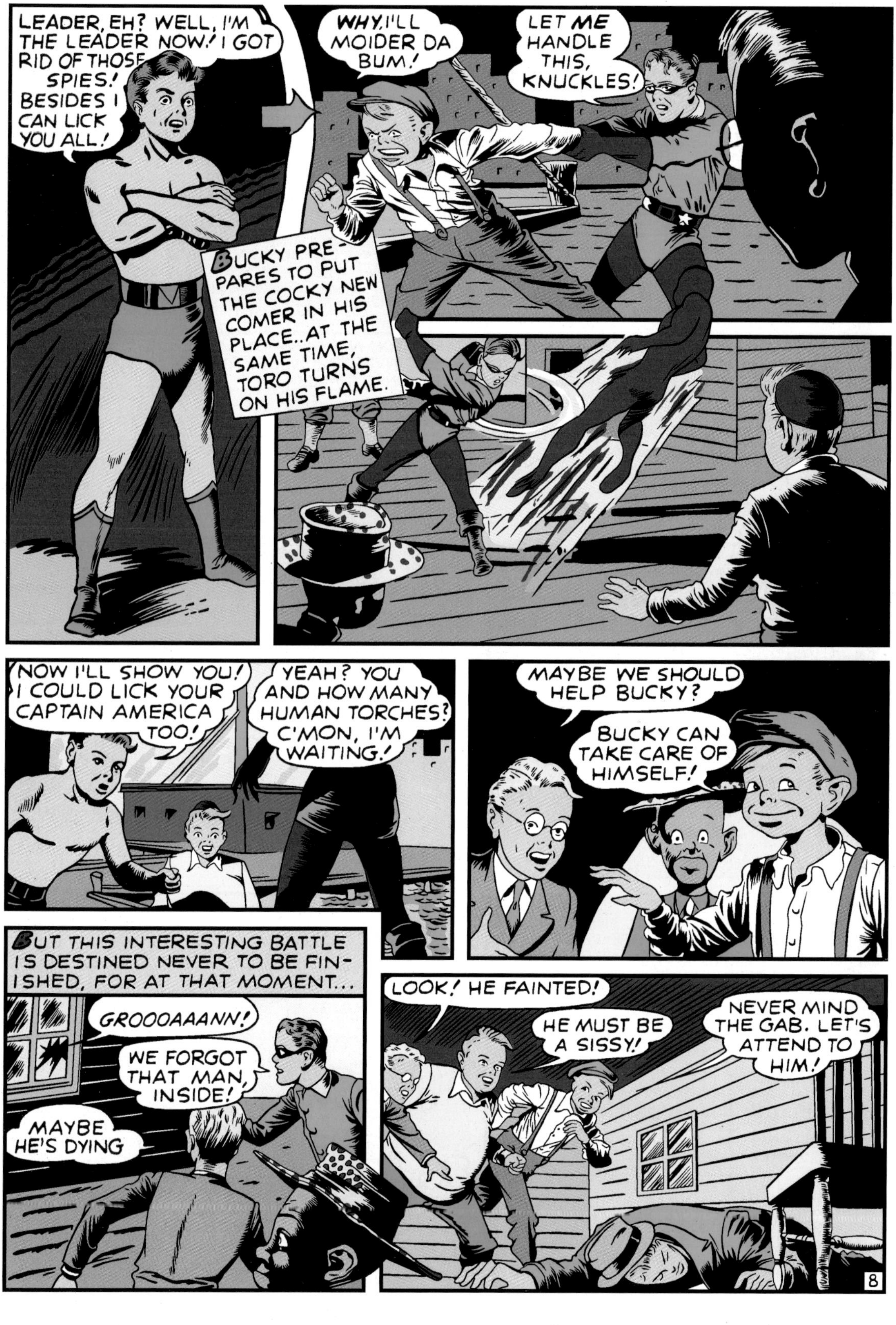
LEADER, EH? WELL, I'M THE LEADER NOW! I GOT RID OF THOSE SPIES! BESIDES I CAN LICK YOU ALL!
WHY, I'LL MOIDER DA BUM!
LET ME HANDLE THIS, KNUCKLES!
BUCKY PREPARES TO PUT THE COCKY NEW COMER IN HIS PLACE..AT THE SAME TIME, TORO TURNS ON HIS FLAME.
NOW I'LL SHOW YOU! I COULD LICK YOUR CAPTAIN AMERICA TOO!
YEAH? YOU AND HOW MANY HUMAN TORCHES? C'MON, I'M WAITING!
MAYBE WE SHOULD HELP BUCKY?
BUCKY CAN TAKE CARE OF HIMSELF!
BUT THIS INTERESTING BATTLE IS DESTINED NEVER TO BE FINISHED, FOR AT THAT MOMENT...
GROOOAAANN!
WE FORGOT THAT MAN, INSIDE!
MAYBE HE'S DYING
LOOK! HE FAINTED!
HE MUST BE A SISSY!
NEVER MIND THE GAB. LET'S ATTEND TO HIM!
8

A SHORT TIME LATER, THE RESCUED MAN REVIVES UNDER THE BOYS' FIRST AID

I'D LIKE TO THANK YOU YOUNG CHAPS...AND... EXCUSE ME FOR FAINTING!

WHAT'S YOUR NAME, SIR?

I CAN'T REVEAL MY REAL NAME. CALL ME - AGENT ZERO.. I WORK FOR THE BRITISH GOVERN - MENT.

I'M BUCKY, I'LL INTRODUCE THE OTHERS.

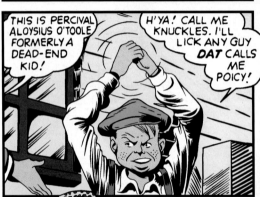

THIS IS PERCIVAL ALOYSIUS O'TOOLE FORMERLY A DEAD-END KID!

H'YA! CALL ME KNUCKLES. I'LL LICK ANY GUY DAT CALLS ME POICY!

JEFFERSON WORTHINGTON SANDERVILT, A BOY INVENTOR WHOSE PARENTS ARE IN WHO'S WHO!

I AM HONORED TO MAKE YOUR ACQUAINTANCE!

WHITEWASH JONES, WHO CAN MAKE A HARMONICA TALK!

YEAH MAN! I IS ALSO GOOD ON DE WATER-MELON!

AND LAST BUT NOT LEAST, HENRY TINKLE, FUGITIVE FROM A CIRCUS. WE CALL HIM TUBBY.

PLEASED TA MEETCHA (MUNCH! MUNCH!)

WE ARE MEMBERS OF THE NATION-WIDE SENTINELS OF LIBERTY CLUB. THIS IS OUR CLUBHOUSE. WE'VE BEEN MEETING HERE EVERY NIGHT, AND PRACTICING WAR MANEUVERS AGAINST IN-VASION. WE CALL OURSELVES THE YOUNG ALLIES.

YOUNG ALLIES! HMMM! PERHAPS YOU CAN HELP ME ... I MUST SEND A MESSAGE

WE HAVE A SHORT WAVE RADIO TRANSMITTER

GOOD THING WE MADE OUR WOODEN GUNS LOOK SO REAL THAT THEY FOOLED THE SPIES!

9

TELL YOUR FRIENDS ABOUT THIS GREAT, NEW, DIFFERENT COMIC MAGAZINE...THE YOUNG ALLIES

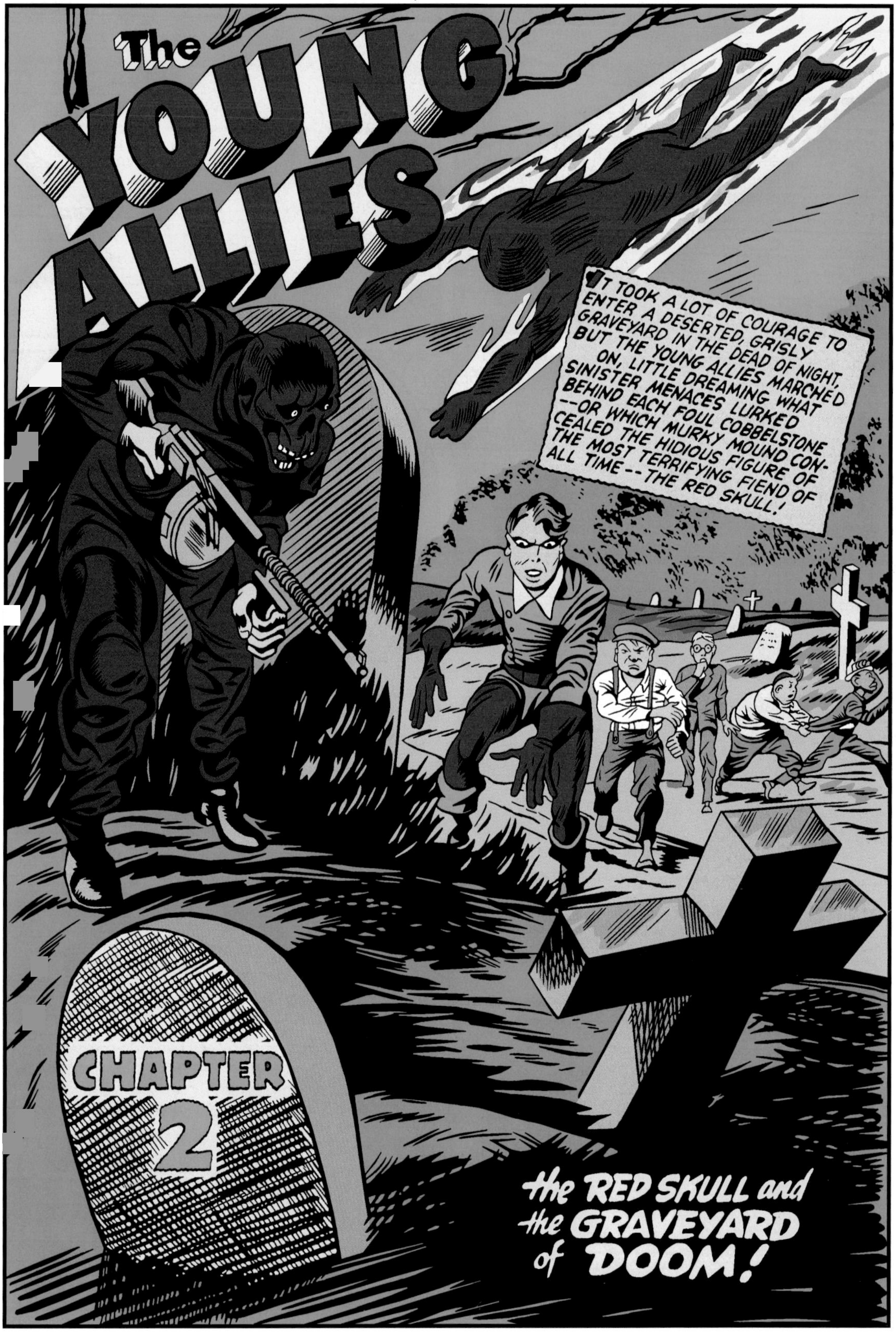
The YOUNG ALLIES
IT TOOK A LOT OF COURAGE TO ENTER A DESERTED, GRISLY GRAVEYARD IN THE DEAD OF NIGHT, BUT THE YOUNG ALLIES MARCHED ON, LITTLE DREAMING WHAT SINISTER MENACES LURKED BEHIND EACH FOUL COBBELSTONE --OR WHICH MURKY MOUND CONCEALED THE HIDIOUS FIGURE OF THE MOST TERRIFYING FIEND OF ALL TIME--THE RED SKULL!
CHAPTER 2
the RED SKULL and the GRAVEYARD of DOOM!

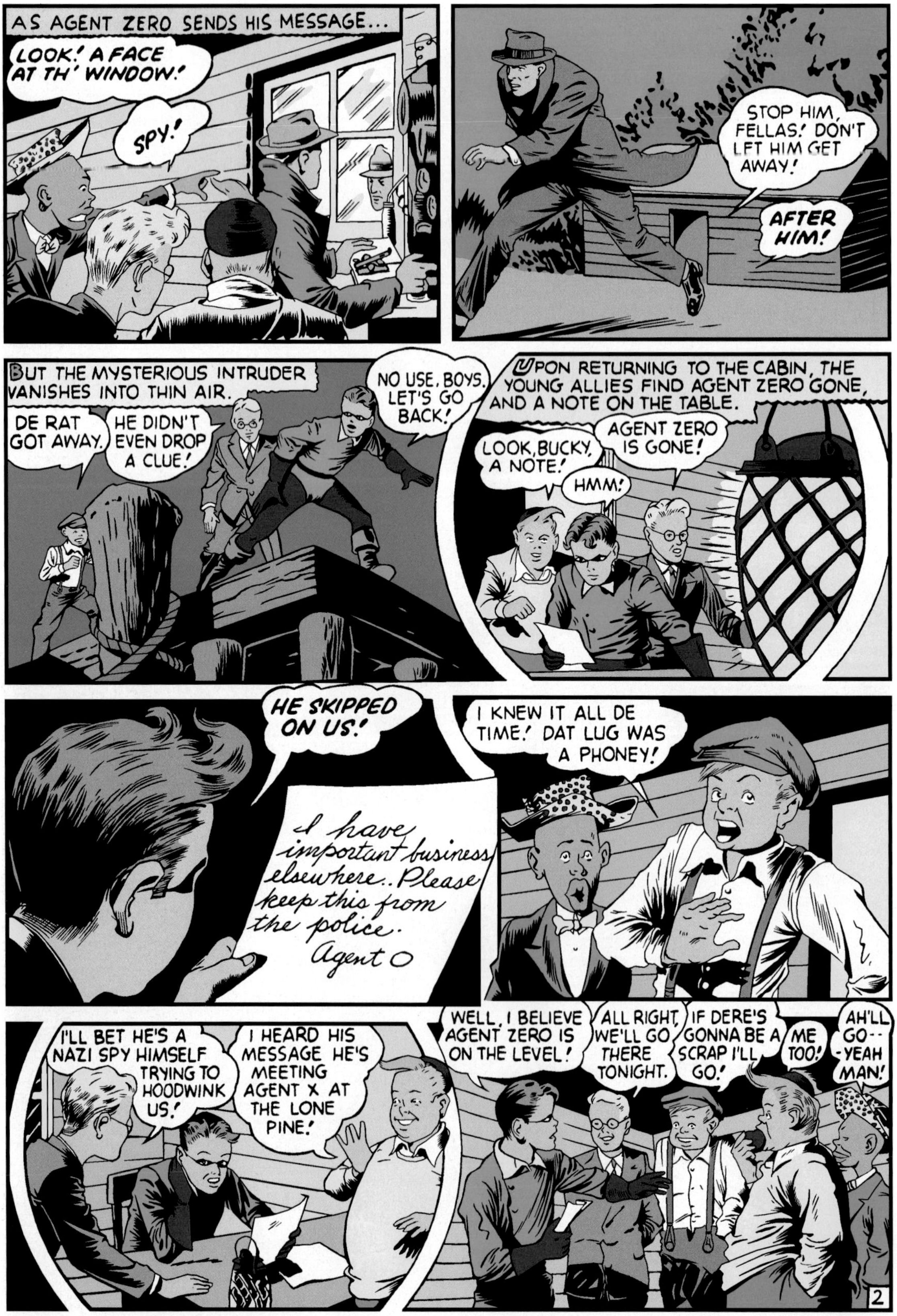
AS AGENT ZERO SENDS HIS MESSAGE...
LOOK! A FACE AT TH' WINDOW!
SPY!
STOP HIM, FELLAS! DON'T LET HIM GET AWAY!
AFTER HIM!
BUT THE MYSTERIOUS INTRUDER VANISHES INTO THIN AIR.
DE RAT GOT AWAY.
HE DIDN'T EVEN DROP A CLUE!
NO USE, BOYS. LET'S GO BACK!
UPON RETURNING TO THE CABIN, THE YOUNG ALLIES FIND AGENT ZERO GONE, AND A NOTE ON THE TABLE.
LOOK, BUCKY, A NOTE!
AGENT ZERO IS GONE!
HMM!
HE SKIPPED ON US!
I have important business elsewhere.. Please keep this from the police. Agent O
I KNEW IT ALL DE TIME! DAT LUG WAS A PHONEY!
I'LL BET HE'S A NAZI SPY HIMSELF TRYING TO HOODWINK US!
I HEARD HIS MESSAGE HE'S MEETING AGENT X AT THE LONE PINE!
WELL, I BELIEVE AGENT ZERO IS ON THE LEVEL!
ALL RIGHT, WE'LL GO THERE TONIGHT.
IF DERE'S GONNA BE A SCRAP I'LL GO!
ME TOO!
AH'LL GO--YEAH MAN!
2

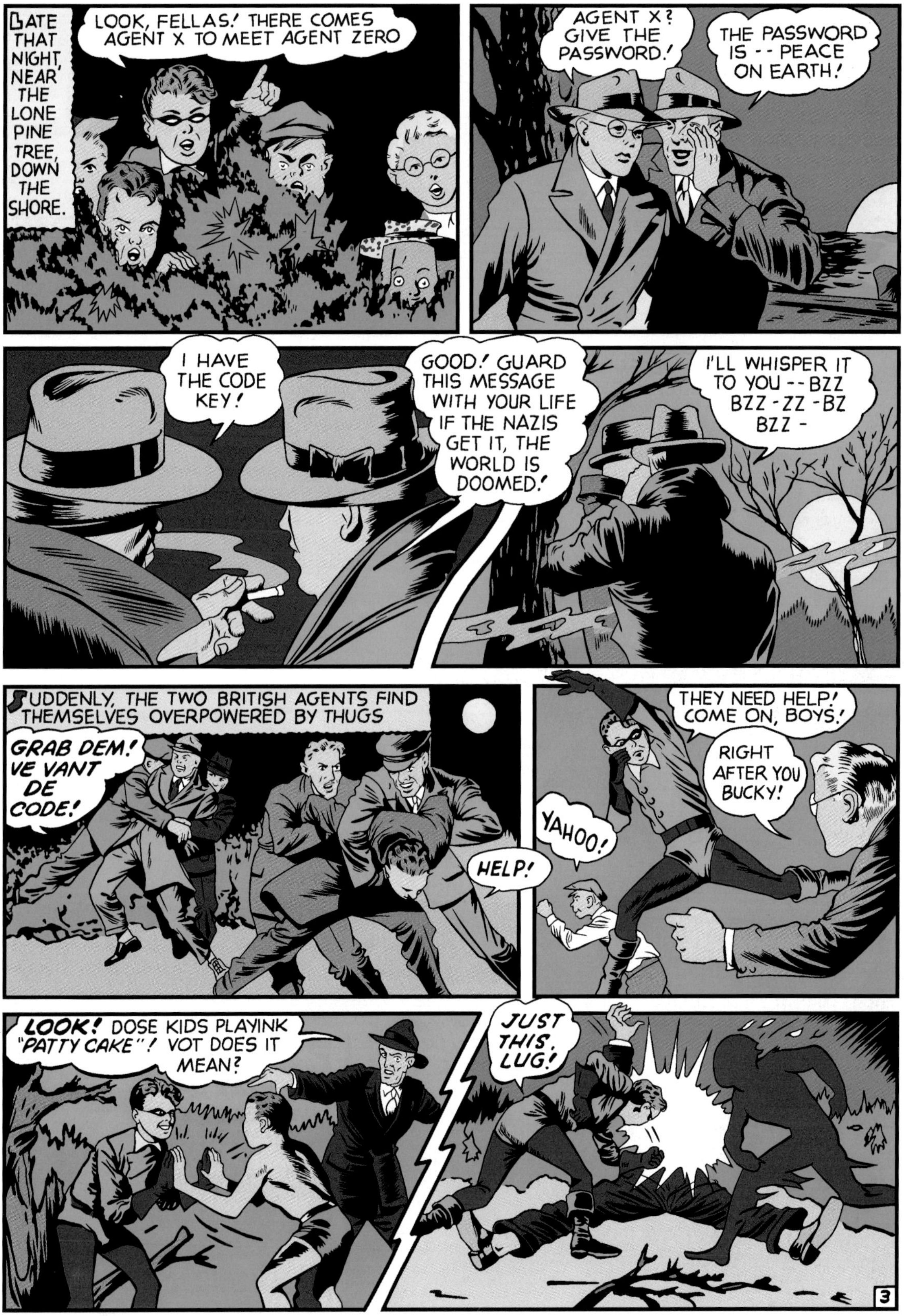
LATE THAT NIGHT, NEAR THE LONE PINE TREE, DOWN THE SHORE.
LOOK, FELLAS! THERE COMES AGENT X TO MEET AGENT ZERO
AGENT X? GIVE THE PASSWORD!
THE PASSWORD IS -- PEACE ON EARTH!
I HAVE THE CODE KEY!
GOOD! GUARD THIS MESSAGE WITH YOUR LIFE IF THE NAZIS GET IT, THE WORLD IS DOOMED!
I'LL WHISPER IT TO YOU -- BZZ BZZ-ZZ-BZ BZZ -
SUDDENLY, THE TWO BRITISH AGENTS FIND THEMSELVES OVERPOWERED BY THUGS
GRAB DEM! VE VANT DE CODE!
HELP!
THEY NEED HELP! COME ON, BOYS!
RIGHT AFTER YOU BUCKY!
YAHOO!
LOOK! DOSE KIDS PLAYINK "PATTY CAKE"! VOT DOES IT MEAN?
JUST THIS, LUG!
3

TELL YOUR FRIENDS ABOUT THIS GREAT, NEW, DIFFERENT COMIC MAGAZINE...THE YOUNG ALLIES

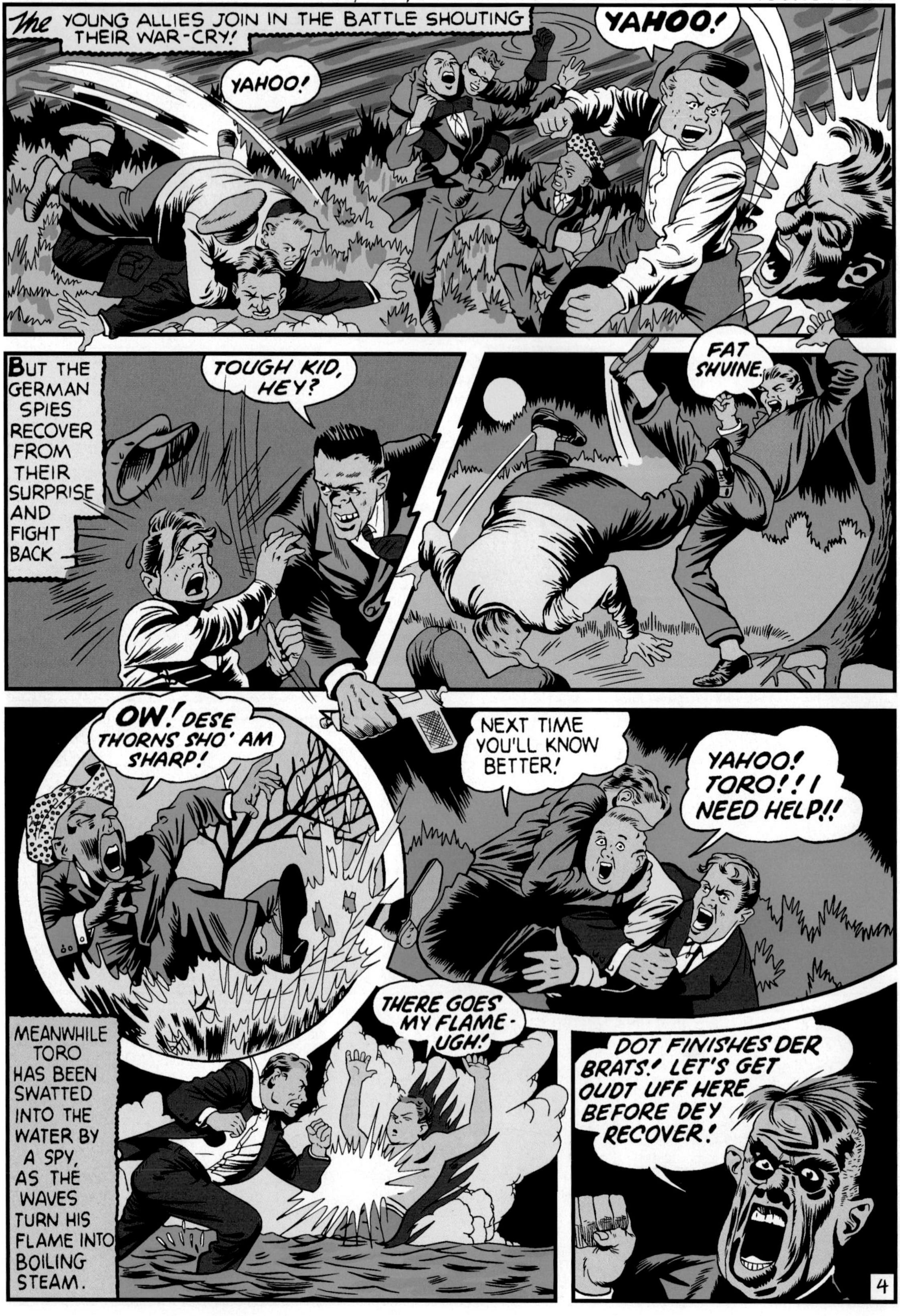
The YOUNG ALLIES JOIN IN THE BATTLE SHOUTING THEIR WAR-CRY!
YAHOO!
YAHOO!
BUT THE GERMAN SPIES RECOVER FROM THEIR SURPRISE AND FIGHT BACK
TOUGH KID, HEY?
FAT SHVINE.
OW! DESE THORNS SHO' AM SHARP!
NEXT TIME YOU'LL KNOW BETTER!
YAHOO! TORO!! I NEED HELP!!
MEANWHILE TORO HAS BEEN SWATTED INTO THE WATER BY A SPY, AS THE WAVES TURN HIS FLAME INTO BOILING STEAM.
THERE GOES MY FLAME-UGH!
DOT FINISHES DER BRATS! LET'S GET OUDT UFF HERE BEFORE DEY RECOVER!
4

TELL YOUR FRIENDS ABOUT THIS GREAT, NEW, DIFFERENT COMIC MAGAZINE...THE YOUNG ALLIES

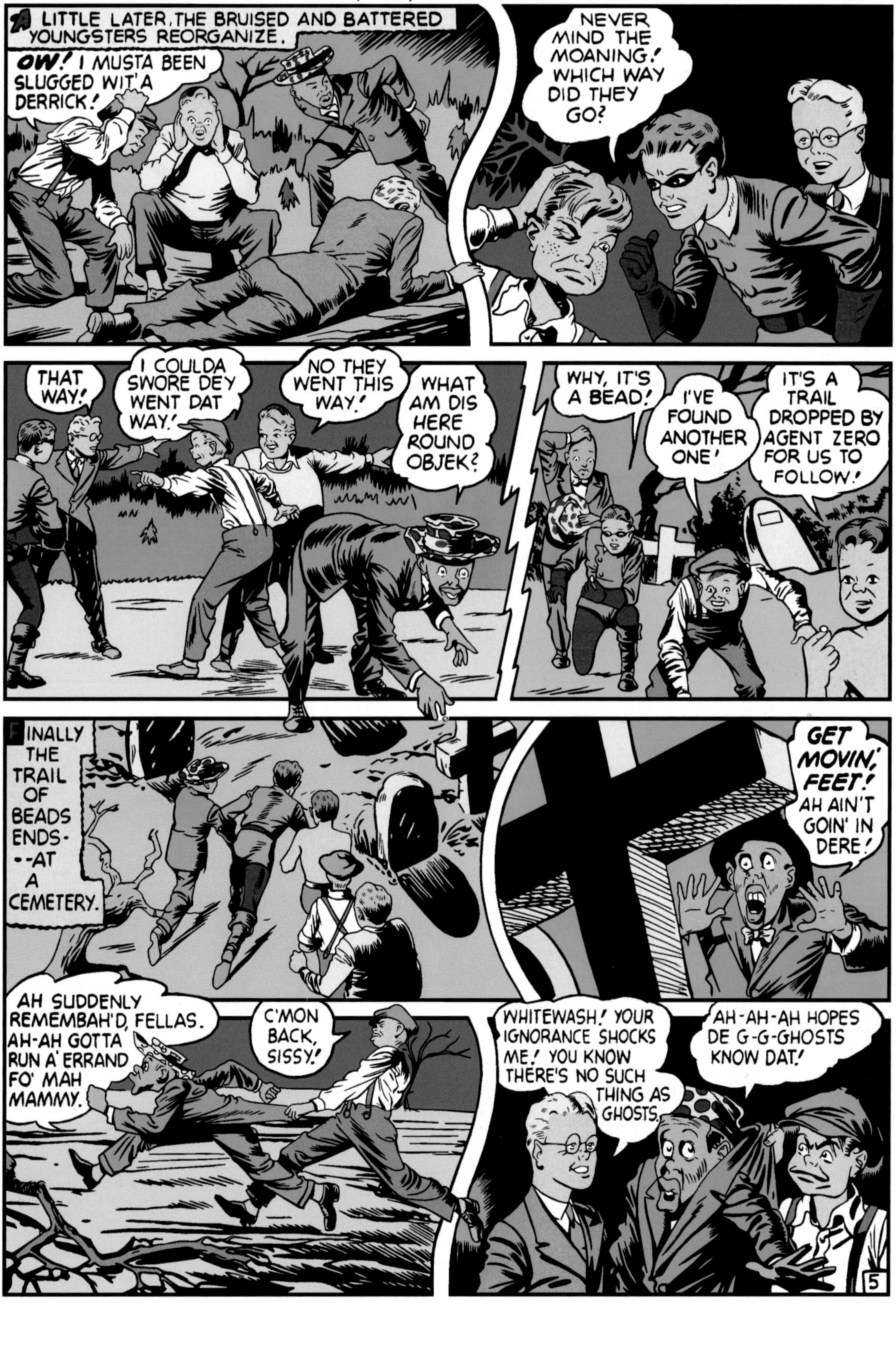
A LITTLE LATER, THE BRUISED AND BATTERED YOUNGSTERS REORGANIZE.
OW! I MUSTA BEEN SLUGGED WIT' A DERRICK!
NEVER MIND THE MOANING! WHICH WAY DID THEY GO?
THAT WAY!
I COULDA SWORE DEY WENT DAT WAY!
NO THEY WENT THIS WAY!
WHAT AM DIS HERE ROUND OBJEK?
WHY, IT'S A BEAD!
I'VE FOUND ANOTHER ONE'
IT'S A TRAIL DROPPED BY AGENT ZERO FOR US TO FOLLOW!
FINALLY THE TRAIL OF BEADS ENDS--AT A CEMETERY.
GET MOVIN', FEET! AH AIN'T GOIN' IN DERE!
AH SUDDENLY REMEMBAH'D, FELLAS. AH-AH GOTTA RUN A' ERRAND FO' MAH MAMMY.
C'MON BACK, SISSY!
WHITEWASH! YOUR IGNORANCE SHOCKS ME! YOU KNOW THERE'S NO SUCH THING AS GHOSTS.
AH-AH-AH HOPES DE G-G-GHOSTS KNOW DAT!
5

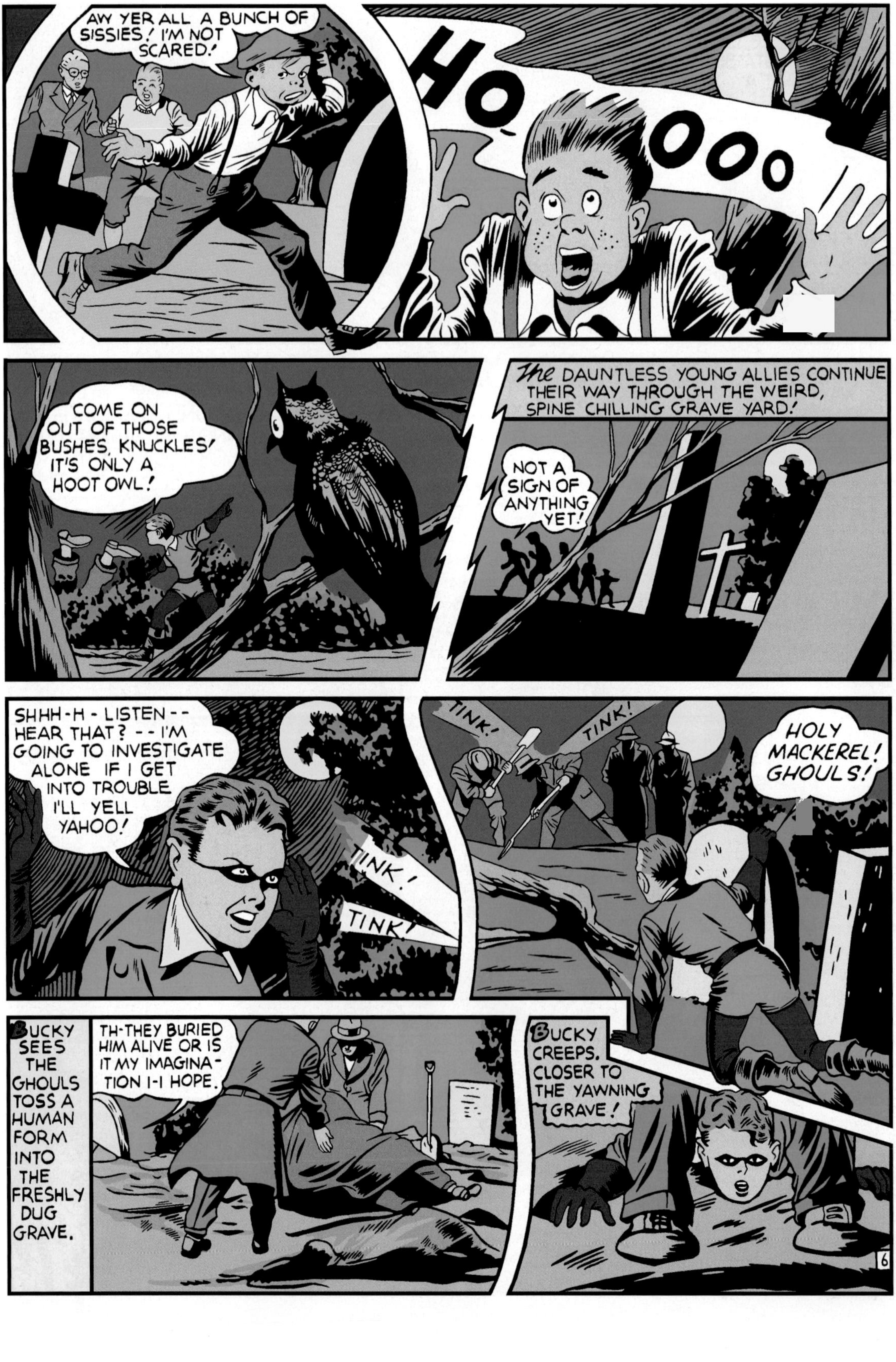
AW YER ALL A BUNCH OF SISSIES! I'M NOT SCARED!
HO-OOOO
COME ON OUT OF THOSE BUSHES, KNUCKLES! IT'S ONLY A HOOT OWL!
THE DAUNTLESS YOUNG ALLIES CONTINUE THEIR WAY THROUGH THE WEIRD, SPINE CHILLING GRAVE YARD!
NOT A SIGN OF ANYTHING YET!
SHHH-H - LISTEN -- HEAR THAT? -- I'M GOING TO INVESTIGATE ALONE IF I GET INTO TROUBLE I'LL YELL YAHOO!
TINK!
TINK!
TINK!
TINK!
HOLY MACKEREL! GHOULS!
BUCKY SEES THE GHOULS TOSS A HUMAN FORM INTO THE FRESHLY DUG GRAVE.
TH-THEY BURIED HIM ALIVE OR IS IT MY IMAGINATION I-I HOPE.
BUCKY CREEPS. CLOSER TO THE YAWNING GRAVE!
6

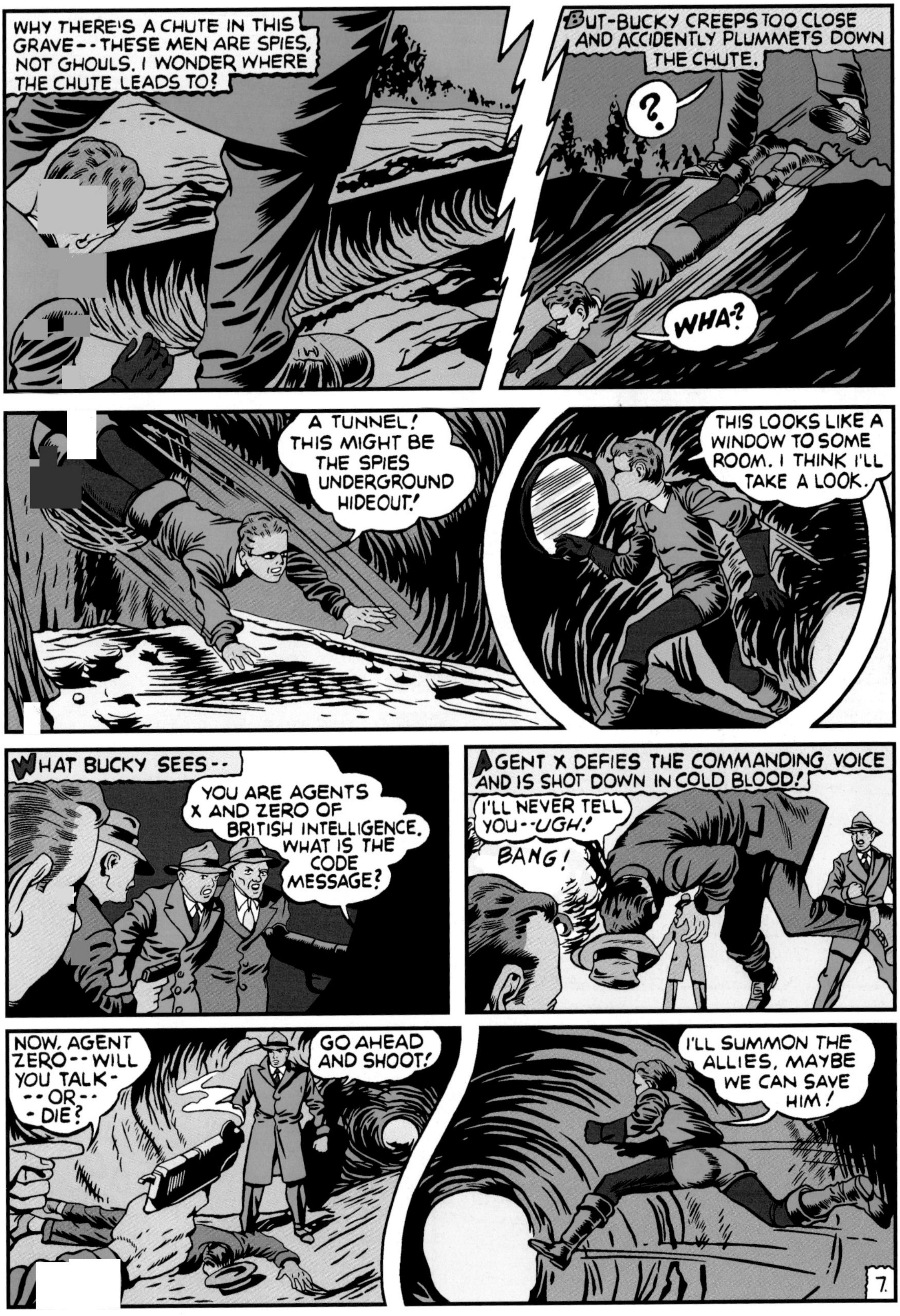
WHY THERE'S A CHUTE IN THIS GRAVE--THESE MEN ARE SPIES, NOT GHOULS. I WONDER WHERE THE CHUTE LEADS TO?
BUT-BUCKY CREEPS TOO CLOSE AND ACCIDENTLY PLUMMETS DOWN THE CHUTE.
?
WHA?
A TUNNEL! THIS MIGHT BE THE SPIES UNDERGROUND HIDEOUT!
THIS LOOKS LIKE A WINDOW TO SOME ROOM. I THINK I'LL TAKE A LOOK.
WHAT BUCKY SEES--
YOU ARE AGENTS X AND ZERO OF BRITISH INTELLIGENCE. WHAT IS THE CODE MESSAGE?
AGENT X DEFIES THE COMMANDING VOICE AND IS SHOT DOWN IN COLD BLOOD!
I'LL NEVER TELL YOU--UGH!
BANG!
NOW, AGENT ZERO--WILL YOU TALK---OR---DIE?
GO AHEAD AND SHOOT!
I'LL SUMMON THE ALLIES, MAYBE WE CAN SAVE HIM!

BUT SUDDENLY LIGHTS FLOOD THE TUNNEL, EXPOSING THE STARTLED BUCKY IN THEIR BLINDING GLARE

AH! WE HAVE CORNERED A LITTLE SNOOPER!

BUCKY WHIRLS AND STARES IN UTTER DISBELIEF AND HORROR AS THE SPY-LEADER CONFRONTS HIM.

HOLY MACKEREL! IT'S-IT'S-

--THE RED SKULL!

WELL! WELL! IF IT ISN'T BUCKY! SO WE MEET AGAIN, EH?

STILL WORKING FOR THE NAZIS, EH, SKULL?

TAKE THIS, BRAT!

THIS TIME CAPTAIN AMERICA ISN'T HERE TO HELP YOU!

UGH

AS THE STEELY FINGERS OF THE RED SKULL MERCILESSLY TIGHTEN, BUCKY GASPS OUT A DESPERATE STRANGLED CRY!

UGG-YAHOO! YAHOO!

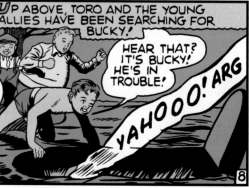

UP ABOVE, TORO AND THE YOUNG ALLIES HAVE BEEN SEARCHING FOR BUCKY!

HEAR THAT? IT'S BUCKY! HE'S IN TROUBLE!

YAHOOO! ARG

8

TELL YOUR FRIENDS ABOUT THIS GREAT, NEW, DIFFERENT COMIC MAGAZINE...THE YOUNG ALLIES

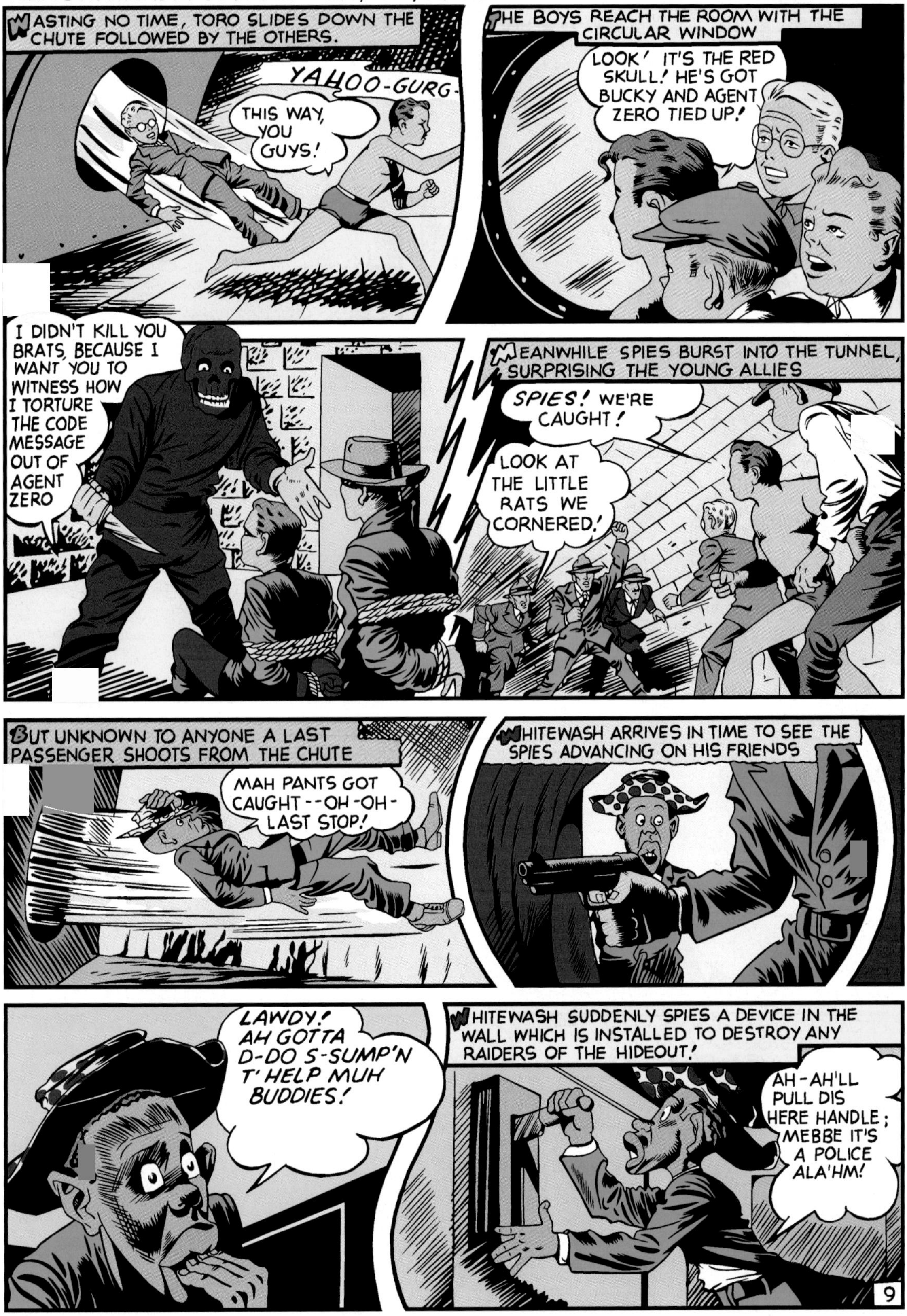
WASTING NO TIME, TORO SLIDES DOWN THE CHUTE FOLLOWED BY THE OTHERS.
YAHOO-GURG-
THIS WAY, YOU GUYS!
THE BOYS REACH THE ROOM WITH THE CIRCULAR WINDOW
LOOK! IT'S THE RED SKULL! HE'S GOT BUCKY AND AGENT ZERO TIED UP!
I DIDN'T KILL YOU BRATS, BECAUSE I WANT YOU TO WITNESS HOW I TORTURE THE CODE MESSAGE OUT OF AGENT ZERO
MEANWHILE SPIES BURST INTO THE TUNNEL, SURPRISING THE YOUNG ALLIES
SPIES! WE'RE CAUGHT!
LOOK AT THE LITTLE RATS WE CORNERED!
BUT UNKNOWN TO ANYONE A LAST PASSENGER SHOOTS FROM THE CHUTE
MAH PANTS GOT CAUGHT--OH-OH-LAST STOP!
WHITEWASH ARRIVES IN TIME TO SEE THE SPIES ADVANCING ON HIS FRIENDS
LAWDY! AH GOTTA D-DO S-SUMP'N T' HELP MUH BUDDIES!
WHITEWASH SUDDENLY SPIES A DEVICE IN THE WALL WHICH IS INSTALLED TO DESTROY ANY RAIDERS OF THE HIDEOUT!
AH-AH'LL PULL DIS HERE HANDLE; MEBBE IT'S A POLICE ALA'HM!

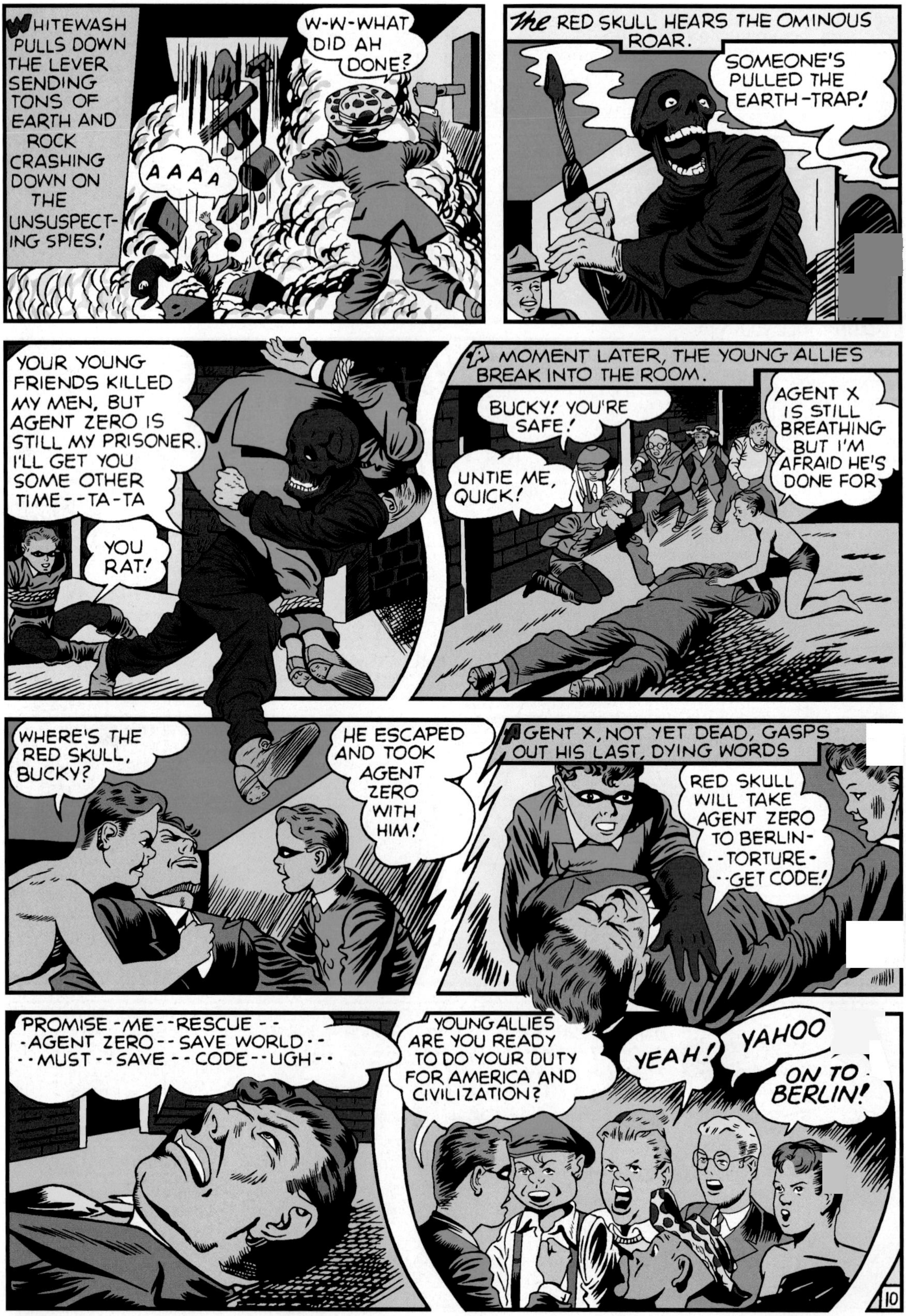
WHITEWASH PULLS DOWN THE LEVER SENDING TONS OF EARTH AND ROCK CRASHING DOWN ON THE UNSUSPECTING SPIES!
W-W-WHAT DID AH DONE?
AAAA
THE RED SKULL HEARS THE OMINOUS ROAR.
SOMEONE'S PULLED THE EARTH-TRAP!
YOUR YOUNG FRIENDS KILLED MY MEN, BUT AGENT ZERO IS STILL MY PRISONER. I'LL GET YOU SOME OTHER TIME--TA-TA
YOU RAT!
A MOMENT LATER, THE YOUNG ALLIES BREAK INTO THE ROOM.
BUCKY! YOU'RE SAFE!
UNTIE ME, QUICK!
AGENT X IS STILL BREATHING BUT I'M AFRAID HE'S DONE FOR
WHERE'S THE RED SKULL, BUCKY?
HE ESCAPED AND TOOK AGENT ZERO WITH HIM!
AGENT X, NOT YET DEAD, GASPS OUT HIS LAST, DYING WORDS
RED SKULL WILL TAKE AGENT ZERO TO BERLIN- -TORTURE- -GET CODE!
PROMISE-ME--RESCUE-- -AGENT ZERO--SAVE WORLD- - --MUST--SAVE--CODE--UGH--
YOUNG ALLIES ARE YOU READY TO DO YOUR DUTY FOR AMERICA AND CIVILIZATION?
YEAH!
YAHOO
ON TO BERLIN!
10

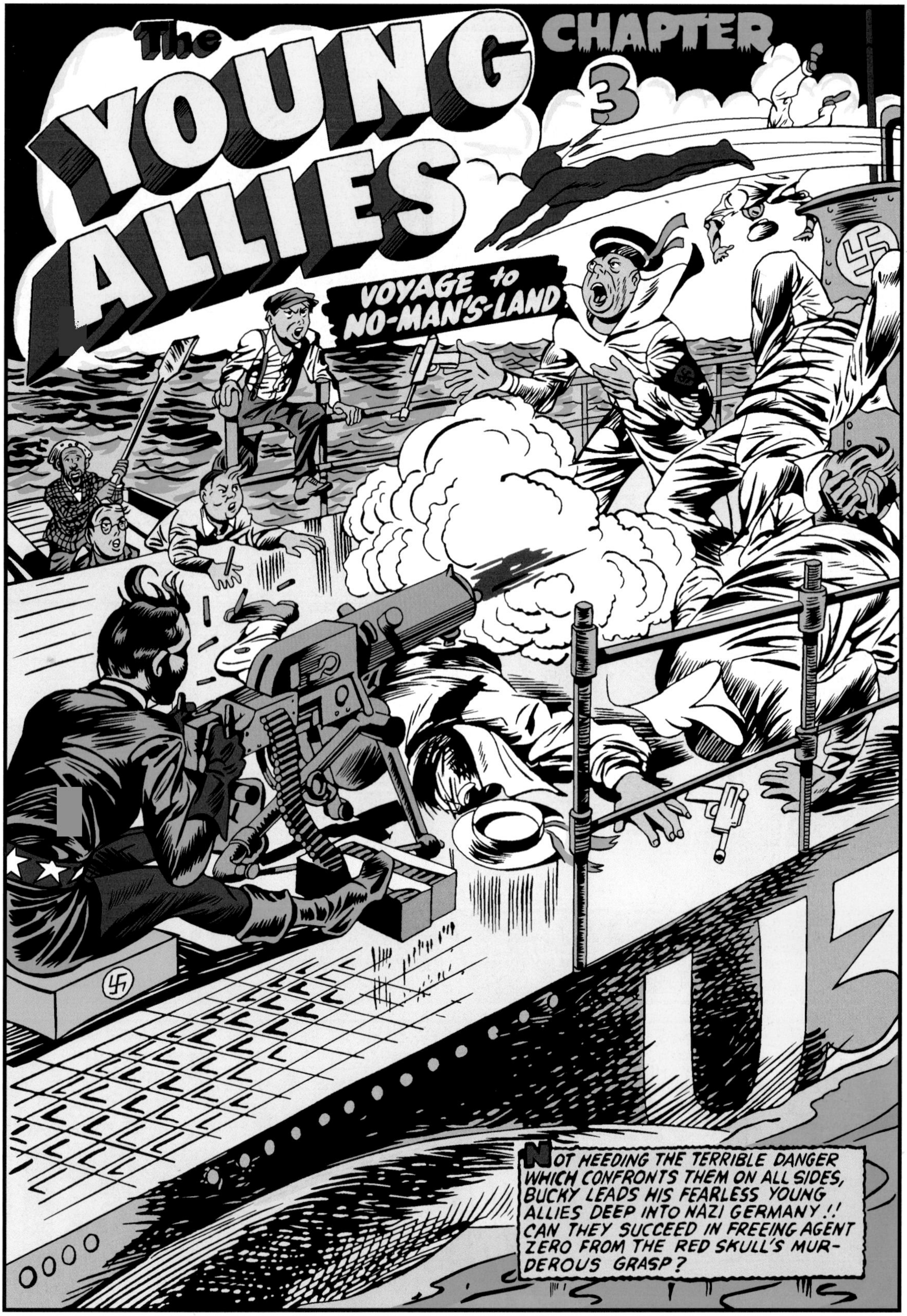
The YOUNG ALLIES
CHAPTER 3
VOYAGE to NO-MAN'S-LAND
NOT HEEDING THE TERRIBLE DANGER WHICH CONFRONTS THEM ON ALL SIDES, BUCKY LEADS HIS FEARLESS YOUNG ALLIES DEEP INTO NAZI GERMANY !! CAN THEY SUCCEED IN FREEING AGENT ZERO FROM THE RED SKULL'S MURDEROUS GRASP?

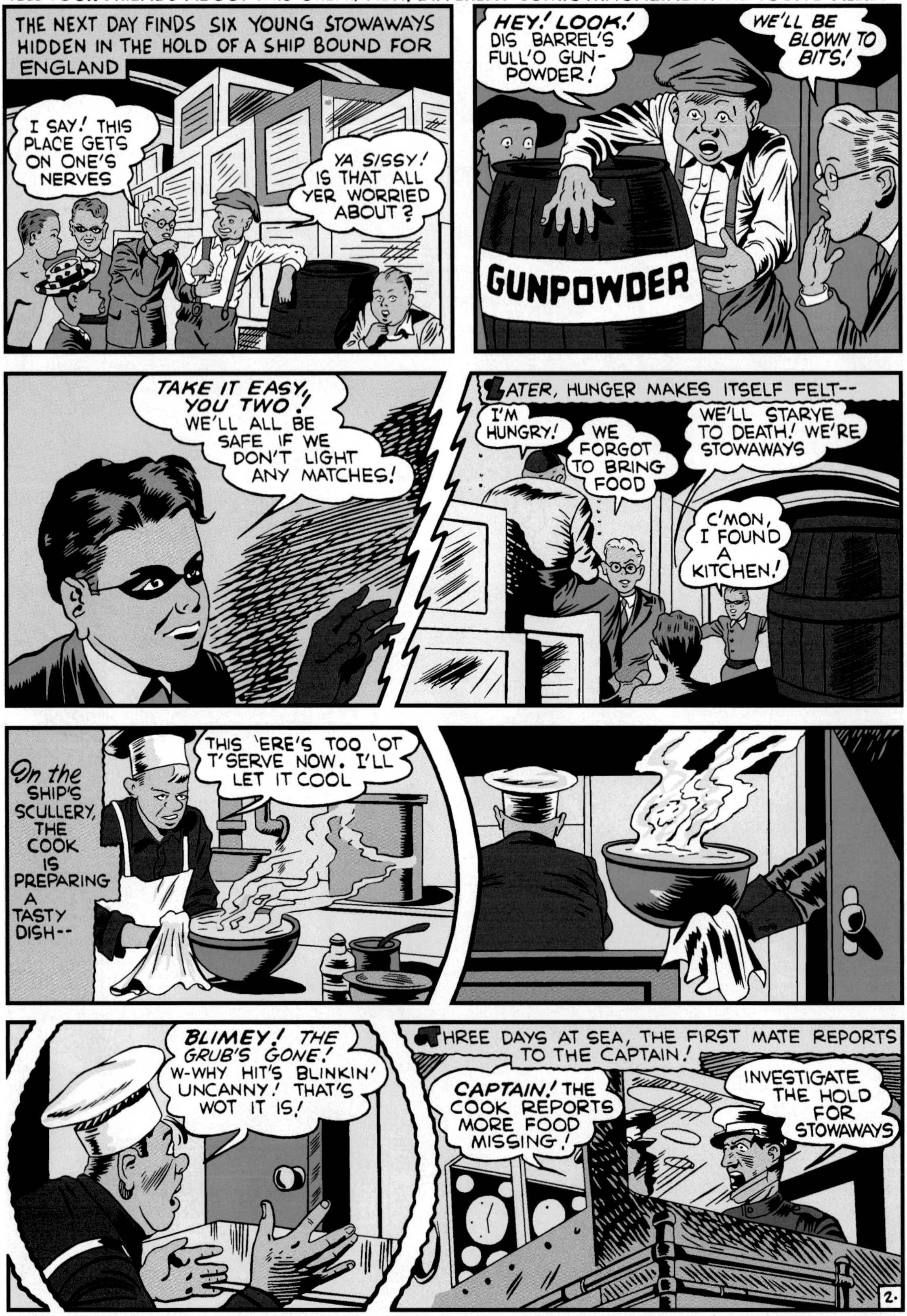
THE NEXT DAY FINDS SIX YOUNG STOWAWAYS HIDDEN IN THE HOLD OF A SHIP BOUND FOR ENGLAND
I SAY! THIS PLACE GETS ON ONE'S NERVES
YA SISSY! IS THAT ALL YER WORRIED ABOUT?
HEY! LOOK! DIS BARREL'S FULL'O GUN-POWDER!
WE'LL BE BLOWN TO BITS!
GUNPOWDER
TAKE IT EASY, YOU TWO! WE'LL ALL BE SAFE IF WE DON'T LIGHT ANY MATCHES!
LATER, HUNGER MAKES ITSELF FELT--
I'M HUNGRY!
WE FORGOT TO BRING FOOD
WE'LL STARVE TO DEATH! WE'RE STOWAWAYS
C'MON, I FOUND A KITCHEN!
In the SHIP'S SCULLERY, THE COOK IS PREPARING A TASTY DISH--
THIS 'ERE'S TOO 'OT T'SERVE NOW. I'LL LET IT COOL
BLIMEY! THE GRUB'S GONE! W-WHY HIT'S BLINKIN' UNCANNY! THAT'S WOT IT IS!
THREE DAYS AT SEA, THE FIRST MATE REPORTS TO THE CAPTAIN!
CAPTAIN! THE COOK REPORTS MORE FOOD MISSING!
INVESTIGATE THE HOLD FOR STOWAWAYS
2.

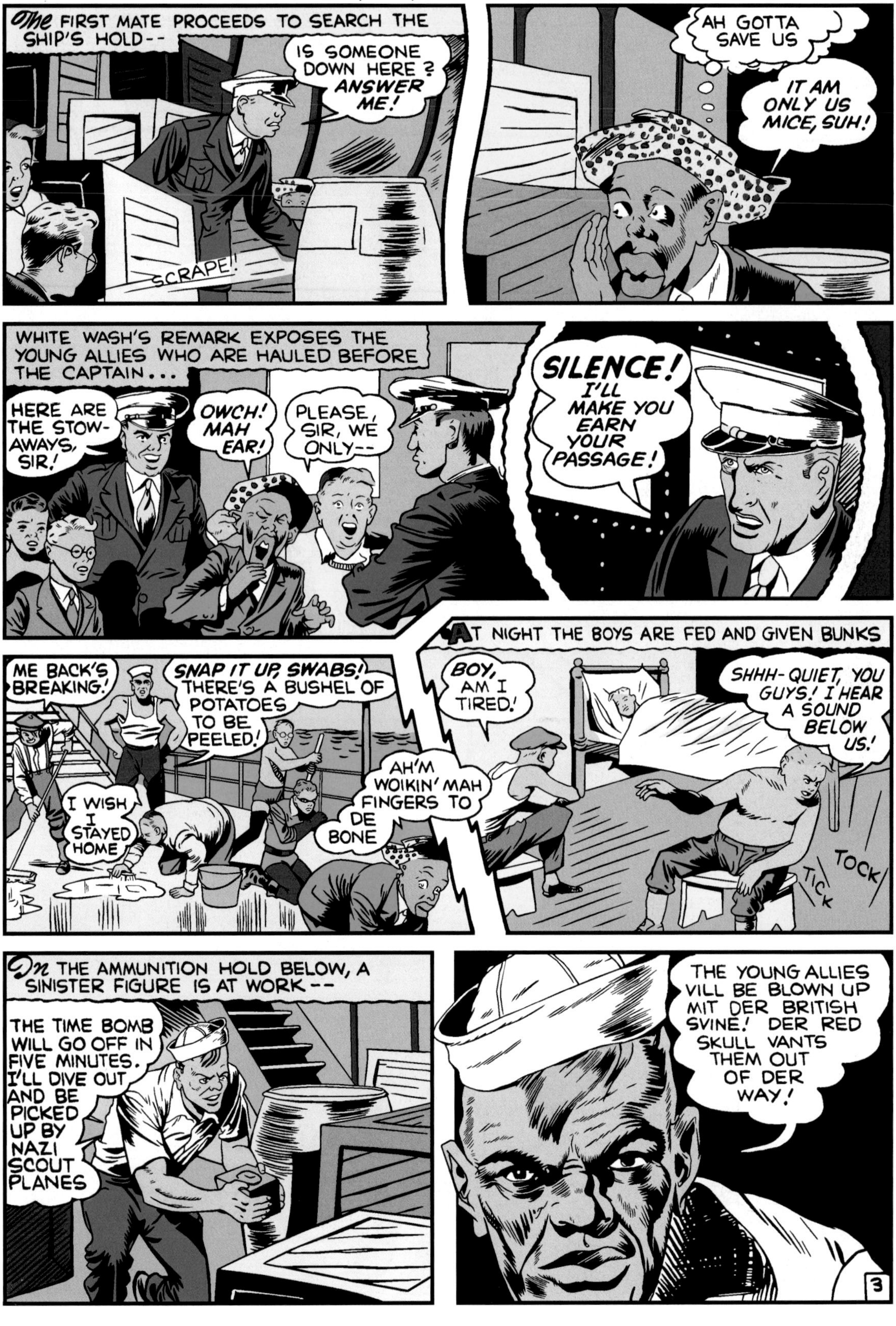
THE FIRST MATE PROCEEDS TO SEARCH THE SHIP'S HOLD--
IS SOMEONE DOWN HERE? ANSWER ME!
SCRAPE!
AH GOTTA SAVE US
IT AM ONLY US MICE, SUH!
WHITE WASH'S REMARK EXPOSES THE YOUNG ALLIES WHO ARE HAULED BEFORE THE CAPTAIN...
HERE ARE THE STOW-AWAYS, SIR!
OWCH! MAH EAR!
PLEASE, SIR, WE ONLY--
SILENCE! I'LL MAKE YOU EARN YOUR PASSAGE!
ME BACK'S BREAKING!
SNAP IT UP, SWABS! THERE'S A BUSHEL OF POTATOES TO BE PEELED!
I WISH I STAYED HOME
AH'M WOIKIN' MAH FINGERS TO DE BONE
AT NIGHT THE BOYS ARE FED AND GIVEN BUNKS
BOY, AM I TIRED!
SHHH-QUIET, YOU GUYS! I HEAR A SOUND BELOW US!
TICK
TOCK
IN THE AMMUNITION HOLD BELOW, A SINISTER FIGURE IS AT WORK--
THE TIME BOMB WILL GO OFF IN FIVE MINUTES. I'LL DIVE OUT AND BE PICKED UP BY NAZI SCOUT PLANES
THE YOUNG ALLIES VILL BE BLOWN UP MIT DER BRITISH SVINE! DER RED SKULL VANTS THEM OUT OF DER WAY!
3

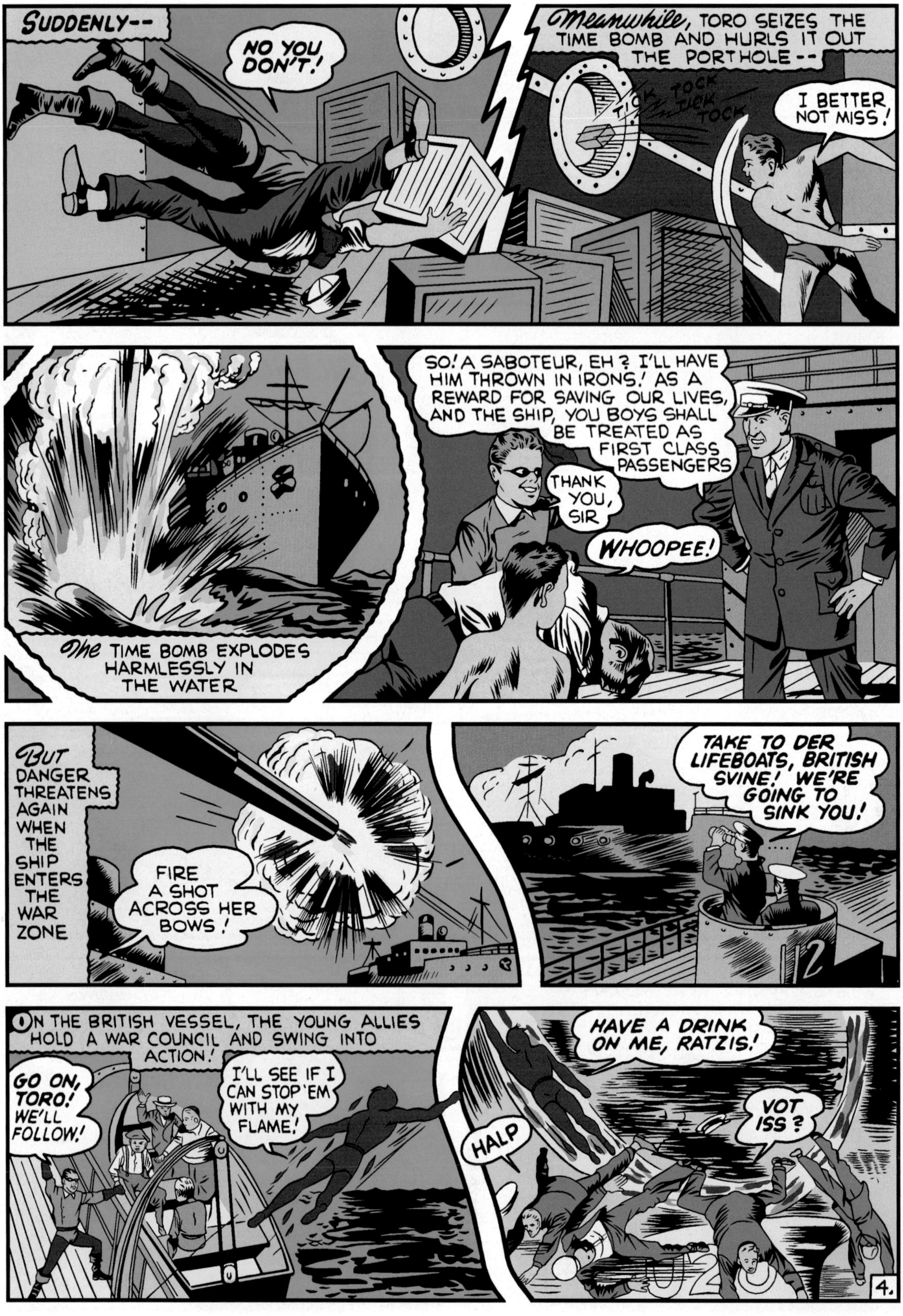
SUDDENLY--
NO YOU DON'T!
Meanwhile, TORO SEIZES THE TIME BOMB AND HURLS IT OUT THE PORTHOLE--
TICK TOCK TICK TOCK
I BETTER NOT MISS!
The TIME BOMB EXPLODES HARMLESSLY IN THE WATER
SO! A SABOTEUR, EH? I'LL HAVE HIM THROWN IN IRONS! AS A REWARD FOR SAVING OUR LIVES, AND THE SHIP, YOU BOYS SHALL BE TREATED AS FIRST CLASS PASSENGERS
THANK YOU, SIR
WHOOPEE!
But DANGER THREATENS AGAIN WHEN THE SHIP ENTERS THE WAR ZONE
FIRE A SHOT ACROSS HER BOWS!
TAKE TO DER LIFEBOATS, BRITISH SVINE! WE'RE GOING TO SINK YOU!
U-2
ON THE BRITISH VESSEL, THE YOUNG ALLIES HOLD A WAR COUNCIL AND SWING INTO ACTION!
GO ON, TORO! WE'LL FOLLOW!
I'LL SEE IF I CAN STOP 'EM WITH MY FLAME!
HAVE A DRINK ON ME, RATZIS!
VOT ISS?
HALP
U-2
4.

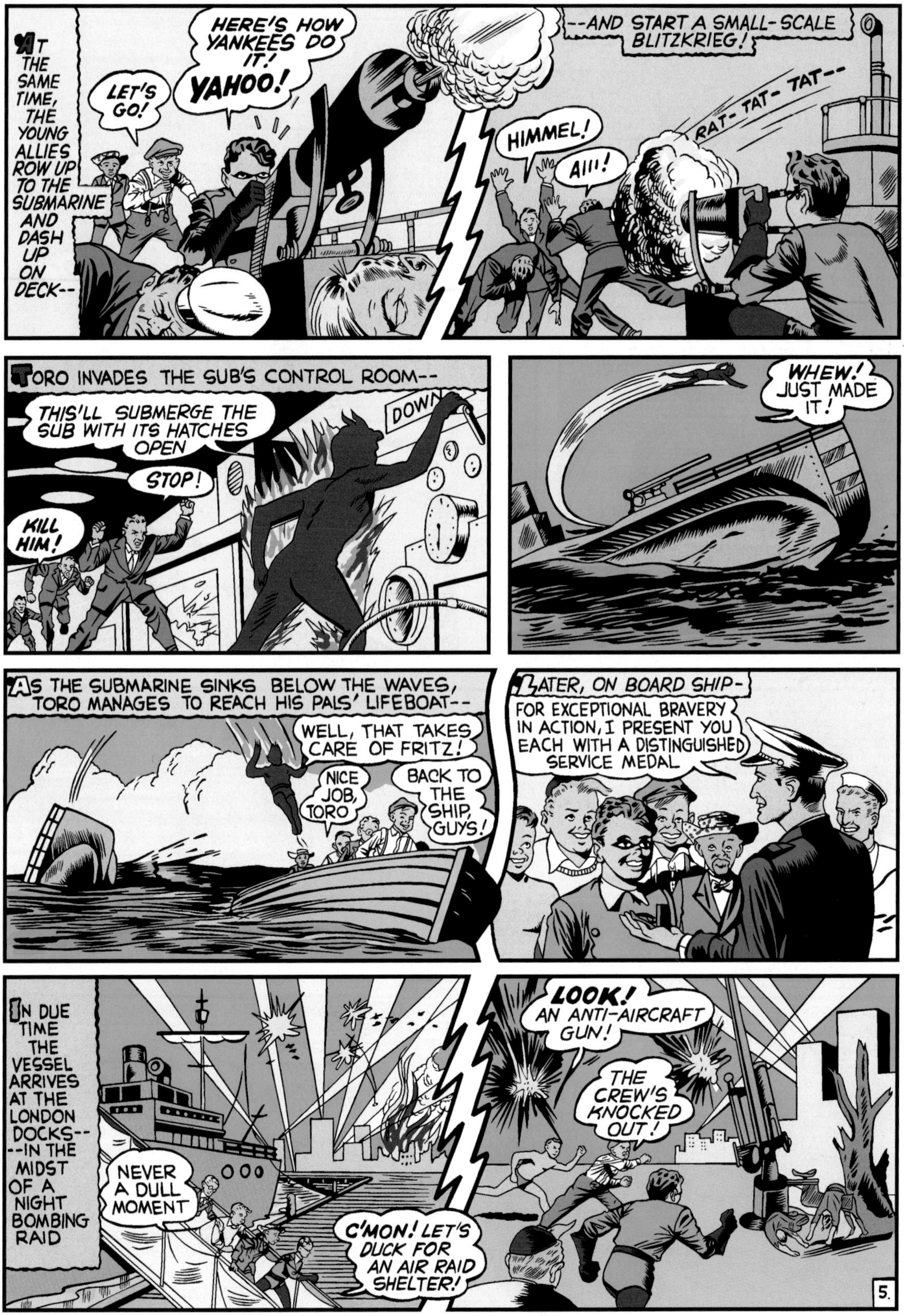
AT THE SAME TIME, THE YOUNG ALLIES ROW UP TO THE SUBMARINE AND DASH UP ON DECK--
LET'S GO!
HERE'S HOW YANKEES DO IT! YAHOO!
--AND START A SMALL-SCALE BLITZKRIEG!
HIMMEL!
AIII!
RAT-TAT-TAT--
TORO INVADES THE SUB'S CONTROL ROOM--
THIS'LL SUBMERGE THE SUB WITH ITS HATCHES OPEN
DOWN
STOP!
KILL HIM!
WHEW! JUST MADE IT!
AS THE SUBMARINE SINKS BELOW THE WAVES, TORO MANAGES TO REACH HIS PALS' LIFEBOAT--
WELL, THAT TAKES CARE OF FRITZ!
NICE JOB, TORO
BACK TO THE SHIP, GUYS!
LATER, ON BOARD SHIP-
FOR EXCEPTIONAL BRAVERY IN ACTION, I PRESENT YOU EACH WITH A DISTINGUISHED SERVICE MEDAL
IN DUE TIME THE VESSEL ARRIVES AT THE LONDON DOCKS-- --IN THE MIDST OF A NIGHT BOMBING RAID
NEVER A DULL MOMENT
C'MON! LET'S DUCK FOR AN AIR RAID SHELTER!
LOOK! AN ANTI-AIRCRAFT GUN!
THE CREW'S KNOCKED OUT!
5.

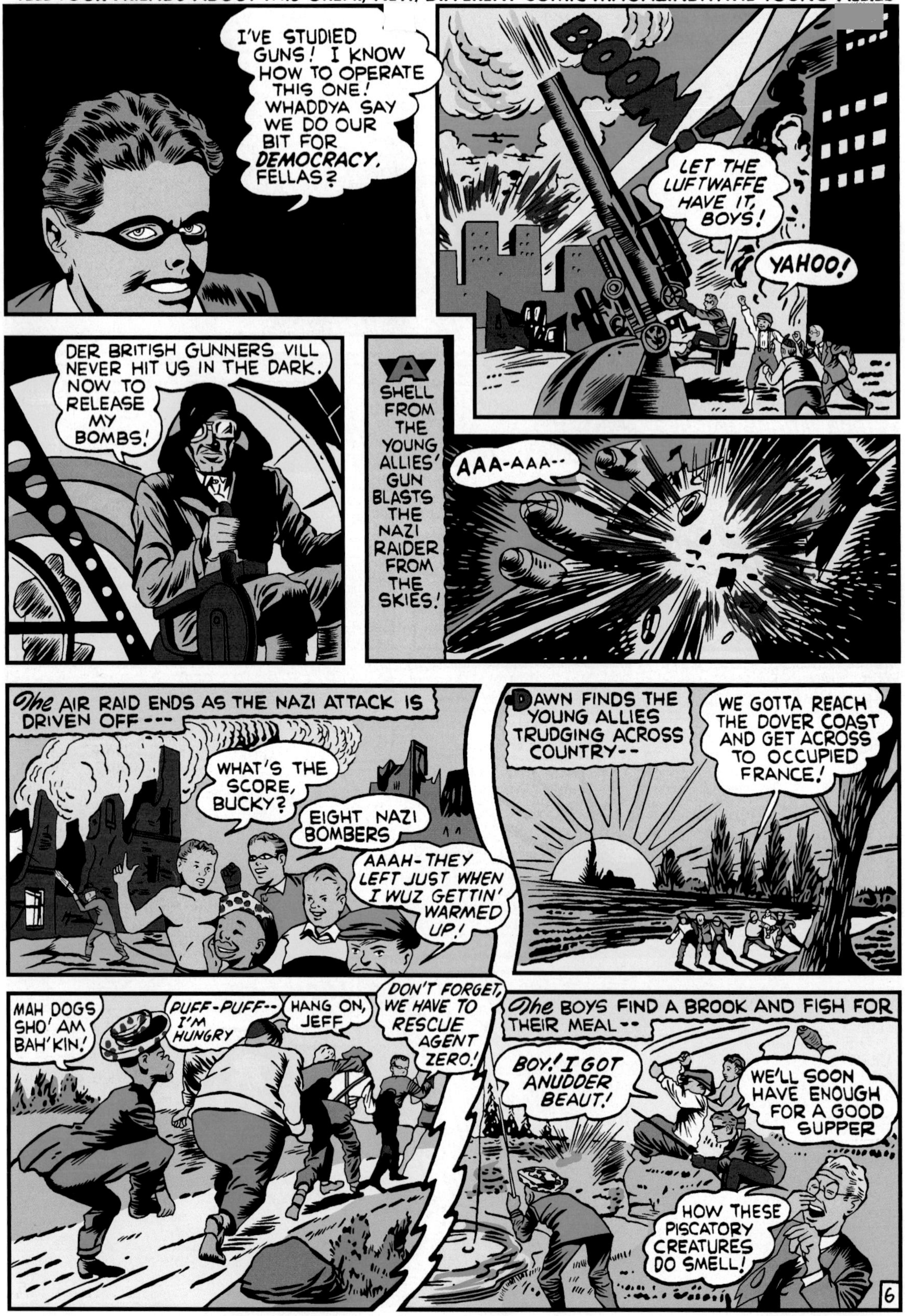
I'VE STUDIED GUNS! I KNOW HOW TO OPERATE THIS ONE! WHADDYA SAY WE DO OUR BIT FOR DEMOCRACY, FELLAS?
BOOM!
LET THE LUFTWAFFE HAVE IT, BOYS!
YAHOO!
DER BRITISH GUNNERS VILL NEVER HIT US IN THE DARK. NOW TO RELEASE MY BOMBS!
A SHELL FROM THE YOUNG ALLIES' GUN BLASTS THE NAZI RAIDER FROM THE SKIES!
AAA-AAA--
The AIR RAID ENDS AS THE NAZI ATTACK IS DRIVEN OFF---
WHAT'S THE SCORE, BUCKY?
EIGHT NAZI BOMBERS
AAAH-THEY LEFT JUST WHEN I WUZ GETTIN' WARMED UP!
DAWN FINDS THE YOUNG ALLIES TRUDGING ACROSS COUNTRY--
WE GOTTA REACH THE DOVER COAST AND GET ACROSS TO OCCUPIED FRANCE!
MAH DOGS SHO' AM BAH'KIN!
PUFF-PUFF-- I'M HUNGRY
HANG ON, JEFF
DON'T FORGET, WE HAVE TO RESCUE AGENT ZERO!
The BOYS FIND A BROOK AND FISH FOR THEIR MEAL--
BOY! I GOT ANUDDER BEAUT!
WE'LL SOON HAVE ENOUGH FOR A GOOD SUPPER
HOW THESE PISCATORY CREATURES DO SMELL!
6

TELL YOUR FRIENDS ABOUT THIS GREAT, NEW, DIFFERENT COMIC MAGAZINE...THE YOUNG ALLIES

Later--

NOT BAD!

THEY TASTE SWELL

AFTER ALL, THE ESKIMOS LIVE MOSTLY ON FISH

AH GUESS AH'M A SORTA DUSKY ESKIMO, KINDA

Upon reaching the Dover coast, the boys build a raft...

THE RAFT'S NEARLY DONE, BUCKY

WE'LL START TONIGHT!

The Young Allies then launch their one-raft invasion of Nazi-held Europe--

WE'RE HALF WAY ACROSS THE CHANNEL NOW!

YEOW! LOOK! A STUKA DIVE BOMBER!

The concussion of the ensuing explosion tears the raft to pieces, tossing the boys into the sea!

The Stuka swoops down again to machine-gun its struggling victims

RAT-TAT-TAT-TAT-TA

HELP!

WHERE'S TORO?

WE'RE COOKED

GOOD THING I LEAPED CLEAR OF THE RAFT BEFORE I COULD GET WET! NOW TO ATTEND TO THAT HEINIE!

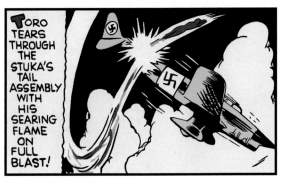

Toro tears through the Stuka's tail assembly with his searing flame on full blast!

The dive-bomber plummets into the sea to a watery grave

7.

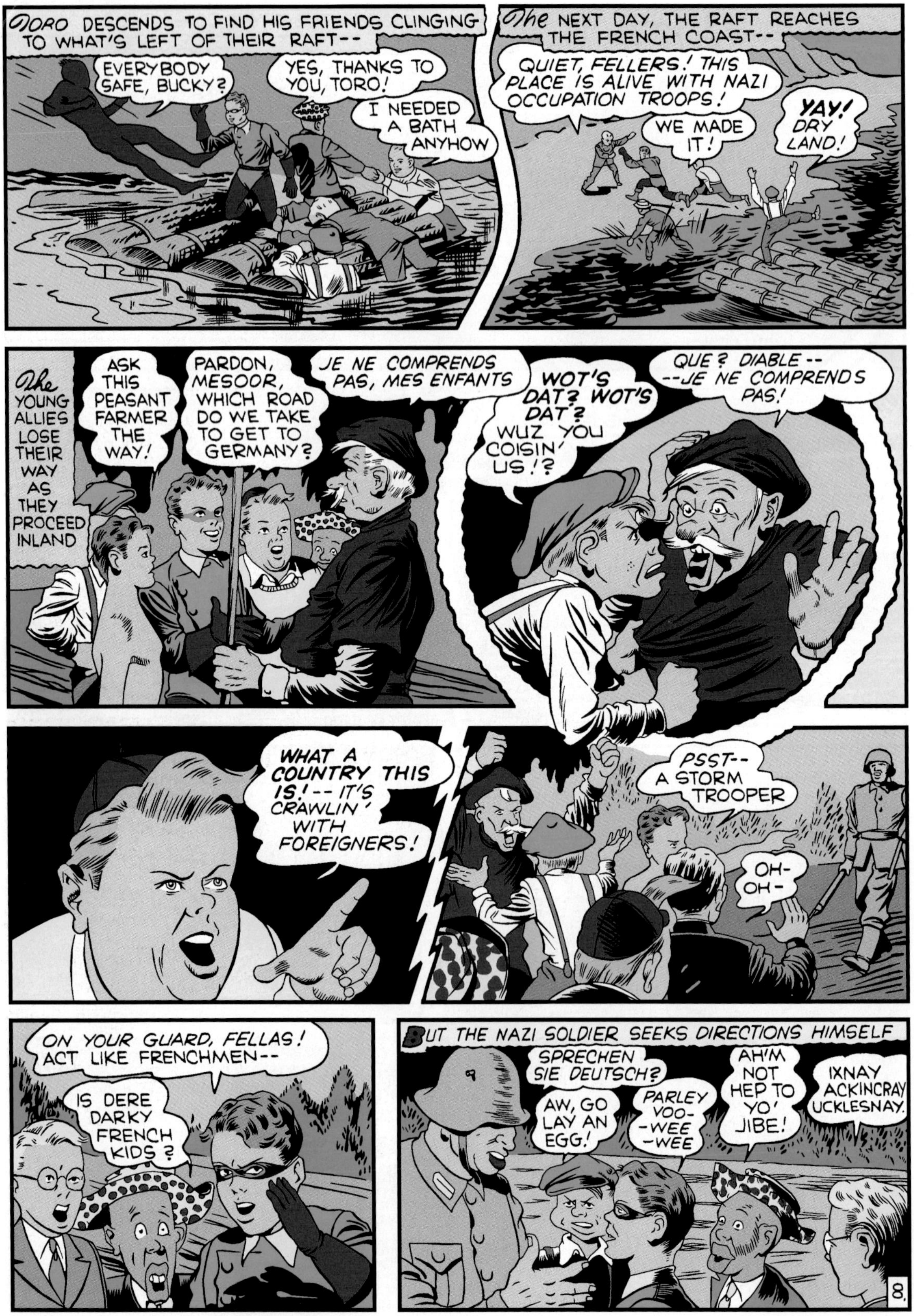
TORO DESCENDS TO FIND HIS FRIENDS CLINGING TO WHAT'S LEFT OF THEIR RAFT--
EVERYBODY SAFE, BUCKY?
YES, THANKS TO YOU, TORO!
I NEEDED A BATH ANYHOW
THE NEXT DAY, THE RAFT REACHES THE FRENCH COAST--
QUIET, FELLERS! THIS PLACE IS ALIVE WITH NAZI OCCUPATION TROOPS!
WE MADE IT!
YAY! DRY LAND!
THE YOUNG ALLIES LOSE THEIR WAY AS THEY PROCEED INLAND
ASK THIS PEASANT FARMER THE WAY!
PARDON, MESOOR, WHICH ROAD DO WE TAKE TO GET TO GERMANY?
JE NE COMPRENDS PAS, MES ENFANTS
WOT'S DAT? WOT'S DAT? WUZ YOU COISIN' US!?
QUE? DIABLE -- --JE NE COMPRENDS PAS!
WHAT A COUNTRY THIS IS! -- IT'S CRAWLIN' WITH FOREIGNERS!
PSST-- A STORM TROOPER
OH- OH-
ON YOUR GUARD, FELLAS! ACT LIKE FRENCHMEN--
IS DERE DARKY FRENCH KIDS ?
BUT THE NAZI SOLDIER SEEKS DIRECTIONS HIMSELF
SPRECHEN SIE DEUTSCH?
AW, GO LAY AN EGG!
PARLEY VOO- -WEE -WEE
AH'M NOT HEP TO YO' JIBE!
IXNAY ACKINCRAY UCKLESNAY.
8.

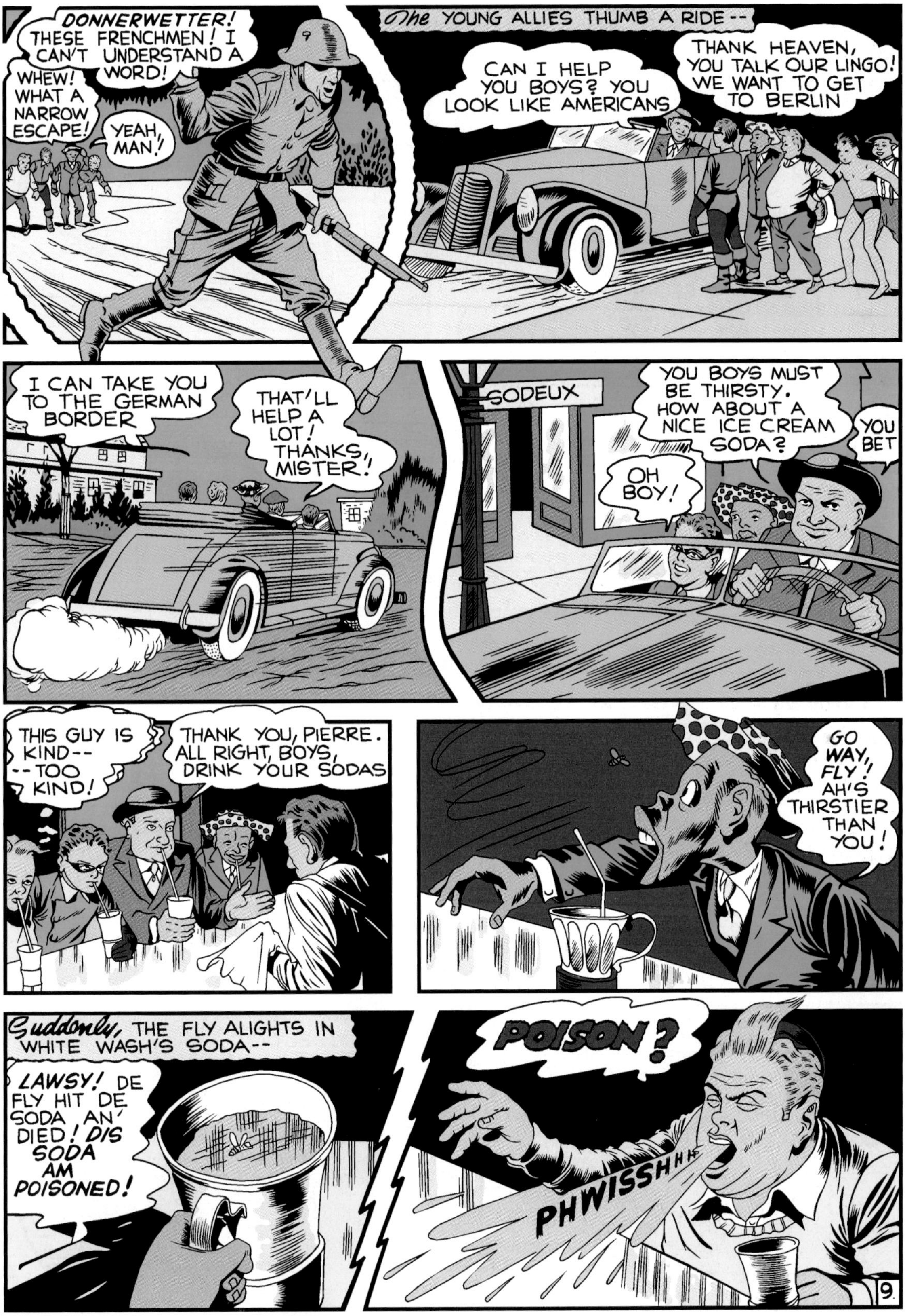
DONNERWETTER! THESE FRENCHMEN! I CAN'T UNDERSTAND A WORD!
WHEW! WHAT A NARROW ESCAPE!
YEAH, MAN!
The YOUNG ALLIES THUMB A RIDE--
CAN I HELP YOU BOYS? YOU LOOK LIKE AMERICANS
THANK HEAVEN, YOU TALK OUR LINGO! WE WANT TO GET TO BERLIN
I CAN TAKE YOU TO THE GERMAN BORDER
THAT'LL HELP A LOT! THANKS, MISTER!
SODEUX
YOU BOYS MUST BE THIRSTY. HOW ABOUT A NICE ICE CREAM SODA?
OH BOY!
YOU BET
THIS GUY IS KIND-- --TOO KIND!
THANK YOU, PIERRE. ALL RIGHT, BOYS, DRINK YOUR SODAS
GO WAY, FLY! AH'S THIRSTIER THAN YOU!
Suddenly, THE FLY ALIGHTS IN WHITE WASH'S SODA--
LAWSY! DE FLY HIT DE SODA AN' DIED! DIS SODA AM POISONED!
POISON?
PHWISSHHH
9.

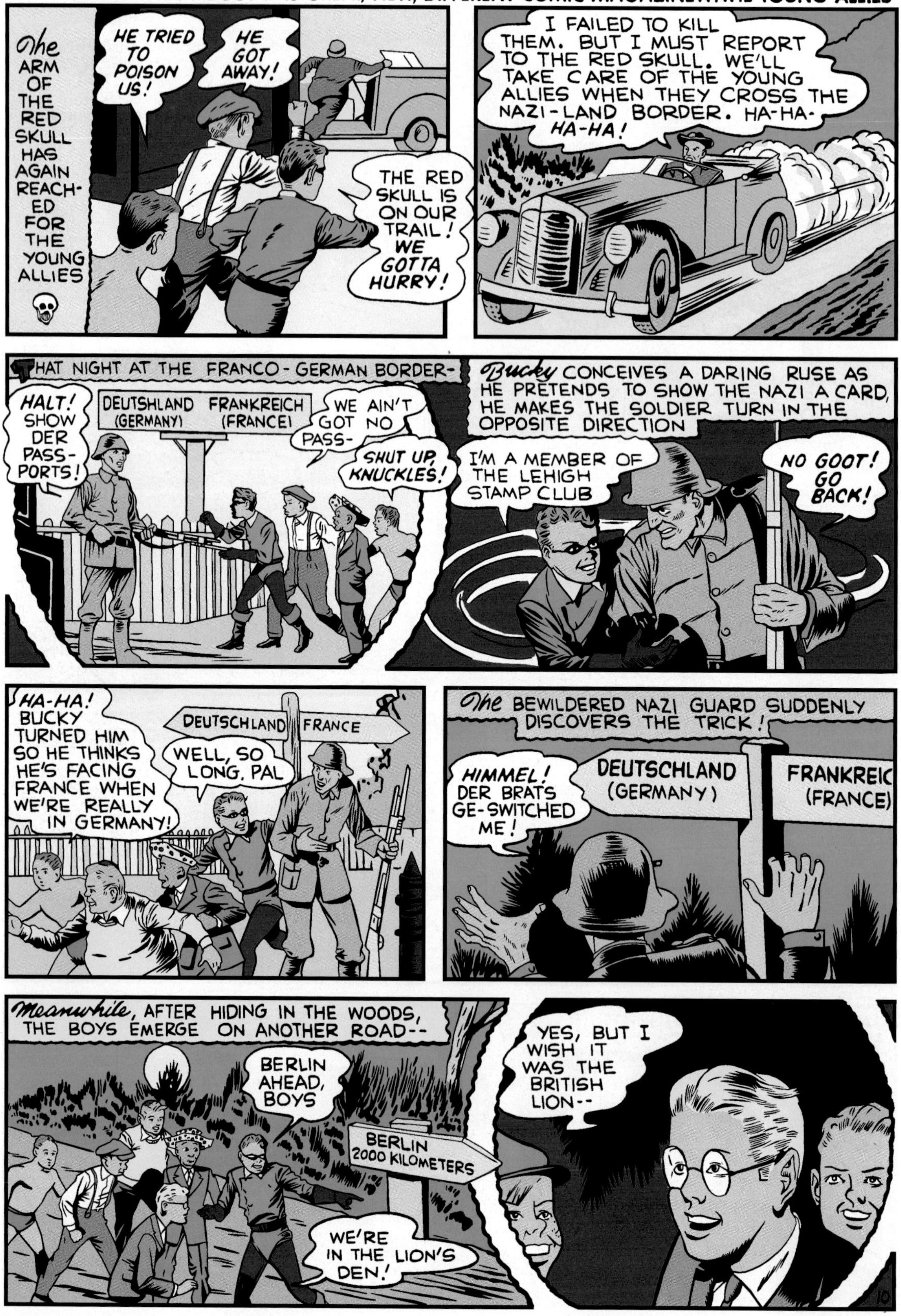
The ARM OF THE RED SKULL HAS AGAIN REACHED FOR THE YOUNG ALLIES
HE TRIED TO POISON US!
HE GOT AWAY!
THE RED SKULL IS ON OUR TRAIL! WE GOTTA HURRY!
I FAILED TO KILL THEM. BUT I MUST REPORT TO THE RED SKULL. WE'LL TAKE CARE OF THE YOUNG ALLIES WHEN THEY CROSS THE NAZI-LAND BORDER. HA-HA-HA-HA!
THAT NIGHT AT THE FRANCO-GERMAN BORDER-
HALT! SHOW DER PASS-PORTS!
DEUTSHLAND (GERMANY) FRANKREICH (FRANCE)
WE AIN'T GOT NO PASS-
SHUT UP, KNUCKLES!
Bucky CONCEIVES A DARING RUSE AS HE PRETENDS TO SHOW THE NAZI A CARD, HE MAKES THE SOLDIER TURN IN THE OPPOSITE DIRECTION
I'M A MEMBER OF THE LEHIGH STAMP CLUB
NO GOOT! GO BACK!
HA-HA! BUCKY TURNED HIM SO HE THINKS HE'S FACING FRANCE WHEN WE'RE REALLY IN GERMANY!
DEUTSCHLAND FRANCE
WELL, SO LONG, PAL
The BEWILDERED NAZI GUARD SUDDENLY DISCOVERS THE TRICK!
HIMMEL! DER BRATS GE-SWITCHED ME!
DEUTSCHLAND (GERMANY)
FRANKREIC (FRANCE)
Meanwhile, AFTER HIDING IN THE WOODS, THE BOYS EMERGE ON ANOTHER ROAD--
BERLIN AHEAD, BOYS
BERLIN 2000 KILOMETERS
WE'RE IN THE LION'S DEN!
YES, BUT I WISH IT WAS THE BRITISH LION--
10

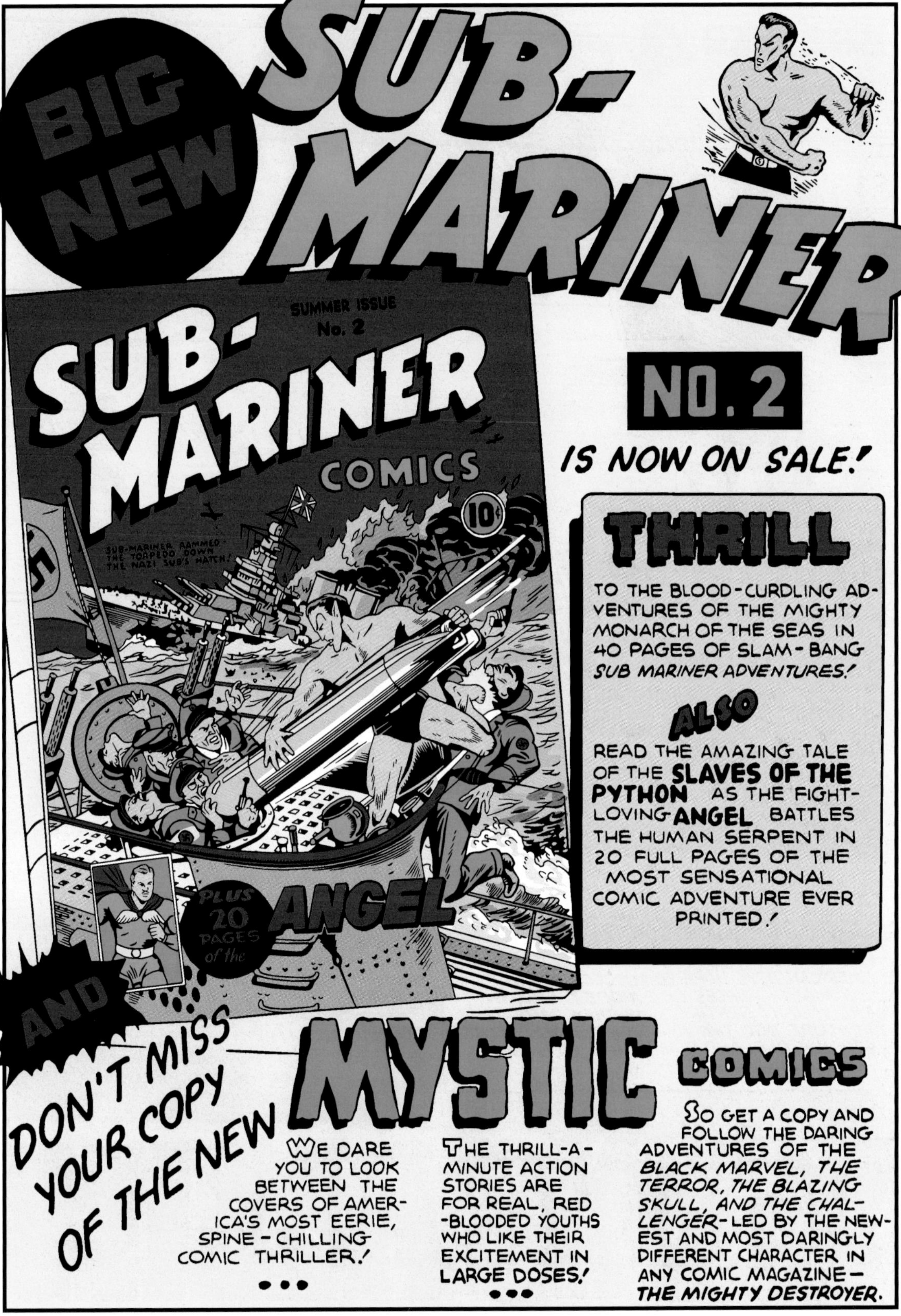

BIG NEW
SUB-MARINER
SUMMER ISSUE No. 2
SUB-MARINER COMICS
10¢
SUB-MARINER RAMMED THE TORPEDO DOWN THE NAZI SUB'S HATCH!
PLUS 20 PAGES of the ANGEL
NO. 2
IS NOW ON SALE!
THRILL
TO THE BLOOD-CURDLING ADVENTURES OF THE MIGHTY MONARCH OF THE SEAS IN 40 PAGES OF SLAM-BANG SUB MARINER ADVENTURES!
ALSO
READ THE AMAZING TALE OF THE SLAVES OF THE PYTHON AS THE FIGHT-LOVING ANGEL BATTLES THE HUMAN SERPENT IN 20 FULL PAGES OF THE MOST SENSATIONAL COMIC ADVENTURE EVER PRINTED!
AND
DON'T MISS YOUR COPY OF THE NEW
MYSTIC COMICS
WE DARE YOU TO LOOK BETWEEN THE COVERS OF AMERICA'S MOST EERIE, SPINE-CHILLING COMIC THRILLER! ...
THE THRILL-A-MINUTE ACTION STORIES ARE FOR REAL, RED-BLOODED YOUTHS WHO LIKE THEIR EXCITEMENT IN LARGE DOSES! ...
SO GET A COPY AND FOLLOW THE DARING ADVENTURES OF THE BLACK MARVEL, THE TERROR, THE BLAZING SKULL, AND THE CHALLENGER-LED BY THE NEWEST AND MOST DARINGLY DIFFERENT CHARACTER IN ANY COMIC MAGAZINE—THE MIGHTY DESTROYER.

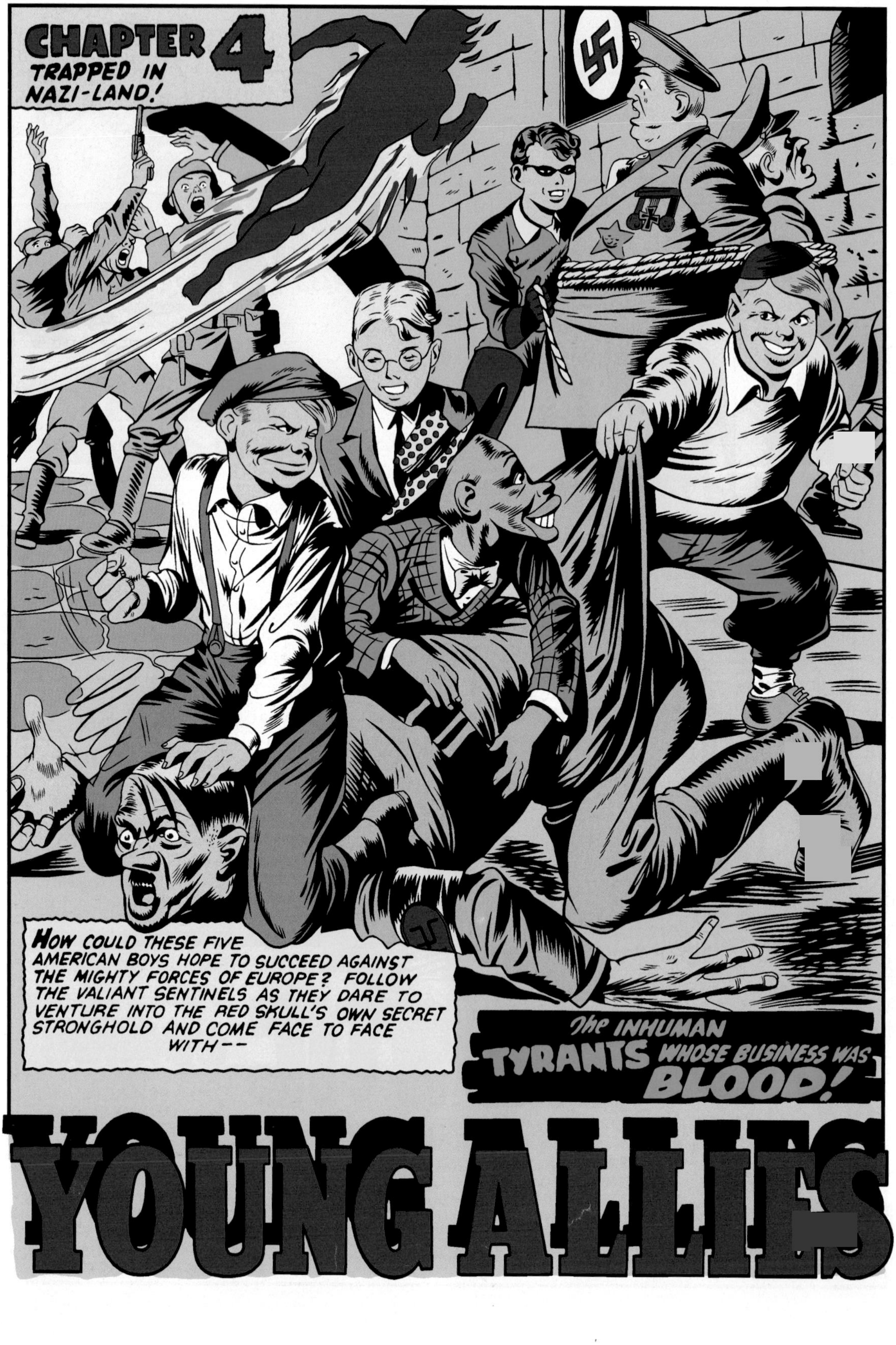
CHAPTER 4
TRAPPED IN NAZI-LAND!
HOW COULD THESE FIVE AMERICAN BOYS HOPE TO SUCCEED AGAINST THE MIGHTY FORCES OF EUROPE? FOLLOW THE VALIANT SENTINELS AS THEY DARE TO VENTURE INTO THE RED SKULL'S OWN SECRET STRONGHOLD AND COME FACE TO FACE WITH--
The INHUMAN TYRANTS WHOSE BUSINESS WAS BLOOD!
YOUNG ALLIES

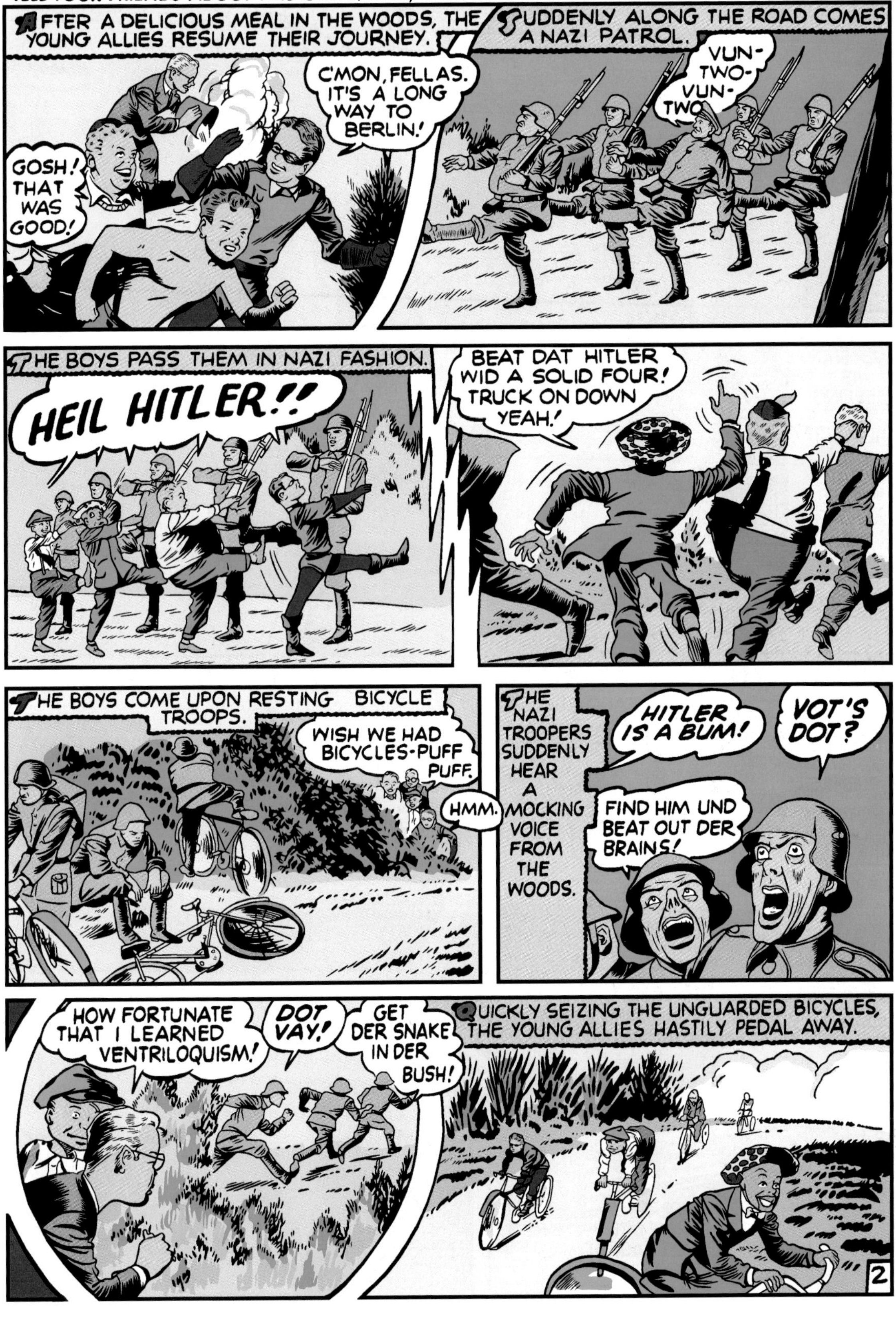
AFTER A DELICIOUS MEAL IN THE WOODS, THE YOUNG ALLIES RESUME THEIR JOURNEY.
C'MON, FELLAS. IT'S A LONG WAY TO BERLIN!
GOSH! THAT WAS GOOD!
SUDDENLY ALONG THE ROAD COMES A NAZI PATROL.
VUN-TWO-VUN-TWO
THE BOYS PASS THEM IN NAZI FASHION.
HEIL HITLER!!
BEAT DAT HITLER WID A SOLID FOUR! TRUCK ON DOWN YEAH!
THE BOYS COME UPON RESTING BICYCLE TROOPS.
WISH WE HAD BICYCLES-PUFF PUFF.
HMM.
THE NAZI TROOPERS SUDDENLY HEAR A MOCKING VOICE FROM THE WOODS.
HITLER IS A BUM!
VOT'S DOT?
FIND HIM UND BEAT OUT DER BRAINS!
HOW FORTUNATE THAT I LEARNED VENTRILOQUISM!
DOT VAY!
GET DER SNAKE IN DER BUSH!
QUICKLY SEIZING THE UNGUARDED BICYCLES, THE YOUNG ALLIES HASTILY PEDAL AWAY.
2

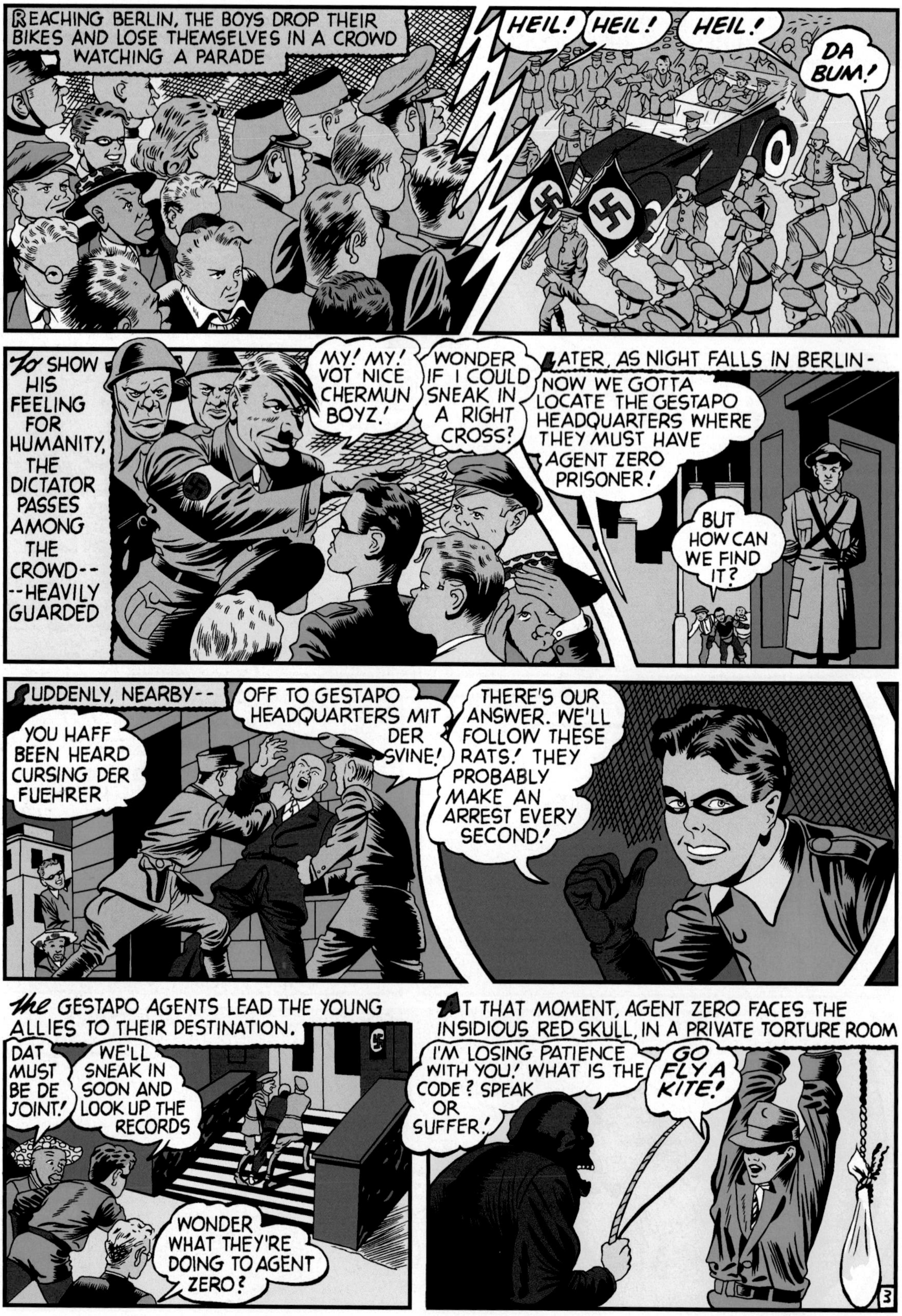
REACHING BERLIN, THE BOYS DROP THEIR BIKES AND LOSE THEMSELVES IN A CROWD WATCHING A PARADE
HEIL! HEIL! HEIL!
DA BUM!
TO SHOW HIS FEELING FOR HUMANITY, THE DICTATOR PASSES AMONG THE CROWD-- --HEAVILY GUARDED
MY! MY! VOT NICE CHERMUN BOYZ!
WONDER IF I COULD SNEAK IN A RIGHT CROSS?
LATER, AS NIGHT FALLS IN BERLIN-
NOW WE GOTTA LOCATE THE GESTAPO HEADQUARTERS WHERE THEY MUST HAVE AGENT ZERO PRISONER!
BUT HOW CAN WE FIND IT?
SUDDENLY, NEARBY--
YOU HAFF BEEN HEARD CURSING DER FUEHRER
OFF TO GESTAPO HEADQUARTERS MIT DER SVINE!
THERE'S OUR ANSWER. WE'LL FOLLOW THESE RATS! THEY PROBABLY MAKE AN ARREST EVERY SECOND!
THE GESTAPO AGENTS LEAD THE YOUNG ALLIES TO THEIR DESTINATION.
DAT MUST BE DE JOINT!
WE'LL SNEAK IN SOON AND LOOK UP THE RECORDS
WONDER WHAT THEY'RE DOING TO AGENT ZERO?
AT THAT MOMENT, AGENT ZERO FACES THE INSIDIOUS RED SKULL, IN A PRIVATE TORTURE ROOM
I'M LOSING PATIENCE WITH YOU! WHAT IS THE CODE? SPEAK OR SUFFER!
GO FLY A KITE!
3

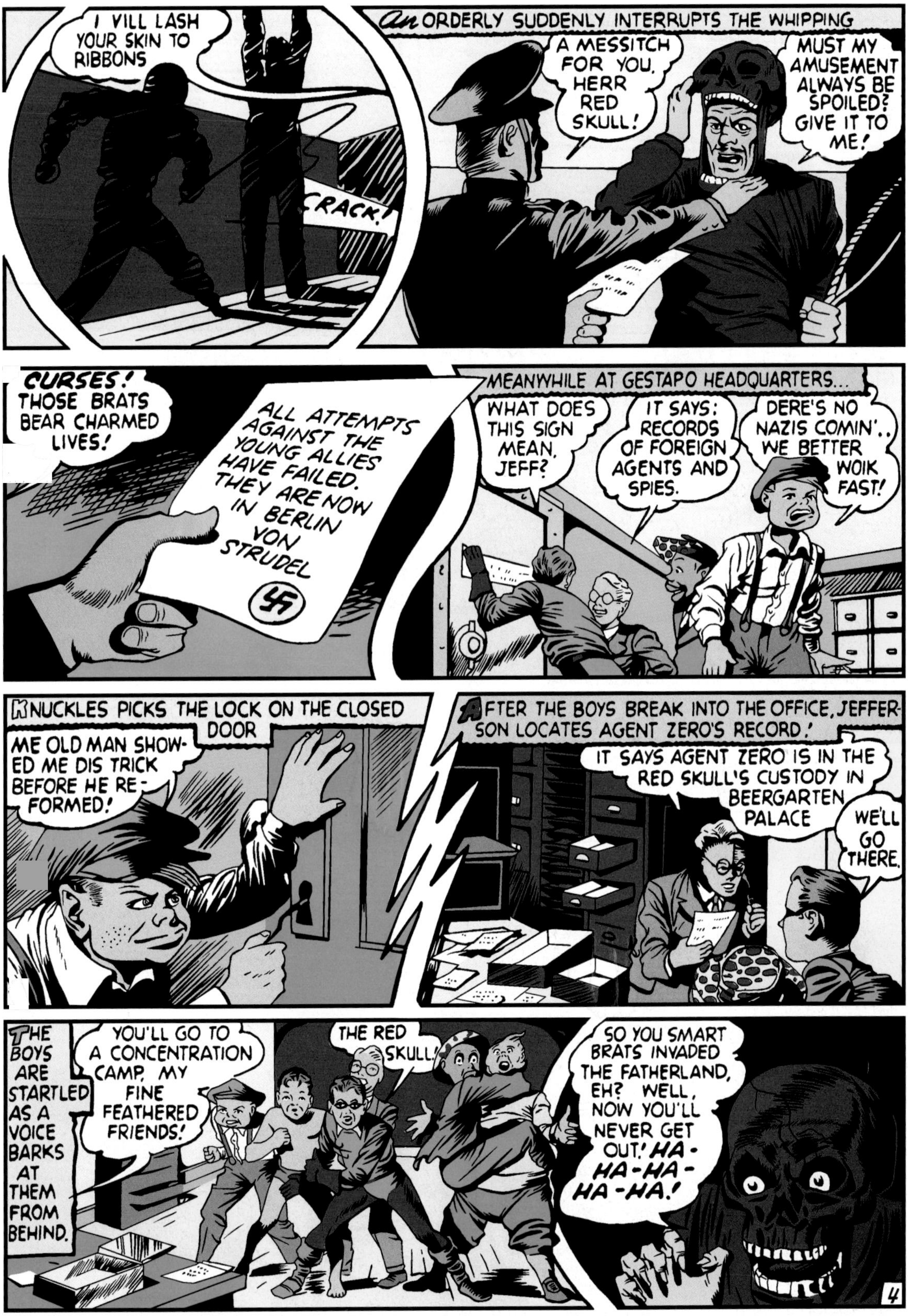
I VILL LASH YOUR SKIN TO RIBBONS
CRACK!
AN ORDERLY SUDDENLY INTERRUPTS THE WHIPPING
A MESSITCH FOR YOU, HERR RED SKULL!
MUST MY AMUSEMENT ALWAYS BE SPOILED? GIVE IT TO ME!
CURSES! THOSE BRATS BEAR CHARMED LIVES!
ALL ATTEMPTS AGAINST THE YOUNG ALLIES HAVE FAILED. THEY ARE NOW IN BERLIN VON STRUDEL
MEANWHILE AT GESTAPO HEADQUARTERS...
WHAT DOES THIS SIGN MEAN, JEFF?
IT SAYS: RECORDS OF FOREIGN AGENTS AND SPIES.
DERE'S NO NAZIS COMIN'.. WE BETTER WOIK FAST!
KNUCKLES PICKS THE LOCK ON THE CLOSED DOOR
ME OLD MAN SHOWED ME DIS TRICK BEFORE HE REFORMED!
AFTER THE BOYS BREAK INTO THE OFFICE, JEFFERSON LOCATES AGENT ZERO'S RECORD!
IT SAYS AGENT ZERO IS IN THE RED SKULL'S CUSTODY IN BEERGARTEN PALACE
WE'LL GO THERE.
THE BOYS ARE STARTLED AS A VOICE BARKS AT THEM FROM BEHIND.
YOU'LL GO TO A CONCENTRATION CAMP, MY FINE FEATHERED FRIENDS!
THE RED SKULL!
SO YOU SMART BRATS INVADED THE FATHERLAND, EH? WELL, NOW YOU'LL NEVER GET OUT! HA-HA-HA-HA-HA!
4

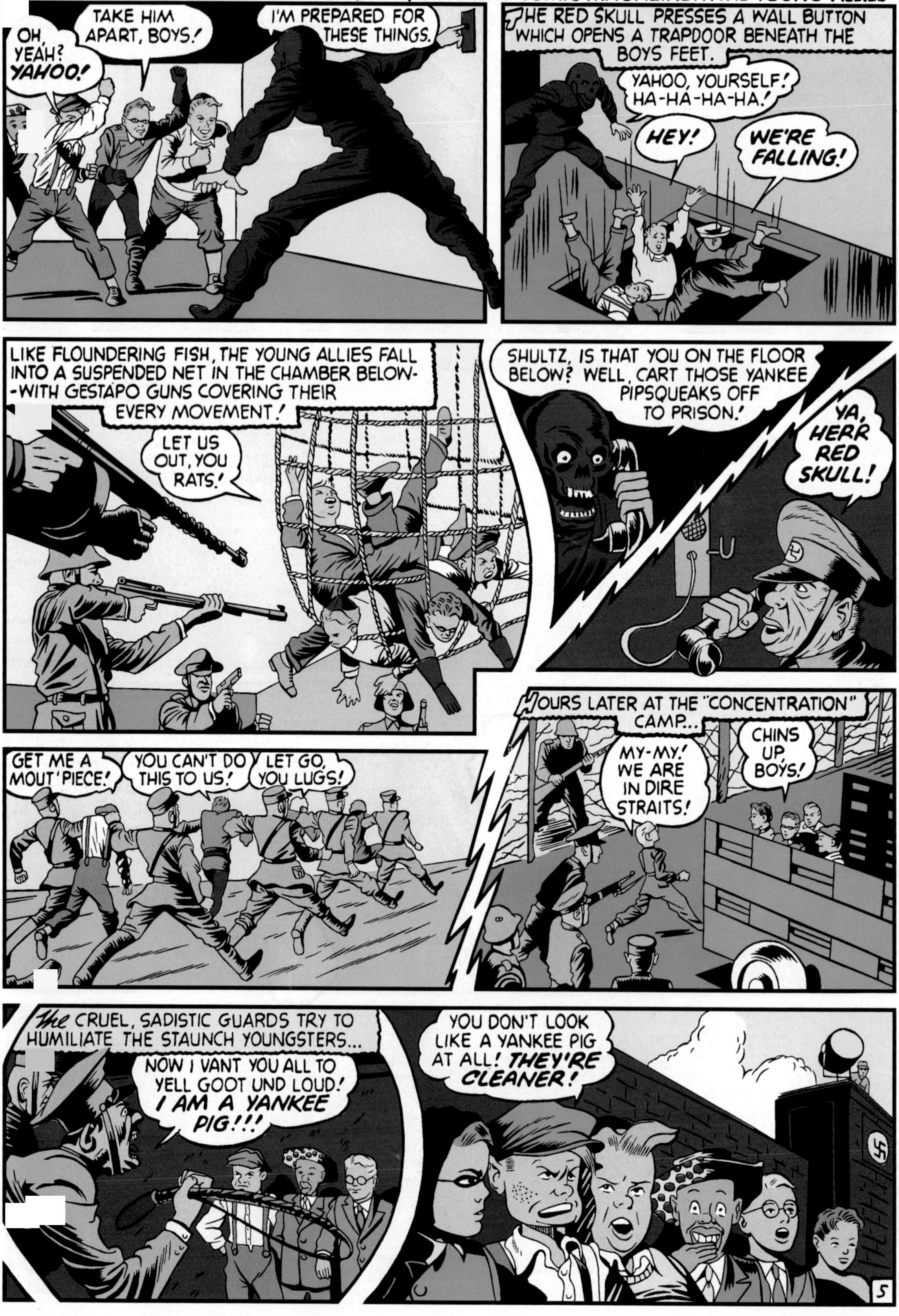
OH, YEAH? YAHOO!
TAKE HIM APART, BOYS!
I'M PREPARED FOR THESE THINGS.
THE RED SKULL PRESSES A WALL BUTTON WHICH OPENS A TRAPDOOR BENEATH THE BOYS FEET.
YAHOO, YOURSELF! HA-HA-HA-HA!
HEY!
WE'RE FALLING!
LIKE FLOUNDERING FISH, THE YOUNG ALLIES FALL INTO A SUSPENDED NET IN THE CHAMBER BELOW- -WITH GESTAPO GUNS COVERING THEIR EVERY MOVEMENT!
LET US OUT, YOU RATS!
SHULTZ, IS THAT YOU ON THE FLOOR BELOW? WELL, CART THOSE YANKEE PIPSQUEAKS OFF TO PRISON!
YA, HERR RED SKULL!
GET ME A MOUT'PIECE!
YOU CAN'T DO THIS TO US!
LET GO, YOU LUGS!
HOURS LATER AT THE "CONCENTRATION" CAMP...
MY-MY! WE ARE IN DIRE STRAITS!
CHINS UP, BOYS!
THE CRUEL, SADISTIC GUARDS TRY TO HUMILIATE THE STAUNCH YOUNGSTERS...
NOW I VANT YOU ALL TO YELL GOOT UND LOUD! I AM A YANKEE PIG!!!
YOU DON'T LOOK LIKE A YANKEE PIG AT ALL! THEY'RE CLEANER!

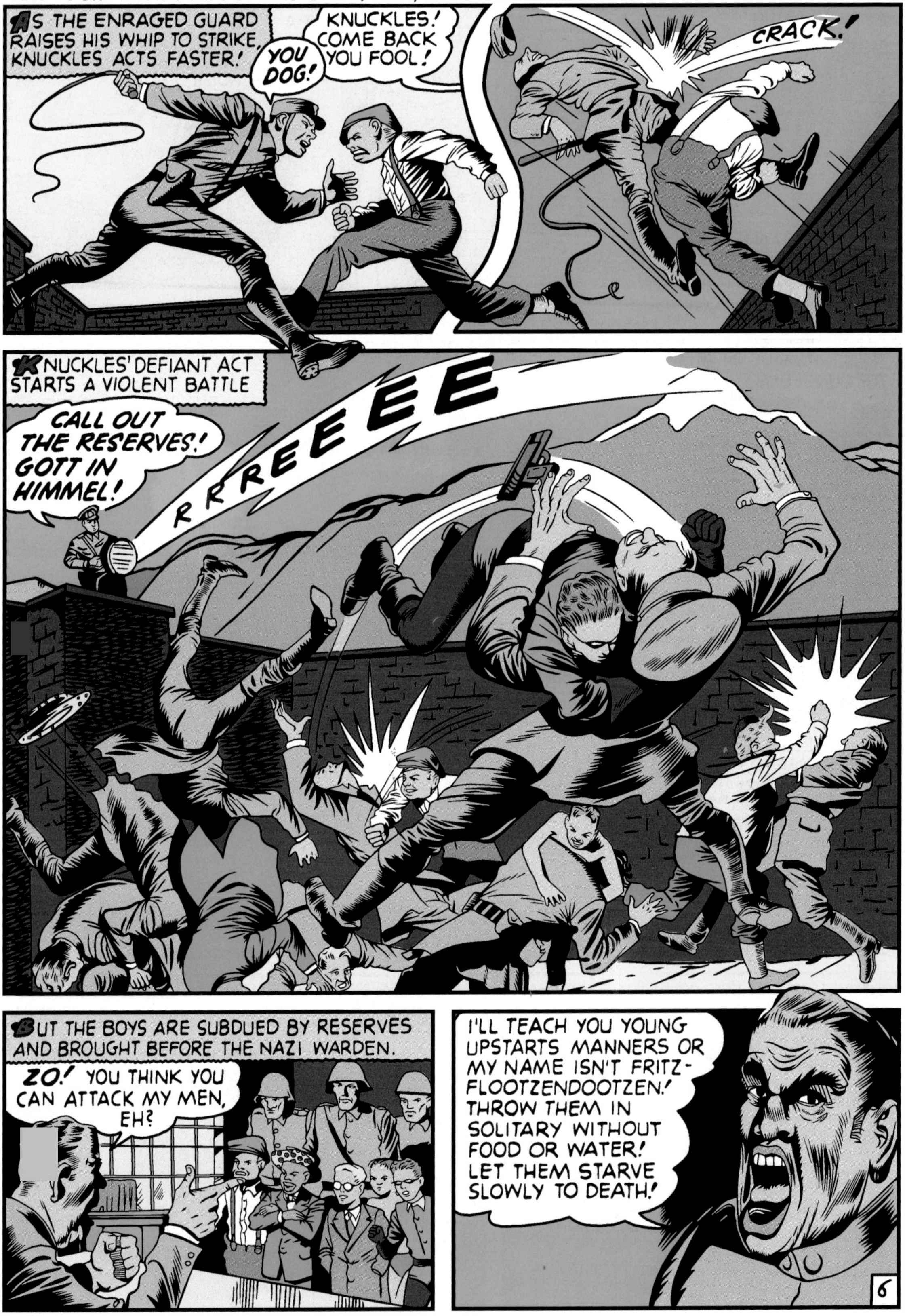
AS THE ENRAGED GUARD RAISES HIS WHIP TO STRIKE, KNUCKLES ACTS FASTER!
YOU DOG!
KNUCKLES! COME BACK YOU FOOL!
CRACK!
KNUCKLES' DEFIANT ACT STARTS A VIOLENT BATTLE
CALL OUT THE RESERVES! GOTT IN HIMMEL!
RRREEEEE
BUT THE BOYS ARE SUBDUED BY RESERVES AND BROUGHT BEFORE THE NAZI WARDEN.
ZO! YOU THINK YOU CAN ATTACK MY MEN, EH?
I'LL TEACH YOU YOUNG UPSTARTS MANNERS OR MY NAME ISN'T FRITZ-FLOOTZENDOOTZEN! THROW THEM IN SOLITARY WITHOUT FOOD OR WATER! LET THEM STARVE SLOWLY TO DEATH!
6

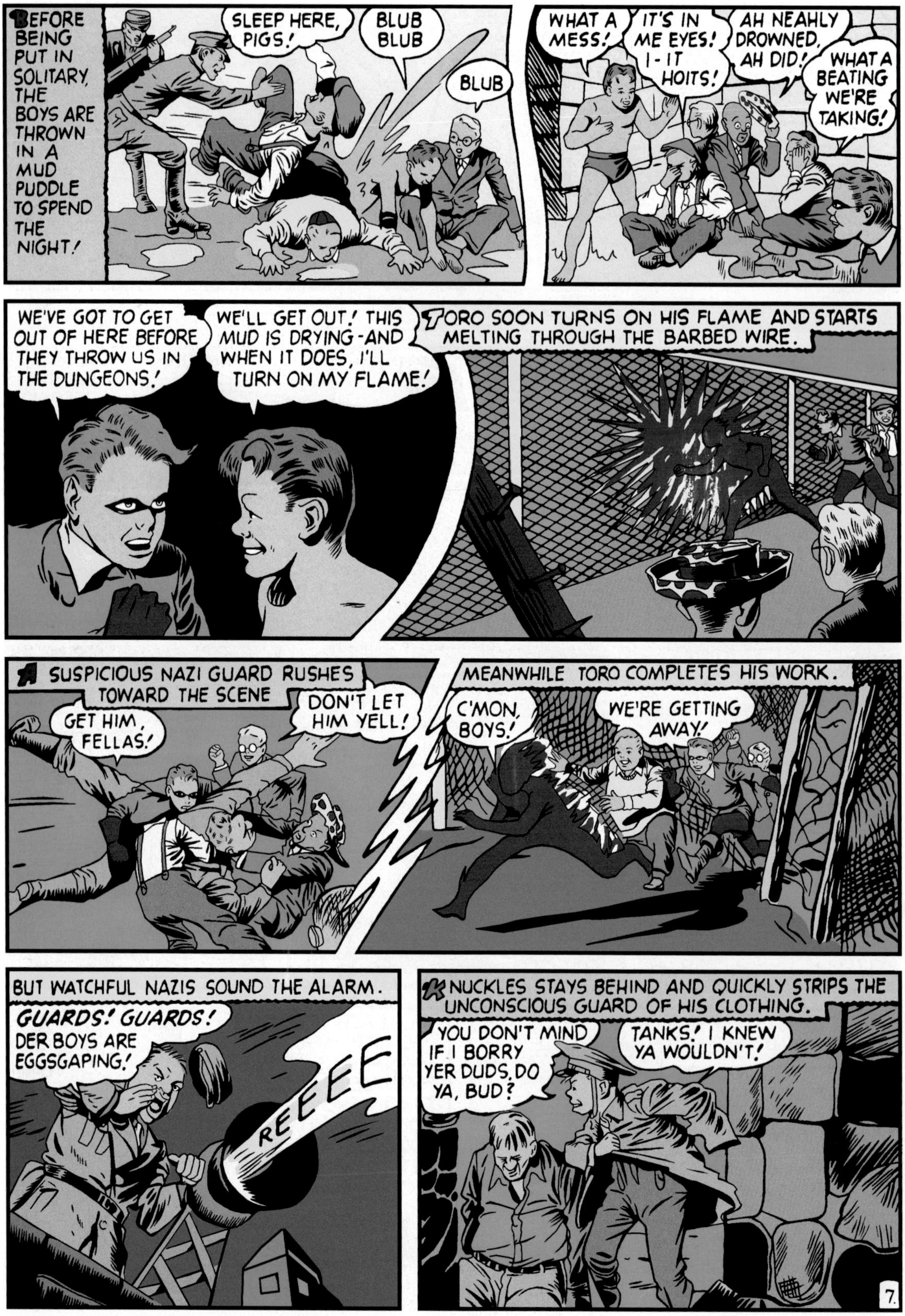

BEFORE BEING PUT IN SOLITARY, THE BOYS ARE THROWN IN A MUD PUDDLE TO SPEND THE NIGHT!
SLEEP HERE, PIGS!
BLUB BLUB
BLUB
WHAT A MESS!
IT'S IN ME EYES! I - IT HOITS!
AH NEAHLY DROWNED, AH DID!
WHAT A BEATING WE'RE TAKING!
WE'VE GOT TO GET OUT OF HERE BEFORE THEY THROW US IN THE DUNGEONS!
WE'LL GET OUT! THIS MUD IS DRYING - AND WHEN IT DOES, I'LL TURN ON MY FLAME!
TORO SOON TURNS ON HIS FLAME AND STARTS MELTING THROUGH THE BARBED WIRE.
A SUSPICIOUS NAZI GUARD RUSHES TOWARD THE SCENE
GET HIM, FELLAS!
DON'T LET HIM YELL!
MEANWHILE TORO COMPLETES HIS WORK.
C'MON, BOYS!
WE'RE GETTING AWAY!
BUT WATCHFUL NAZIS SOUND THE ALARM.
GUARDS! GUARDS! DER BOYS ARE EGGSGAPING!
REEEEE
KNUCKLES STAYS BEHIND AND QUICKLY STRIPS THE UNCONSCIOUS GUARD OF HIS CLOTHING.
YOU DON'T MIND IF I BORRY YER DUDS, DO YA, BUD?
TANKS! I KNEW YA WOULDN'T!

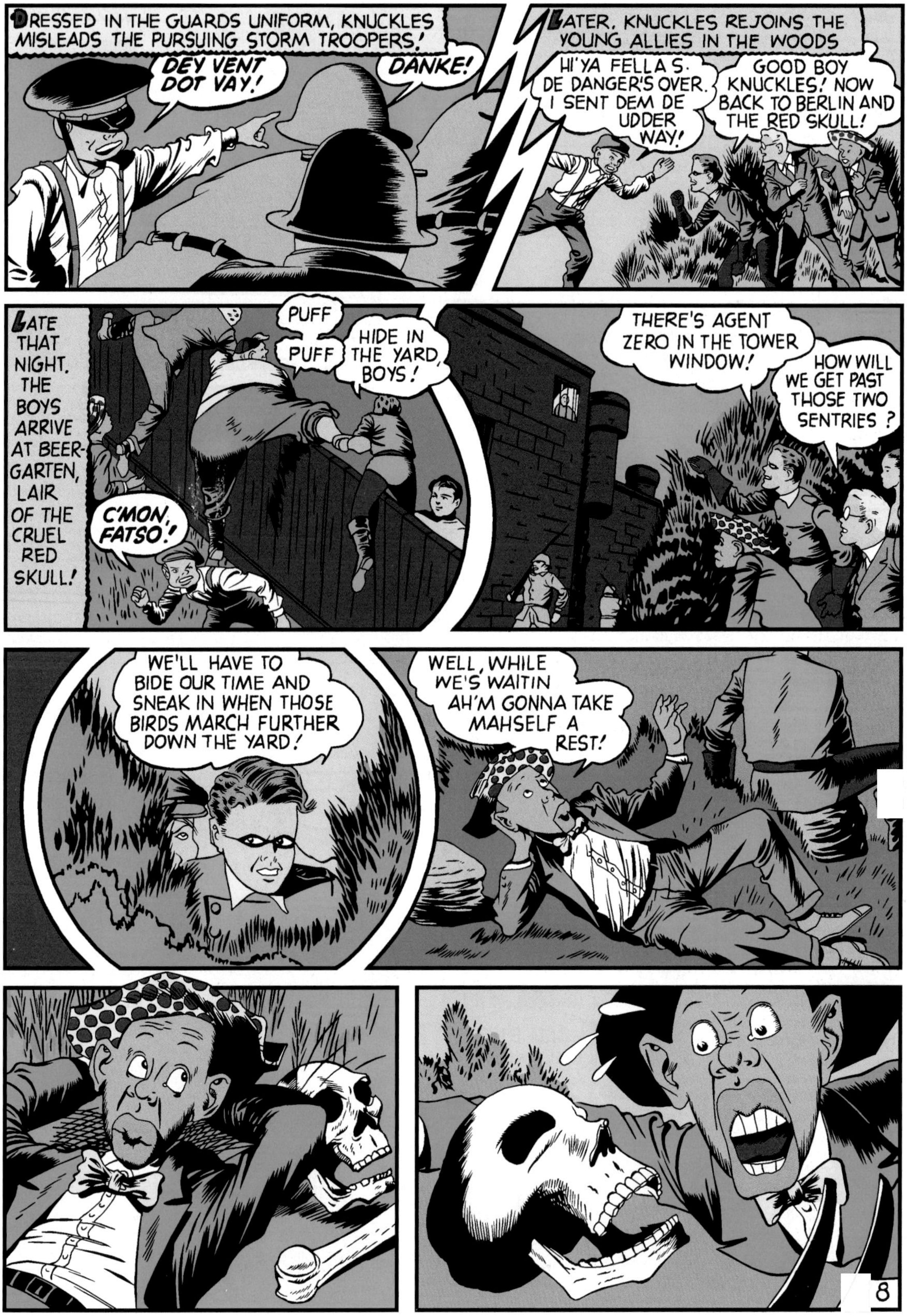
DRESSED IN THE GUARDS UNIFORM, KNUCKLES MISLEADS THE PURSUING STORM TROOPERS!
DEY VENT DOT VAY!
DANKE!
LATER, KNUCKLES REJOINS THE YOUNG ALLIES IN THE WOODS
HI'YA FELLA'S. DE DANGER'S OVER. I SENT DEM DE UDDER WAY!
GOOD BOY KNUCKLES! NOW BACK TO BERLIN AND THE RED SKULL!
LATE THAT NIGHT, THE BOYS ARRIVE AT BEER-GARTEN, LAIR OF THE CRUEL RED SKULL!
PUFF
PUFF
HIDE IN THE YARD, BOYS!
C'MON, FATSO!
THERE'S AGENT ZERO IN THE TOWER WINDOW!
HOW WILL WE GET PAST THOSE TWO SENTRIES ?
WE'LL HAVE TO BIDE OUR TIME AND SNEAK IN WHEN THOSE BIRDS MARCH FURTHER DOWN THE YARD!
WELL, WHILE WE'S WAITIN AH'M GONNA TAKE MAHSELF A REST!

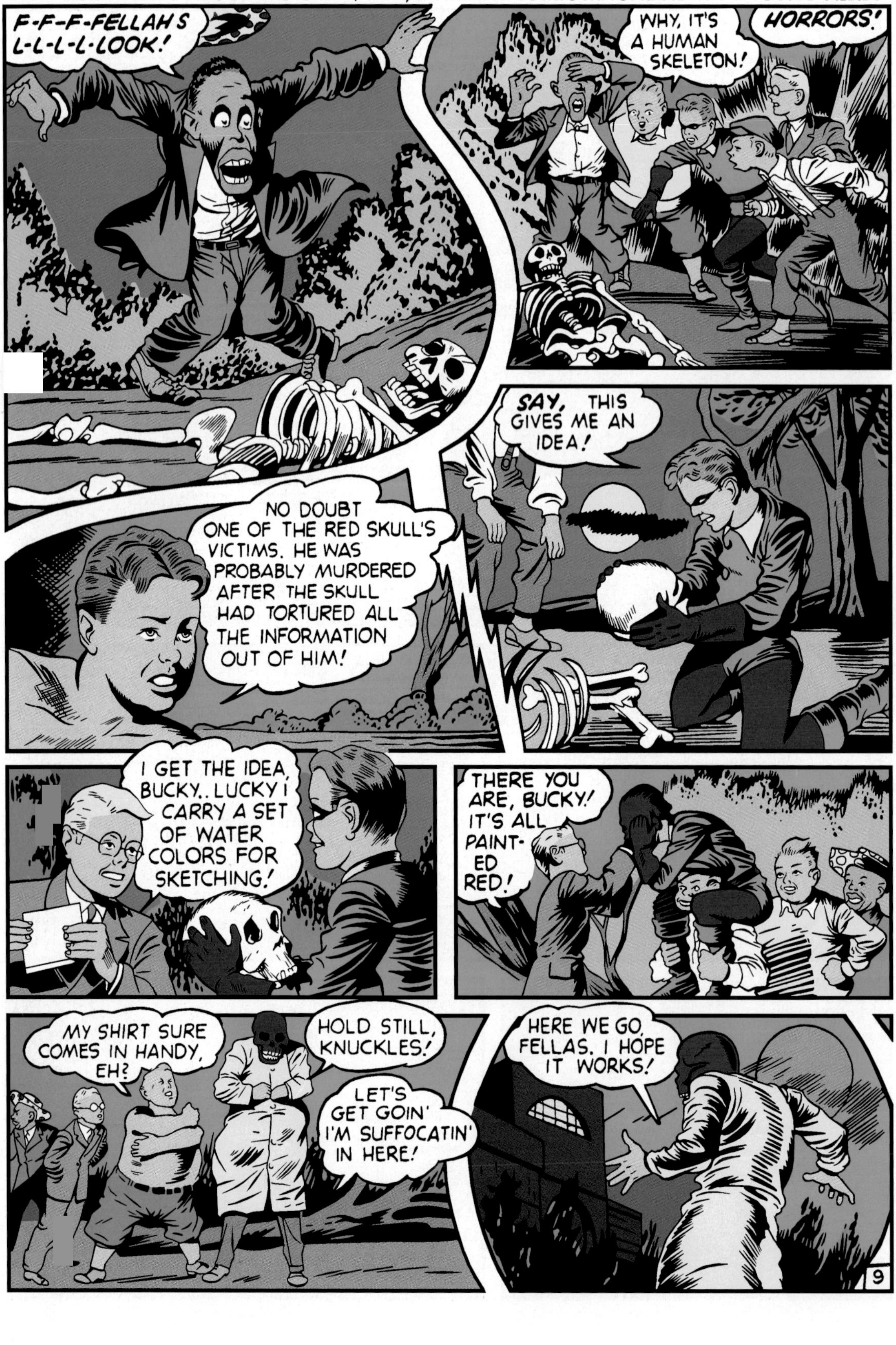
F-F-F-FELLAH S L-L-L-L-LOOK!
WHY, IT'S A HUMAN SKELETON!
HORRORS!
NO DOUBT ONE OF THE RED SKULL'S VICTIMS. HE WAS PROBABLY MURDERED AFTER THE SKULL HAD TORTURED ALL THE INFORMATION OUT OF HIM!
SAY, THIS GIVES ME AN IDEA!
I GET THE IDEA, BUCKY.. LUCKY I CARRY A SET OF WATER COLORS FOR SKETCHING!
THERE YOU ARE, BUCKY! IT'S ALL PAINT-ED RED!
MY SHIRT SURE COMES IN HANDY, EH?
HOLD STILL, KNUCKLES!
LET'S GET GOIN' I'M SUFFOCATIN' IN HERE!
HERE WE GO, FELLAS. I HOPE IT WORKS!

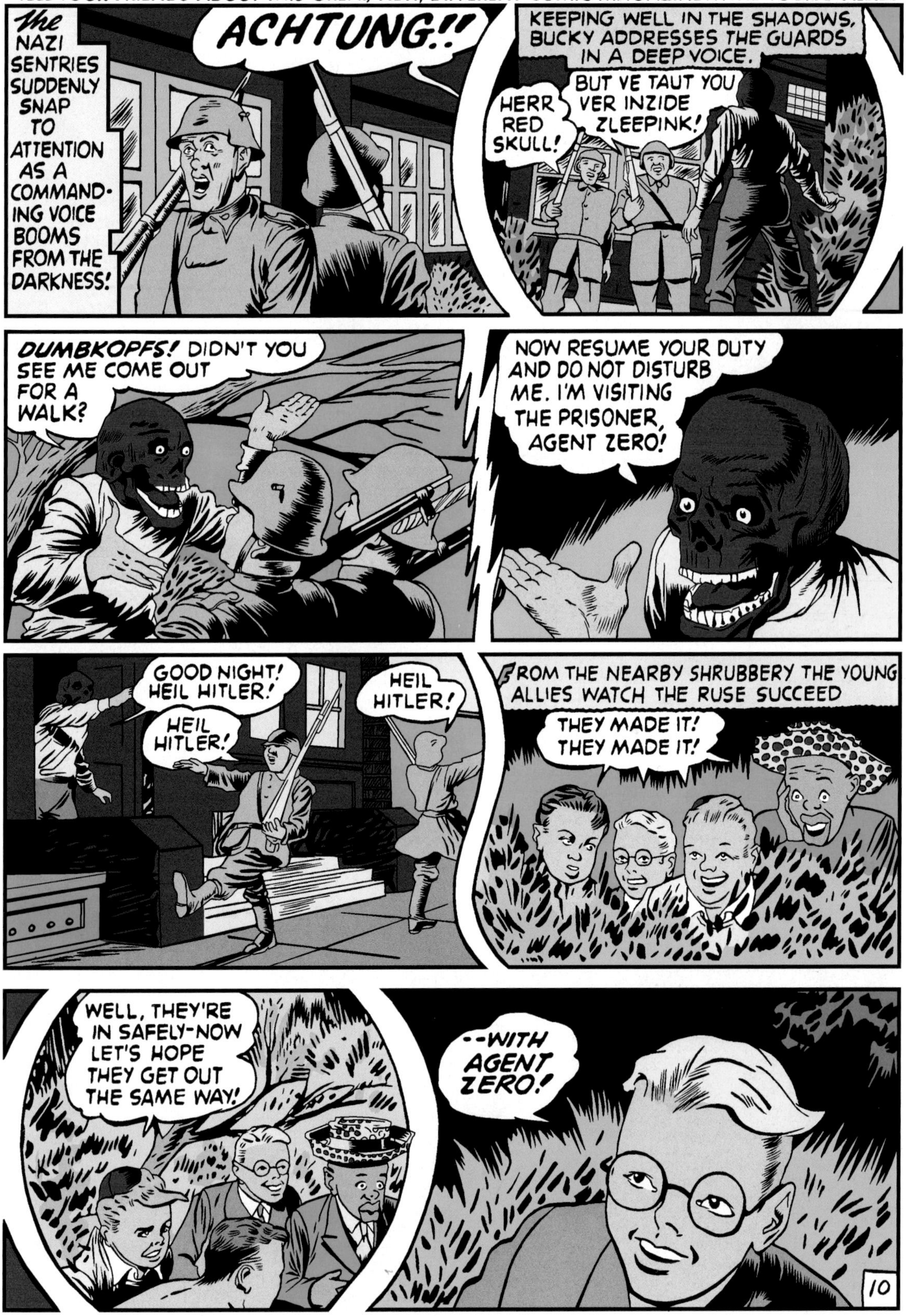
The NAZI SENTRIES SUDDENLY SNAP TO ATTENTION AS A COMMANDING VOICE BOOMS FROM THE DARKNESS!
ACHTUNG!!
KEEPING WELL IN THE SHADOWS, BUCKY ADDRESSES THE GUARDS IN A DEEP VOICE.
HERR RED SKULL!
BUT VE TAUT YOU VER INZIDE ZLEEPINK!
DUMBKOPFS! DIDN'T YOU SEE ME COME OUT FOR A WALK?
NOW RESUME YOUR DUTY AND DO NOT DISTURB ME. I'M VISITING THE PRISONER, AGENT ZERO!
GOOD NIGHT! HEIL HITLER!
HEIL HITLER!
HEIL HITLER!
FROM THE NEARBY SHRUBBERY THE YOUNG ALLIES WATCH THE RUSE SUCCEED
THEY MADE IT! THEY MADE IT!
WELL, THEY'RE IN SAFELY-NOW LET'S HOPE THEY GET OUT THE SAME WAY!
--WITH AGENT ZERO!
10

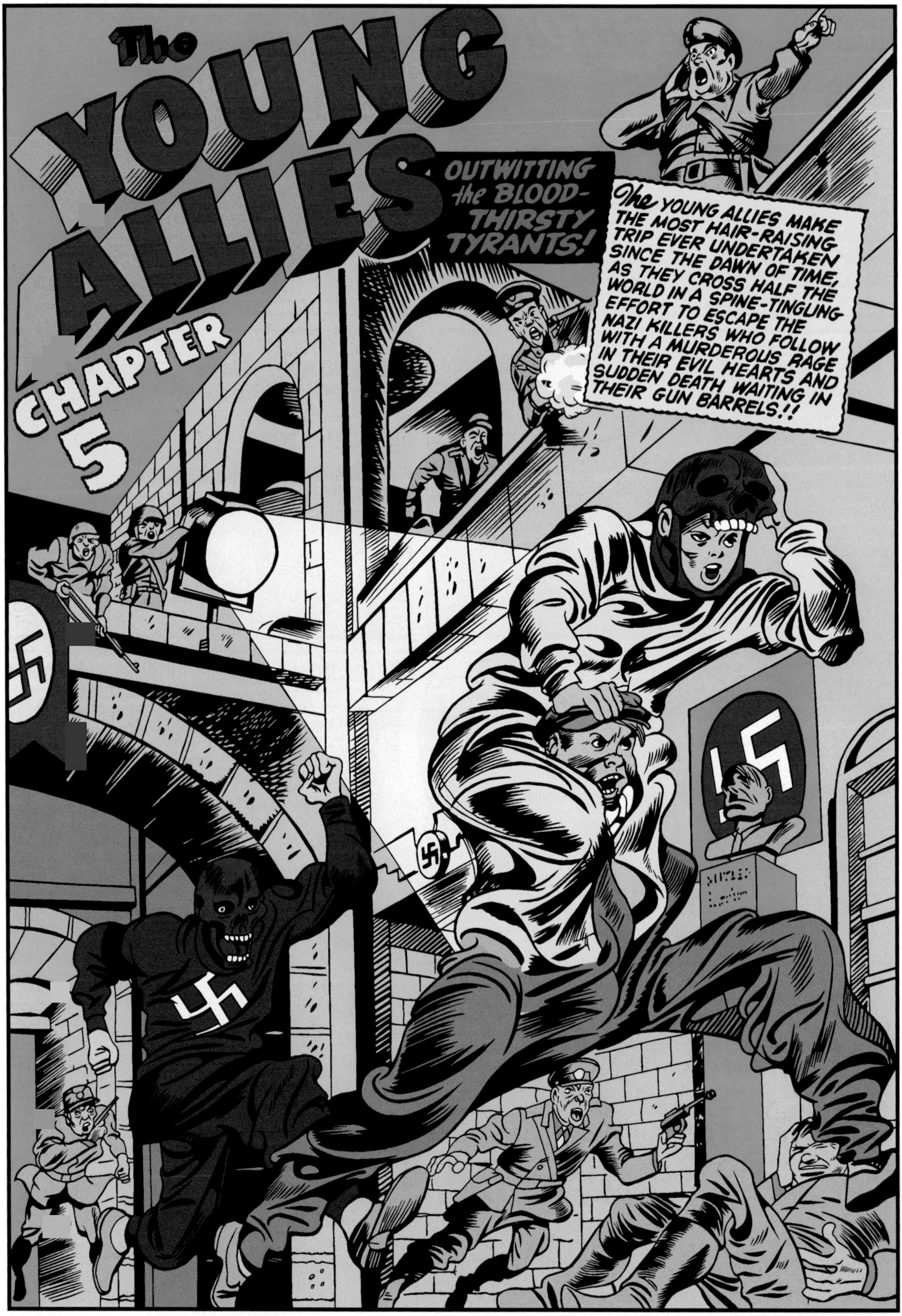
The YOUNG ALLIES
CHAPTER 5
OUTWITTING the BLOOD-THIRSTY TYRANTS!
The YOUNG ALLIES MAKE THE MOST HAIR-RAISING TRIP EVER UNDERTAKEN SINCE THE DAWN OF TIME, AS THEY CROSS HALF THE WORLD IN A SPINE-TINGLING EFFORT TO ESCAPE THE NAZI KILLERS WHO FOLLOW WITH A MURDEROUS RAGE IN THEIR EVIL HEARTS AND SUDDEN DEATH WAITING IN THEIR GUN BARRELS!!

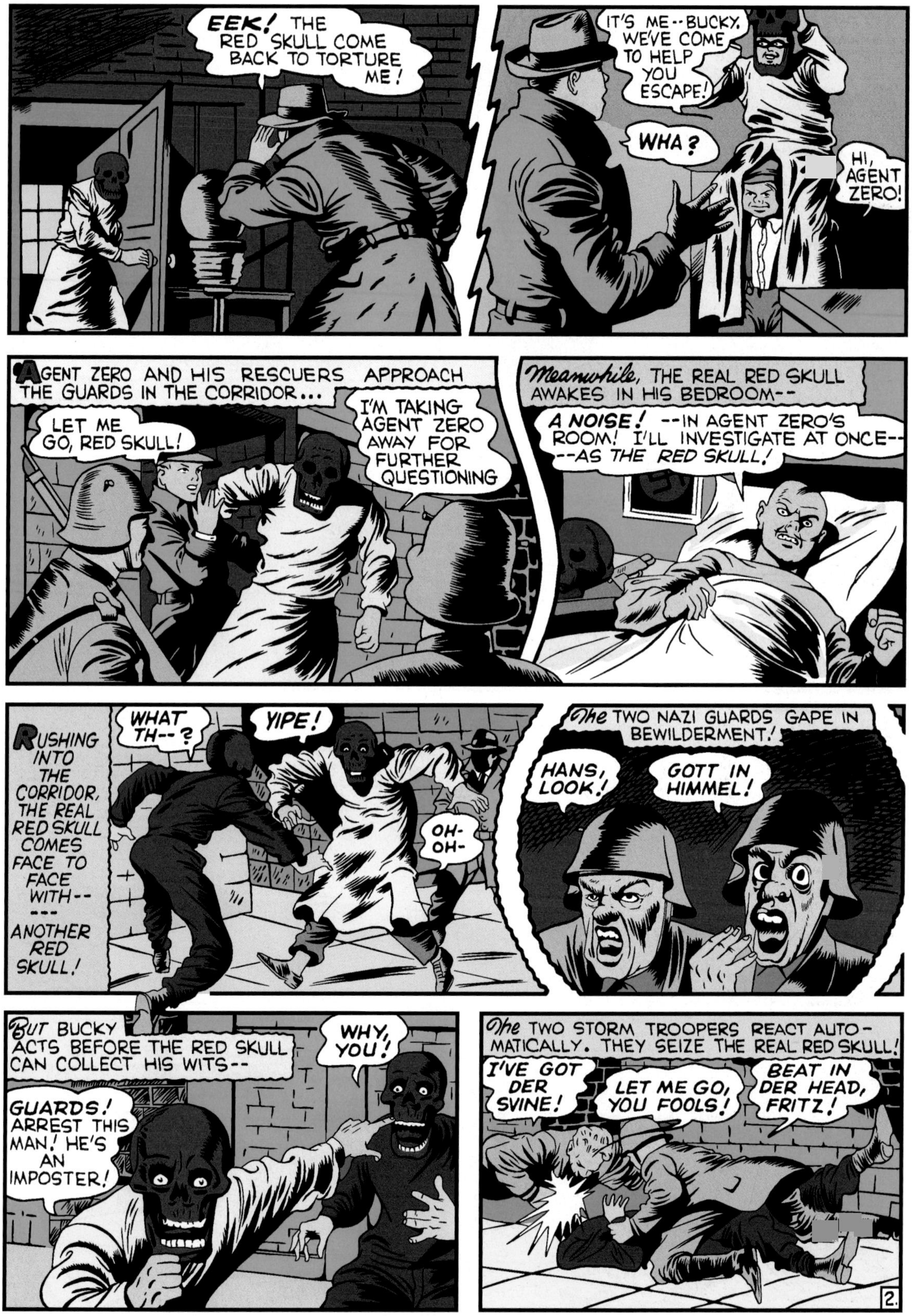

EEK! THE RED SKULL COME BACK TO TORTURE ME!
IT'S ME--BUCKY. WE'VE COME TO HELP YOU ESCAPE!
WHA?
HI, AGENT ZERO!
AGENT ZERO AND HIS RESCUERS APPROACH THE GUARDS IN THE CORRIDOR...
LET ME GO, RED SKULL!
I'M TAKING AGENT ZERO AWAY FOR FURTHER QUESTIONING
Meanwhile, THE REAL RED SKULL AWAKES IN HIS BEDROOM--
A NOISE! --IN AGENT ZERO'S ROOM! I'LL INVESTIGATE AT ONCE-- --AS THE RED SKULL!
RUSHING INTO THE CORRIDOR, THE REAL RED SKULL COMES FACE TO FACE WITH-- --- ANOTHER RED SKULL!
WHAT TH--?
YIPE!
OH-OH-
The TWO NAZI GUARDS GAPE IN BEWILDERMENT!
HANS, LOOK!
GOTT IN HIMMEL!
BUT BUCKY ACTS BEFORE THE RED SKULL CAN COLLECT HIS WITS--
WHY, YOU!
GUARDS! ARREST THIS MAN! HE'S AN IMPOSTER!
The TWO STORM TROOPERS REACT AUTOMATICALLY. THEY SEIZE THE REAL RED SKULL!
I'VE GOT DER SVINE!
LET ME GO, YOU FOOLS!
BEAT IN DER HEAD, FRITZ!
2.

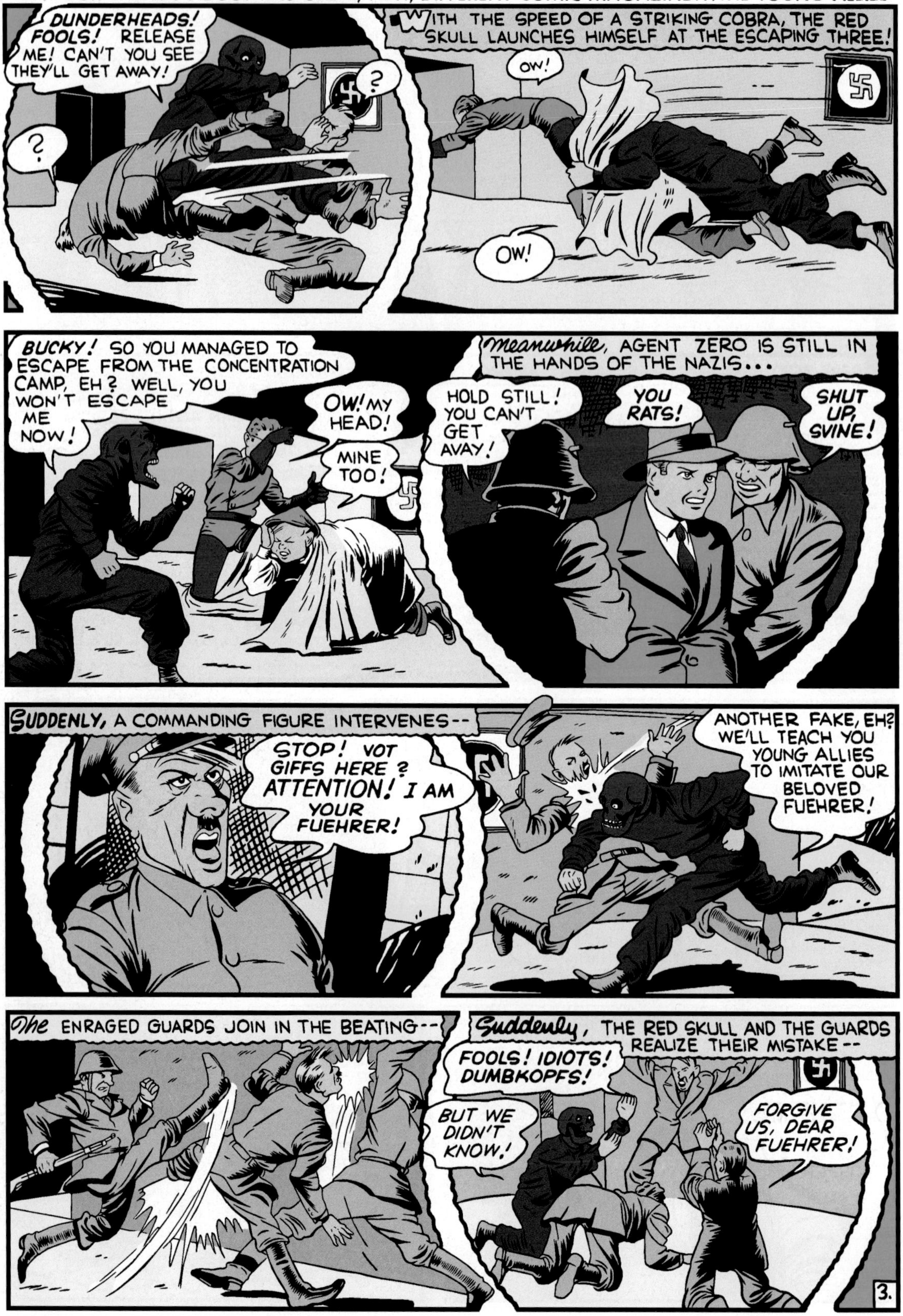
DUNDERHEADS! FOOLS! RELEASE ME! CAN'T YOU SEE THEY'LL GET AWAY!
?
?
WITH THE SPEED OF A STRIKING COBRA, THE RED SKULL LAUNCHES HIMSELF AT THE ESCAPING THREE!
OW!
OW!
BUCKY! SO YOU MANAGED TO ESCAPE FROM THE CONCENTRATION CAMP, EH? WELL, YOU WON'T ESCAPE ME NOW!
OW! MY HEAD!
MINE TOO!
MEANWHILE, AGENT ZERO IS STILL IN THE HANDS OF THE NAZIS...
HOLD STILL! YOU CAN'T GET AVAY!
YOU RATS!
SHUT UP, SVINE!
SUDDENLY, A COMMANDING FIGURE INTERVENES--
STOP! VOT GIFFS HERE? ATTENTION! I AM YOUR FUEHRER!
ANOTHER FAKE, EH? WE'LL TEACH YOU YOUNG ALLIES TO IMITATE OUR BELOVED FUEHRER!
THE ENRAGED GUARDS JOIN IN THE BEATING--
SUDDENLY, THE RED SKULL AND THE GUARDS REALIZE THEIR MISTAKE--
FOOLS! IDIOTS! DUMBKOPFS!
BUT WE DIDN'T KNOW!
FORGIVE US, DEAR FUEHRER!

TELL YOUR FRIENDS ABOUT THIS GREAT, NEW, DIFFERENT COMIC MAGAZINE...THE YOUNG ALLIES

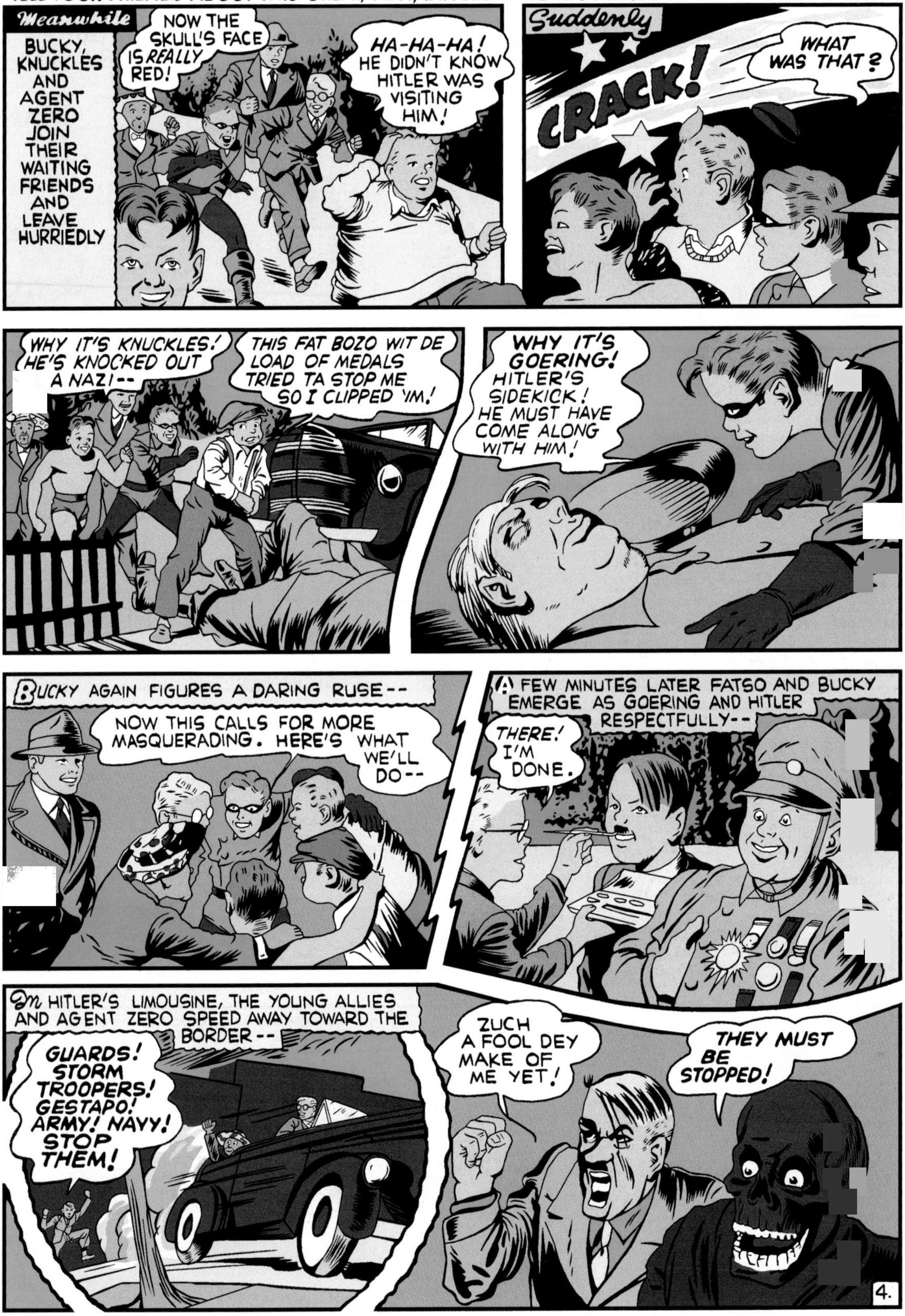

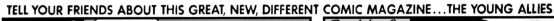

Meanwhile
BUCKY, KNUCKLES AND AGENT ZERO JOIN THEIR WAITING FRIENDS AND LEAVE HURRIEDLY
NOW THE SKULL'S FACE IS REALLY RED!
HA-HA-HA! HE DIDN'T KNOW HITLER WAS VISITING HIM!
Suddenly
CRACK!
WHAT WAS THAT?
WHY IT'S KNUCKLES! HE'S KNOCKED OUT A NAZI--
THIS FAT BOZO WIT DE LOAD OF MEDALS TRIED TA STOP ME SO I CLIPPED 'IM!
WHY IT'S GOERING! HITLER'S SIDEKICK! HE MUST HAVE COME ALONG WITH HIM!
BUCKY AGAIN FIGURES A DARING RUSE--
NOW THIS CALLS FOR MORE MASQUERADING. HERE'S WHAT WE'LL DO--
A FEW MINUTES LATER FATSO AND BUCKY EMERGE AS GOERING AND HITLER RESPECTFULLY--
THERE! I'M DONE.
IN HITLER'S LIMOUSINE, THE YOUNG ALLIES AND AGENT ZERO SPEED AWAY TOWARD THE BORDER--
GUARDS! STORM TROOPERS! GESTAPO! ARMY! NAVY! STOP THEM!
ZUCH A FOOL DEY MAKE OF ME YET!
THEY MUST BE STOPPED!

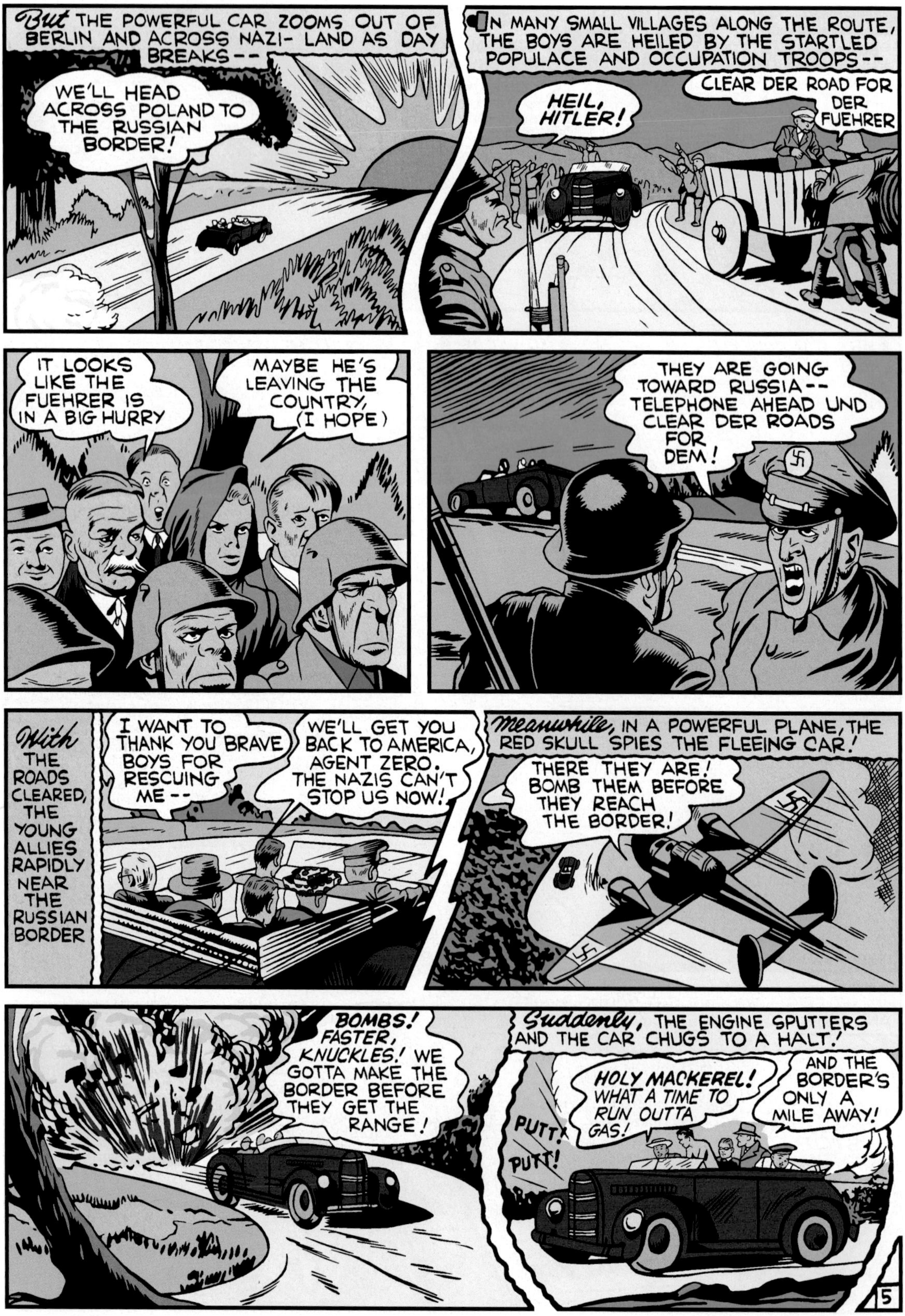

But THE POWERFUL CAR ZOOMS OUT OF BERLIN AND ACROSS NAZI- LAND AS DAY BREAKS--
WE'LL HEAD ACROSS POLAND TO THE RUSSIAN BORDER!
IN MANY SMALL VILLAGES ALONG THE ROUTE, THE BOYS ARE HEILED BY THE STARTLED POPULACE AND OCCUPATION TROOPS--
HEIL, HITLER!
CLEAR DER ROAD FOR DER FUEHRER
IT LOOKS LIKE THE FUEHRER IS IN A BIG HURRY
MAYBE HE'S LEAVING THE COUNTRY, (I HOPE)
THEY ARE GOING TOWARD RUSSIA-- TELEPHONE AHEAD UND CLEAR DER ROADS FOR DEM!
With THE ROADS CLEARED, THE YOUNG ALLIES RAPIDLY NEAR THE RUSSIAN BORDER
I WANT TO THANK YOU BRAVE BOYS FOR RESCUING ME--
WE'LL GET YOU BACK TO AMERICA, AGENT ZERO. THE NAZIS CAN'T STOP US NOW!
Meanwhile, IN A POWERFUL PLANE, THE RED SKULL SPIES THE FLEEING CAR!
THERE THEY ARE! BOMB THEM BEFORE THEY REACH THE BORDER!
BOMBS! FASTER, KNUCKLES! WE GOTTA MAKE THE BORDER BEFORE THEY GET THE RANGE!
Suddenly, THE ENGINE SPUTTERS AND THE CAR CHUGS TO A HALT!
HOLY MACKEREL! WHAT A TIME TO RUN OUTTA GAS!
AND THE BORDER'S ONLY A MILE AWAY!
PUTT! PUTT!

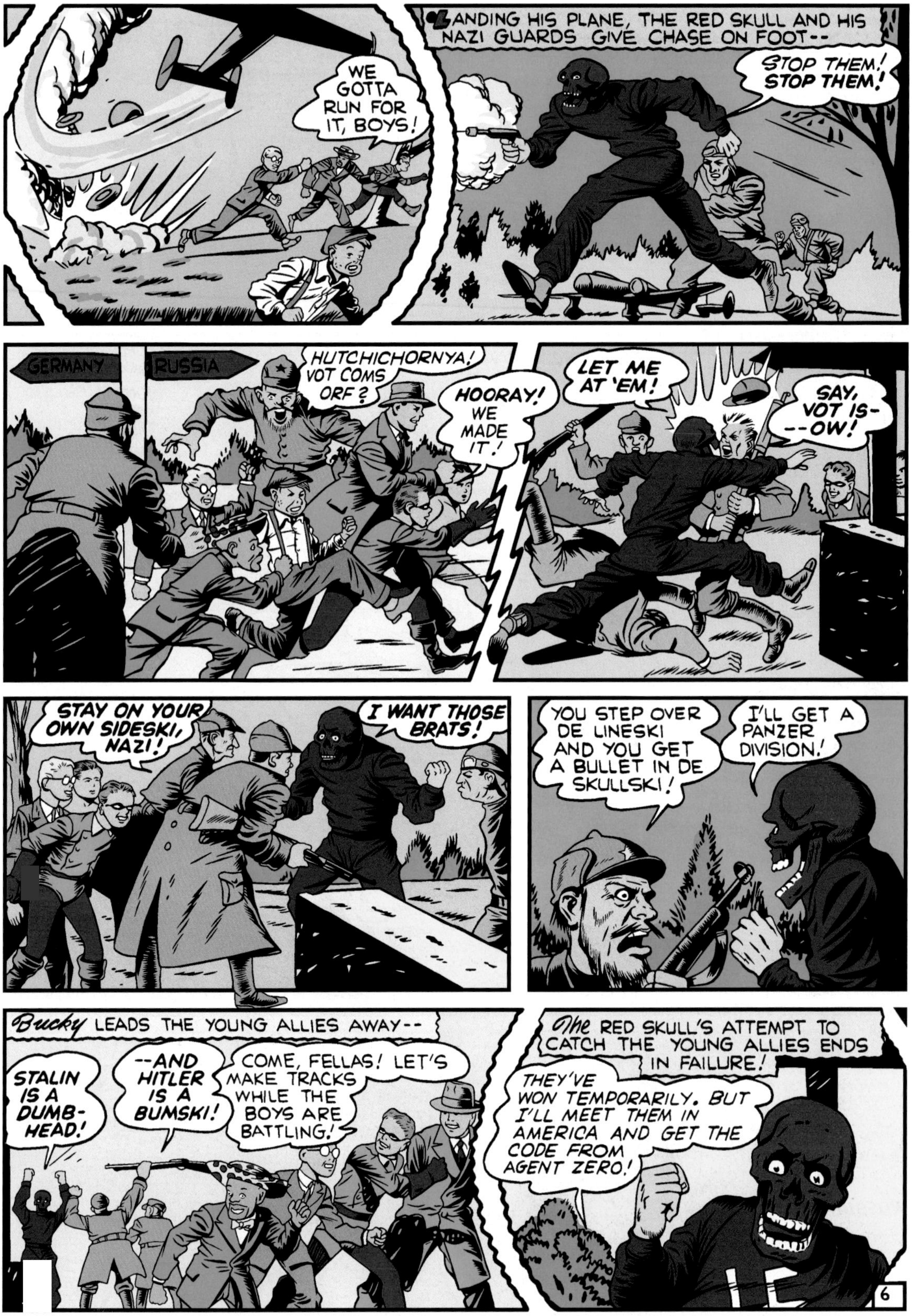
WE GOTTA RUN FOR IT, BOYS!
LANDING HIS PLANE, THE RED SKULL AND HIS NAZI GUARDS GIVE CHASE ON FOOT--
STOP THEM! STOP THEM!
GERMANY
RUSSIA
HUTCHICHORNYA! VOT COMS ORF?
HOORAY! WE MADE IT!
LET ME AT 'EM!
SAY, VOT IS--OW!
STAY ON YOUR OWN SIDESKI, NAZI!
I WANT THOSE BRATS!
YOU STEP OVER DE LINESKI AND YOU GET A BULLET IN DE SKULLSKI!
I'LL GET A PANZER DIVISION!
Bucky LEADS THE YOUNG ALLIES AWAY--
STALIN IS A DUMB-HEAD!
--AND HITLER IS A BUMSKI!
COME, FELLAS! LET'S MAKE TRACKS WHILE THE BOYS ARE BATTLING!
The RED SKULL'S ATTEMPT TO CATCH THE YOUNG ALLIES ENDS IN FAILURE!
THEY'VE WON TEMPORARILY. BUT I'LL MEET THEM IN AMERICA AND GET THE CODE FROM AGENT ZERO!
6

TELL YOUR FRIENDS ABOUT THIS GREAT, NEW, DIFFERENT COMIC MAGAZINE...THE YOUNG ALLIES

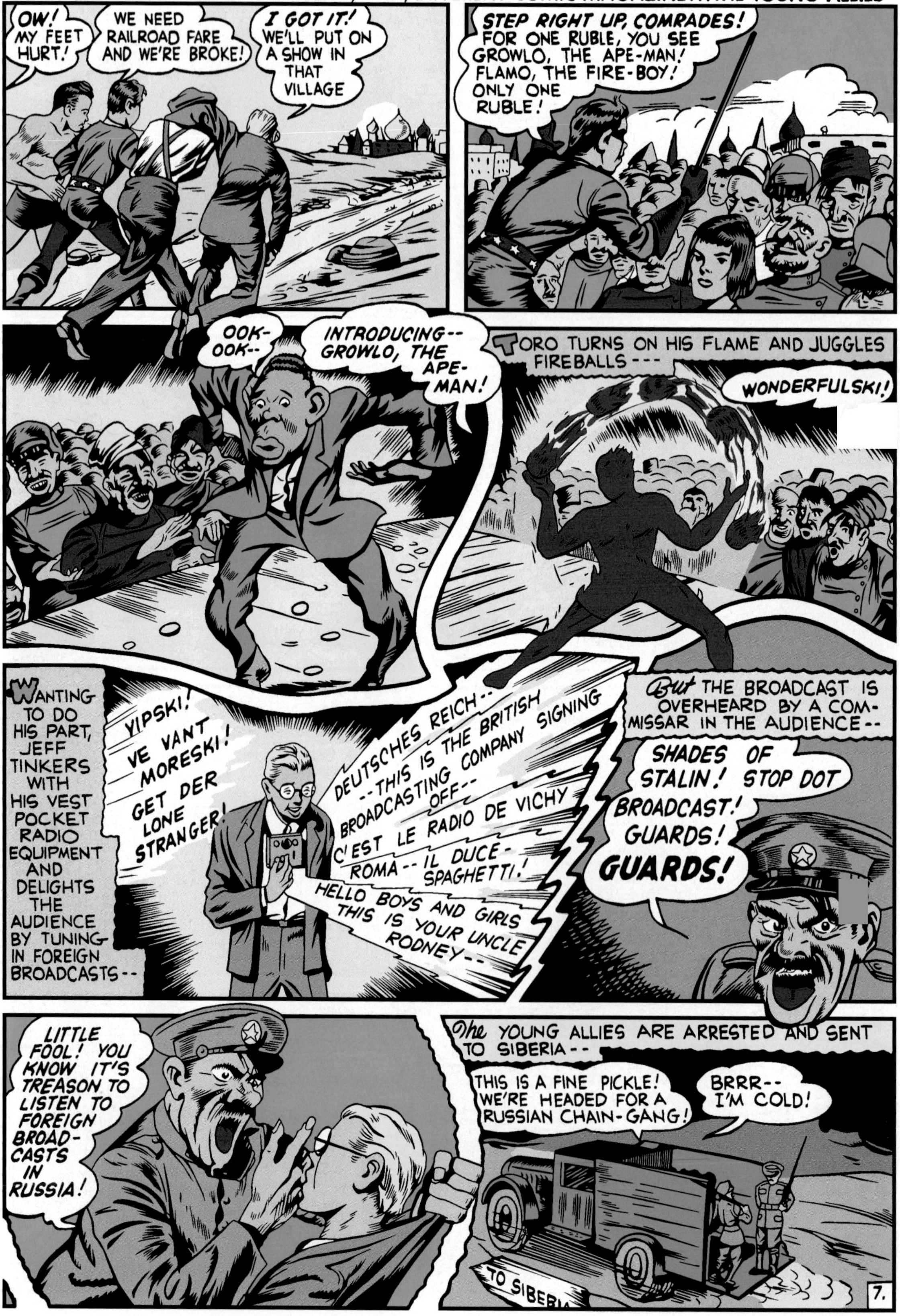

OW! MY FEET HURT!
WE NEED RAILROAD FARE AND WE'RE BROKE!
I GOT IT! WE'LL PUT ON A SHOW IN THAT VILLAGE
STEP RIGHT UP, COMRADES! FOR ONE RUBLE, YOU SEE GROWLO, THE APE-MAN! FLAMO, THE FIRE-BOY! ONLY ONE RUBLE!
OOK-OOK--
INTRODUCING--GROWLO, THE APE-MAN!
TORO TURNS ON HIS FLAME AND JUGGLES FIREBALLS---
WONDERFULSKI!
WANTING TO DO HIS PART, JEFF TINKERS WITH HIS VEST POCKET RADIO EQUIPMENT AND DELIGHTS THE AUDIENCE BY TUNING IN FOREIGN BROADCASTS--
YIPSKI!
VE VANT MORESKI!
GET DER LONE STRANGER!
DEUTSCHES REICH--
--THIS IS THE BRITISH BROADCASTING COMPANY SIGNING OFF--
C'EST LE RADIO DE VICHY
ROMA--IL DUCE-SPAGHETTI!
HELLO BOYS AND GIRLS THIS IS YOUR UNCLE RODNEY--
BUT THE BROADCAST IS OVERHEARD BY A COMMISSAR IN THE AUDIENCE--
SHADES OF STALIN! STOP DOT BROADCAST! GUARDS! GUARDS!
LITTLE FOOL! YOU KNOW IT'S TREASON TO LISTEN TO FOREIGN BROADCASTS IN RUSSIA!
THE YOUNG ALLIES ARE ARRESTED AND SENT TO SIBERIA--
THIS IS A FINE PICKLE! WE'RE HEADED FOR A RUSSIAN CHAIN-GANG!
BRRR--I'M COLD!
TO SIBERIA
7.

TELL YOUR FRIENDS ABOUT THIS GREAT, NEW, DIFFERENT COMIC MAGAZINE...THE YOUNG ALLIES

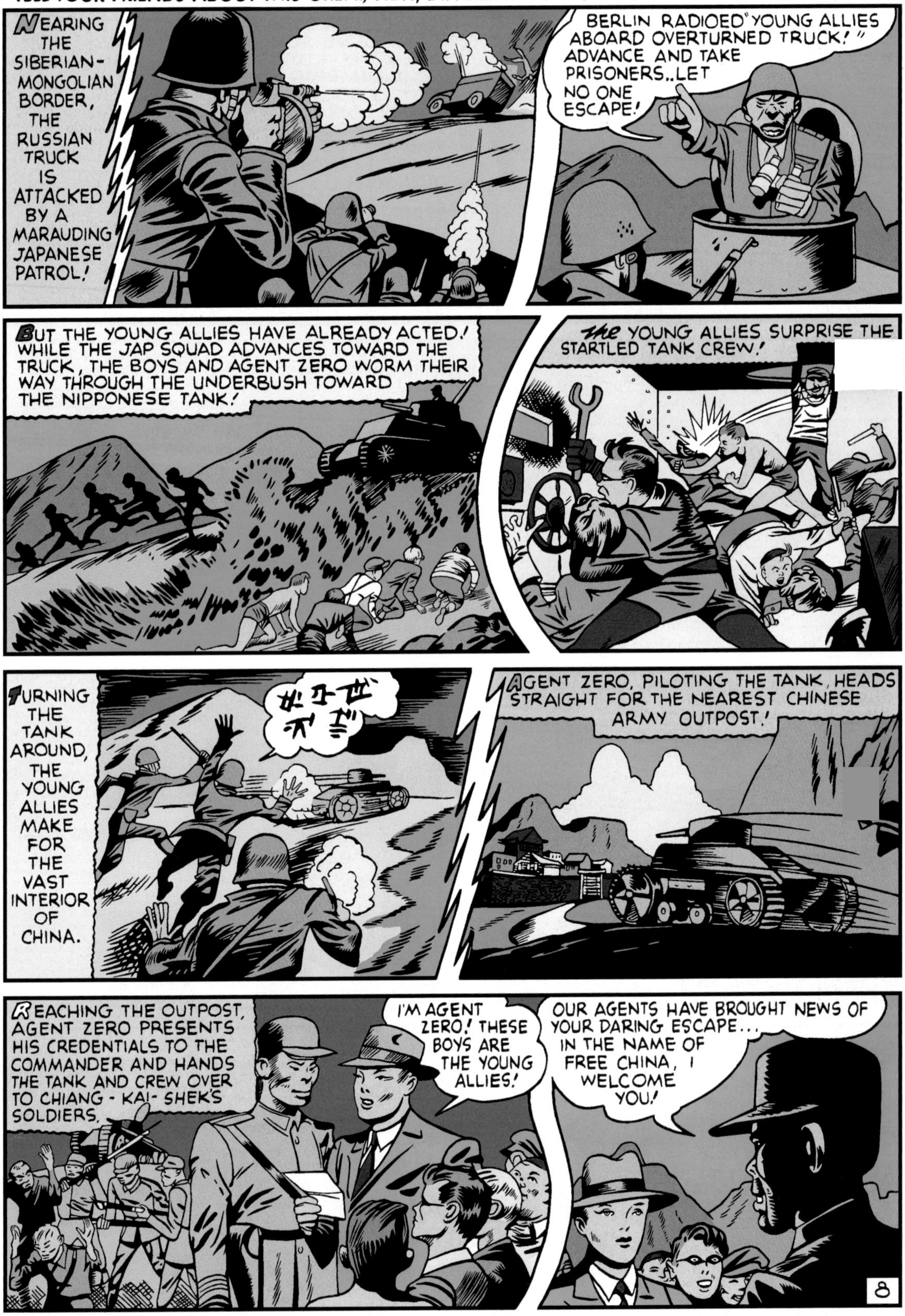
NEARING THE SIBERIAN-MONGOLIAN BORDER, THE RUSSIAN TRUCK IS ATTACKED BY A MARAUDING JAPANESE PATROL!
BERLIN RADIOED "YOUNG ALLIES ABOARD OVERTURNED TRUCK!" ADVANCE AND TAKE PRISONERS..LET NO ONE ESCAPE!
BUT THE YOUNG ALLIES HAVE ALREADY ACTED! WHILE THE JAP SQUAD ADVANCES TOWARD THE TRUCK, THE BOYS AND AGENT ZERO WORM THEIR WAY THROUGH THE UNDERBUSH TOWARD THE NIPPONESE TANK!
THE YOUNG ALLIES SURPRISE THE STARTLED TANK CREW!
TURNING THE TANK AROUND, THE YOUNG ALLIES MAKE FOR THE VAST INTERIOR OF CHINA.
AGENT ZERO, PILOTING THE TANK, HEADS STRAIGHT FOR THE NEAREST CHINESE ARMY OUTPOST!
REACHING THE OUTPOST, AGENT ZERO PRESENTS HIS CREDENTIALS TO THE COMMANDER AND HANDS THE TANK AND CREW OVER TO CHIANG-KAI-SHEK'S SOLDIERS.
I'M AGENT ZERO! THESE BOYS ARE THE YOUNG ALLIES!
OUR AGENTS HAVE BROUGHT NEWS OF YOUR DARING ESCAPE... IN THE NAME OF FREE CHINA, I WELCOME YOU!
8

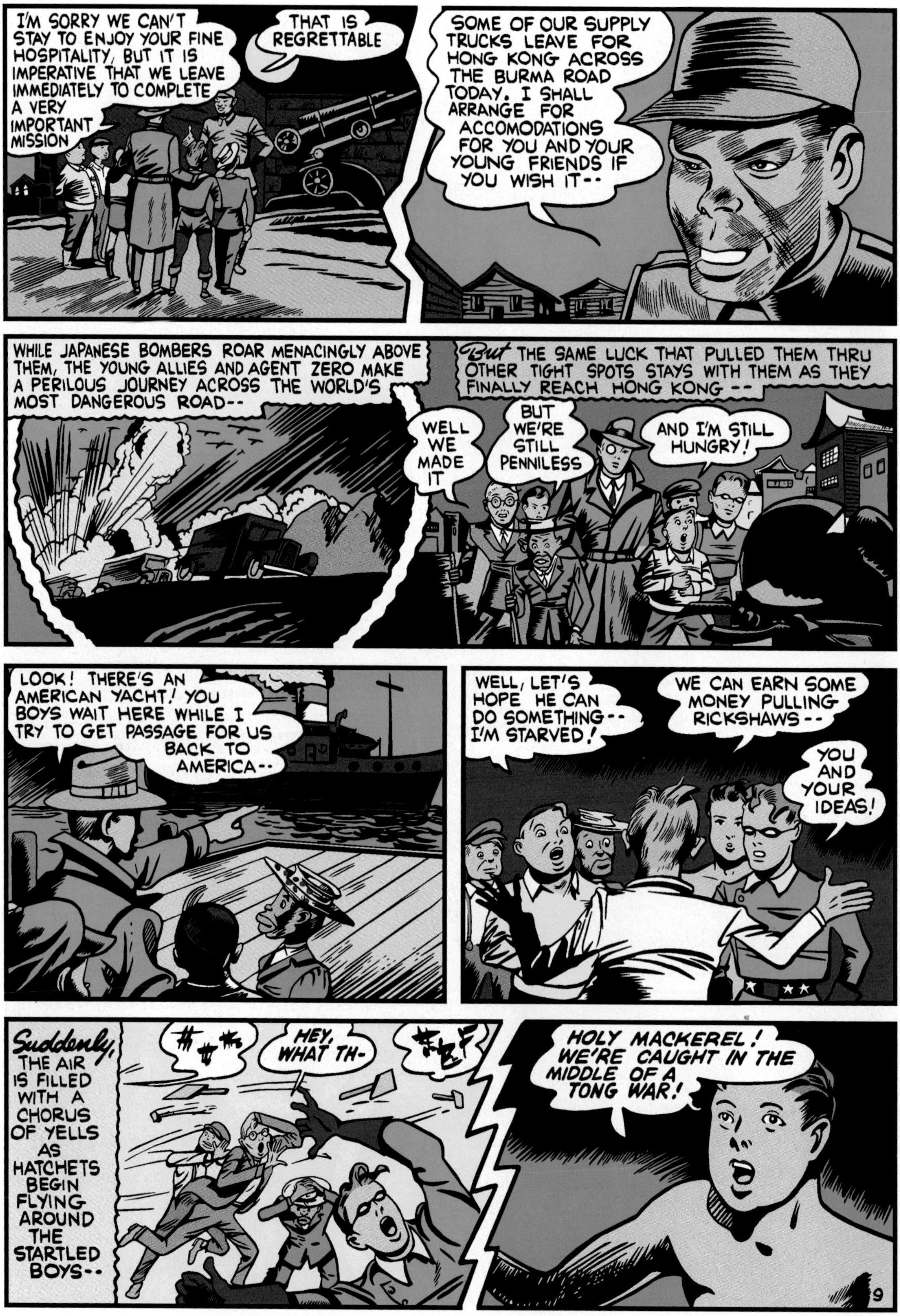
I'M SORRY WE CAN'T STAY TO ENJOY YOUR FINE HOSPITALITY, BUT IT IS IMPERATIVE THAT WE LEAVE IMMEDIATELY TO COMPLETE A VERY IMPORTANT MISSION
THAT IS REGRETTABLE
SOME OF OUR SUPPLY TRUCKS LEAVE FOR HONG KONG ACROSS THE BURMA ROAD TODAY. I SHALL ARRANGE FOR ACCOMODATIONS FOR YOU AND YOUR YOUNG FRIENDS IF YOU WISH IT--
WHILE JAPANESE BOMBERS ROAR MENACINGLY ABOVE THEM, THE YOUNG ALLIES AND AGENT ZERO MAKE A PERILOUS JOURNEY ACROSS THE WORLD'S MOST DANGEROUS ROAD--
But THE SAME LUCK THAT PULLED THEM THRU OTHER TIGHT SPOTS STAYS WITH THEM AS THEY FINALLY REACH HONG KONG --
WELL WE MADE IT
BUT WE'RE STILL PENNILESS
AND I'M STILL HUNGRY!
LOOK! THERE'S AN AMERICAN YACHT! YOU BOYS WAIT HERE WHILE I TRY TO GET PASSAGE FOR US BACK TO AMERICA--
WELL, LET'S HOPE HE CAN DO SOMETHING-- I'M STARVED!
WE CAN EARN SOME MONEY PULLING RICKSHAWS --
YOU AND YOUR IDEAS!
Suddenly, THE AIR IS FILLED WITH A CHORUS OF YELLS AS HATCHETS BEGIN FLYING AROUND THE STARTLED BOYS--
HEY, WHAT TH-
HOLY MACKEREL! WE'RE CAUGHT IN THE MIDDLE OF A TONG WAR!

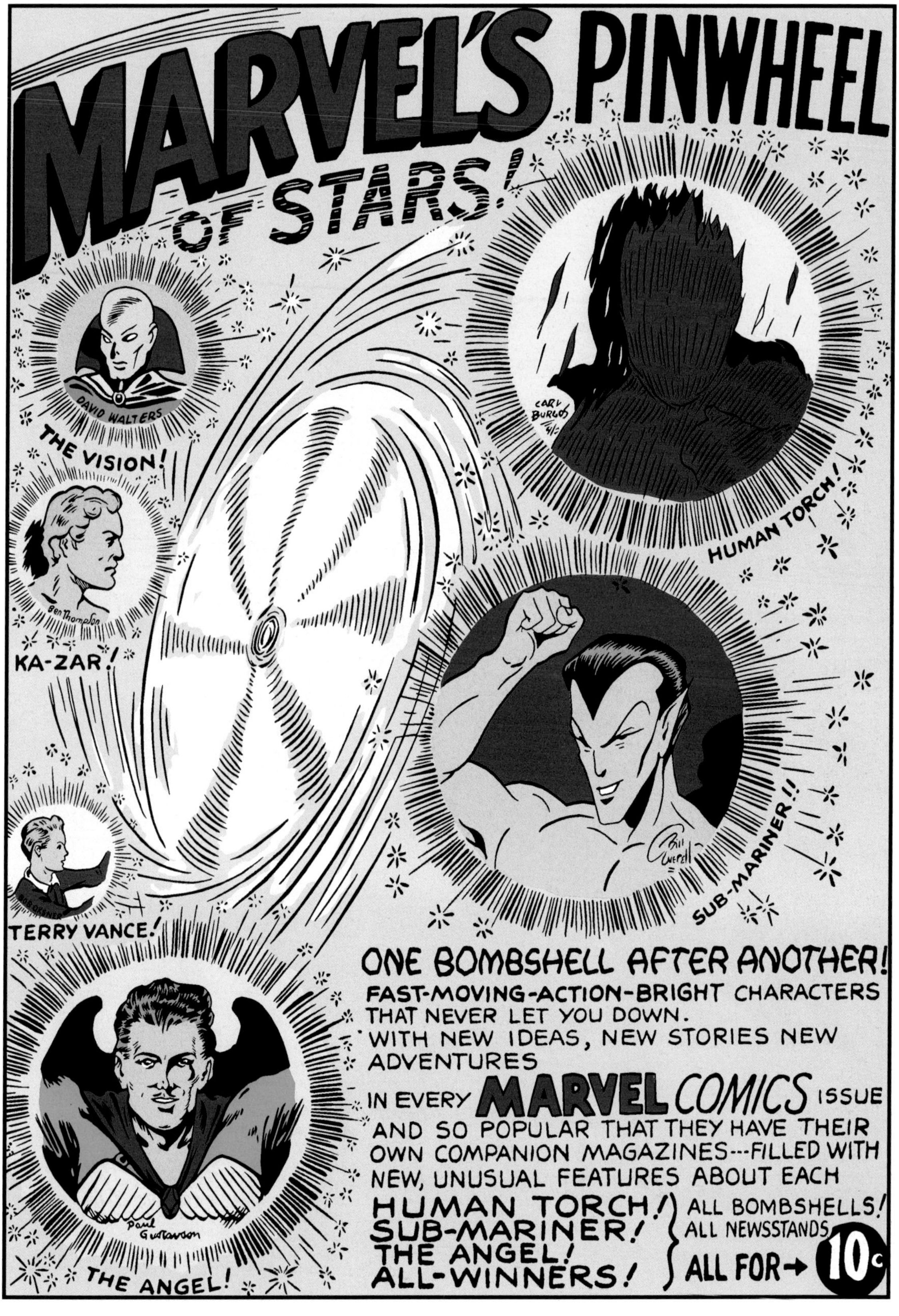

MARVEL'S PINWHEEL OF STARS!
DAVID WALTERS
THE VISION!
CARL BURGOS
HUMAN TORCH!
Ben Thompson
KA-ZAR!
Bill Everett
SUB-MARINER!!
TERRY VANCE!
Paul Gustavson
THE ANGEL!
ONE BOMBSHELL AFTER ANOTHER!
FAST-MOVING-ACTION-BRIGHT CHARACTERS THAT NEVER LET YOU DOWN.
WITH NEW IDEAS, NEW STORIES NEW ADVENTURES
IN EVERY MARVEL COMICS ISSUE
AND SO POPULAR THAT THEY HAVE THEIR OWN COMPANION MAGAZINES---FILLED WITH NEW, UNUSUAL FEATURES ABOUT EACH
HUMAN TORCH! SUB-MARINER! THE ANGEL! ALL-WINNERS!
ALL BOMBSHELLS! ALL NEWSSTANDS
ALL FOR → 10¢

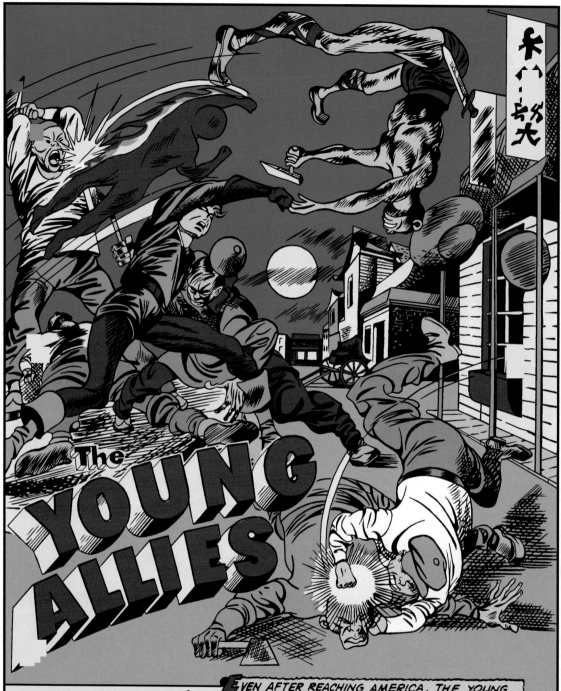

The YOUNG ALLIES

CHAPTER 6

CAPTAIN AMERICA *and the* HUMAN TORCH *to the* RESCUE!!

EVEN AFTER REACHING AMERICA, THE YOUNG ALLIES AREN'T SAFE FROM THE MENACE OF THE RED SKULL, WHO STRIKES AGAIN! BUCKY AND THE SENTINELS SOON FIND THEMSELVES IN THEIR MOST DANGEROUS POSITION, WITH DEATH PEERING AT THEM AT EVERY TURN! CAN THE MIGHTY CAPTAIN AMERICA AND THE DARING HUMAN TORCH COME TO THE RESCUE BEFORE THEY DISAPPEAR FOREVER DOWN THE DIM MYSTERIOUS ALLEYS OF CHINATOWN?

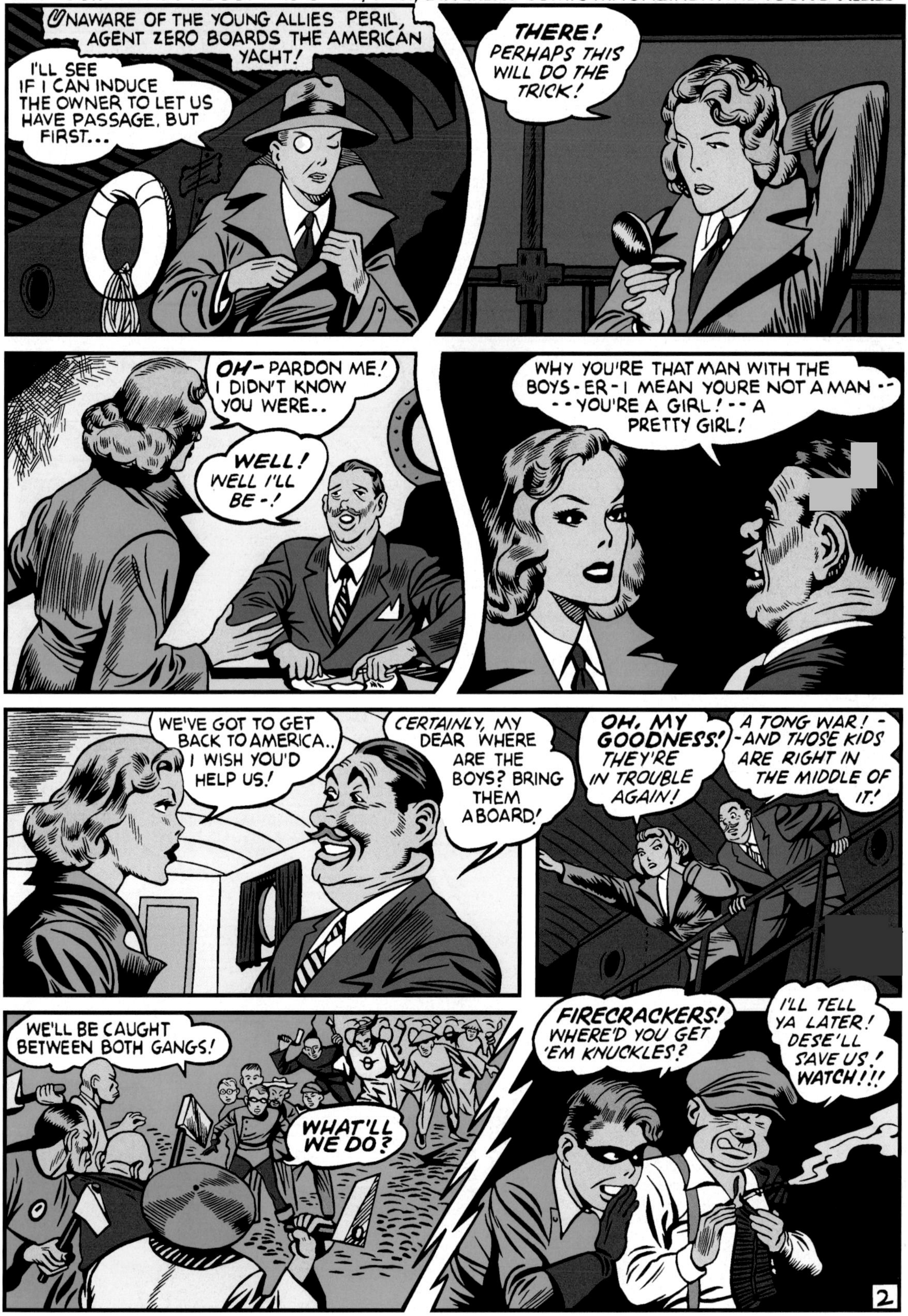
UNAWARE OF THE YOUNG ALLIES PERIL, AGENT ZERO BOARDS THE AMERICAN YACHT!
I'LL SEE IF I CAN INDUCE THE OWNER TO LET US HAVE PASSAGE, BUT FIRST...
THERE! PERHAPS THIS WILL DO THE TRICK!
OH- PARDON ME! I DIDN'T KNOW YOU WERE..
WELL! WELL I'LL BE-!
WHY YOU'RE THAT MAN WITH THE BOYS-ER-I MEAN YOURE NOT A MAN-- --YOU'RE A GIRL!--A PRETTY GIRL!
WE'VE GOT TO GET BACK TO AMERICA.. I WISH YOU'D HELP US!
CERTAINLY, MY DEAR WHERE ARE THE BOYS? BRING THEM ABOARD!
OH, MY GOODNESS! THEY'RE IN TROUBLE AGAIN!
A TONG WAR!--AND THOSE KIDS ARE RIGHT IN THE MIDDLE OF IT!
WE'LL BE CAUGHT BETWEEN BOTH GANGS!
WHAT'LL WE DO?
FIRECRACKERS! WHERE'D YOU GET 'EM KNUCKLES?
I'LL TELL YA LATER! DESE'LL SAVE US! WATCH!!!

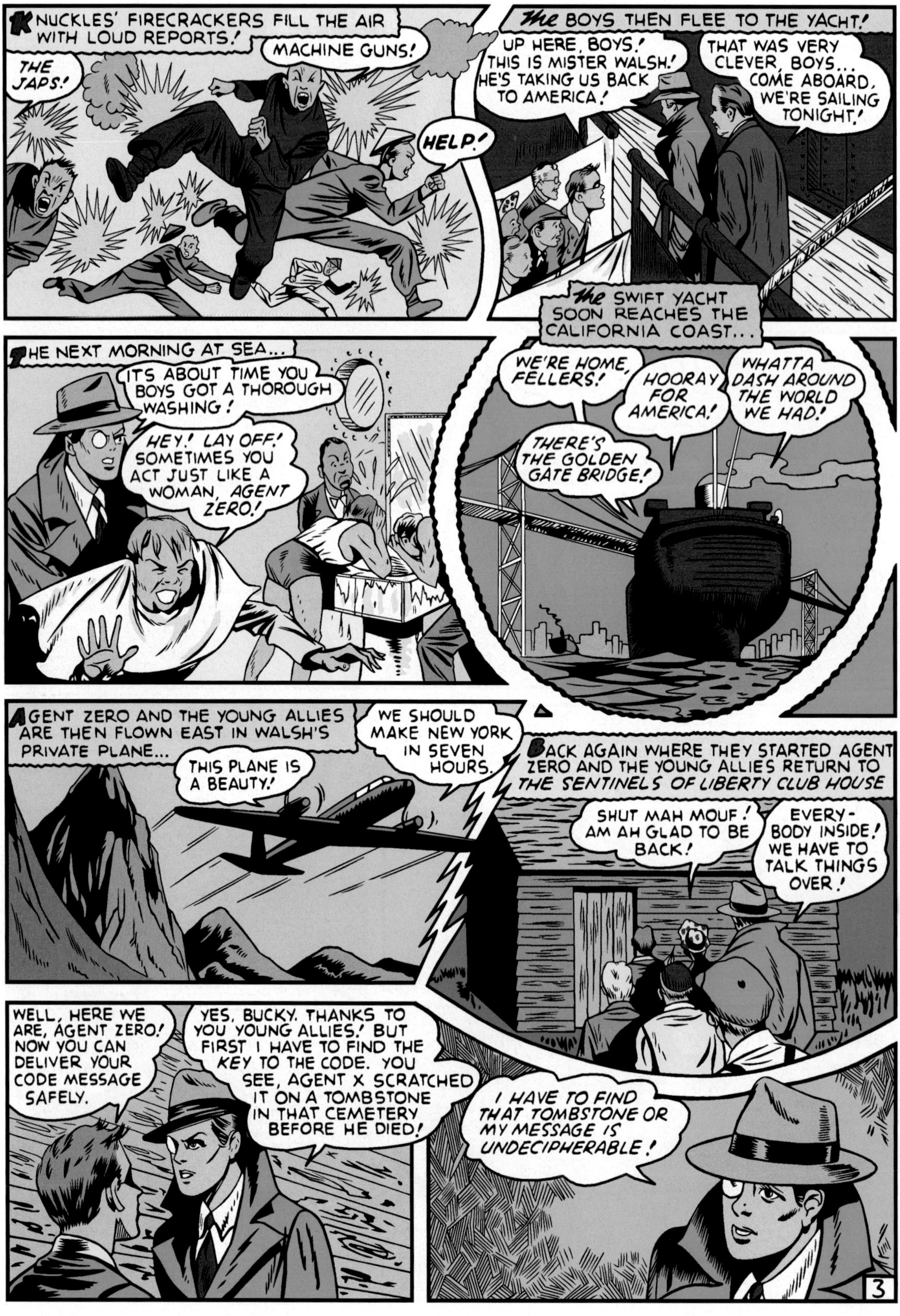
KNUCKLES' FIRECRACKERS FILL THE AIR WITH LOUD REPORTS!
THE JAPS!
MACHINE GUNS!
HELP!
THE BOYS THEN FLEE TO THE YACHT!
UP HERE, BOYS! THIS IS MISTER WALSH! HE'S TAKING US BACK TO AMERICA!
THAT WAS VERY CLEVER, BOYS... COME ABOARD, WE'RE SAILING TONIGHT!
THE SWIFT YACHT SOON REACHES THE CALIFORNIA COAST...
THE NEXT MORNING AT SEA...
ITS ABOUT TIME YOU BOYS GOT A THOROUGH WASHING!
HEY! LAY OFF! SOMETIMES YOU ACT JUST LIKE A WOMAN, AGENT ZERO!
WE'RE HOME, FELLERS!
HOORAY FOR AMERICA!
WHATTA DASH AROUND THE WORLD WE HAD!
THERE'S THE GOLDEN GATE BRIDGE!
AGENT ZERO AND THE YOUNG ALLIES ARE THEN FLOWN EAST IN WALSH'S PRIVATE PLANE...
WE SHOULD MAKE NEW YORK IN SEVEN HOURS.
THIS PLANE IS A BEAUTY!
BACK AGAIN WHERE THEY STARTED AGENT ZERO AND THE YOUNG ALLIES RETURN TO THE SENTINELS OF LIBERTY CLUB HOUSE
SHUT MAH MOUF! AM AH GLAD TO BE BACK!
EVERY-BODY INSIDE! WE HAVE TO TALK THINGS OVER!
WELL, HERE WE ARE, AGENT ZERO! NOW YOU CAN DELIVER YOUR CODE MESSAGE SAFELY.
YES, BUCKY. THANKS TO YOU YOUNG ALLIES! BUT FIRST I HAVE TO FIND THE KEY TO THE CODE. YOU SEE, AGENT X SCRATCHED IT ON A TOMBSTONE IN THAT CEMETERY BEFORE HE DIED!
I HAVE TO FIND THAT TOMBSTONE OR MY MESSAGE IS UNDECIPHERABLE!
3

OUTSIDE THE WINDOW, A SINISTER FIGURE LISTENS TO THE CONVERSATION.

I MUST REPORT THIS TO DER RED SKULL AT ONCE!

MEANWHILE, AGENT ZERO LEAVES ON HER MISSION...

FOR PURPOSES OF SECRECY I MUST GO ALONE!

WE UNDERSTAND GOOD LUCK!

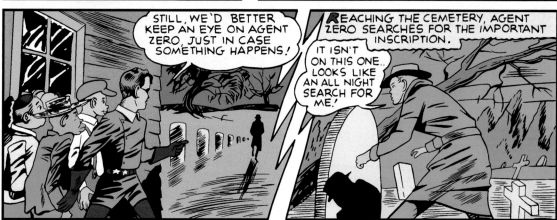

STILL, WE'D BETTER KEEP AN EYE ON AGENT ZERO, JUST IN CASE SOMETHING HAPPENS!

REACHING THE CEMETERY, AGENT ZERO SEARCHES FOR THE IMPORTANT INSCRIPTION.

IT ISN'T ON THIS ONE.. LOOKS LIKE AN ALL NIGHT SEARCH FOR ME!

I'LL SAVE YOU THE TROUBLE, AGENT ZERO!

THE RED SKULL!

I'VE BEEN WAITING FOR YOU SINCE YOU ESCAPED NAZI-LAND, AGENT ZERO! YOU WON'T GET AWAY THIS TIME!

THE YOUNG ALLIES WITNESS THE SCENE FROM BEHIND A TOMBSTONE...

I THOUGHT THERE'D BE TROUBLE! COME ON, FELLAS!

SUDDENLY, THE BOYS ARE SURROUNDED BY MACHINE GUNS!

ULP! ULP! ULP!

VOT'S DER HURRY BOYS?

4

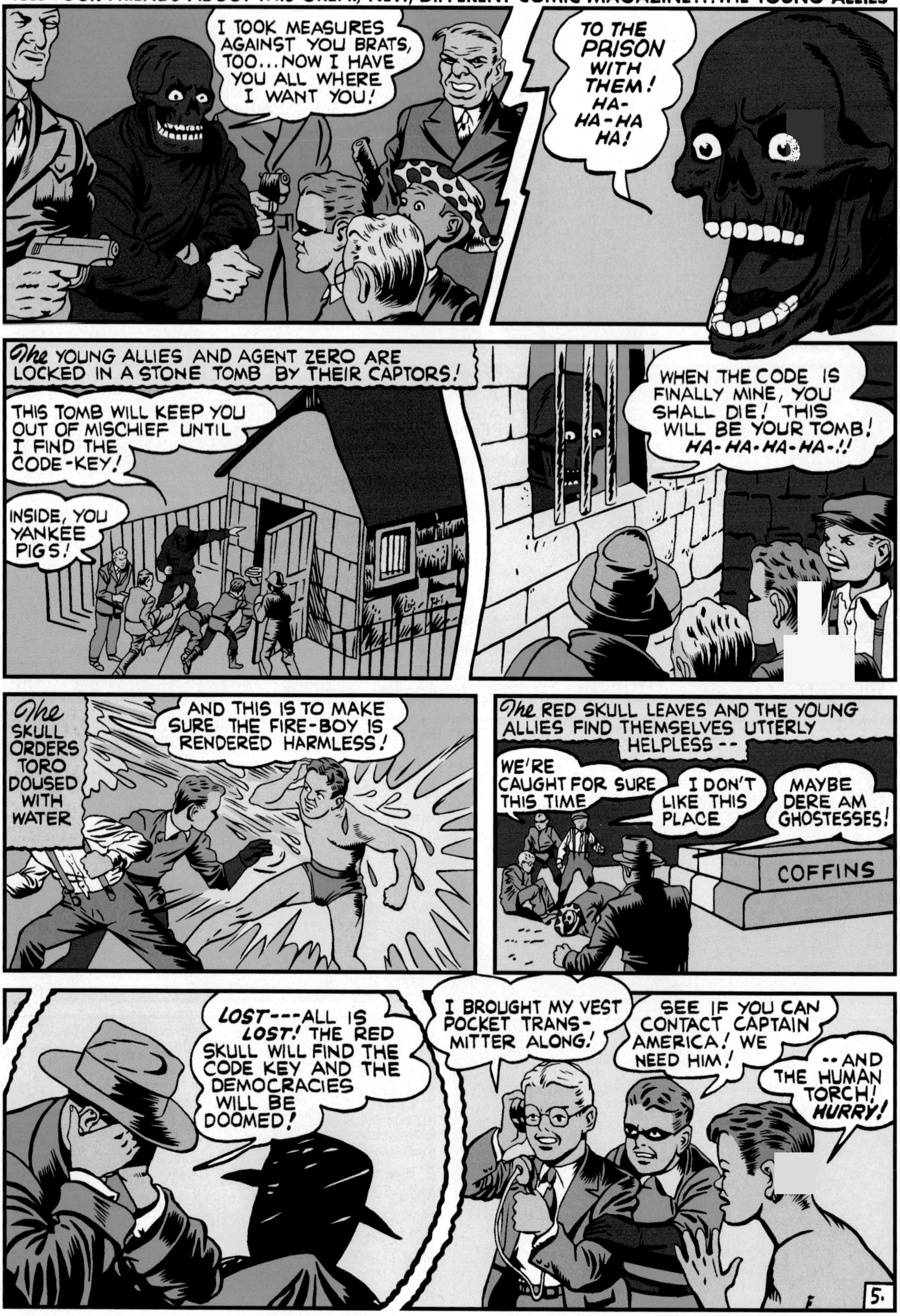
I TOOK MEASURES AGAINST YOU BRATS, TOO... NOW I HAVE YOU ALL WHERE I WANT YOU!
TO THE PRISON WITH THEM! HA-HA-HA HA!
The YOUNG ALLIES AND AGENT ZERO ARE LOCKED IN A STONE TOMB BY THEIR CAPTORS!
THIS TOMB WILL KEEP YOU OUT OF MISCHIEF UNTIL I FIND THE CODE-KEY!
INSIDE, YOU YANKEE PIGS!
WHEN THE CODE IS FINALLY MINE, YOU SHALL DIE! THIS WILL BE YOUR TOMB! HA-HA-HA-HA-!!
The SKULL ORDERS TORO DOUSED WITH WATER
AND THIS IS TO MAKE SURE THE FIRE-BOY IS RENDERED HARMLESS!
The RED SKULL LEAVES AND THE YOUNG ALLIES FIND THEMSELVES UTTERLY HELPLESS --
WE'RE CAUGHT FOR SURE THIS TIME
I DON'T LIKE THIS PLACE
MAYBE DERE AM GHOSTESSES!
COFFINS
LOST---ALL IS LOST! THE RED SKULL WILL FIND THE CODE KEY AND THE DEMOCRACIES WILL BE DOOMED!
I BROUGHT MY VEST POCKET TRANS-MITTER ALONG!
SEE IF YOU CAN CONTACT CAPTAIN AMERICA! WE NEED HIM!
--AND THE HUMAN TORCH! HURRY!

TELL YOUR FRIENDS ABOUT THIS GREAT, NEW, DIFFERENT COMIC MAGAZINE...THE YOUNG ALLIES

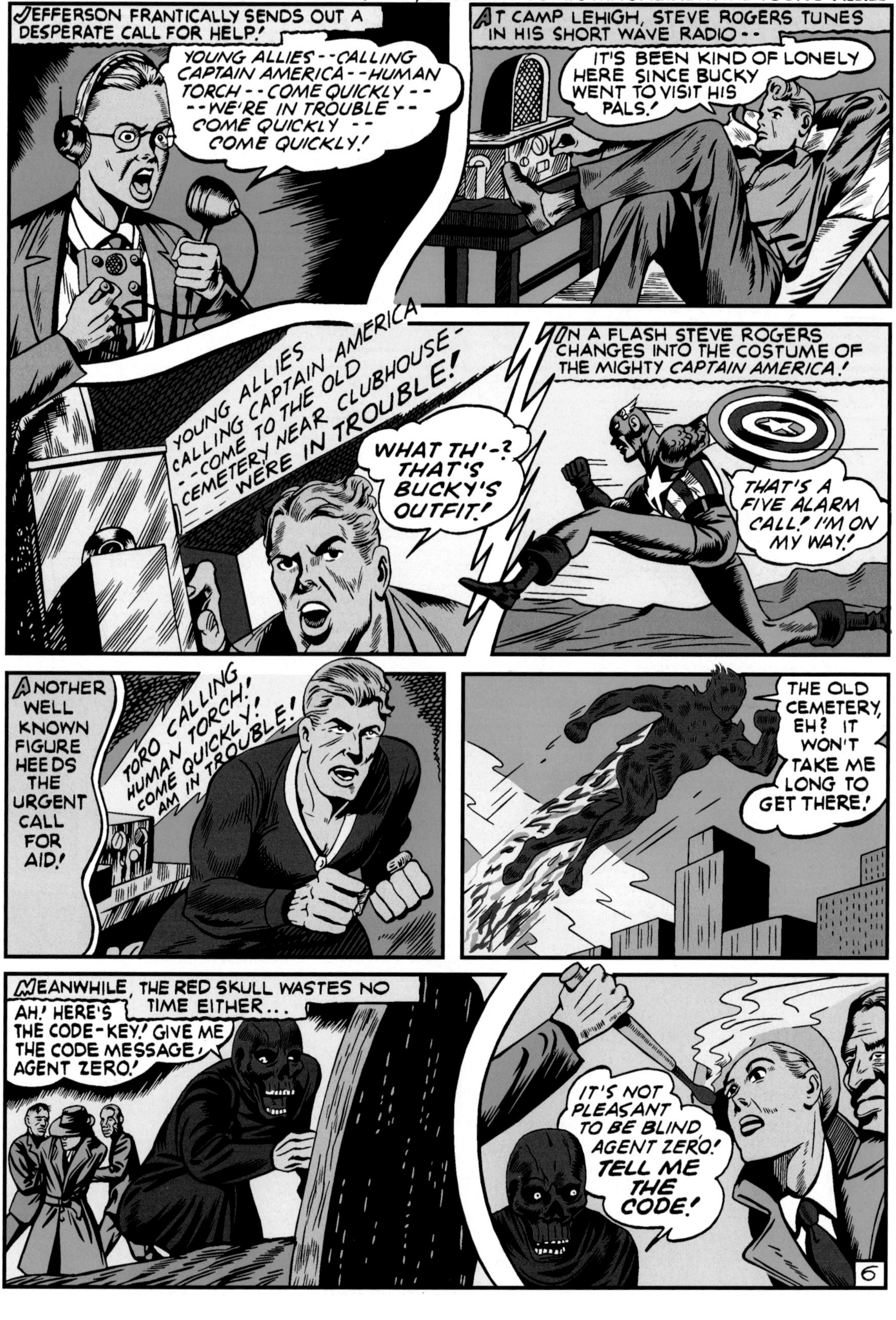

JEFFERSON FRANTICALLY SENDS OUT A DESPERATE CALL FOR HELP!
YOUNG ALLIES--CALLING CAPTAIN AMERICA--HUMAN TORCH--COME QUICKLY----WE'RE IN TROUBLE--COME QUICKLY--COME QUICKLY!
AT CAMP LEHIGH, STEVE ROGERS TUNES IN HIS SHORT WAVE RADIO--
IT'S BEEN KIND OF LONELY HERE SINCE BUCKY WENT TO VISIT HIS PALS!
YOUNG ALLIES CALLING CAPTAIN AMERICA --COME TO THE OLD CEMETERY NEAR CLUBHOUSE-WE'RE IN TROUBLE!
WHAT TH'-? THAT'S BUCKY'S OUTFIT!
IN A FLASH STEVE ROGERS CHANGES INTO THE COSTUME OF THE MIGHTY CAPTAIN AMERICA!
THAT'S A FIVE ALARM CALL! I'M ON MY WAY!
ANOTHER WELL KNOWN FIGURE HEEDS THE URGENT CALL FOR AID!
TORO CALLING HUMAN TORCH! COME QUICKLY! AM IN TROUBLE!
THE OLD CEMETERY, EH? IT WON'T TAKE ME LONG TO GET THERE!
MEANWHILE, THE RED SKULL WASTES NO TIME EITHER...
AH! HERE'S THE CODE-KEY! GIVE ME THE CODE MESSAGE, AGENT ZERO!
IT'S NOT PLEASANT TO BE BLIND, AGENT ZERO! TELL ME THE CODE!
6

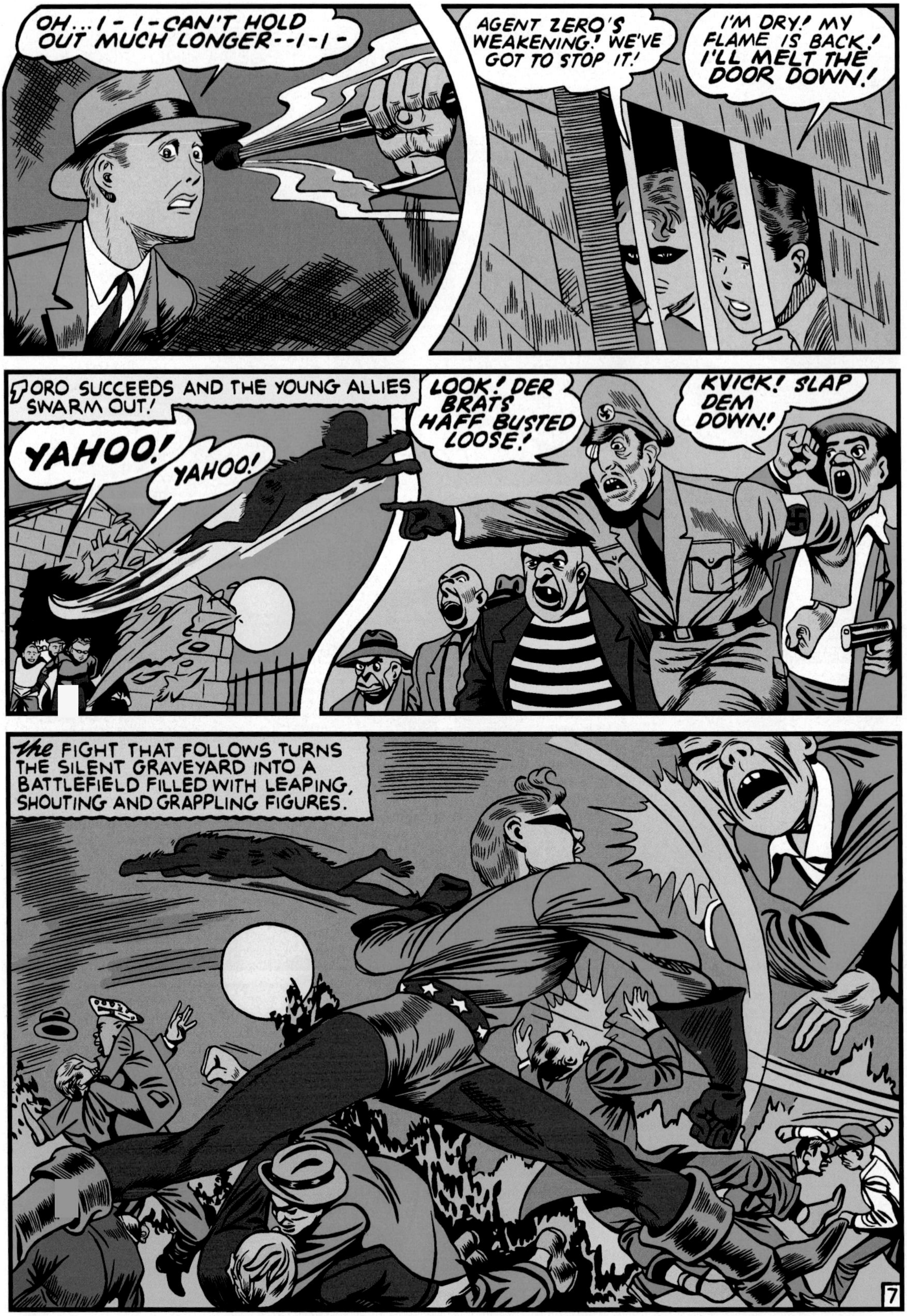

OH... I - I - CAN'T HOLD OUT MUCH LONGER - - I - I -
AGENT ZERO'S WEAKENING! WE'VE GOT TO STOP IT!
I'M DRY! MY FLAME IS BACK! I'LL MELT THE DOOR DOWN!
TORO SUCCEEDS AND THE YOUNG ALLIES SWARM OUT!
YAHOO!
YAHOO!
LOOK! DER BRATS HAFF BUSTED LOOSE!
KVICK! SLAP DEM DOWN!
THE FIGHT THAT FOLLOWS TURNS THE SILENT GRAVEYARD INTO A BATTLEFIELD FILLED WITH LEAPING, SHOUTING AND GRAPPLING FIGURES.
7

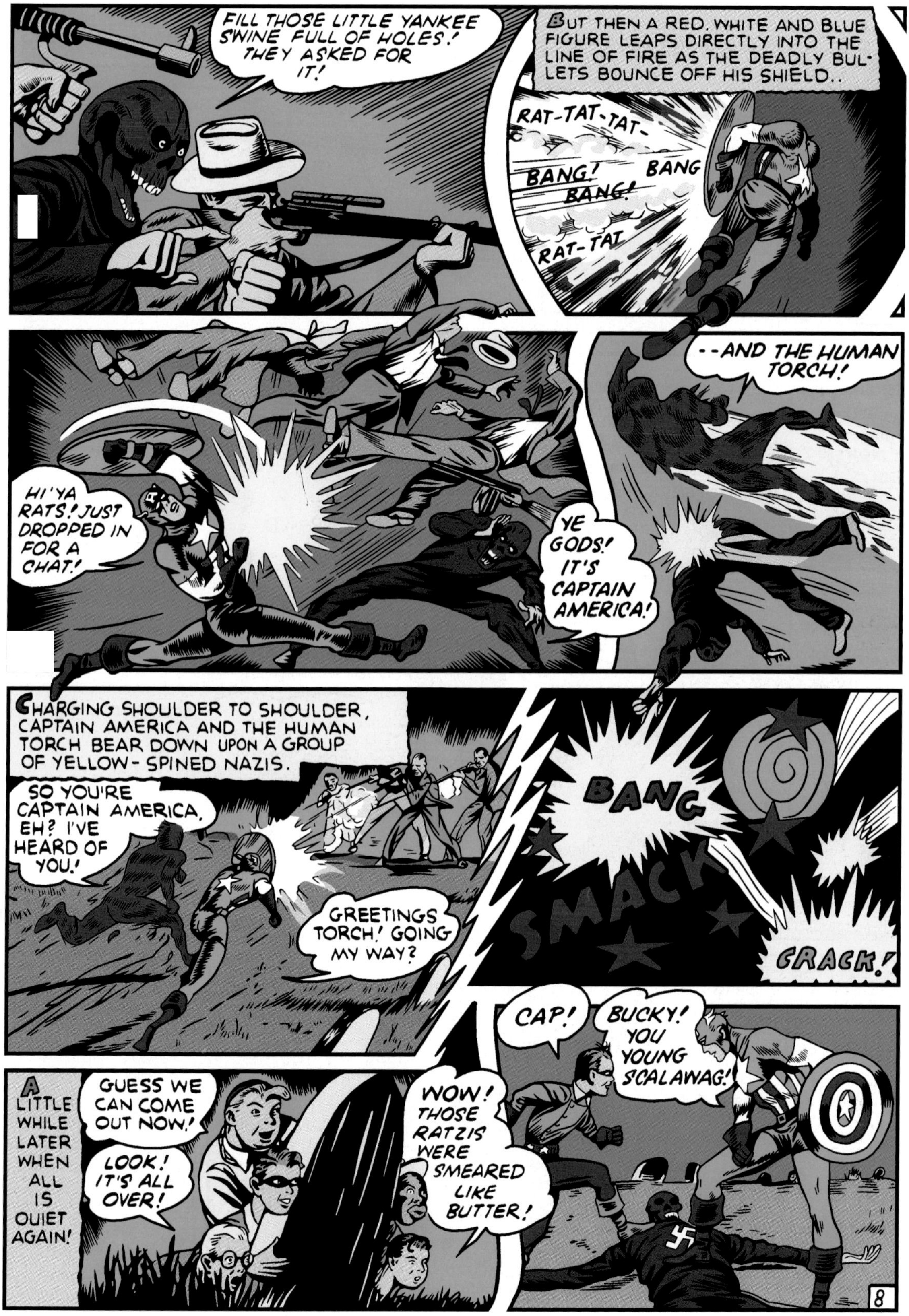
FILL THOSE LITTLE YANKEE SWINE FULL OF HOLES! THEY ASKED FOR IT!
BUT THEN A RED, WHITE AND BLUE FIGURE LEAPS DIRECTLY INTO THE LINE OF FIRE AS THE DEADLY BULLETS BOUNCE OFF HIS SHIELD..
RAT-TAT-TAT-
BANG! BANG! BANG
RAT-TAT
HI'YA RATS! JUST DROPPED IN FOR A CHAT!
YE GODS! IT'S CAPTAIN AMERICA!
--AND THE HUMAN TORCH!
CHARGING SHOULDER TO SHOULDER, CAPTAIN AMERICA AND THE HUMAN TORCH BEAR DOWN UPON A GROUP OF YELLOW-SPINED NAZIS.
SO YOU'RE CAPTAIN AMERICA, EH? I'VE HEARD OF YOU!
GREETINGS TORCH! GOING MY WAY?
BANG
SMACK
CRACK!
A LITTLE WHILE LATER WHEN ALL IS QUIET AGAIN!
GUESS WE CAN COME OUT NOW!
LOOK! IT'S ALL OVER!
WOW! THOSE RATZIS WERE SMEARED LIKE BUTTER!
CAP!
BUCKY! YOU YOUNG SCALAWAG!
8

TELL YOUR FRIENDS ABOUT THIS GREAT, NEW, DIFFERENT COMIC MAGAZINE...THE YOUNG ALLIES

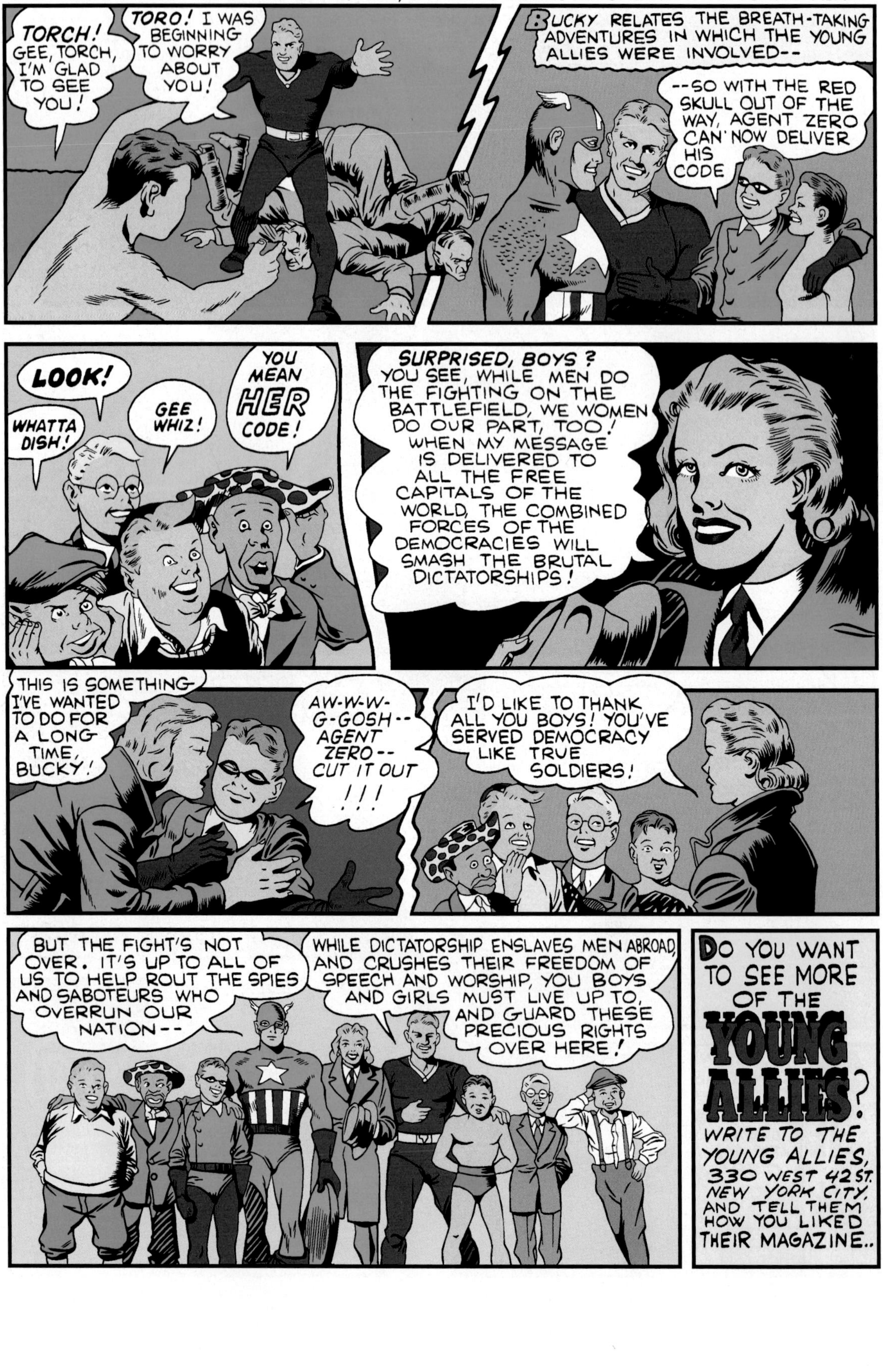

TORCH! GEE, TORCH, I'M GLAD TO SEE YOU!
TORO! I WAS BEGINNING TO WORRY ABOUT YOU!
BUCKY RELATES THE BREATH-TAKING ADVENTURES IN WHICH THE YOUNG ALLIES WERE INVOLVED--
--SO WITH THE RED SKULL OUT OF THE WAY, AGENT ZERO CAN NOW DELIVER HIS CODE
LOOK!
WHATTA DISH!
GEE WHIZ!
YOU MEAN HER CODE!
SURPRISED, BOYS? YOU SEE, WHILE MEN DO THE FIGHTING ON THE BATTLEFIELD, WE WOMEN DO OUR PART, TOO! WHEN MY MESSAGE IS DELIVERED TO ALL THE FREE CAPITALS OF THE WORLD, THE COMBINED FORCES OF THE DEMOCRACIES WILL SMASH THE BRUTAL DICTATORSHIPS!
THIS IS SOMETHING I'VE WANTED TO DO FOR A LONG TIME, BUCKY!
AW-W-W-G-GOSH-- AGENT ZERO-- CUT IT OUT !!!
I'D LIKE TO THANK ALL YOU BOYS! YOU'VE SERVED DEMOCRACY LIKE TRUE SOLDIERS!
BUT THE FIGHT'S NOT OVER. IT'S UP TO ALL OF US TO HELP ROUT THE SPIES AND SABOTEURS WHO OVERRUN OUR NATION--
WHILE DICTATORSHIP ENSLAVES MEN ABROAD, AND CRUSHES THEIR FREEDOM OF SPEECH AND WORSHIP, YOU BOYS AND GIRLS MUST LIVE UP TO, AND GUARD THESE PRECIOUS RIGHTS OVER HERE!
DO YOU WANT TO SEE MORE OF THE YOUNG ALLIES? WRITE TO THE YOUNG ALLIES, 330 WEST 42 ST. NEW YORK CITY, AND TELL THEM HOW YOU LIKED THEIR MAGAZINE..

CROOKS ARE COWARDS

"WHAT!" Biff Jenkins cried. "Come again?" Biff was a star reporter for the World Wide Tribune and a bit of a sleuth thrown in.

"I said the Billingslys were just held up for everything they had on them. They were on the way to the yacht hotel from the race track," Burt Higgins told him. "I ran across them on my beat and I'm on my way to call headquarters. Gotta rush. Y'owe me a fiver for this!"

Burt beat it on to the nearest telephone. Biff stood lost in thought for a moment then turned and ran after him. "How much loot did the thugs get?" he asked Burt as they ran side by side.

"Don't know. Didn't take time to question them."

"That's all I want'a know," Biff said, then struck out for the yacht hotel. He had little trouble finding the whereabouts of the frantic couple, although he was afraid at first that they would already be on their yacht, then he probably couldn't have seen them.

"Yes," Mr. Billingsly stated, "You're the first we've released any facts about the robbery to, except to tell the officer that we were robbed."

"Well, listen folks," Biff said,

"I have a plan by which the thugs can be brought to justice if you'll work with me."

"Shoot, sonny," the wealthy old man said quickly. "Let's have it."

"D-d-deah me. M-my deah boy," the prostrated Mrs. Billingsly said nervously. "D-do let's have it!"

"Okay," Biff shot. "Listen—"

The Tribune the next morning carried the huge headline: "BILLINGSLYS ROBBED OF 200,000 DOLLARS IN JEWELS".

Biff threw his long legs across his little desk the next morning as he read his own work and a smile wrinkled his freckled nose. "If the executive editor knew what I did," he thought, "he would give me my time and a swift kick!" Now that his little plan was working, Biff didn't feel so bold about having done it. In fact, he was more than a little nervous. But Biff thought he knew who did that job, and if he was right, this was the best way to get them. They were too smart to play the ordinary way. The two Anson brothers were tough, too, and he knew that he was playing with dynamite.

But when the Tribune carried

a smaller headline that afternoon: "BILLINGSLY ROBBERS STILL AT LARGE", he smiled again. So far so good.

Biff then went to police headquarters and asked for a couple of men to go with him.

"Ok, Biff," Chief Wells agreed. "But what for?"

"Rather not tell you yet, Chief. I might be wrong, and I wouldn't want to get your hopes aroused."

But Biff didn't admit even to himself that he stood much chance of being wrong. His plans had to work out, because if they didn't, the story would get out and he would lose his job and maybe get into serious trouble. No, he had to be right!

Biff knew John Athey and Bob Robins, the two plain clothes men the chief had let him have. He knew them well; they were two good men and would be right there in case of trouble — which Biff expected — even hoped for. The three of them went through the city that Saturday night in Biff's car, Biff being the only one knowing their destination. And his companions did not ask.

On the outer edge of the business district Biff pulled up in front of a small jewelry store. It was the only jewelry store that wasn't right in the middle of the business district and Biff was certain that if the robbers did as he expected, they would come here. He parked his car and told the plain clothes men

"John, you stroll down one way and you the other, Bob. I expect the two thugs who robbed the Billingslys last night, or more likely just one of them, to come here any minute. If we're careful they won't notice us, it being Saturday night and the streets so crowded. In case of trouble, Bob, you come on in the store right away, and John, you guard the entrance — and don't let anybody out!"

"Wow!" Bob Robins exclaimed. "This *is* something!"

"Boy, oh boy!" John Athey confirmed. "How right you are! And Biff, I hope you're right, too!"

"Not half as much as I do," Biff answered Then suddenly he stiffened — his body tensed. "Oh-oh! Boys, I think we might be late for the party!"

At the same time as his words a shot rang out from the store. A couple of women screamed and people cleared out in front of the place. Biff and his two companions leaped into action. John was the first out of the car and he went bounding into the store.

It was a brave thing to do, but a dangerous one, for a bullet from the thug's gun caught John in the shoulder and knocked him backwards. He fell to the hard marble floor at the entrance to the store and blood spouted from a hole in his vest. You cowards, Bob Robins screamed, as he let go a volley of slugs at the man who had downed John. That man

was disappearing through a door in the back of the jewelry store's front room, and so far as Biff could see he had not been hit. Biff yelled at a couple of pedestrians to take care of John and shot after Bob Robins, his pet twenty-five automatic in his hand.

By the time Biff caught up with Bob they were both at the door that entered into the front of the jewelry store, and the thug — there was only one — was going out the back door that opened into the alley. Heavy brick buildings lined the alley on each side. Before running into the alley he poured a couple of bullets back at the two men after him. Both bullets went wild, the closest crashing through the door Biff had just come through.

Biff was the first to the back door and when he raced through it and into the alley the robber was already far down the alley. Biff took careful aim and fired. But the short little automatic was made only for close range and the thug kept running. Soon he would be at the end of the alley and lost in the Saturday night crowds. This was one time Biff felt like swearing. There was only one thing to do; run after the fellow.

But just as Biff started to run there was a blast at his shoulder that felt as though it would break his eardrums. The report of Bob Robin's service revolver.

The hands of the man at the end of the alley reached frantically toward the skies for something that wasn't there. He careened crazily, then fell flat on his face. Biff reached around and grabbed Bob's hand, shook it. "Nice work," he complimented.

"But Biff," Chief Wells asked later. "How did you happen to

know the thug would be at that jewelry store?"

They were standing beside John Athey's bed at the hospital. Will, smiling, said: "Yeah, I think I deserve to know that, too." The doctor had said John would be OK in a few weeks.

"You certainly do!" Biff admitted. "Well, you see, I asked the Billingslys to let me state in my story that the jewels the thugs took from them were worth two hundred thousand, when in reality they were worth only a thousand bucks. I knew when the thugs read that in the paper they would think they got more than they expected, thus demand more of their fence. But their fence would tell them the stuff wasn't worth what they wanted, and naturally the thugs wouldn't believe him. They'd rather take a chance on going to some small jewelry store and getting the stuff evaluated. To play safe they'd pick a place as far out from town as possible, so if the jeweler became suspicious and called the law, or they had to quiet him they'd be on their way out of town. The little place where we nabbed the thief was the only logical one I could figure, the only one not in the middle of town. Need I say more?"

"Well I'll be darned," Chief Wells exclaimed.

"All thieves are cowards and all cowards get caught in the end," Biff Jenkins explained. "So with the other thug in irons from the confession of his buddy and John here getting better every day, and the little jeweler the same way, I'd better go do a little explaining to the executive editor!"

THE END

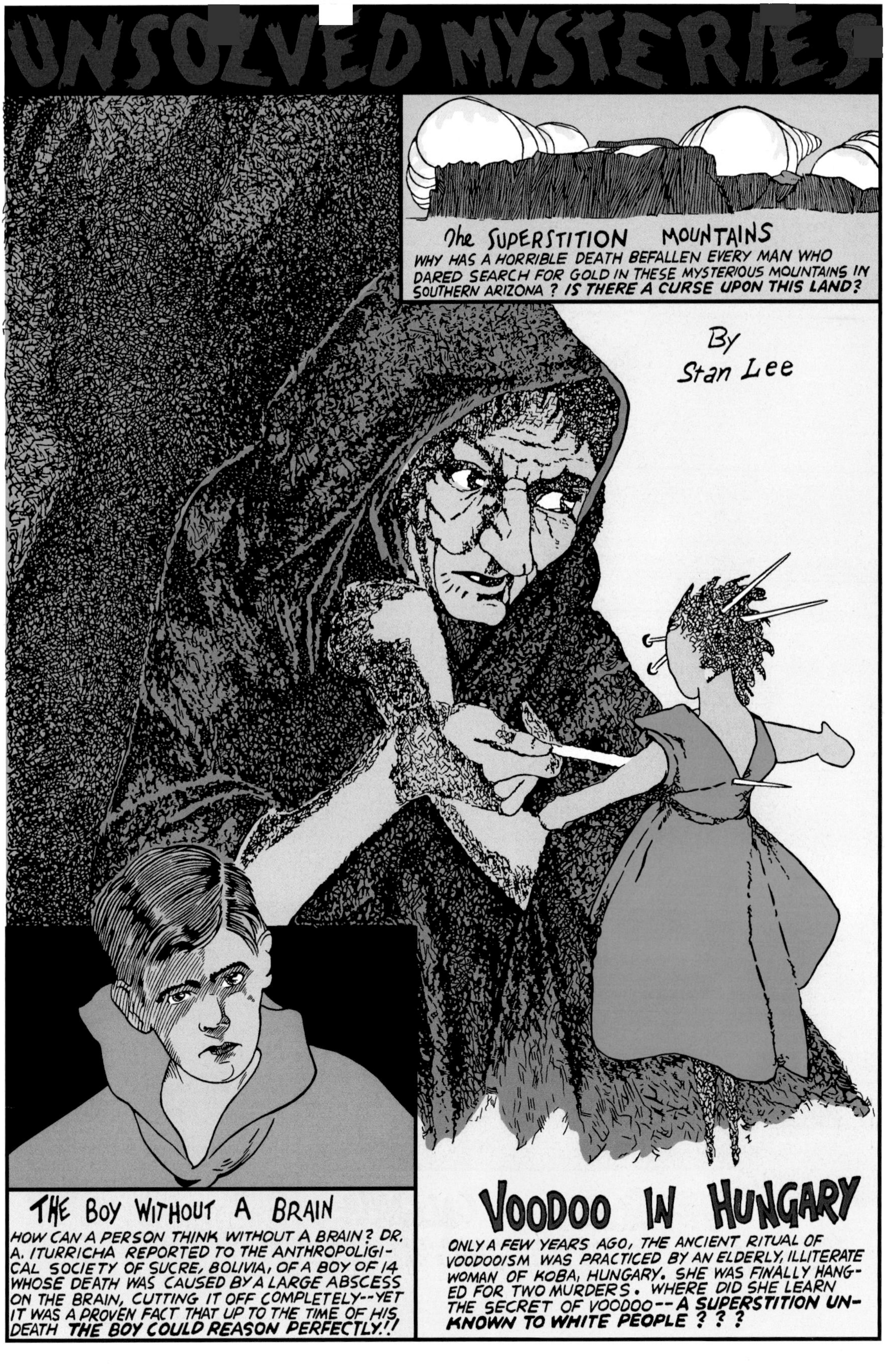
UNSOLVED MYSTERIES
The SUPERSTITION MOUNTAINS
WHY HAS A HORRIBLE DEATH BEFALLEN EVERY MAN WHO DARED SEARCH FOR GOLD IN THESE MYSTERIOUS MOUNTAINS IN SOUTHERN ARIZONA ? IS THERE A CURSE UPON THIS LAND?
By Stan Lee
THE BOY WITHOUT A BRAIN
HOW CAN A PERSON THINK WITHOUT A BRAIN? DR. A. ITURRICHA REPORTED TO THE ANTHROPOLIGI-CAL SOCIETY OF SUCRE, BOLIVIA, OF A BOY OF 14 WHOSE DEATH WAS CAUSED BY A LARGE ABSCESS ON THE BRAIN, CUTTING IT OFF COMPLETELY--YET IT WAS A PROVEN FACT THAT UP TO THE TIME OF HIS DEATH THE BOY COULD REASON PERFECTLY!!
VOODOO IN HUNGARY
ONLY A FEW YEARS AGO, THE ANCIENT RITUAL OF VOODOOISM WAS PRACTICED BY AN ELDERLY, ILLITERATE WOMAN OF KOBA, HUNGARY. SHE WAS FINALLY HANG-ED FOR TWO MURDERS. WHERE DID SHE LEARN THE SECRET OF VOODOO--A SUPERSTITION UN-KNOWN TO WHITE PEOPLE ? ? ?

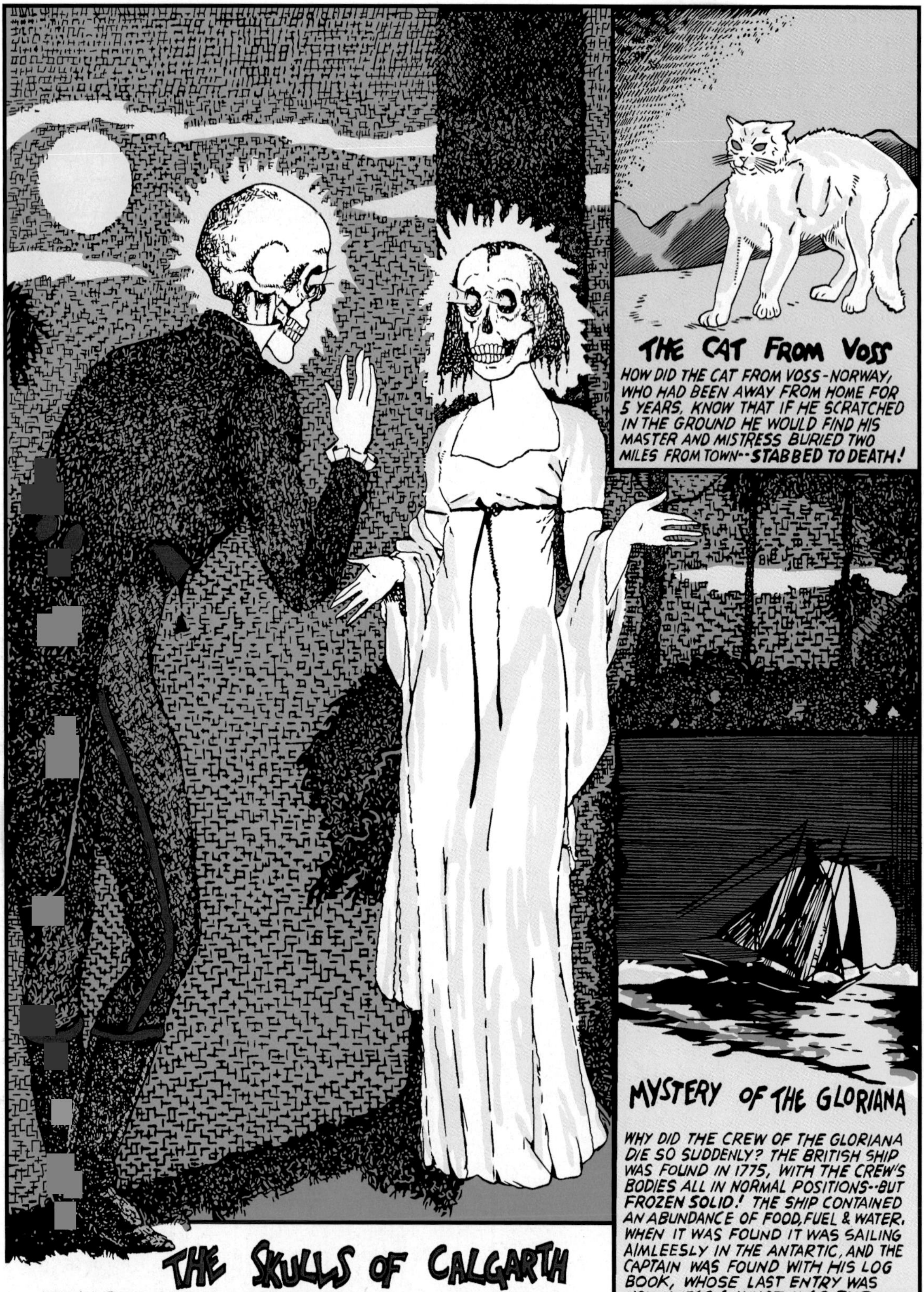
THE SKULLS OF CALGARTH
WHY HAVE THE SKULLS OF CALGARTH, SEEN FOR 100 YEARS AT THE WILDEMERE LAKE REGION IN ENGLAND, FAILED TO APPEAR SINCE THE FIRST NAZI BOMBS FELL IN THAT SECTION ? ? ?
THE CAT FROM VOSS
HOW DID THE CAT FROM VOSS-NORWAY, WHO HAD BEEN AWAY FROM HOME FOR 5 YEARS, KNOW THAT IF HE SCRATCHED IN THE GROUND HE WOULD FIND HIS MASTER AND MISTRESS BURIED TWO MILES FROM TOWN--STABBED TO DEATH!
MYSTERY OF THE GLORIANA
WHY DID THE CREW OF THE GLORIANA DIE SO SUDDENLY? THE BRITISH SHIP WAS FOUND IN 1775, WITH THE CREW'S BODIES ALL IN NORMAL POSITIONS--BUT FROZEN SOLID! THE SHIP CONTAINED AN ABUNDANCE OF FOOD, FUEL & WATER. WHEN IT WAS FOUND IT WAS SAILING AIMLEESLY IN THE ANTARTIC, AND THE CAPTAIN WAS FOUND WITH HIS LOG BOOK, WHOSE LAST ENTRY WAS NOV. 11, 1762! WHAT WAS THE CAUSE OF THEIR DEATHS ????

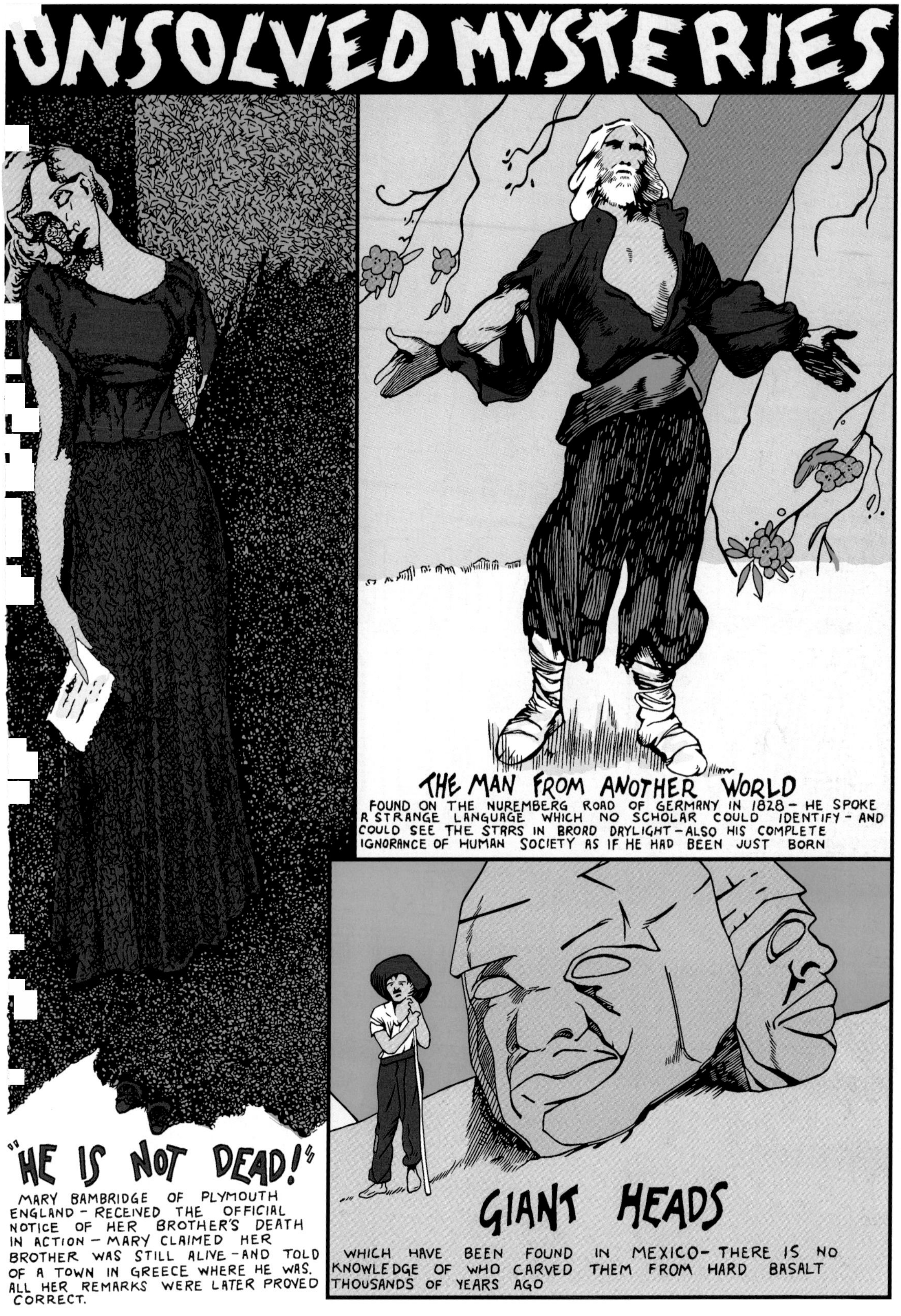

UNSOLVED MYSTERIES
THE MAN FROM ANOTHER WORLD
FOUND ON THE NUREMBERG ROAD OF GERMANY IN 1828 - HE SPOKE A STRANGE LANGUAGE WHICH NO SCHOLAR COULD IDENTIFY - AND COULD SEE THE STARS IN BROAD DAYLIGHT - ALSO HIS COMPLETE IGNORANCE OF HUMAN SOCIETY AS IF HE HAD BEEN JUST BORN
"HE IS NOT DEAD!"
MARY BAMBRIDGE OF PLYMOUTH ENGLAND - RECEIVED THE OFFICIAL NOTICE OF HER BROTHER'S DEATH IN ACTION - MARY CLAIMED HER BROTHER WAS STILL ALIVE - AND TOLD OF A TOWN IN GREECE WHERE HE WAS. ALL HER REMARKS WERE LATER PROVED CORRECT.
GIANT HEADS
WHICH HAVE BEEN FOUND IN MEXICO - THERE IS NO KNOWLEDGE OF WHO CARVED THEM FROM HARD BASALT THOUSANDS OF YEARS AGO

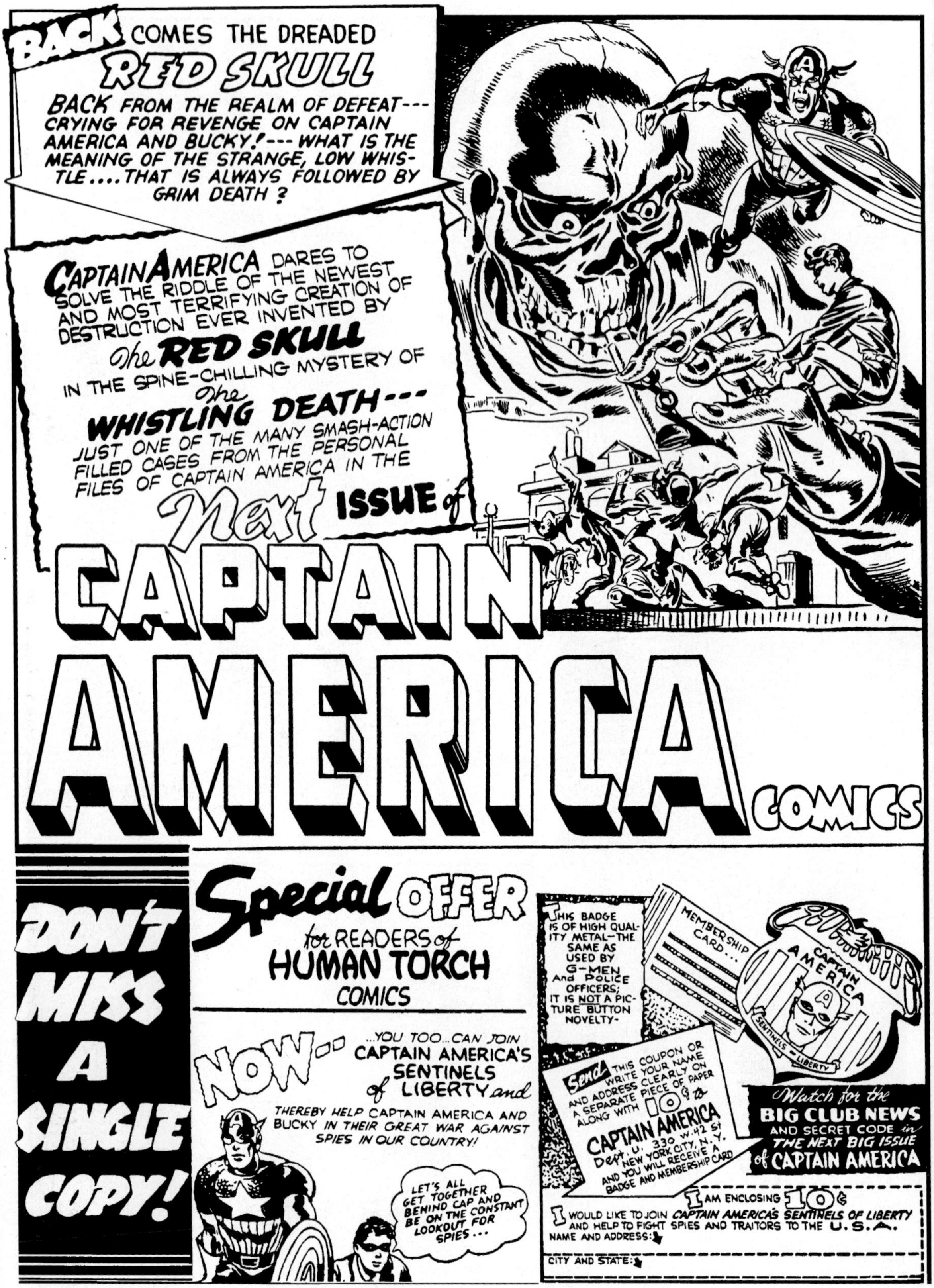
BACK COMES THE DREADED
RED SKULL
BACK FROM THE REALM OF DEFEAT--- CRYING FOR REVENGE ON CAPTAIN AMERICA AND BUCKY!--- WHAT IS THE MEANING OF THE STRANGE, LOW WHISTLE.... THAT IS ALWAYS FOLLOWED BY GRIM DEATH?
CAPTAIN AMERICA DARES TO SOLVE THE RIDDLE OF THE NEWEST AND MOST TERRIFYING CREATION OF DESTRUCTION EVER INVENTED BY
The RED SKULL
IN THE SPINE-CHILLING MYSTERY OF
The WHISTLING DEATH---
JUST ONE OF THE MANY SMASH-ACTION FILLED CASES FROM THE PERSONAL FILES OF CAPTAIN AMERICA IN THE
Next ISSUE of
CAPTAIN AMERICA COMICS
DON'T MISS A SINGLE COPY!
Special OFFER
for READERS of HUMAN TORCH COMICS
NOW-- ...YOU TOO...CAN JOIN CAPTAIN AMERICA'S SENTINELS of LIBERTY and
THEREBY HELP CAPTAIN AMERICA AND BUCKY IN THEIR GREAT WAR AGAINST SPIES IN OUR COUNTRY!
LET'S ALL GET TOGETHER BEHIND CAP AND BE ON THE CONSTANT LOOKOUT FOR SPIES...
THIS BADGE IS OF HIGH QUALITY METAL-THE SAME AS USED BY G-MEN And POLICE OFFICERS; IT IS NOT A PICTURE BUTTON NOVELTY-
MEMBERSHIP CARD...
CAPTAIN AMERICA
SENTINELS of LIBERTY
Send THIS COUPON OR WRITE YOUR NAME AND ADDRESS CLEARLY ON A SEPARATE PIECE OF PAPER ALONG WITH 10¢ to
CAPTAIN AMERICA Dept. U. 330 W. 42 St. NEW YORK CITY, N.Y. AND YOU WILL RECEIVE A BADGE AND MEMBERSHIP CARD
Watch for the BIG CLUB NEWS AND SECRET CODE in THE NEXT BIG ISSUE of CAPTAIN AMERICA
I AM ENCLOSING 10¢
I WOULD LIKE TO JOIN CAPTAIN AMERICA'S SENTINELS OF LIBERTY AND HELP TO FIGHT SPIES AND TRAITORS TO THE U.S.A.
NAME AND ADDRESS:
CITY AND STATE:

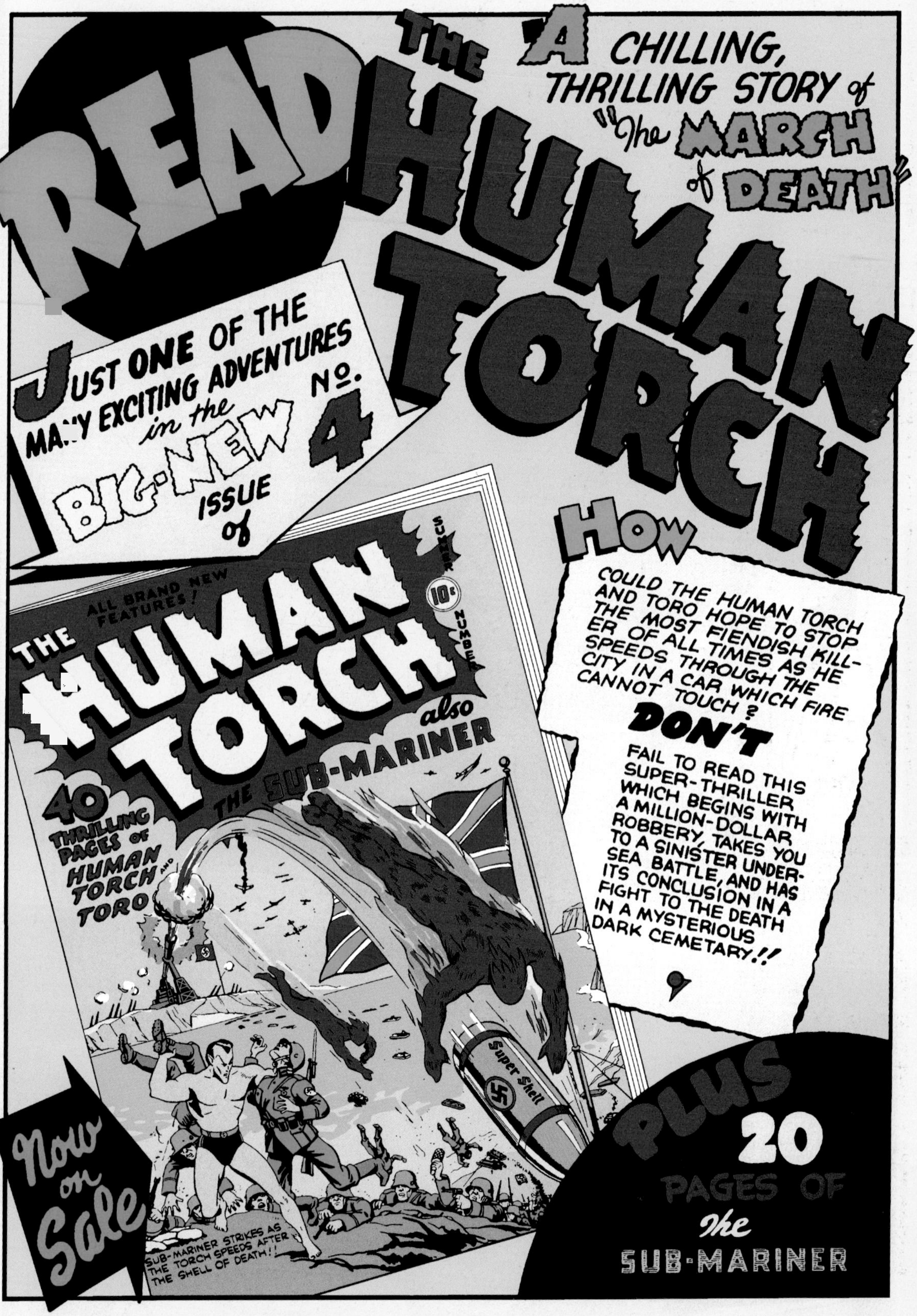

READ THE HUMAN TORCH
A CHILLING, THRILLING STORY of "The MARCH of DEATH"
JUST ONE OF THE MANY EXCITING ADVENTURES in the BIG-NEW NO. 4 ISSUE of
ALL BRAND NEW FEATURES!
THE HUMAN TORCH also THE SUB-MARINER
SUMMER
10¢
NUMBER
40 THRILLING PAGES OF HUMAN TORCH AND TORO
Super Shell
SUB-MARINER STRIKES AS THE TORCH SPEEDS AFTER THE SHELL OF DEATH!!
HOW
COULD THE HUMAN TORCH AND TORO HOPE TO STOP THE MOST FIENDISH KILL-ER OF ALL TIMES AS HE SPEEDS THROUGH THE CITY IN A CAR WHICH FIRE CANNOT TOUCH?
DON'T
FAIL TO READ THIS SUPER-THRILLER WHICH BEGINS WITH A MILLION-DOLLAR ROBBERY, TAKES YOU TO A SINISTER UNDER-SEA BATTLE, AND HAS ITS CONCLUSION IN A FIGHT TO THE DEATH IN A MYSTERIOUS DARK CEMETARY.!!
Now on Sale
PLUS 20 PAGES OF The SUB-MARINER

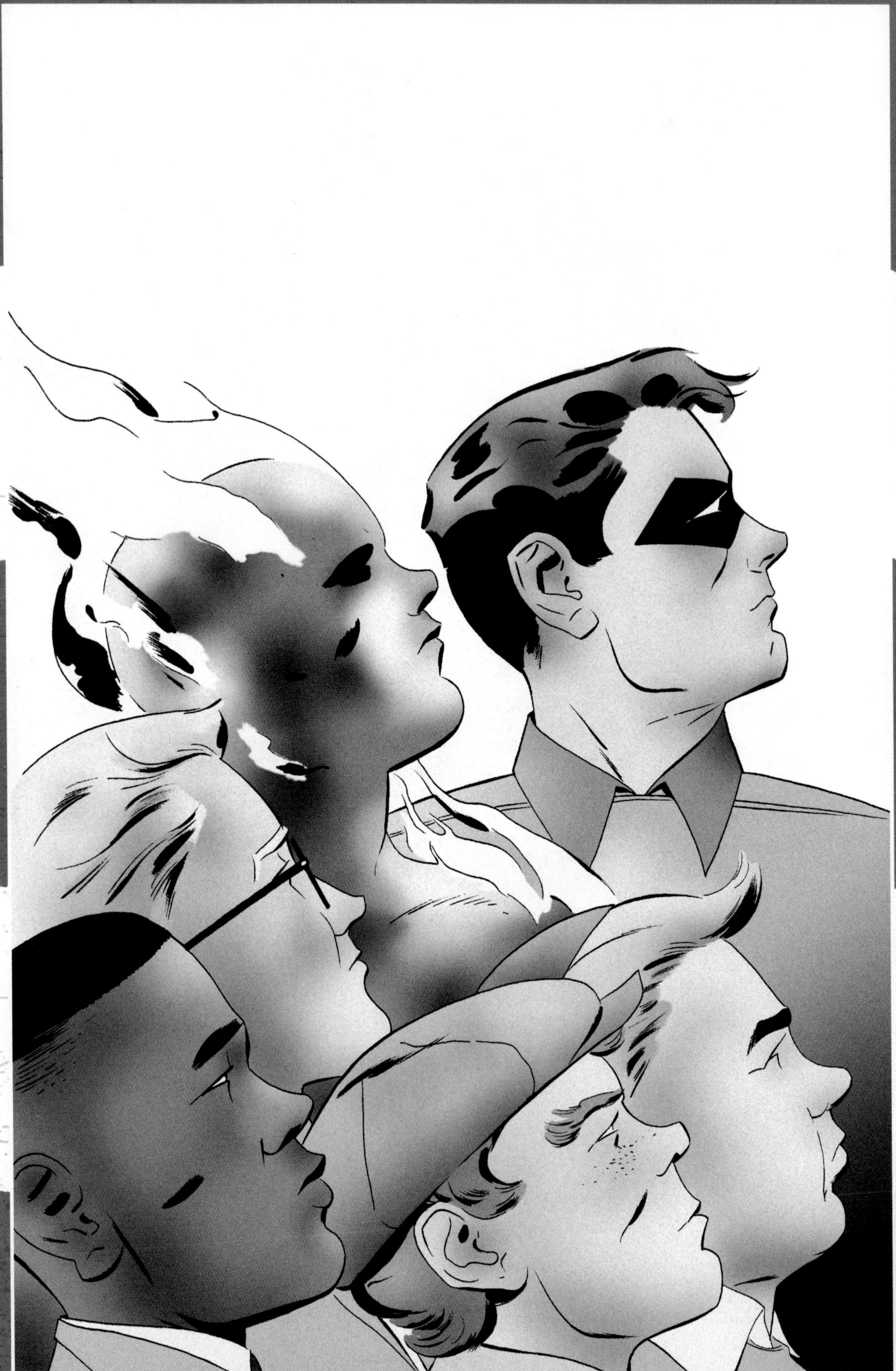

YOUNG ALLIES COMICS 70TH ANNIVERSARY SPECIAL #1
VARIANT BY MARCOS MARTIN

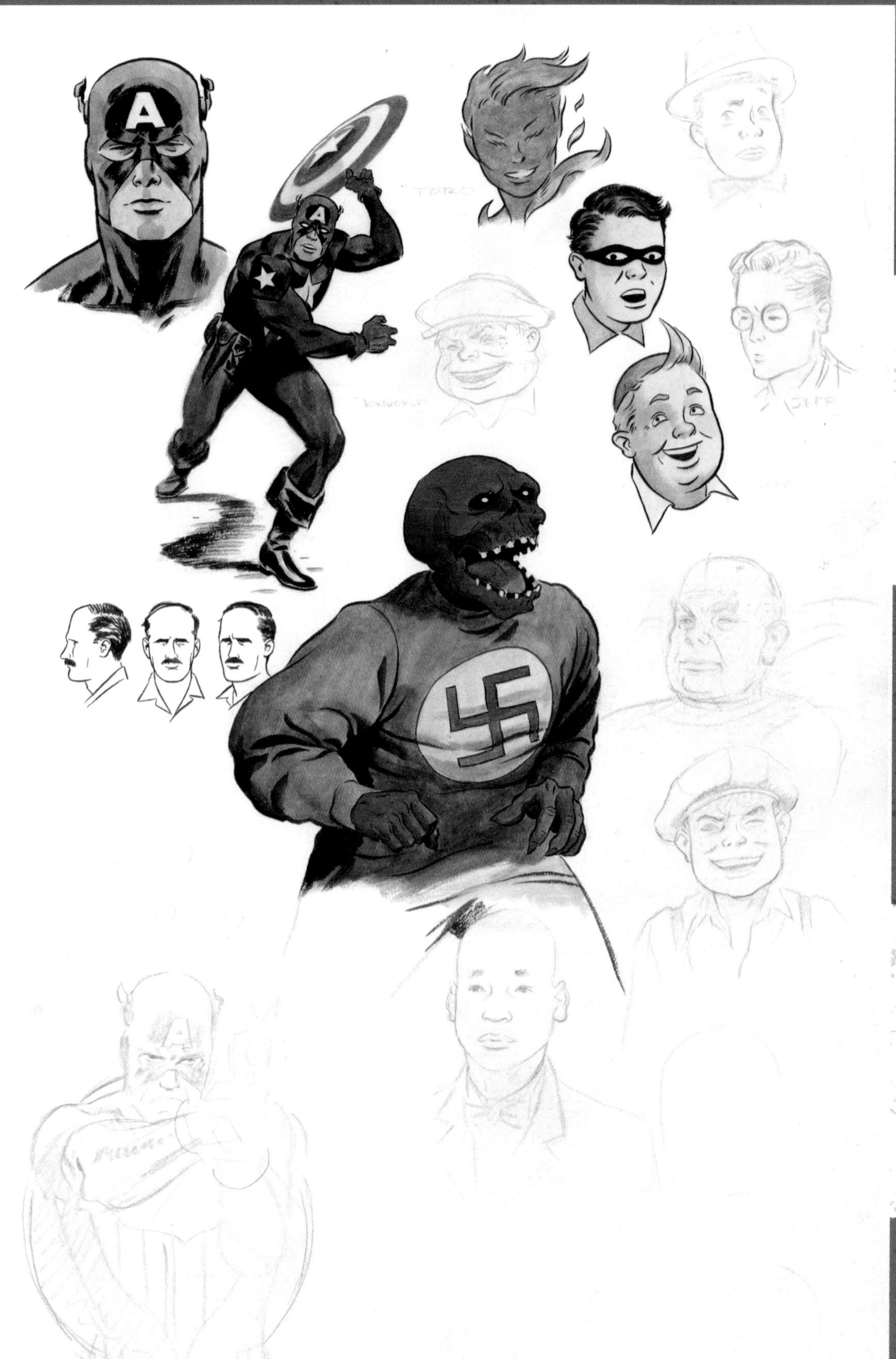
TORO
JEFF

Character Designs BY NICK DRAGOTTA

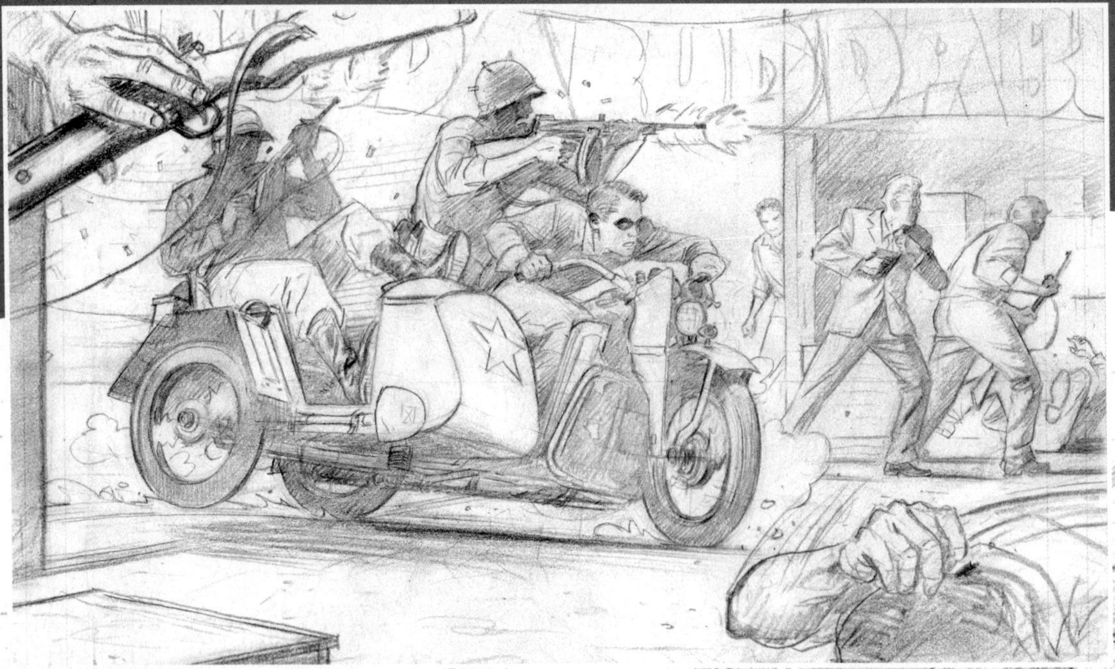

Young Allies
Comics #1 70th
Anniversary Special
page 13, panel 3
pencils by
NICK DRAGOTTA

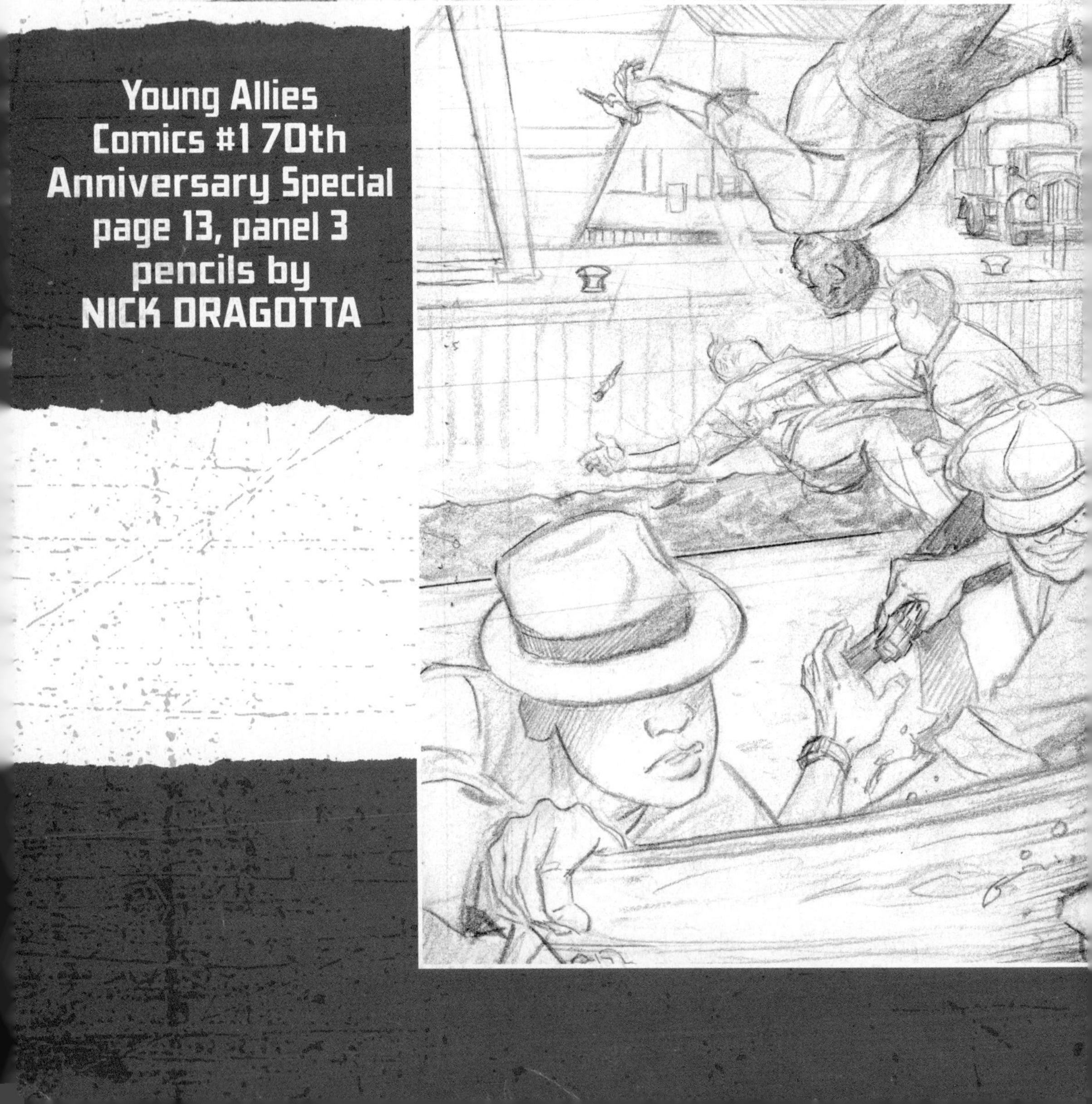

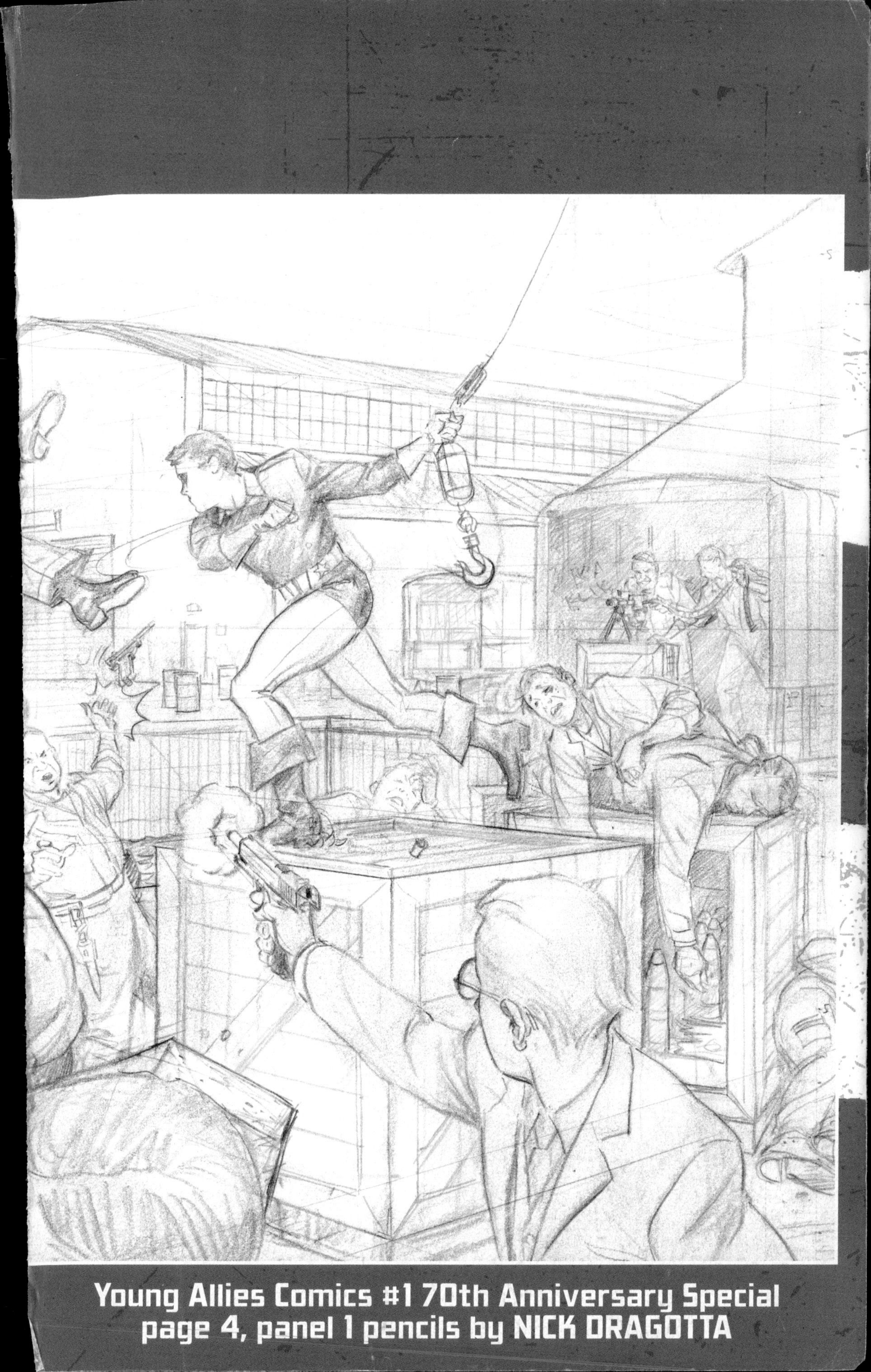

Young Allies Comics #1 70th Anniversary Special
page 4, panel 1 pencils by NICK DRAGOTTA

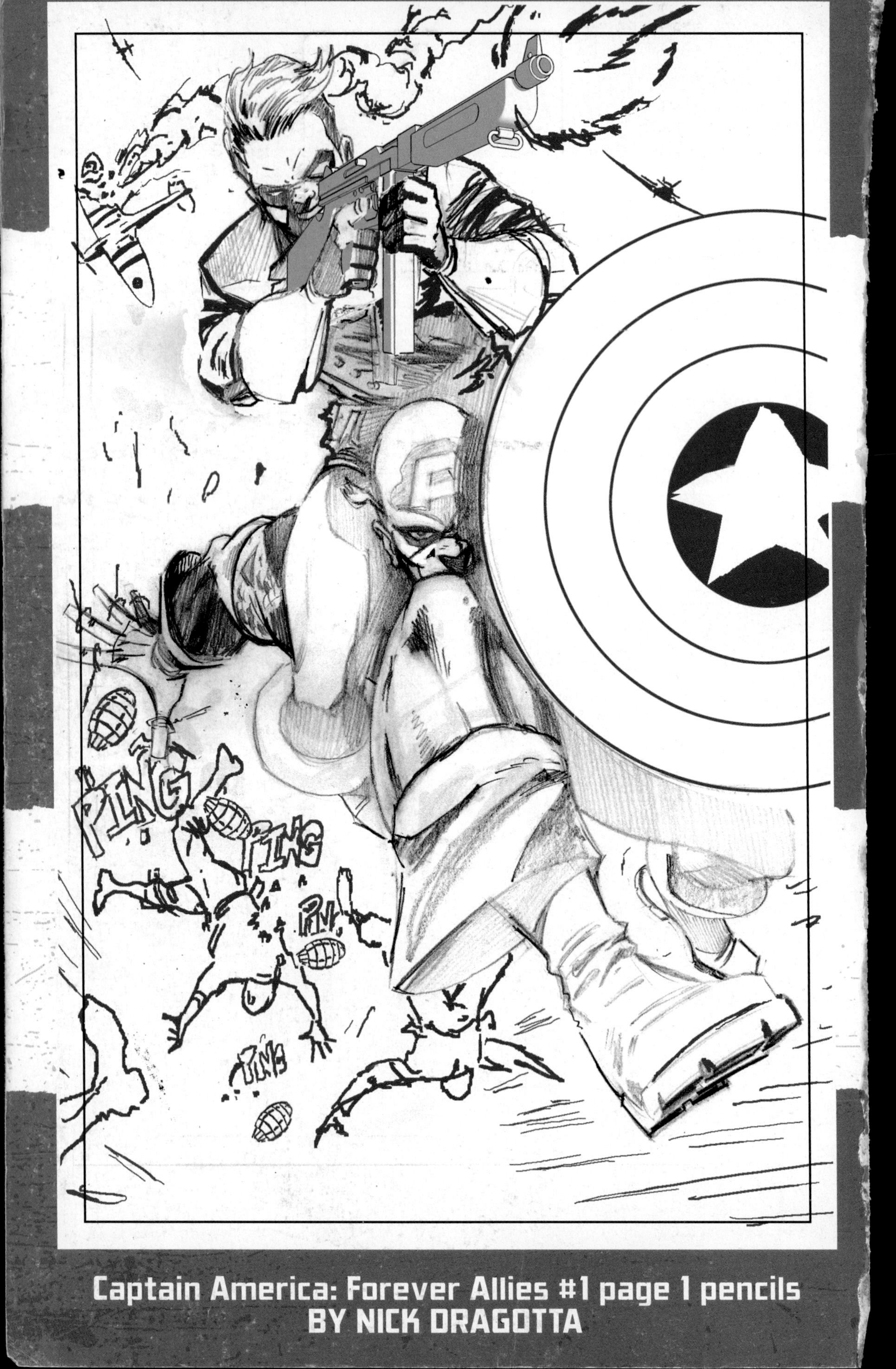
PING
PING

Captain America: Forever Allies #1 page 1 pencils
BY NICK DRAGOTTA